PARLIAMENT
A QUESTION OF MANAGEMENT

PARLIAMENT
A QUESTION OF MANAGEMENT

V M BARRETT

Australian
National
University

ANU PRESS

Australian
National
University

ANU PRESS

Published by ANU Press
The Australian National University
Canberra ACT 2600, Australia
Email: anupress@anu.edu.au

Available to download for free at press.anu.edu.au

ISBN (print): 9781760465452
ISBN (online): 9781760465469

WorldCat (print): 1346132397
WorldCat (online): 1346132305

DOI: 10.22459/PQM.2022

Cover design and layout by ANU Press. Cover photographs: © UK Parliament/Jessica Taylor and AUSPIC © Commonwealth of Australia.

This book is published under the aegis of the Public Policy Editorial Board of ANU Press.

Contents

Abbreviations

ANAO	Australian National Audit Office
CPA	Commonwealth Parliamentary Association
DDC	Digital Democracy Commission
DPS	Department of Parliamentary Services
HCPACAC	House of Commons Public Administration and Constitutional Affairs Committee
HOCGC	House of Commons Governance Committee
ICT	information and communications technology
IPEA	Independent Parliamentary Expenses Authority
IPSA	Independent Parliamentary Standards Authority
IT	information technology
JCPAA	Joint Committee of Public Accounts and Audit
MP	member of parliament
NPM	new public management
NSW	New South Wales
PBO	Parliamentary Budget Office
PGPA Act	*Public Governance, Performance and Accountability Act 2013*
PSC	Parliamentary Service Commissioner
SFPALC	Senate Finance and Public Administration Legislation Committee
UCL	University College London
UK	United Kingdom
UN	United Nations

List of boxes

List of tables

Acknowledgements

First, I acknowledge my excellent supervisors during this study: professors John Wanna, John Uhr and Meg Russell. I have benefited immensely from their formidable knowledge, encouragement and insightful advice, and I thank each of them for all that I have learned. I am most grateful for the outstanding support I have received from The Australian National University (ANU), including a postgraduate award and assistance with travel expenses and copyediting. I also acknowledge support from other universities including Exeter, Hull and University College London (UCL).

Current and former clerks and their staff in the Australian and UK parliaments and the Secretary of the Australian Department of Parliamentary Services provided access to the parliamentary buildings and to resources, material and interview discussions that were crucial to this research. I have the highest regard for the work they perform on behalf of us all and I thank them wholeheartedly. Thanks go to many interviewees—members of parliament, officials, academics and commentators—for giving up their valuable time to discuss candidly their perspectives on parliament's administrative challenges. I have appreciated also the growing contribution to the topic of parliamentary administration from a range of parliamentary scholars and authors and from institutions including the Hansard Society, the Institute for Government, the Crick Centre and the UCL Constitution Unit. Their work has highlighted the many different priorities of parliamentary actors and the importance of supporting parliamentary democracy through all available means.

To my ANU colleagues and my wonderful family and friends, I extend my deepest appreciation for their patience, support and forbearance through this extended undertaking. Special thanks go to John Templeton, a pioneer in the art of parliamentary management.

I have received a great deal of help in writing this book. All errors and omissions are my own.

Preface

The research that led to this book was inspired by my interest in public management theory and practice during a long career serving the Parliament of Australia and the Legislative Assembly for the Australian Capital Territory. As a senior administrator, I faced constant choices between the individual and collective interests of members of parliament, the institutional interests of parliamentary officials and the public interest. Was I a guardian of parliamentary traditions and practices or an agent of change in the pursuit of efficiency and public value? If the answer was both, how would I navigate a path between these different goals? And was this dilemma different for an Australian Parliamentary Service official than for any public administrator? Why is parliament considered unique and why do parliaments appear to resist or even defy attempts to manage them more effectively? Business as usual, an emphasis on efficiency and routine, and a low appetite for risk often seemed like the least controversial choices.

My attempt at answering these questions followed the award of a Senior Executive Fellowship by the Australian Public Service Commission in 1999 to study the impact of public management reforms on parliaments in the United Kingdom, Australia, Canada and Singapore. In the research for this book, completed more than 20 years later, I have explored new questions and analysed evidence from an array of sources in an attempt to provide a greater understanding of what it means to manage a parliament effectively, and how the beliefs and actions of a parliament's many actors can work against each other to diminish its reputation and lessen the public's trust. By viewing this evidence in the light of public management approaches, rather than through traditional lenses of parliamentary reform, I have sought to present new perspectives on parliamentary management to academic researchers and parliamentary practitioners in the interests of advancing this essential institution.

My later study took place between 2015 and 2019 and was confined to two national parliaments: those in the United Kingdom and Australia. Most of the events I have recorded occurred within this time frame. The topic of parliamentary administration has, however, become increasingly dynamic. Events post 2019 included the re-election of the Johnson government with a large majority in the United Kingdom and its withdrawal from the European Union; the global Covid-19 outbreak, which disrupted the operation of all parliaments; and, in Australia, the damaging exposure of a crisis in parliamentary culture. These unfolding events, I suggest, have not changed the key arguments in this book. If anything, they have magnified them.

For centuries, scholars and practitioners have studied parliament and its reform from an institutional perspective, but few have addressed the internal relationships among parliamentary actors, their competing beliefs or their influence on parliament's effectiveness. The research leading to this book was precipitated by evidence of a dissensus in management priorities among officials and members, a purported decline in public confidence in democracy and a lack of public engagement with parliament. I used a qualitative, interpretative and exploratory methodology to compare the two parliaments. This involved spending a lot of time in both institutions holding informal discussions with colleagues, analysing a range of literature in parliamentary and university libraries and conducting more than 90 formal interviews with parliamentary officials, members of parliament and other parliamentary actors, exploring dilemmas relating to governance, management and procedural and cultural change.

Initially, I wanted to test my perception that 'management' as a concept was considered less important than 'procedure', especially by members themselves. I wondered whether structural differences in the organisation of management and procedural functions in the two parliaments had contributed to the level of understanding and appreciation of the importance of the management role. The 'simple' answers appeared to be 'yes' and 'not necessarily'. The real answers were far more complex and contestable. My extensive analysis of hours of interview transcripts, historical and recent management reports and parliamentary literature revealed much about the beliefs and actions of parliamentary actors and commentators and uncovered simmering tensions between the upholders and would-be reformers of parliamentary traditions. In conjunction, I studied the trajectory of public management reforms in both the United Kingdom and Australia to better understand their relevance to parliamentary management, including how they have been applied in the past and whether more contemporary approaches might be applied in the future.

The research drew four main conclusions, which have implications for the future management of parliaments. First, parliament is overwhelmingly an agonistic institution and competition between parliamentary actors for status, resources, influence and control has pervaded its administration and impeded reform. Second, in the context of parliament's role as a deliberative forum and broker of ideas, managing public expectations remains a principal challenge for its administrators. Third, parliament's claims to be unique and a consequent emphasis on differences rather than similarities with other public organisations have reduced the potential for learning from others. Fourth, a lack of constructive engagement with administrative issues from members of parliament has contributed to a vacuum of leadership in an institution in which no one has overall authority.

This book may have raised more questions than it has answered. Readers may have different interpretations of the events described within it. I hope those questions and differences will contribute to ongoing discussion about the vital role of parliament in our democratic system and how it might be more effectively managed into the future.

1

An introduction

Managing parliament: Why is this problematic?

Parliaments appear to struggle with the concept of institutional management. Parliament's supposedly sovereign role ensures its place at the apex of the constitutional constellation, along with the other two branches of government: the executive and the judiciary. The doctrine of exclusive cognisance means that parliament, and only parliament, retains control of its internal business. Moreover, the doctrine of the separation of powers, while not strictly applicable in the loosely defined Westminster system of government,[1] is often called on to support the belief that the management of parliament, including decisions on its funding, should be carried out independently of the executive even though their powers are closely intertwined (Benwell and Gay 2011). Parliament is indeed unique—or is it?

Many views have been put forward over the years about the effectiveness of parliamentary management. On the one hand, there is evidence that parliament's internal management has been insular, self-serving and elitist. Parliament has been likened to a gentlemen's club, with its members holding on nostalgically to dominant traditions, resenting intrusions into mysterious practices and failing to communicate effectively with the public (Crick 1968; Reid and Forrest 1989; DDC 2015; Patience 2019). Parliamentary actors have traditionally been concerned with institutional

---

1   Russell and Serban (2020) argue the Westminster model is no longer useful for comparative purposes and can lead to flawed inferences and false generalisations.

continuity and preservation and rather less so with innovation and change. Conversely, the story of parliament is seen as a struggle by its members, representing the people who elect them—and sometimes its officials, representing the institution—against potential misuse of power by a dominant and authoritarian government. The struggle is aided by conventions and practices built up over centuries, reflecting hard-won concessions towards a devolution of power from the rulers to the ruled and from government to parliament. Seen in this light, the role of parliamentary actors in defending parliament from being sidelined by a rampant executive is, indeed, a noble pursuit and warrants the most sceptical questioning of parliamentary reformers, especially those proposing greater efficiency with apparent disregard for parliament's effectiveness in carrying out its key roles (Evans 2003, 2004).

A third, less discussed, factor is the complexity of our understanding of the term 'management', which is often conflated with related concepts of 'administration' and 'governance'. Management means different things to different people and many parliamentary actors are ambivalent about management theory and practice in the context of running the parliamentary institution. Contest between traditional long-serving parliamentary administrators and lately arrived management 'technocrats', perceived failures of new public management (NPM) and scepticism about the relevance and applicability of new forms of value-creating and collaborative management, with greater citizen involvement, appear to have limited enthusiasm among parliamentary actors for the take-up of new management ideas.

Fourth, and perhaps most importantly, public perceptions of the relevance and effectiveness of parliament have declined and the deference that politicians, institutions and officials could once count on has all but disappeared. Members of the public do not appear to appreciate the enduring significance of the contest between a government's prerogative and a parliament's right to scrutinise, viewing it instead as the pursuit of power and self-interest by politicians from opposing political parties. This phenomenon has been accelerated in no small part by the rise of social media, enhanced mainstream media scrutiny and, paradoxically, even by the broadcasting of parliamentary proceedings themselves. It seems that the more people know about politics (and by extension parliament), the more disaffected they become (Segal, in Crick 1968; Winnett and Rayner 2009; Fox 2012a). Parliament's public standing is also complicated by the fact that many people conflate parliament, government and adversarial politics, consigning them all to the same fate of poor public opinion, distrust and disenchantment (Stoker et al. 2018). But the problem is also part of the cure: it is widely held that a lack of awareness and understanding about how politics and parliament work can equally feed into public disaffection (Lusoli et al. 2005; Stoker 2006b; Fox 2009; Leston-Bandeira 2014; Jennings et al. 2016). Accordingly, parliaments tend to remain committed to public engagement strategies while remaining unclear about their effectiveness (Kelso 2007b; Uberoi 2017; Weerasinghe and Ramshaw 2018).

In this book, I examine parliamentary management/administration (I talk about this distinction shortly) in the UK and Australian national parliaments. I attempt to provide a relatable account of how parliamentary officials and members of parliament (MPs) carry out their respective institutional roles, cognisant of the complexity and contradictions inherent in those roles. My aim is to enhance understanding of how parliament is managed and engender an appreciation of the difficulties faced by parliamentary actors who are committed to the ongoing effectiveness of the parliamentary institution. But in so doing I go beyond institutional description and validation, taking a critical approach at times given a demonstrated lack of collective responsibility, a culture of avoidance and a failure to appreciate the need for parliamentary actors, both officials and members, to see their roles more broadly as responsible public managers.

Parliament remains an essential institution in our democratic system. It does many things well. We may not know much about it, but we should be glad it is there (Uhr and Wanna 2000). This book is, indeed, a defence of parliament, notwithstanding its acknowledgement of widespread criticism through the decades. But it also argues that for parliament to remain relevant, inclusive and publicly respected, it must enhance its management capability.

Defining the problem

If I want to elevate the management role in parliament, I first need to be clear about nomenclature and how to distinguish between the terms 'public management' and 'public/parliamentary administration'. Second, I need to demonstrate a relationship between 'public management' and 'parliamentary management'. I can turn to the public management literature for guidance. Lynn (2012: 18), for example, has asked: '[W]hen we talk of "public management" or of "public administration" are we talking of the same subject or of different subjects?' According to dictionary definitions, the distinction appears to be arbitrary,[2] but there are competing views as to whether public management and public administration are different concepts or whether one is a subset of the other. Early commentaries referenced by Lynn (2006) either viewed the two terms as synonymous or regarded management as the more general concept.[3] Other scholars have claimed that management and administration are fundamentally different and have relegated management to a subordinate and even stigmatised status.[4] Lynn suggested the subordination of public management in favour of public administration may be a reaction to the perceived appropriation of the former by graduate schools of public policy, which have tended to move political thinking about public managers towards a distinction between those who are able to change an organisation and those who play a custodial role (see also Moore 1995).

While the older view of public management may have been concerned with the responsible exercise of administrative discretion, the newer behavioural approach has emphasised the strategic political role of the public manager and placed a lower priority on institutional capacity and durable democratic values (Lynn 2012; Keulen and Kroeze 2014). Rosenbloom (1998, in Lynn 2012) claims the term 'administration' conveys more respect for the constitutional and political foundations of governance than does 'management'. This approach seems particularly relatable to parliamentary administration when read in conjunction with governance reports in the Australian and UK parliaments and it also provides some insights into conflicting beliefs about the management role. Parliamentary 'administration' has tended to privilege maintenance and preservation over (public) 'management' concepts of leadership and results, the latter being viewed with suspicion in some parliamentary quarters (Barrett 1999; and later chapters of this volume). However, to Raadschelders (1999: 289), administrative legitimacy rests 'with

---

2   Cambridge Online Dictionary (2018, available from: dictionary.cambridge.org/dictionary/english/) definitions of administration include: 'the arrangements and tasks needed to control the operation of a plan or organization'; 'the people in an organization who manage its business and operations'. Oxford Online Dictionary (2018, available from: www.oed.com/) definitions of administration include: 'the process or activity of [or the people responsible for] running a business, organization, etc'; or 'the management of public affairs; government'.

3   Lynn cites works by Fayol (1930); Martin (1940); Van Riper (1990); and Waldo (1984).

4   Lynn cites Perry and Kraemer (1983); Rainey (1990); and Ott Hyde and Shafritz (1991); but see also Savoie (2006).

the swiftness and adequacy of its response to changing environmental conditions'. Shergold (1997) also argued that the relationship between the administrative and political domains is not linear but involves a 'strategic conversation' between all stakeholders, including the public.[5] Sowa and Lu (2017) highlighted a focus on strategy, rather than managerial processes, and on interorganisational rather than intra-organisational relations. They drew on Hill and Lynn (2009) to advocate a holistic approach to public management—one that includes personnel and strategic dimensions within a larger system of resources, strategies and other components necessary to achieve legitimate goals. The problem can be summed up thus: How can a parliament balance the routine and strategic dimensions of its administrative roles? How can its administrators and managers play a strategic and political role while preserving institutional capacity and democratic values as well as responding swiftly to changing environmental conditions (Keulen and Kroeze 2014; Raadschelders 1999)? How can they conduct public strategic conversations between all stakeholders while minimising the risk of crossing the political/administrative divide (Shergold 1997)? These complexities would seem remarkably familiar to all public managers, whether in the parliamentary sphere or the wider public/civil service.

The theoretical dichotomy between the 'old' institutionally based administration and the 'new' action-oriented public management becomes especially interesting, and tricky, when it emerges within the parliament—an institution with the sometimes competing purposes of both enabling and holding to account the elected policymakers, as well as representing and supporting the democratic rights of citizens. I have touched on differing perceptions of the value of the more traditional specialist procedural and political skills when judged against calls for a more 'professional' approach to the management of the institution itself (HOCGC 2014). These perceptions are more fully exposed by interviews with parliamentary actors and other events discussed in following chapters. For the moment, we should at least be aware that parliamentary management is a broader concept than the provision of routine support services. My use of the term throughout this book favours the scholarly view of 'management' as a more general concept than 'administration', although I use the latter term where it seems more appropriate to the

---

5   Shergold credits Alex Matheson with describing this space as the 'purple zone' where the 'blue' of political strategy and 'red' of public administration merge in 'strategic conversation'.

events described. As I have noted already, 'management' means different things to different people. In the parliamentary context, it might be thought of as managing practice and procedure through the routines and protocols that are consistently followed. Or it might be considered the efficient organisation of the functions or operations of service delivery. At its highest level, it might be synonymous with the exercise of overall authority or institutional governance. From an academic or practitioner perspective, it might include the adoption of management theory and techniques that could contribute to improving the effectiveness, efficiency, coordination and quality of the services parliament provides. This book takes a broad view in encompassing all these interpretations and the tensions among them. It includes examples of how opportunities for improved management have been ignored, sidelined, resisted or ineffectually implemented and what factors might have contributed.

I begin the account by recalling well-publicised events in the UK and Australian parliaments when the question of effective management was brought into the spotlight. They followed the attempt in 2014 by former UK Speaker John Bercow to replace the outgoing Clerk of the House of Commons, Sir Robert Rogers, with Carol Mills, the former Secretary of the Australian Department of Parliamentary Services (DPS). Mills had served as a senior executive in the NSW public sector but before her appointment to DPS had no parliamentary experience. Her appointment to the House of Commons was terminated and she was also later dismissed from the Australian Parliamentary Service following a series of senate committee inquiries.[6] To say these events inspired this work would be an overstatement, yet they did serve as a useful illustration of the tensions that have long existed among those responsible for carrying out parliament's multifaceted roles. The following quotations from long-serving and vocal former members of each parliament are telling examples of what was seen at the time as a paucity of effective parliamentary management:

> [T]here is a serious problem to address in the management in the House [of Commons]. The House is a loveable shambles. Waste is everywhere. There is an absence of clear chains of command for many of the functions that are provided. The security arrangements are quite extraordinary ... [T]he House is vulnerable to criticism once it has a budget of several hundred million, which is one of the reasons why the legislature needs to pay attention to the

---

6   The events became known as 'the Mills affair' and are described in detail in later chapters.

problem. It works despite, not because of, its organisational and management structure. It works because people are so deeply committed to making it work and to ensuring that the legislature functions. (HOCGC 2014: 92)

Over recent years … I have raised concerns about the senior management of the Department of Parliamentary Services. I have said in the past I consider DPS to be the worst run government [*sic*] department in the Commonwealth of Australia. Unfortunately, nothing has changed … This raises very serious questions about the probity and transparency of decision making in the Department of Parliamentary Services. I can assure the Senate that its Finance and Public Administration Committee will not let these serious questions go unanswered. (Australia, Senate 2014: 8785)

The first-cited criticism came from Andrew Tyrie, who, until his retirement in 2017, was a Conservative member of the UK House of Commons and chair of several influential committees. The second came from Labor Senator John Faulkner, who, until his retirement in 2015, was among the Australian Senate's better-known critics of both public and parliamentary administration. He was scathing about the performance of the DPS, which was tasked with providing support services to members of parliament and those occupying and visiting Australia's Parliament House. Both members were speaking from years of parliamentary experience and providing evidence to important inquiries into the effectiveness of each parliament's management. They were not alone in their observations: through the decades, there have been many criticisms of the services that support the functioning of parliament.[7] These criticisms from members, who are the recipients of parliamentary services as well as the custodians and overseers of the parliamentary institution, give early insights into the difficulties parliamentary administrators face in supporting parliamentarians and the institution itself—essentially involving issues of power and politics (Geddes and Mulley 2018; Geddes 2019b).

A generalised perception is that the UK and Australian parliaments are not well managed on several fronts, including accountability and transparency, efficiency and the effective use of resources.[8] These parliaments also appear to be failing to secure the trust, support and engagement of citizens,

---

7   These are contained in early literature, parliamentary committees of inquiry, management reviews, audit reports and newspaper articles.
8   See, for instance, HOCGC (2014); SFPALC (2012a, 2012b, 2015a, 2015b).

thereby further reducing their effectiveness (Evans et al. 2013, 2017, 2019; Hansard Society 2019). Less publicly visible but also relevant are calls for procedural and other reforms to enhance parliamentary effectiveness both in holding the executive to account and in facilitating effective lawmaking (Kelso 2007a, 2009; Winetrobe 2013, 2014; Hansard Society 2014). Successive internal and external reviews over decades have done little to belie the impression that parliamentary management has been internally focused and insular, concerned with preserving the status quo, self-serving and resisting the changes confronting all public institutions. Of note are disturbing claims of bullying, harassment and sexual assault in both parliaments and subsequent investigations of workplace culture (Cox 2018; Ellenbogen 2019; AHRC 2021).

Despite continuing calls for reform, it is not clear what effective parliamentary management looks like and who should be held responsible and accountable. Indeed, management appears to have been viewed with suspicion by conservative 'elites' and some parliamentary officials. Administrative change has often only followed a crisis or critical juncture rather than taking a planned and strategic approach (Russell 2011b; Flinders et al. 2018a; Petit and Yong 2018). Little regard has been paid to the proposition that the public management requirements of a parliament, as a key public institution, should be taken as seriously as its political management. Instead, political and procedural outcomes have been accorded priority over policy outcomes and parliamentary actors have not taken sufficient account of their interrelationships.

Rogers and Walters (2015), former clerks in the House of Commons and House of Lords, argued that the more effective a parliament is, the better it will serve its real 'owners': the people. Yet, few informed observers are likely to agree that parliaments operate effectively (Uhr and Wanna 2000; Evans et al. 2013, 2017, 2019; Oliver 2014; Hansard Society 2015, 2017, 2019). Even fewer will have considered how parliaments could be better managed. It is only when something goes wrong—when the media reports on the misuse of members' entitlements, when a security project runs into trouble, when the Speaker makes a seemingly partisan statement about a head of state or selects a controversial amendment, when Big Ben stops chiming, when MPs or officials are forced to resign due to a process failure or shortfall in behaviour or when a serious crime is alleged to have been committed in the parliamentary building—that we sit up and take notice.[9] Even then we are inclined to blame the self-interest, incompetence and venality of political elites (Fox 2009; Allen 2011; Negrine and Bull 2014; Snow and Robertson 2015). Little constructive thought goes into how parliament as an institution could be better managed to achieve its deliberative, legislative, scrutiny and representational functions.

The problem is exacerbated when there appears to be no clear line of authority or responsibility for the effective performance of parliament and differing views on how effectiveness can be achieved. When things go wrong, who do we blame? Who is responsible for running the institution, enhancing its reputation and making sure it can carry out its functions effectively? How does parliament operate? What role should a parliament's members play? Should a parliament be managed like any other public institution? Perhaps more problematic is the lack of agreement *within* parliaments as to what parliamentary management even means. To some, it is seen as the provision of facilities and catering services, information technology (IT) support, keeping the lights on and providing comfort to the parliamentary building's occupants. This view of 'management' as the provision of administrative support services relegates the concept to a subordinate function that can oversee service provision and perform necessary tasks and routines, enabling the 'real' activities of parliamentary staff—providing procedural advice to the government and its opponents—to proceed untrammelled by lesser concerns. Others take a more holistic view of parliament and see their roles as part of a larger engagement with members and the public to ensure members can operate effectively, to maintain and preserve the parliamentary building (both physically and symbolically) and to promote the institution of parliament as the pinnacle of democracy. From this perspective, a critical task is to acquire and effectively manage political backing and resources (CPA 2005; IPU and UNDP 2017). MPs also regard themselves as individual officeholders—a view that can obscure a wider institutional responsibility to act and lead to perceptions of poor governance (HOCGC 2014). These competing views do not always reconcile and competition between them does not assist effective parliamentary management.

At risk of oversimplifying the challenges of parliamentary management, we can think of them in terms of the need to prioritise and contribute to fulfilling parliament's roles. The key functions of parliament are to: 1) form

---

9   See, for instance, Winnett and Rayner (2009); The Independent (2017); Swinford (2017); Meakin (2017a); Bagshaw (2019); Perkins (2019); Murphy (2021); and later chapters.

government and enable it to achieve its mandated program, including authorising spending; 2) allow scrutiny of an incumbent government's policy proposals and their implementation and administration; and 3) provide a public forum for deliberation, policymaking and addressing public concerns. When we think of management in the context of the first two functions, we are immediately drawn to the concept of 'political management' and the agonistic contest between opposing political parties, which is exacerbated during periods of instability and small government majorities. We might have some awareness of the need for managing the support services that allow this contest to proceed and turn our minds to the myriad underlying 'operational' and 'routine' management functions, encompassing finance and budgeting, human resources, and building and facilities management. Some might argue these functions could be successfully outsourced, but all of us would at least recognise that they must be carried out efficiently and with an eye to the future and accept the need for parliaments to adopt business and strategic planning methods like any other organisation. We might also think of 'political' management in terms of the procedures and structures that allow governments to govern and parliaments to scrutinise. Parliamentary 'governance' also comes to mind during and after a crisis, particularly of an administration's own making—think of recent scandals involving parliamentary expenses or examples of bullying and harassment within the two parliaments. But we might be less inclined here to see the corollary between effective strategic governance and management and parliament's ongoing legitimacy, relevance and public standing. We might overlook the need for MPs and officials to exercise agency in building and maintaining public trust in the institution of parliament, rather than seeking to avoid public scrutiny and opprobrium at all costs. During a major national or international crisis, such as the Covid-19 pandemic, we might be inclined to overlook parliament's scrutiny role while placing our faith in the government's ability to wield extensive emergency powers in our collective interest.

Regarding the third parliamentary function I have ascribed, we might reject altogether the prospect of a parliamentary institution that fosters effective public debate and input into policymaking, arguing that citizens have little opportunity to participate in or influence the course of policy and politics; they elect politicians to do that (assuming each eligible citizen places an informed vote). Indeed, the Hansard Society in its annual series of parliamentary audits has produced much evidence of a lack of public engagement and efficacy and an abundance of apathy and disengagement.

The Democracy 2025 project in Australia, while not focusing directly on parliament, draws similar conclusions (Stoker et al. 2018). In this respect, we could conclude that parliament is not effectively fulfilling its role as a deliberative forum and broker of ideas (Crick 1968), it will continue to serve only as a forum for adversarial politics and parliamentary government will continue to fail to solve society's most pressing problems. We might never have considered whether new approaches to managing public institutions could enhance parliamentary effectiveness in each of its roles.

Despite all the signs of a lack of engagement with parliament and disaffection with adversarial politics, there is evidence to suggest that 'parliament matters' (Norton 1993). Uhr and Wanna contend that although 'people are ignorant of what [parliament] does [they] are nevertheless glad that it is there' (2000: 23). The Hansard Society (2017) found that most people believe parliament is essential to democracy.[10] Flinders and Kelso (2011: 249) claimed the 'parliamentary decline thesis' is exacerbated by political scientists who reinforce the perception of an 'eviscerated and sidelined parliament', thus perpetuating and fuelling public disengagement and disillusionment. If, as parliamentary scholars and practitioners, we hold to the view that the more effective parliament is, the better it will serve the constituencies it represents (Rogers and Walters 2015), it would seem necessary, at the very least, for scholars and practitioners to engender a greater understanding and appreciation of the management challenges of delivering a 'thriving parliamentary democracy'[11] to an increasingly sceptical public.

Encouragingly, recent publications suggest the study of parliament's administration is gaining in popularity; they emphasise the importance of understanding parliamentary reform from an administrative or management perspective (Besly et al. 2018; Geddes and Meakin 2018; Leston-Bandeira and Thompson 2018; Meakin and Geddes 2020). Leston-Bandeira and Thompson (2018), in their book *Exploring Parliament*, presented perspectives from parliamentary scholars and practitioners on many aspects of parliamentary activity. Their central purpose was 'to bring the study of Parliament as a constitutional entity together with the study of Parliament as a multi-layered and complex actor which shapes, and is shaped by the life of the nation' (p. 10). I have drawn

---

10   Although later audits challenge this finding (Hansard Society 2019a).
11   A key aspiration in the *Strategy for the House of Commons Service 2016–2021* (House of Commons Commission 2016).

heavily on their excellent publication. Also in 2018, Marc Geddes and Alexandra Meakin presented a paper to the Political Studies Association International Annual Conference on the dilemmas of managerial reform in the UK House of Commons in which they acknowledged that exploration of the administrative and managerial organisation of the UK Parliament was largely missing. Drawing on Bevir and Rhodes (2003, 2006), they used an interpretive approach to demonstrate how the concept of dilemma, in concert with a focus on the beliefs and everyday practices of parliamentary actors, can explain how change occurs. This approach was further developed in Geddes's work on the influence of power relations on practice (2019b; see also Meakin and Geddes 2020).

My contribution to the field complements these contemporary works: first, by illuminating management practices in the UK and Australian national parliaments (influenced in part by a related 'crisis' or 'critical juncture');[12] and second, by placing parliament within the context of public management theory rather than adopting the path-dependent institutional approach traditionally associated with parliamentary practice. I have taken a broad view of 'management' to include procedural and cultural management and reform and the influences of power, authority and relationships. I have drawn on Bevir and Rhodes (2003, 2006) and Geddes and Rhodes (2018), whose work has provided an ideal interpretive framework for examining the roles and actions of parliamentary actors in the context of traditional beliefs and practices and the potential for situated agency. The discussion in Chapters 5 to 7 is structured in terms of specific dilemmas arising from three key elements of managing a parliament: governance, operational management, and procedural and cultural reform. These dilemmas emerged from wide-ranging interviews with parliamentary actors, academic literature and parliamentary and media reports. As well as illustrating conflicts that have emerged between existing beliefs and traditions, they offer the potential to consider and deploy newer and more generalised approaches to parliamentary reform.

---

12   The 'Mills affair' (see Chapter 4).

Why choose the UK and Australian national parliaments?

The national parliaments of Australia and the United Kingdom have a longstanding relationship. They both have a common heritage in what is often called the 'Westminster family' of parliamentary democracies. The UK Parliament is often regarded as the 'mother of parliaments',[13] while many of the Australian Parliament's practices and procedures, particularly in the House of Representatives, are modelled on the United Kingdom's Westminster system. Each parliament closely monitors and sometimes adopts the other's procedural and management reforms[14] and information is shared regularly through meetings of members, clerks, officials and academics.[15] Both institutions are bound by tradition; parliamentary reform in the Westminster system is slow to materialise (Kelso 2009).

When viewed through a historical institutionalist lens, the change process within the two institutions is seen to be gradual and incremental but also characterised by 'drift' due to shifts in the environment and operating within a context that favours certain strategies over others (Hay and Wincott 1998; Streeck and Thelen 2005; Mahoney and Thelen 2010). The patterns followed are broadly similar: the two parliaments have experienced repeated reviews of structure and organisation and they provide a large source of comparable data (Bottomley 1975; House of Commons Commission 1990, 2007a; Braithwaite 1999; Adams 2002; House of Lords 2002; Podger 2002; HOCGC 2014; departmental annual reports). Yet, while they might come from the same Westminster family, they are nevertheless different in their constitutional, structural, governance and financial arrangements and this provides the potential for differences in observable outcomes (Anckar 2008; Keman 2011). Although both parliaments are bicameral, the House of Lords is not elected

---

13   Although Chris Bryant, former Shadow Leader of the House, has pointed out that the term 'mother of parliaments' was coined by John Bright in the nineteenth century to criticise not to praise it (Bryant 2015).

14   Examples include the introduction into the UK House of Commons in 1999 of Westminster Hall debates—an opportunity for backbench MPs to discuss uncontroversial matters of local or national interest in a 'second chamber'. This followed an earlier reform by the Australian House of Representatives that introduced the Main Committee (since renamed the Federation Chamber) to provide more debating time for backbench members (Parliament of Australia 2017a; TheyWorkForYou 2017; UK Parliament 2017).

15   Examples include the Commonwealth Parliamentary Association, the Society of Clerks-at-the-Table in Commonwealth parliaments, conferences of presiding officers and clerks, and the Study of Parliament groups.

and therefore lacks the democratic legitimacy claimed by the Australian Senate. Also significant are the differences in each nation's electoral system. In the United Kingdom's first-past-the-post and voluntary voting system, a dominant executive is more likely to result.[16] Voting is compulsory in Australia and a system of preferential voting in the House of Representatives tends to reduce government majorities while proportional representation in the Senate usually precludes executive control.

The principal difference in financial terms is in the ability of the House of Commons to decide its own funding (the budget put forward by the House of Lords administration is also rarely challenged). The Australian Parliament relies on the executive government for its funding. The structural and governance arrangements are also quite different in each parliament and these are addressed in detail later in the book. The main difference is that, historically, the House of Commons and House of Lords have retained separate control over their support services, whereas in the Australian Parliament the House of Representatives and the Senate have been served by separate service-related departments. An outcome of this key structural difference appears to be a greater division of responsibility between the management and procedural functions in the Australian Parliament with an increasing propensity to 'blame it on the manager' (Keulen and Kroeze 2014). These arrangements have evolved over time under pressure from both internal and external factors, as the next few chapters will show.

Both parliaments have been affected by a series of events and missteps that publicly highlighted management failures and I recount these in detail in later chapters. That these events were characterised by their capacity to change the structural influences bearing on each parliament and expand the choices open to parliamentary actors would justify their classification as parliamentary 'critical junctures'.[17] For those inside the two parliaments, the episodes and their consequences highlighted pre-existing underlying tensions relating to the constitutional roles of the two parliaments and their management trajectories. For those outside, each event provided yet another example of a parliamentary brouhaha increasing public cynicism. From an academic perspective, they provided a catalyst for engendering a

---

16   Although note occurrences of non-majority government—in particular, the 2010 Conservative–Liberal Democrat coalition government and the 2017 minority Conservative government (Maer and Kelly 2017).

17   See Capoccia and Kelemen (2007) for a comprehensive explanation of critical junctures in historical institutionalism.

greater interest in the administration and management of parliaments—an observation borne out by the emergence of relevant literature during this study.

The number of reports that have questioned the effective management of both national parliaments also provides a rich field for analysing management practices within them, including the beliefs and actions of parliamentary actors that have influenced them. The reports have highlighted difficulties in managing parliaments that may not be encountered within mainstream public sector organisations, including:

- ad hoc, piecemeal and often reactive approaches to procedural reform (Winetrobe 2013)
- a lack of high-level managerial expertise at senior levels and complexity of governance arrangements, particularly at the 'interface' between parliamentary actors and the institution (Winetrobe 2014)
- a governance structure inadequate to deal with a mammoth workload, split between constitutional and strategic management roles (Hansard Society 2014)
- inherent conflict between clerks and managers (Mulgan 2014)
- combining effective decision-making with transparent accountability; matching best-practice governance in the public sector; developing skills; and preparing for future challenges (HOCGC 2014)
- alleged misleading of a senate committee by a parliamentary official (SFPALC 2012a, 2012b)
- possible improper interference with the performance of a senator during a disciplinary investigation (Senate Committee of Privileges 2014; SFPALC 2015a)
- managing assets and contracts in Parliament House (ANAO 2015)
- allegations of poor workplace culture in both parliaments (Cox 2018; Ellenbogen 2019; AHRC 2021).

These related examples have raised important questions about the management and administrative functions within the two parliaments including:

1. How do competing beliefs about the relative value of procedural and management skills influence effective management in the UK and Australian parliaments?

2. To what extent do MPs engage constructively in managing their parliaments?

3. How do structural and other differences between the two parliaments inhibit or facilitate effective management and governance?

4. Is managing parliaments similar to managing other complex organisations, and could contemporary public management approaches be usefully applied?

A new approach to the study of parliaments

I have two main purposes in writing this book. One is simply to engender a greater understanding and appreciation of the challenges and complexities of managing a parliament; the other is to consider whether these challenges are unique to the parliamentary environment or whether they can be addressed within the wider context of public management theory and practice. A third concomitant purpose has emerged, which is highlighted but not fully explored here—that is, the connection between parliamentary management, public policymaking and broader democratic reform. I hope this work will at least serve as a building block for further research.

A typical 'historical institutionalist' approach to writing about parliaments would seek to describe their evolution and reform and explain how and why changes have come about (Kelso 2009; see also Geddes and Rhodes 2018). This is important and I am not dismissive of this approach. Understanding the past is an essential element in explaining reform and shaping the future. But this approach also needs to acknowledge and analyse the inherent complexities and tensions that arise from parliament's multifaceted and competing roles and the beliefs and actions of the members and officials who perform them.

This study is cognisant of a traditional division in scholarship of parliamentary reform between ideas of attitude (or agency) and context (or institutional settings). Proponents of attitudinal change (Norton 1983, 2000; Russell 2011b) assert that political will, especially when combined with a coherent reform agenda and a window of opportunity, can bring about meaningful change. Others (Kelso 2003, 2009; Wright 2004) argue that in the parliamentary institution change is constrained by party politics and the lack of a collective parliamentary voice or agenda. In this sense, the evolving and sometimes conflicting roles of parliamentary actors can be overlooked or even dismissed. Integrating these two schools of thought, however, is the acceptance by interpretive scholars that the dilemmas that arise from the need to make choices between outcomes that may be undesirable, at least to one set of interests, are built on webs of belief, or traditions, which are influenced by the context in which individual actors find themselves (situated agency) and which play out in everyday practice (Meakin and Geddes 2020). It is only by elucidating these dilemmas and examining the relationships among parliamentary actors—influenced by their beliefs and actions—that it is possible to consider ways in which they might be mutually resolved or at least accommodated within the constraints of the parliamentary environment.

My research approach draws from the work of Bevir and Rhodes (2006) on interpretive political science, taking up, specifically, three of their arguments. First, they acknowledge that beliefs and practices are constitutive of each other: the way people act depends on what they believe. Second, they assert that beliefs are inherently holistic and each belief or meaning is located within a wider web of beliefs or meaning. In the parliamentary context, what parliamentary actors believe about the effective management of a parliament will depend on what they think about its multifaceted roles and how they should be prioritised, what they think about their own roles, whether they are attracted to management theory and practice, public or private—in short, a host of relevant and influential beliefs that interact with one another to inform and motivate behaviour, relationships and actions. Third, Bevir and Rhodes conclude that practices, while arising from individual beliefs or meanings, are not fixed but are affected by the contingencies of political (and social) life. Parliamentary management is complicated by unpredictable political events to which parliamentary actors are required to respond or exercise their 'situated agency'.

In seeking to explain the challenges of managing parliament, including differing interpretations of parliamentary effectiveness, this narrative adheres to Bevir and Rhodes' interpretive concepts of traditions, beliefs and dilemmas. But it also seeks to place parliamentary traditions, beliefs and concepts within a public management framework to offer a path towards a new set of traditions, beliefs and practices for parliamentary actors in ways that move beyond an overreliance on institutionalised structures, cultures and discourse. This approach sits well with Bevir and Rhodes' notion that situated agents use their conscious and subconscious reasoning to adjust existing beliefs and practices and to question traditions. It also suggests that the beliefs and traditions held and practised by parliamentary actors within their institutional settings could be influenced beneficially by a greater knowledge, appreciation and application of public management approaches—by learning from outside. An emergence of new beliefs and practices could enhance parliamentary effectiveness, particularly in the degree to which parliament remains publicly relevant and valued.

A word here on 'effectiveness': a basic conundrum is that parliamentary effectiveness will always be a contested concept in a legislative context given parliament's conflicting roles.[18] Measuring parliamentary effectiveness is difficult. This research will not alter either of these truisms, nor does it shy away from them. Its twin purposes, as outlined, are to understand the dilemmas and offer a new perspective on their mutual resolution or accommodation.

To summarise, parliaments have traditionally resisted external intrusions into their internal operations; at the same time, they have resisted administrative change and forestalled reforms, in effect consigning the concept of management to a subordinate and technocratic status. Despite this insularity, such reforms as have been achieved have often been driven by exogenous factors, particularly after a crisis. Procedural reforms have tended to arise from the political contest between governments and oppositions in performing two key parliamentary roles: government and scrutiny. Cultural reforms have been resisted, with parliaments using their 'uniqueness' as a defence against calls for reform of all public institutions. In the case of the most widespread management reforms achieved during the past half-century, most have related to organisational efficiency, 'doing more with less', 'letting the managers manage', mimicking the slogans of new public management and managerialism. Managers have been seen as technocrats with little understanding of the political dimensions of parliamentary administration. To a large extent, 'management' has been compartmentalised and reduced to measures of efficiency: reduced spending, greater outputs, activity-based costing, greater use of technology, business planning and avoidance of risk.[19] Of course, these are important aims; the public expects the parliament to operate

---

18   M. Flinders, pers. comm., 23 March 2020.
19   There is a huge array of literature on new public management. Sources on which I drew included: Hood (1991, 2005); Osborne and Gaebler (1993); Pollitt (2003); Dunleavy et al. (2006); Savoie (2006); Halligan (2012); Moynihan (2012); Rainey (2012); de Vries and Nemec (2013); Esmark (2016).

efficiently at the least cost to taxpayers. But thinking of the management task in such narrow terms begs the much larger question of whether parliament remains relevant and effective in representing the interests of the public in an era of greater public and media scrutiny, adversarial, divisive and populist politics, and public disengagement and cynicism. Neither the preservation of traditions nor a narrow pursuit of efficiency appears to have enhanced public perceptions of parliament's effectiveness in upholding the United Kingdom's or Australia's democratic systems, particularly in the context of parliament's key role in providing a forum for public participation and deliberative policymaking (Crick 1968). This will become apparent from a reading of the various dilemmas I address throughout this book, which highlight the failure of both parliaments to exemplify a respectful, safe and inclusive workplace culture and to achieve a less divisive and more deliberative public discourse. Addressing these dilemmas will require parliamentary actors to understand and accept new beliefs, practices and traditions, as practice and theory in managing all public institutions evolve.

These are bold and simplified claims that require justification. Managing parliament is complex; the parliamentary *context* is unique, the wholesale adoption of private or public sector management models would not be appropriate and parliament must retain its independence and legitimacy. But it can be argued that these factors demand greater, not less, attention to management theory and practice. Parliament is a key public institution that requires effective public management if it is to remain relevant and play its part in our democratic system.

Outline of the book

In writing about an institution steeped in history and precedent, it is important to look to the past. Reinforcing the need to understand the historical context of parliamentary reform, Chapter 2 provides an account of the nature of reforms in each parliament through the previous century. It highlights an ongoing conflict between government efficiency (in achieving its legislative mandate and securing re-election) and parliamentary scrutiny, and notes parliament's limited relationship with the public. It introduces the important and symbolic role of the parliamentary buildings and the complexities surrounding their preservation and security.

It is also important to understand the administrative context in the two national parliaments: the parliamentary actors and their roles, the internal management structures and the governance arrangements. These are described in some detail throughout this book, starting in Chapter 3, which also provides a historical and institutional perspective of administrative reform in each parliament. Chapter 4 examines each parliament's management challenges in a contemporary political context, addressing in detail controversial events that have spurred wider public interest in parliamentary management. They go to the heart of the tensions that exist among the roles and priorities of parliament's many actors.

Chapters 5 to 7 unravel key administrative dilemmas characterised in terms of governance, management and procedural and cultural reforms. These dilemmas help to illustrate the differing beliefs, actions and practices of parliamentary actors as well as the ways in which they have influenced change (Bevir and Rhodes 2006). On governance (Chapter 5), the absence of definitive administrative authority has contributed to inertia and avoidance and a lack of collective responsibility and advocacy for parliamentary administration. The capacity for effective management (Chapter 6) has been diminished by the difficulties encountered in establishing a shared parliamentary identity across multiple roles and conflicting goals—exacerbated by strident scrutiny from the media, the public and internal critics. The dilemmas recounted in Chapter 7 include the capacity for the parliament to meet public expectations by changing behaviours to become more inclusive, representative and respectful, and by expanding the opportunities for public engagement and participation. The chapter also highlights the dilemma of leaving decisions in the 'too-difficult box'. Chapter 8 summarises the two parliaments' management challenges before addressing differences between parliamentary and public management. It discusses the potential benefit of public management approaches—in particular, public value, collaboration and co-production—to improve parliament's management processes and outcomes and allow the institution to play a more influential role in broader democratic reform.

Last, in the Epilogue, I reflect on unfolding events and suggest a future research path for parliamentary management.

2

Calls for parliamentary reform: A brief review

Overview

Calls for reform are a continuing theme in the evolution of parliaments, particularly in the United Kingdom (understandably, noting its long history), and in any study of the struggle between the traditionalists and the reformers it is important to gain an understanding of the antecedents to more recent criticism of parliamentary effectiveness. The following discussion highlights recurring themes in continuing calls for reform, including parliament's relationship with the public and other public institutions, its relationship with the executive, a lack of governance authority within the parliament, limited interest by parliament's members in administrative matters and calls to increase the resources and capacity of its members. It also introduces the challenges surrounding the management of symbolic parliamentary buildings.

The nature of reform in the UK Parliament

In the United Kingdom, Walter Bagehot's *The English Constitution* is acknowledged as a classic and seminal work (St John-Stevas 1959) in explaining how English government worked, famously referring to the fusion of executive and legislative functions—'the efficient secret of the English Constitution' (Benwell and Gay 2011)—to better depict parliamentary politics in England.[1] Bagehot was not a great supporter of the democratic theory and would probably have struggled with contemporary calls for greater public participation, particularly from a public that was not well informed. Jennings' (1941, 1961) work on parliament was 'groundbreaking' in terms of his efforts to marshal parliamentarians towards improving the effectiveness of parliament (Tomkins 2004). He was a promoter of public engagement and the public's right to question and criticise and was concerned that ordinary people should not be denied the opportunity of learning about government policy. On public administration generally, he believed in the maintenance of efficient and effective procedures but was derisory about the 'excessive timidity' of the civil service, partly due to the promotion of 'safe' men rather than those with 'energy and initiative'—criticisms reflecting the Northcote–Trevelyan report on the civil service (Northcote et al. 1854) a century earlier and relatable to the parliamentary environment. It was to the public that Jennings appealed in his call for parliament to be reformed, claiming the quality of government depends essentially on the quality of the House of Commons and the influence that public opinion brings to bear:

> If they regard 'politics' as a matter for a few enthusiasts; if they insist that 'all politicians are the same'; if they pretend that the racing and football results are more important than the most urgent questions of public policy ... our democracy must inevitably be inadequate. Politics in a democracy is not a game but a matter of bread and butter and the future of our children ... This means that they must use the books in the public libraries and read the more intelligent bits in the more intelligent newspapers. (Jennings 1941: 61–63)

Jennings' seemingly elitist view (not too far from Bagehot's perhaps) is easily distilled to a question for today: should we read *The Guardian* or the *Daily Mail*, the *Sydney Morning Herald* or *The Daily Telegraph*? It reflects a contemporary problem of public engagement and perceptions in the context of the 'Westminster bubble' and the 'Canberra bubble' (see Chapter 7).

Hill and Whichelow's *What's Wrong with Parliament?* (1964) was a 'benchmark piece' in the analysis of all that was problematic with Westminster at the start of the 1960s (Kelso 2009: 91). They noted a significant decline in the reputation of parliament in the postwar years

---

1   See also Shugart (2005) on comparative constitutional design.

and offered examples of unfavourable commentary from the media and ubiquitous pessimism from authors about parliament's future survival. To improve that reputation, they looked for ways of making parliament work more effectively, making the point that adequate facilities should be made available to elected members at Westminster. Some of their proposals were outwardly focused and included a revitalisation of the public petitions system, televising of parliamentary proceedings and an edited version, or precis, of the daily *Hansard* to attract greater interest given its falling readership. (The first two of these proposals were adopted, though only latterly in the case of parliamentary petitions.) Crick (1968) also expressed concerns about the decline of popular esteem and crumbling parliamentary effectiveness. He saw the then reputation of the House of Commons as 'far in excess of its merits', claiming it had 'fallen hideously behind the times both in its procedures and in the facilities it extends to its members' (Crick 1968: 11). Crick was aware of an increasing public hostility towards and a lack of knowledge of the methods by which parliament fulfilled its function. He claimed this was because

> the Mother of Parliaments has not been shy of hinting that the way she conducts her business is the wonder of the wise; partly because the study of parliamentary procedure seems to many just so dry and dull; and partly because there is widespread confusion about what the functions of parliament should be. (Crick 1968: 12)

Crick (1968: 161) was scathing about parliament's 'arrogant', 'feckless' and 'ultimately dangerous' lack of concern for public opinion and public understanding of its proper functioning, likening it to an isolated club, nostalgically holding on to dominant procedural traditions and viewing public concern as an 'ignorant intrusion into private mysteries' (p. 162). To him, the mutual back-scratching in debates on parliamentary reform about parliament's past glories 'makes the flesh creep' (p. 162). He noted that not only was parliament symbolic of Britain's three curses— amateurism, inner-circle secrecy and snobbery—it also was helping to perpetuate them by example (p. 252).

Highlighting the relationships between 'managerial' and 'procedural' functions, Hill and Whichelow (1964) and Crick (1968) pointed to the potential to increase the effectiveness of House of Commons scrutiny by increasing the capacity of members to contribute. Crick sought to counter the view that providing facilities and resources to backbench members could lead to a dangerous counter-bureaucracy. He was clear that parliament's most important function was not its capacity to threaten the government or to refuse to pass legislation but to act as a broker of ideas and information so the electorate could sit in judgement. He was concerned that reform would be *internalised* within an isolated Palace of Westminster rather than *externalised* to serve public purposes, and his calls for better facilities for members were intended to allow them to carry out their very public function. Menhennet and Palmer (1967) were two House of Commons Library staff who argued that it was misleading and futile to look back to a golden age when parliament worked perfectly. Instead, they claimed that contemporary pressure for reform required continuing evolution and a strengthening of the working efficiency of all members. Like Jennings (1961), they maintained that members' (and therefore parliament's) effectiveness depended on public acceptance of the responsibilities as well as the privileges of a democracy and that the people themselves could be guilty of a dereliction of their duties to parliament.

The Study of Parliament Group was founded in the United Kingdom in 1964 by Fellowes, Ryle and Crick—clerks who were concerned about the surprisingly few contemporary studies of parliament compared with historical studies (Englefield 1985). In 1974, the group commissioned an investigation into the working environment in which members of the UK House of Commons conducted their business (Rush and Shaw 1974). The investigation resulted in a detailed exposition of each of the then five departments and their functions, and drew attention to an inefficient use of space, largely due to the duplication of services in a bicameral parliament—still prevalent today—and a lack of facilities normally required by any 'managerial or professional man' (Crick 1968: 67; see also HOCGC 2014). Rush and Shaw (1974) also cited several negative assessments of facilities by members, including from one MP that his office accommodation was 'ideal for a suicide' (in Hill and Whichelow 1964: 85). In comparison with other legislatures, they concluded, the United Kingdom's appeared to rank in the middle when it might be expected to rank higher, concurring with Hanson's (1963: 279) view that there were disadvantages in being ancient: 'admiration for the long-established inhibits a willingness to change'. Norton (1993), like others (Menhennet and Palmer 1967; Crick 1968), was also dismissive of an earlier 'golden age' of parliament and cited the positive developments in parliamentary administration in the twentieth century such as the increase in numbers of career politicians and the expansion of physical resources, including office space (new accommodation in Parliament

Street, Millbank and Portcullis House) and research support. But in his view, the end of the twentieth century was a lost opportunity in terms of the political will required to strengthen the parliament's resources.

In terms of the use of technology in enabling a more externally focused public-facing parliament, Seaward (2009), a parliamentary historian, described the House of Commons' move into the new media age as extremely tentative and the UK Parliament's attempts to assert its right to be the principal forum for political debate as absurd. Proceedings were not broadcast on radio until 1975 and on television until 1989, although the House of Lords agreed to televising proceedings in 1983 (UK Parliament 2019c). The parliament seemed threatened by the challenge from the media and Segal, a scholar in political sociology, made an early case for *not* televising parliament despite repeated demands (in Crick 1968). He argued that there was little evidence to suggest it would lead to a new political reality, enhancing democratic process or make parliament's public figures behave more reasonably. Puttnam (Hansard Society 2005), as chair of the United Kingdom's Hansard Society Commission on the Communication of Parliamentary Democracy, argued that parliament consistently failed to present itself as the sum of its parts. The commission's report stated that parliament's communication was still organised around inward-looking procedures and had failed to link its work to other representative bodies in discussing public issues. It urged that the extra costs involved in improving communication, such as a new parliamentary website, should be regarded as an 'investment in modern democracy, not a charge against it' (Hansard Society 2005: vii). Discussion of whether parliament's communications are fit for purpose are ongoing (Williamson and Fallon 2011; DDC 2015; Leston-Bandeira 2015; Uberoi 2017).

Kelso (2009) has provided a detailed analysis, through a historical institutionalist lens, of more than a century of procedural reform at Westminster, in both the House of Commons and the House of Lords.[2] Her excellent account explains the paradox of parliamentary reform within the context of efficiency reforms proposed by a dominant executive to expedite its legislative program versus effectiveness reforms designed to increase legislative and policy scrutiny and effectively balance executive–legislative relations. Effectiveness reforms are less likely to succeed as they threaten to destabilise the normative values of the dominant elite—those

---

2   See also Dorey (2009) on the House of Lords' experience of 'punctuated equilibrium'.

who privilege the role of the executive in providing strong government—over those who believe that a parliament's primary function is to act as a check on the executive. According to Kelso, the paradox lies in the fact that the effectiveness reformers tend to argue that a strong parliament will sustain strong government—an acceptance that the political system of party government and partisanship is unlikely to change. Kelso's somewhat fatalistic and two-dimensional approach does not deal specifically with administrative or cultural reforms[3] nor is it focused on the role of public opinion, but she does address the role of agency in achieving effectiveness reforms and notes the (recent) influence of extra-parliamentary organisations in shaping the reform debate.

Contemporary scholars have continued the emphasis on procedural and behavioural reform (for example, Russell 2000, 2011a; Russell and Sandford 2002; Cowley and Stuart 2003, 2004; Kelso 2007a, 2009), including relationships between parliament's members and the executive (see Norton 2000; Russell and Cowley 2016, 2018) and between parliament and the public (Kelso 2007b; Wright 2015), particularly after the widely condemned 'cash for comment' and expenses scandals (see Oliver 1997; Winnett and Rayner 2009; vanHeerde-Hudson 2011).[4] These themes are explored in detail in later chapters.

The nature of reform in the Australian Parliament

Reid and Forrest (1989), in their seminal, comprehensive work on Australia's parliament, observed that its administrative arrangements were as important to parliamentarians as were those of executive government to ministers of state, devoting a whole chapter to the topic. But they also noted that although Australia had a written constitution, unlike the United Kingdom, it was silent on administrative matters and provided 'only the most rudimentary guide to the financial processes of government'

---

3   Kelso acknowledges this necessary omission in her comprehensive analysis. She also concludes that in the context of achieving institutional change, the process of reform is more significant than the outcome, citing changes to the House of Commons' select committee system and the composition of the House of Lords.

4   The cash-for-comments crisis led to the Nolan Inquiry and the establishment of the Committee on Standards in Public Life (Oliver 1997). The misuse of entitlements by members of both parliaments (see Chapter 4) has arguably brought more publicity to the quality of parliament's administration than any other issue.

(Reid and Forrest 1989: 347).[5] They observed little evidence of any resistance to executive domination during the parliament's establishment in 1901: '[I]n so far as its staffing and appropriations were concerned, [it] was dominated by the executive government from the beginning, without so much as a murmur, much less a fight' (p. 400). Parliamentarians who were not members of the executive played very little part in the development of the overall administrative arrangements and almost anything to do with the library, the buildings or facilities needed the prime minister's imprimatur. Officials were organised from the beginning into five small departments, making it unlikely that one would overshadow the other four, and officials were encouraged to develop limited, inward-looking relationships and loyalties to their own departments rather than to the parliament as a whole (pp. 400–3). These early proclivities were to have a profound long-term effect. Reid and Forrest also offered insights into the 'recurrent and increasingly important difficulty' of parliament's communication with the public. Designed in 'an age of communication by the written word', it was now required to function in 'an age of instantaneous electronic communication', but despite these dramatically different circumstances, parliamentary procedures in 1988 were 'essentially those introduced in 1901' (p. 8).

Wiltshire (1982: 305) lamented the ambivalence of 'lame-duck' presiding officers as a basic cause of the inability of parliaments to accept responsibility for 'all matters related to the running of the house'. He criticised the cautious approach to reform of the 1981 Senate Select Committee on Parliament's Appropriations and Staffing (the Jessop report) and the reluctance of the presiding officers to confront the executive over questions of staffing and appropriations—a problem highlighted by then senators Gareth Evans, Alan Missen and Kathy Martin.[6] Uhr (1982) related parliament's scrutiny role to the effectiveness of its internal management, providing a useful link to the arguments in this book:

> [I]t is unrealistic to expect [the parliament] to exercise an intelligent and respectable oversight of the executive departments when it was not even master of the five small departments which administer Parliament House … [I]n the sorry spectacle of parliament's

---

5   Nevertheless, it appears that, as in the United Kingdom, constitutional factors are often called on in arguments for conservatism (Reid 1966; HOCGC 2014).
6   Of relevance to later discussion, the committee did not endorse the establishment of a commission similar to the United Kingdom's, stating that it would produce a rigid, structured approach rather than the flexibility required.

inability to manage its own appropriation and staffing, one does see a number of the central problems of legislative–executive relations in Australia. (Uhr 1982: 28)

Problems Uhr cited included a demarcation between members who complained about the subservience of parliament to the executive and those who defended the executive's responsibility for the conduct of public administration. No one could realistically expect a dominant executive to grant additional powers (or resources) to parliament to enable it to wield more authority (Uhr 1982: 29)—and, potentially, emerge as Crick's (1968) counter-bureaucracy.

Nethercote (1982) heralded the great inroads the Australian Parliament had made in scrutinising executive government but also warned of the challenges to parliament's authority from non-parliamentary institutions, such as the Office of the Ombudsman, the Administrative Appeals Tribunal and the Australian Law Reform Commission. Aldons (2001b), a former parliamentary official, also noted the presence of external scrutiny bodies, but, unlike Nethercote, he took a more inclusive view, claiming they could bolster, rather than threaten, the legitimacy of the political system, of which parliament was a key but not the only part. According to Reid and Forrest (1989), the Senate's extensive use of standing committees from 1970 revolutionised the overall effectiveness of the parliament, but they were less impressed with the House of Representatives' committee system.[7] Like Nethercote (1982) and Aldons (2001b), they also noted new administrative law enacted since 1976 that provided for redress of grievances and additional scrutiny *external* to the two houses of parliament. They regarded the quest for parliamentary control in the Australian Parliament 'by nineteenth-century means' as a 'useful way of diverting twentieth-century politicians from effectiveness in a late twentieth-century parliament' (Reid and Forrest 1989: 388)—in other words, the Australian Parliament's administrators had done little to increase the effectiveness of its members, preferring to maintain the practices of the past. Unlike Segal (in Crick 1968) in the United Kingdom, Reid and Forrest argued for parliament's control function (to influence,

---

7   They attributed the demise of that House's legislation and estimates committees to a lack of backbench support, no entrenchment in Standing Orders and their perceived threat to party cohesion and executive power.

advise and criticise) to be transferred to the television screen and, indirectly, to the public, emphasising the continuing tension between the inward-looking and outward-facing approaches of parliamentary actors.

On procedural reform, former Clerk of the Senate Harry Evans, well-known as the guardian of the Senate's practice and procedure and advocate for its powerful constitutional role, conceded that some procedures and practices were valued simply because they were 'traditional and quaint' while having no substantial legislative value. Although he was referring to the vestiges of traditions inherited from the United Kingdom, perhaps reflecting the Senate's early decision not to tie itself procedurally to Westminster (Reid and Forrest 1989; Fewtrell et al. 2008), he was, however, concerned that radical hostility towards an 'obscurantist Bagehotian philosophy' of symbols and rituals could sweep away useful procedures and preference legislative efficiency over deliberation and scrutiny (Evans 2009).

Reid and Forrest (1989) made farsighted predictions for the Australian Parliament in the next century. They saw the lack of a spokesperson for the parliament as a significant weakness, claiming the machinery for introspection, including about its relationship with the public, was lacking. The administrative structure of five separate parliamentary departments was keeping the elected houses weak; they thought a longstanding proposition for a single parliamentary department would 'offer the Parliament an organisational and public identity it had not previously enjoyed' (p. 484). Such observations resonate not only with recent UK literature (Norton 2017; Judge and Leston-Bandeira 2018), but also with a recommendation by the Australian National Commission of Audit (Officer 1996) for a single parliamentary department in the Australian Parliament. The commission's proposal was fiercely opposed by the Senate (see Chapter 3) and similar proposals, directed largely at efficiency, were not taken up (Malcolmson 1999).[8]

Research by practitioners in Australia has often concentrated on the need for governance reform. Some argue that the Australian Parliament should be financed independently of government, as occurs in the United Kingdom; others have provided good reasons why this is all but impossible, including the requirement for constitutional change

8 Malcolmson suggested a variation of the commission's proposal, which would have established one corporate administration department. Two small chamber departments would have been managed by each clerk, who would have no other administrative responsibilities.

(Verrier 2007, 2008; Sloane 2014; Breukel et al. 2017). Elder (2006), a former clerk of the House of Representatives, noted shortcomings in the governance arrangements for the delivery of cross-parliamentary services. Parliamentary entitlements have also been the subject of adverse media comment and numerous official reports (see Committee for the Review of Parliamentary Entitlements 2010; Remuneration Tribunal 2011; Fels 2015). Governance issues are further discussed in Chapter 5.

None of the foregoing claims should surprise anyone with a contemporary interest in parliamentary administration; indeed, they would sound familiar even decades later. They emphasise the ongoing need to manage parliament's internal functions in the context of increasing public expectations.

Managing an iconic workplace: The symbolism of parliamentary buildings

The ongoing debate about the effectiveness or otherwise of the buildings that house the two parliaments is of sufficient significance to warrant a separate discussion at this point. The priorities attached by each parliament to the preservation, maintenance and renewal of the parliamentary buildings are central to the argument that management challenges are not subsidiary issues. (Conflicting priorities towards managing the parliamentary buildings are discussed in Chapter 6.) As Parkinson (2012) argued, effective democracy depends on and is influenced by the physical space in which it is practised. In this respect, I note a continuing disinclination to address building deficiencies, particularly in the United Kingdom, and also point to the architectural and symbolic influences the parliamentary buildings bring to bear on institutional effectiveness.

An Amsterdam-based architectural firm, XML, has studied the relationships between space, decision-making and democracy in the plenary chambers of the state legislature of every UN member. Mulder (2017), one of its founding partners, summed up these relationships thus:

> Parliament is the space where politics literally takes shape. Here, collective decisions take form in a specific setting where relationships between various political actors are organized through architecture. The architecture of spaces of political congregation is not only an abstract expression of a political culture—it participates in politics.

This is perhaps a present-day confirmation of the oft-quoted view of Winston Churchill that 'we shape our buildings and afterwards our buildings shape us' (HC Debates 1943). Churchill was a devotee of the agonistic model of opposing benches in the House of Commons chamber while Mulder favoured more consensual designs for parliamentary chambers such as the semicircular shape that is now dominant around the world, particularly in Europe. The horseshoe shape of the two chambers in the Australian Parliament is a mixture of adversarial and consensual models (Parkinson 2012). Crosby (2016) extols the virtues of consensual designs for debating chambers, including in the Scottish Parliament, the Welsh National Assembly and London's City Hall. Discussions about the design of plenary chambers alone, important as they are, do not necessarily take account of other important building influences, including the efficiency of members' offices in serving constituents; informal spaces for meetings and deliberation; public access, including security issues; and parliamentary efficiency. In both parliaments, reviews of annual reports indicate progress through the years in the support given to members through accommodation and office resources. In the United Kingdom, this includes the completion of Portcullis House in 2001 and the ongoing acquisition and refurbishment of offices in the parliamentary estate. In Australia, the resources available to members increased exponentially when the new purpose-built Parliament House was opened in 1988. Few would now disagree that the level of resources, including communication channels, available to members has improved significantly; paradoxically, the demands on politicians' time and attention have increased exponentially (Flinders et al. 2018b).

Material defects in the Palace of Westminster remain, however, and much has been written on the subject by scholars and practitioners alike (see Childs 2016; Gay 2016; Flinders 2016, 2019; Meakin 2017a, 2017b, 2018, 2020; Crick Centre 2018; Flinders et al. 2018a, 2019; R. Kelly 2018; Meakin et al. 2020). Prominent among early critics was Cocks (1977), a former clerk, who described the Palace of Westminster as a legislature that was admired and copied around the world, but which had been unable to put its own house in order. His criticism of the role of members in its rebuilding and modernisation, supervised by Charles Barry following the major fire in 1834, was coruscating. Shenton (2012, 2017) chronicled the battleground of the UK Parliament building's design and construction and the associated personal and political conflicts, lamenting its current dire condition (see also Eagles 2017). Related observations have also emerged from a new history of parliament by the British Academy and Wolfson Foundation Research:

> The constantly postponed parliamentary 'Restoration and Renewal' project offers an irresistible metaphor for the battered state of the Westminster Parliament. For over the last decade, if not more, Britain's venerable legislature has been beset with a series of challenges to its reputation, authority and effectiveness every bit as dangerous as its mouldering masonry and chaotic cabling … Parliament … frequently appears to be an incoherent collection of individuals and cultures with competing and often incompatible aims and objectives, underlining a sense of chaos and confusion. (Seaward 2017)

The case for the United Kingdom's crumbling parliament symbolising a crumbling democracy continues to be prosecuted (see Flinders 2016, 2019; Higgins 2017; Anderson and Meakin 2019). Scholars lament a missed opportunity to overcome internal resistance and use the building's restoration and renewal to improve the parliament's culture and effectiveness and open its environs to the public (Hansard Society 2011;[9] Flinders 2016; Flinders et al. 2018a, 2018b, 2019; Meakin 2017b; Crook and Harrison 2018; McCarthy-Cotter et al. 2018). Many intimates of the existing building have resisted the potential loss of the building's historical connections, particularly if members are forced to 'decant' during its restoration (see D'Arcy 2015; HC Debates 2017a; Moore 2018). Norton (2018b) reinforced the notion that informal meeting spaces for members are an intrinsic part of parliamentary life, meriting serious analysis in the restoration debate. He cited informal meetings in division lobbies as an argument against the perceived efficiency of electronic voting. Childs (2016), on the other hand, was more concerned about opportunities for greater inclusivity, including for the public, than maintaining the existing culture, calling for more flexible and welcoming meeting places, including the layout of the House of Commons. The debate about the restoration and renewal of the Palace of Westminster continues.[10]

---

9   It should be noted that the Hansard Society's proposal was put forward before the 2017 Westminster terrorist attack.
10   See R. Kelly (2018, 2022) for a full history.

The Australian experience is quite different, given the Australian Parliament's relatively recent history. Nevertheless, concerns about the effectiveness and symbolism of the parliamentary building have similarly evolved, and the planning and construction of Australia's federal capital and its national buildings were not without controversy, even if their designer, Walter Burley Griffin, was not subject to the extent of hostility meted out to Barry.[11] The first meeting of the Australian Parliament took place on 9 May 1901 at the Exhibition Building in Melbourne; its first purpose-built home in Canberra, the 'provisional' Parliament House, was opened on 9 May 1927. Plans for its permanent location were caught up in controversy relating to aspects of Griffin's design for Canberra, but eventually the 'new and permanent' Parliament House opened on 9 May 1988. As described by then prime minister Bob Hawke:

> It is a building for the entire Australian community, a workplace for the community's elected representatives and a free and open forum for resolving the community's concerns … [T]he symbolic and practical importance of the building, as well as the very high standard of excellence of its construction and finish, will be a great source of pride to all Australians now and in the future. (in McCann et al. 2018)

Kouzmin (1979) likened the building of the new Australian Parliament House to Sydney's Opera House project, citing incompatibility between architectural idealism and political necessity. Disney and Nethercote (1996) offered the reflections of its occupants as an assessment of the effectiveness of parliament's structures and processes, including the observation that the building's excessive space was impersonal and isolating (Hutchison 1996; see also Uhr and Wanna 2000). Annual reports from the former Department of the Parliamentary Library (DPL) evidenced dismay from librarians when members eschewed the longer distances between their offices and the library and submitted their requests by electronic means rather than in person (DPL 1989). Many participants in a roundtable discussion on architecture and parliament also commented on the effect of the distance between functional areas in the new Parliament House

---

11   For a full account of controversies in both parliaments, see Cocks (1977) and McCann et al. (2018).

(Fewtrell et al. 2008).[12] The much-lamented non-members' bar in the former building was one of the Australian Parliament's important informal spaces (see Norton 2018b); its successor in the new building was underutilised and later housed parliament's childcare centre. 'Aussie's' coffee shop, while popular, was only a partial substitute. The building's workplace culture has been heavily criticised in recent times (including widely publicised allegations of sexual assault; AHRC 2021), marking another similarity with the Palace of Westminster (O'Malley 2018; Warhurst 2018; Prasser 2019).

Aside from the historical and physical differences between the two parliamentary buildings, a symbolic difference lies in the newly housed Australian Parliament's relationship with the public. Its architect, Romaldo Giurgola, believed it was important that the new building was seen to be inviting all citizens to visit and see democracy working. The descending arms of the forecourt walls were described as a gesture of welcome and the position of the building, nestled into Capital Hill, symbolised the rise of democracy rather than the imposition of government over the people. Public access was estimated to extend to one-fifth of the building. However, public access has been progressively restricted in the first 30 years of the building's life, due to security concerns—ironically, from public protests as well as potential terrorist attacks (Bennett 2008). These restrictions are seen to have contributed to a deterioration of the relationship between parliament and the public (The Canberra Times 2017; Day 2017; Fewtrell 2017). A further difference is the presence in the Australian Parliament of the executive's ministerial offices—seen as both a boon and a disadvantage by its occupants (Fewtrell et al. 2008) and a factor of significance in recent workplace culture inquiries (AHRC 2021).

Dilemmas in the management of the United Kingdom's and Australia's symbolic, iconic parliamentary buildings continue to arise, including in the context of the Covid-19 pandemic and concerns about a debilitating parliamentary workplace culture. These are discussed in later chapters on governance, management and procedural and cultural reform.

---

12   The roundtable discussion brought together original planners and architects, academics, parliamentary officials and members of the public and revealed useful insights into the new building's symbolic influences, including its differences from Westminster and its capacity to adapt to future requirements.

Conclusion

As we can see, calls for parliamentary reform have been manifest. Those I have documented—they are by no means exhaustive—detail a long chronology of criticisms over many decades going to the heart of parliament's conflicting roles and an apparent inability or resistance among parliamentary officials and elected members to bring about meaningful reform. There is, of course, a story to tell about repeated attempts in both parliaments to improve their administrative efficiency and these attempts are described in the next chapter, along with insights into the specialised nature and roles of parliamentary administration.

3

The 'specialised little world' of parliamentary administration

Overview

The calls for reform of parliament documented in the previous chapter came largely from external actors concerned particularly with public engagement, executive–legislative relations, governance and resourcing. Not all these calls went unheeded and we have seen, over the decades, significant improvements in communications and in the facilities and resources available to members. But claims that the two parliaments have always been insular, self-serving and elitist cannot be easily dismissed. In this chapter, I establish the context within which administrative reform has occurred and bring to the account an understanding of the specialised nature of parliamentary management and the traditions, beliefs and practices of parliamentary administrators that have influenced the pace of reform. The chapter describes a culture of 'uniqueness' that has resisted calls for greater attention to be paid to effective management practices. It begins with insights into the specialised nature of the roles of parliamentary officials and, in the second half, provides a historical trajectory of administrative reform in the two legislatures.

The UK Parliament

Much has been written about Parliament—Parliament as a place of legislature, as court of law, as defender of the liberties of the people (and their oppressor at times) … but the great machinery of Parliament, as distinct from the machinery of government, is not kept running by politicians, nor does it run itself; it is kept in motion, cared for and continually brought up to date by men who are carefully chosen and meticulously trained to carry out this peculiarly subtle task … Seen against the background of contemporary politics, the internal organisation of Parliament … may appear complicated—to some, even chaotic—but the endless efficiency of the machine itself is undeniable. And this efficiency, which has been maintained through every crisis thrust upon it by Parliament and the nation's affairs, is simply the product of the efforts of all those men who are part of this specialised little world. (Marsden 1979: 11)

Marsden's idealised account of the roles of parliamentary administrators noted the 'unique' characteristics of officers of the parliament: they were almost religiously non-political; professionally expert with a reputation second to none; unmercenary;[1] discreet, knowledgeable, instinctive and prescient; and devoted to duty—characteristics suggestive of the archetypal Weberian bureaucrat. But it was only through living and working in 'the very special atmosphere that [existed] uniquely within the walls of Westminster' that they began to absorb that 'intangible "something"' and then to act in the way it demanded (Marsden 1979: 16). There can be no doubting Marsden's view of the parliament and its administrators as *sui generis*. Rydz (1979) also gave useful insights into the early development of the clerk's role. In describing how the clerks of the House of Commons once acted as parliamentary agents by exploiting their privileged positions to extract fees from the proponents of private bills introduced into the parliament, he demonstrated how influential they have been since the earliest days of the institution in providing procedural advice—a clerk's principal role (see also Williams 1954).

The early parliamentary literature examined in this study focused mainly on procedural reform. Michael Ryle—a clerk in the House of Commons from 1951 to 1989, co-founder of the Study of Parliament Group in

---

1   Which Marsden defines as being willing to work for more than 80 hours a week, month after month, for no extra pay (1979: 16).

1964 and joint author of an authoritative work on parliamentary functions, processes and procedures (Griffith and Ryle 1989)—noted the contribution of 50 years of procedural reform to the growing influence and effectiveness of parliament, and he strongly defended the institution's relevance. But he also urged the House of Commons to 'take itself and its practices more seriously' (Griffith and Ryle 1989: 10) and suggested ways in which the House's modernisation and procedure committees could achieve further legislative reform. However, Johnson (2005)—an emeritus fellow of Nuffield College, Oxford—questioned the assumption of many political and parliamentary practitioners that procedural change and adaptation had, in fact, strengthened parliament's effectiveness. He believed the challenge was not just to change the balance of power between government and parliament by reforming procedures, but also to rethink what parliament 'can and cannot do' in a more complex environment where it seemed increasingly disconnected from the real citizens. He advocated 'standing back from the preoccupations of politicians and officials *who work the system as it now is*' (Johnson 2005: 19; emphasis added) to adopt practices that wider society might understand and recognise. Among the uncomfortable questions parliamentary institutions should ask themselves, Johnson listed: 'Could not officials discharge some of the functions presently reserved for the most part to political appointees, many of whom are ill-prepared for the managerial functions to which they often lay claim?' (2005: 20). We see here a call for greater agency for parliamentary officials and perhaps an early connection with Moore's (1995) concept of public value and subsequent criticisms of unelected officials crossing the political divide (Shergold 1997; Rhodes and Wanna 2007, 2009).

Blackburn et al. (2003: vii), in their preface to the second edition of Griffith and Ryle's work, also acknowledged the concept of self-interest in their study of how the rules, processes and procedures affecting the work of parliament were 'employed in practice and *manipulated* by the participants at Westminster in order to further their own vested interests and objectives' (emphasis added). Readers cannot avoid inferring that traditional parliamentary practitioners, including proponents of procedural reform, sought principally to preserve the institution of parliament in their own image, rather than pursuing Crick's ideal of reaching out to the public—a theme that is explored throughout this account.

Crewe (2015, 2017) offered a different perspective: a strong defence of the roles and culture of clerks, sweeping aside perceptions that they remain backward-looking, tradition-bound and opposed to innovation, and that they make poor managers. On the contrary, she argued, they are at risk of being pressured into following external organisational norms, becoming bureaucrats and losing the detailed knowledge of the rules that is required for flexibility and innovation (Crewe 2017: 65). Crewe likened the clerks to either Magi or mandarins—on the one hand, protecting parliamentary rules and knowledge; on the other, managing the rulers—concluding that, in fact, they are neither. To her, the mix of improvisation, innovation and interpretation that clerks have to master sets them apart from priests and, unlike the mandarins of the civil service, they are not involved in developing or implementing government policies or services. Rather, they are both custodians *and* reformers and their goals are to win support for the institution and serve its members. Crewe's (2017) work on the clerks' roles and culture was insightful but also seemingly dismissive of the strategic or managerial role they perform, appearing to offer instead a defence of process over outcome. It also contrasted with research that found that House of Commons administrators themselves saw the need for improved professional management, long-term planning, economy and efficiency—albeit within the context of parliament's independence and a sensitivity to members' demands—provided they could maintain their distinction from the civil service (Barrett 1999).

Blackburn et al. (2003: 203) also explained that the functions of officeholders in parliament—to exercise authority, speak on its behalf, administer its business and serve its members—are, in fact, divided among elected MPs and permanent officers and staff employed by the House, often for the whole of their career. This explanation provides an important allusion to the distinct role elected members do (and should) play in the parliament's administration, as well as in the lawmaking, scrutiny, representational and grievance-airing roles typically associated with MPs. It links the management of the business of the House with the administrative requirements and processes that support its functioning. This link is germane to articulating a comprehensive understanding of parliamentary administration—one that includes management of both the business of parliament and the administrative support underpinning all its functions. As this book argues, the history of management reform in the two parliaments has tended to view management as a separate and subsidiary function and has failed to acknowledge the relationship between political and institutional reform and effective public management.

The business relationship also comes to mind when considering the political role of the whips, whose principal duties are to keep MPs informed about forthcoming parliamentary business, to ensure they attend important debates and vote in support of their parties and to pass on to the party leadership the opinions of backbench members (Walpole et al. 2008). The traditional hunting analogy of a whipper-in who ensures the hounds do not stray remains a preferred description of the whips' role (Renton 2004; Crewe 2015), and their influence in managing the business of the House and its members' responses through 'the usual channels' is well documented (Walpole et al. 2008; Crewe 2015; Rogers and Walters 2015). Less has been written about when the whips' roles extend into administrative activity. One prominent example is the 2009 expenses scandal in the UK House of Commons.[2] Crewe (2015) recounted that, before the scandal and the subsequent transfer of responsibility for the oversight of parliamentary expenses to an external body, the whips would use their knowledge of individual members' expenses claims and other personal affairs to offer a form of protection in return for party loyalty. She claimed they retain an ability to offer rewards to loyal members, such as a good office within the parliamentary estate (Crewe 2015: 136). However, rising independence among backbenchers and an increase in cross-party cooperation have reduced the power and authority of the whips over the management of parliamentary business and contributed to the erosion of their influence (House of Commons Reform Committee 2009; House of Commons Political and Constitutional Reform Committee 2013).[3]

The Speaker's role (and the roles of other presiding officers) is central to the effectiveness of parliamentary administration, as will become apparent. But early scholars were divided about the professional standing of this high office. According to Cocks (in Laundy 1964: vii), the Speaker in the mid-twentieth century did not appear to be burdened by managerial responsibilities outside their notably antiquated and dignified position in the chamber. In contrast, Laundy (1979), in Walkland's collection of essays on the House of Commons by the Study of Parliament Group, gave a spirited defence of the onerous duties of the office—the principal ones being to apply and interpret the rules and practice of the House and maintain order in debate. He sought to demolish the 'fallacy' put forward

---

2   For a full account, see Winnett and Rayner (2009) and vanHeerde-Hudson (2014).
3   This followed the procedural reforms arising from the expenses scandal, including the creation of the Backbench Business Committee and changes to the selection process for committee chairs. But note the heightened power of the 'usual channels' during sittings of the Covid-19 hybrid parliament.

by Jennings (1961: 65) that the qualities required of a Speaker were not very high and any reasonable person could make a success of the office. The only administrative duties Laundy mentioned were those pertaining to being head of the five departments forming the House of Commons administration (in effect, the Speaker's counsel acted as de facto head and relieved the Speaker of the day-to-day administration).[4] He did note, however, that in 1973, the Speaker ordered a 'thorough-going review of the structure, organisation and co-ordination of the services provided by the five departments' (Laundy 1979: 198). This was known as the Compton review (1974); it was the start of a series of management reviews that led to the establishment of the House of Commons Commission and which have progressively modernised the House of Commons' administration.

Responsibility for responding to members' demands, as well as maintaining order, security and ceremony, lay with the Serjeant-at-Arms. The role's multiple domestic oversight tasks included accommodation, cleaning, laundry, stationery, telephones and division bells, but not catering services, which were provided by professional managerial staff appointed by a select committee but who did 'not enjoy the status of House officials' (Marsden 1979: 239). Marsden wryly recorded that although these 'routine tasks' could be undertaken by staff 'in their stride', the Serjeant, as the contact point for users of the services, was the constant recipient of everyone's complaints and suggestions; 'the trouble [was], from his point of view, that he generally [had] to *do* something about them' (Marsden 1979: 211; emphasis in original). The 1974 Compton review included sweeping changes to the Serjeant's remit, but, as we will learn, the review attracted strident criticism from staff, and only led to further investigations. Today, the Serjeant's non-ceremonial role is principally related to access to and within the parliamentary building.

---

4   Laundy (1964: 67) cited the source of the Speaker's authority as emanating from the House itself—he was the servant, not its master—and that authority, exercised in accordance with the wishes of the House, extended to regulating the course of debate, calling on members to speak, ensuring established conventions were observed and using the Standing Orders to interpret and implement the House's will. A compelling source for this view comes from Speaker Lenthall's defiance of the King in upholding the privileges of parliament in 1642: 'I have neither eyes to see nor tongue to speak in this place, but as the house is pleased to direct me, whose servant I am here' (UK Parliament 2018b). Other authors (Niven et al. 1959; Marsden 1979; Lloyd 1976) have described the institutional authority of the Speaker and other official roles modelled on the Westminster system without shedding any light on management aspects.

The library and Hansard functions have also received some attention in parliamentary literature. Marsden (1979) noted that the House of Commons Library emerged from a small collection of records, pamphlets and assorted books stored in a warehouse in the custody of the Clerk of the Journals. It was officially established in 1818 in a 1.6-square-metre room in the Palace of Westminster and rehoused following the Great Fire of 1834 into a noble suite of rooms in the finest position in the palace. Notwithstanding that the first librarian was reported to have died from overwork, the life of successive librarians continued at a steady pace and they were able to preside with 'leisured dignity' from their desk in the library itself (Marsden 1979: 177). The library was the responsibility of the Speaker and was 'governed' by a series of standing committees until 1862, after which it was left to its own devices. In 1922, it came under the direct control of a committee appointed by the House to advise the Speaker on library affairs. With the influx of new and more demanding members in the 1945 parliament, a select committee was appointed to oversee it and it expanded rapidly thereafter (see also Menhennet and Palmer 1967). Gay (2017), a former senior library staffer and scholar, provided a contemporary account of the development of the House of Commons Library with a specific focus on House-wide corporate management and service improvement. She claimed that interdepartmental rivalries and jealousies, particularly from within the clerk's department, inhibited change—resistance being the product of an excessive emphasis on hierarchy and departmentalism that existed until the 1990s. She did, however, praise the largely unrecognised role of the Study of Parliament Group for fostering parliamentary reform that was more broadly based than simply procedural reform, and she highlighted technology and the appointment of non-librarians as factors contributing to the library taking on outreach and public engagement roles.

The story of Hansard as the publisher of a near-verbatim report of parliamentary debates has been well documented by parliament's officials (Weatherston 1975; Marsden 1979; Church 1991; Holland 1991; Barrett 2010; Sutherland and Farrell 2013). Although the service could be considered 'ancient', and has generally been highly regarded, Hansard staff have not retained the same cachet as other long-established parliamentary staff. The service and its staff are particularly vulnerable to technological innovation and efficiency initiatives, including contracting out.

I have touched briefly on the characteristics and administrative roles of officers and members of the House of Commons, influenced by the 'special' nature of parliamentary administration; the importance of maintaining order, security and ceremony; an increasing level of dissatisfaction from members with the services offered; and, from a scholarly perspective, questions about the nature and effectiveness of administrative reform. Central to this picture is an ethos epitomised by the need to hold the executive to account, as summed up by MP Hugh Munro-Lucas-Tooth:

> It is not the mere existence of Parliament which ensures our freedom but the way in which we do our job here. If Parliament becomes inefficient or impotent, the first thing which will suffer will be our personal freedom as citizens. I will not base my argument on the view that the power of the executive is too great. On the contrary, I recognise that the power of the executive is great … [W]hether we like it or not, it will grow greater … But if it is inevitable, then that is the best reason why we should ensure that we make the machinery for the supervision of the executive by Parliament as modern and as strong as it can be. (in Menhennet and Palmer 1967)

For an outline of the history of administrative practice in the House of Lords, the research notes provided by the House of Lords Library are an excellent resource (Brown and Evennett 2015; James et al. 2017; Torrance 2017). The Select Committee on the House of Lords' Offices (the Offices Committee) was established shortly after the *Clerk of the Parliaments Act* was enacted in 1824 to supervise appointments and conditions of employment in what were then the only two offices in the House of Lords: the Clerk of the Parliaments and the Black Rod. Thereafter the committee of more than 60 members presided over the House of Lords Library, refreshments, works of art, staff, finance and administration. In 1965, responsibility was formally vested in the Lord Chancellor, acting as Speaker of the House of Lords. He delegated his authority to the Offices Committee, with the Black Rod acting as its agent. Following the *Constitution Reform Act 2005*, the lords resolved that they should elect their own presiding officer (House of Lords Select Committee on the Speakership of the House 2005). The first Lord Speaker was elected in July 2006 but with a very different role from that of the Speaker of the House of Commons. The House of Lords is self-regulating and the Lord Speaker has no power to rule on matters of order; his or her primary role in presiding is to assist proceedings. During question time, the Leader of the House continues to advise the House (Brown and Evennett 2015).

The leaders and whips of the main political parties within the House of Lords (sometimes including the Convenor of the Crossbench Peers) are also known as the 'usual channels'. They play a key role in decision-making about the governance and administration of the House, including facilities and services for members. In 2002, the Offices Committee was replaced with a new House Committee, which was tasked with providing leadership and strategic planning for the House of Lords' administration, reflecting earlier widespread dissatisfaction with service delivery and the standard of accommodation (Blackburn et al. 2003). Crewe (2005: 174) noted that the 'usual channels' were not much interested in managing the House of Lords during the 1990s; Labour managers had enough on their plate; Conservatives did not see much wrong with it; and the Liberal Democrats, who complained about inefficiency, were ignored. The path to management reform in the House of Lords is discussed later in this chapter.

The position of Clerk of the Parliaments (the title being indicative of the tenure of the clerk through successive parliaments) was once considered a sinecure (Bond 1958), although administrative changes have since added considerably to the procedural functions of the office. Crewe's (2005) anthropological study of rituals and politics in the House of Lords provided insights into the hierarchical nature of the various administrative offices. As a group, the clerks have been criticised for their snobbery, privileges, exclusiveness and intolerance of mistakes, including by staff within the semi-autonomous fiefdoms of the library, the parliamentary archives, Hansard and the refreshment department, who themselves have exhibited traits of exclusivity and remoteness. Rivalries between those facilitating the business of the House and those concerned with maintaining the building and looking after the peers stemmed partly from the backgrounds of staff. Overall, Crewe concluded, management has been inconsistent, tending towards conservatism; nevertheless, the changes that most public institutions in the United Kingdom have undergone have also affected the House of Lords.

From this overview of both houses, we are left with an impression of a parliament with two separate administrations, each inculcating specialised tasks and fiefdoms, the existence of self-serving social hierarchies and an environment resembling a gentlemen's club. We are also aware of an institution facing increasing external pressures for change.

The Australian Parliament

Reid and Forrest's (1989) single chapter on parliamentary administration is surprisingly candid, perhaps reflecting Reid's later career as a political scientist, following his official roles in the House of Representatives. It noted a complete lack of early planning for how the new Commonwealth Parliament would operate from its inception in 1901, citing widespread confusion among parliamentarians about their administrative roles and responsibilities. Members and senators were indifferent to staffing and administration arrangements for the two houses, being content to leave those matters to the presiding officers. Then prime minister, Edmund Barton, capitalised on this confusion to great effect, appointing a new Clerk of the House of Representatives against the advice of the Speaker and maintaining control over the officers of the library and parliamentary reporting staff until arrangements were finalised under the *Public Service Act* in 1902. Although members were said to regard the clerks as overpaid, with what little work they had to do being of a routine and clerical nature, the powers of the clerks were significant and the two house departments became 'insular and deferential' and displayed 'intense hostility' to any measures that might have threatened their limited scope for advancement (Reid and Forrest 1989: 416–17). Jealousies, suspicion and politicking between departments stymied attempts at reform and raised questions about who *should* be in control of parliament's administrative affairs. For more than 60 years, the five departments remained almost unchanged structurally, with hierarchical and slow progression of officials to senior levels.

Reid and Forrest succinctly encapsulated the effect of early administrative decisions resulting from a culture of insularity, exclusivity and hostility towards outsiders, and even one's own colleagues, combined with a lack of support and engagement from both the presiding officers and other members:

> In matters of parliamentary administration, organisation and staffing, the executive arm of government has exploited the weaknesses of the five parliamentary departments and their employees. The latter have suffered the disability of organisational fragmentation and an absence of leadership and representation within the Cabinet and the party rooms. The party affiliations of the respective presiding officers and the temporary nature of their appointments have consistently placed the parliamentary

organisations they are required to administer at a considerable disadvantage. *The resort to rhetoric about parliamentary independence in budgetary management has not helped*; neither has the predisposition of parliamentary officials to have their organisational arrangements and salary classification tied to public service criteria and public service recommendations. *The lack of a person authorised to advocate, negotiate and plan in the interests of Parliament as an institution has greatly impeded the growth of an effective parliamentary administration.* (Reid and Forrest 1989: 433; emphasis added)

There are elements of self-interest within this historical account of parliamentary administration in Australia, as in earlier references to the UK Parliament (Rydz 1979; Blackburn et al. 2003; Crewe 2005; Gay 2017). Continued politicking among officials and members within the two houses has also hampered the progress of structural reforms on efficiency grounds, as discussed later in this chapter.

More recent commentary on the role of officers in the House of Representatives sheds little light on the execution of their managerial responsibilities but offers some insights into procedural roles. Wright, former clerk of the House of Representatives and editor of *House of Representatives Practice*, drew on Laundy's work on the historical development of the Speaker's role in the United Kingdom. He echoed the latter's description of the speakership as being 'an office of great importance not only in its significant and onerous duties but particularly for what it is held to represent' and noted that the Speaker is not extraordinary but an 'ordinary person of the highest calibre' (Wright and Fowler 2012: 161–63). Wright drew also on Erskine May to highlight differences in the degree of impartiality exercised by the Speaker in the House of Commons in the UK Parliament and the Speaker of the House of Representatives in the Australian Parliament. In the latter case, the Speaker, although ostensibly impartial while in the chair, remains politically affiliated with his or her party and is not considered independent. This important difference in the way the Speaker's role is executed is discussed further in Chapter 5. The powers and functions of the presiding officers under the *Parliamentary Service Act 1999* parallel those of a government minister, but responsibility for day-to-day administrative matters is delegated to the clerks of the two houses and to the Secretary of the Department of Parliamentary Services, which provides services and facilities to both houses. The Speaker has *ex officio* membership of the House Committee and the House Appropriations and Administration Committee.

PARLIAMENT: A QUESTION OF MANAGEMENT

Like Marsden (1979), Wright emphasised the distinction between parliamentary staff and those serving the executive, highlighting their impartiality and professional expertise. He described the procedural role of the Clerk of the House in some detail, but did not elaborate on the management role, merely stating that it 'covers the usual range of departmental functions including staffing matters, financial management and so on' (Wright and Fowler 2012: 207). This is not a surprising observation but is illustrative of the differing emphasis placed on procedural and management roles, particularly in the Australian Parliament with its separate services department. Wright outlined the historical role of the Serjeant-at-Arms: as in the House of Commons, it is principally concerned with the ceremony of parliament and the preservation of order. In practice, duties also include serving on the parliament's Security Management Board and providing a range of support services to members.

Laing (2013), a former senate clerk, in an address to the 44th Presiding Officers and Clerks Conference, stated that continuing to give advice, whether the advice was contested or acted on, was possibly the most important function clerks performed, both to support individual members to be effective parliamentarians and for institutional purposes by ensuring that important things (powers, practices and procedures) were not forgotten. Patmore (2017), a former member of the Tasmanian Parliament, told a workshop of parliamentary scholars and parliamentarians that the clerks are vital in supporting the concepts of the separation of powers and responsible government; he saw their role as going beyond the purely administrative and advisory. As editor of *Odger's Australian Senate Practice*, Laing (2016b) provided a brief account of the management roles of the Senate's senior offices. The president is responsible for the proper conduct of proceedings of the Senate and the interpretation and application of its rules, in addition to 'ministerial-type functions' (Laing 2016b: 146). The president chairs the Standing Committee on Appropriations, Staffing and Security, which determines the budget and oversees the Senate's organisational structure, and is also concerned with seating arrangements in the chamber, room allocations and certain entitlements of senators. The incumbent has joint administrative responsibility with the Speaker for the joint department (the Department of Parliamentary Services) and joint control of the parliamentary precincts. The Clerk of the Senate, as the departmental head of the Department of the Senate, exercises the powers of a departmental secretary and is responsible for the budget, staffing and management of the department. The perennial problem of the dependence of the parliament on the executive for funding is addressed in a brief history of the establishment of the Senate Appropriations and Staffing Committee and the introduction of a separate appropriation bill for the parliament (Laing 2016b: 156).

In many ways, the administrative roles of officials and members in the Australian Parliament are similar to those of their counterparts in the UK Parliament; indeed, as the discussion above makes clear, the House of Representatives draws much of its organisation and characteristics from the House of Commons. But there are also differences. In the Senate in particular, much store is set on its independence from the executive, not just in budgetary matters, but also in organisational and structural issues. As an elected chamber, its powers are vastly greater than those of the House of Lords and, under existing electoral arrangements, its legislative independence from the executive is largely guaranteed. The presiding officers in the Australian Parliament also retain their affiliation with their party. The effects of these differences will become apparent later in this account. For now, we can look at the pattern of administrative reviews in each parliament, commencing in the 1970s, to see evidence of resentment among parliamentary officials and members towards the management function; a lack of interest by members in the administrative complexities of the services provided to them—at least until they become the subject of public criticism, usually after some type of failure; the slow pace of management reform; and continuing concerns about governance and strategy.

Chronicling administrative reforms: A historical and institutional perspective

House of Commons Service

Moroney (1997) described early attempts at reform precipitated by the inadequate accommodation available to members in the outdated Palace of Westminster. Control of the palace passed from the monarch to the two houses in 1965 but there was still no clear line of authority for the administration of the parliament, and the *House of Commons Act 1812*, which had established a 13-member commission, made no provision for the appropriate representation of members. The parliament had 'little control over its own budget, an ineffective committee system and outdated staff supervisory arrangements' (Moroney 1997: 23). Constant lobbying achieved some small concessions, such as secretarial support and office facilities, but the pressure for reform grew, including from proponents of procedural reform who were able to draw links between administrative structures, members' services and facilities and parliamentary effectiveness (Jennings 1941; Hill and Whichelow 1964; Crick 1968). The Compton review (1974) recommended, among other things, a unified house service under a new chief officer and interchanges between the house service and the civil service, but the review was roundly condemned by members and staff and was quickly succeeded by an internal investigation headed by a House of Commons member. Bottomley (1975) reported that even though the Compton review had received little input from members, it had been criticised for its failure to avoid executive government control, its underestimation of the differences between the requirements of the House and the wider civil service, its proposed appointment of a 'chief officer' (likened to a 'fifth wheel on the coach'; p. 9), its underestimation of the relative importance of procedural services and its proposals on the pay, grading and retirement of officials. Although Bottomley rejected much of Compton's civil service approach to parliamentary administration, the groundwork was laid (Moroney 1997) and, two years later, the *House of Commons (Administration) Act 1978* was passed, establishing the House of Commons Commission, with the Speaker as chair and appropriate member representation. The commission became responsible for the employment of staff in a unified service, with the clerk as accounting officer. The first annual report of the commission was presented in 1979.

Boulton (1991), a former clerk of the House, saw the passing of the *House of Commons (Administration) Act* as a watershed—the most significant change in the organisation of house services in modern times. Lacking radical tendencies, it nonetheless presaged the assertion by the House of Commons of its right to control its internal affairs. It did not, however, lead to a unified hierarchy: each head of department retained significant independence, and although the clerk was the senior officer of the House, they had no power to intervene in the affairs of their colleagues.[5] No one was in charge.

---

5   The House of Commons has yet to appoint a woman to the role of Clerk of the House.

An examination of the commission's annual reports over the decade following their inception in 1979 does not bear out the initial enthusiasm for the changes brought about by the new administration. Despite repeated assurances from successive accounting officers (the Clerk of the House) that the 'authorities of the House' considered themselves to be under a moral obligation to scrutinise expenditure, particularly on staff numbers, as 'thoroughly and strictly as possible' (House of Commons Commission 1979: 6), ensuing reports revealed growing concerns about staffing costs, pay and grading, recruitment, accommodation, the introduction of technology and financial management, particularly within the refreshments department.

In 1990, Sir Robin Ibbs was invited to conduct a short but detailed review of the provision of services to members to address divided responsibilities and to ensure a coordinated decision-making structure that could respond to, and prioritise, the demands by members for services. Ibbs (House of Commons Commission 1990) pointed to continuing widespread dissatisfaction from members, particularly about accommodation and catering, which was exacerbated by the increasing gap between the House's need for accommodation and facilities and the original design of the Palace of Westminster, and the lack of control by the House over its works program.[6] The review drew attention to shortcomings in the management structures and the lack of effective financial control and oversight. Ibbs emphasised the need for greater clarity among members on how the House operated administratively; a survey of members conducted during the review found that although 58 per cent claimed to understand the way services were managed, the majority of them were ignorant about the role of the commission. It also found a positive correlation between knowledge of the way services were managed and the level of satisfaction expressed by members—an important observation in terms of the value of members' engagement in administration.

The Ibbs 'settlement' included a more strategic role for the commission, an enhanced corporate management role for the management board, a new financial management system, the appointment of a finance director, clarity around the role of the Clerk of the House as *primus inter pares* in executing policy on service delivery, transferring to the House of

---

6   The vote for expenditure on works until 1992 was controlled by the Department of Environment and the House's influence on decisions on how and when money was spent was minimal (House of Commons Commission 1990; Torrance 2017).

Commons Commission responsibility for all Commons expenditure except members' salaries, and regular examination of the House's accounts and performance by the National Audit Office and Public Accounts Committee. The commission welcomed the recommendations and noted the House's general support. It was enthusiastic about the review's evolutionary nature yet reassured that 'the main procedural, library and accountancy services were the subject of so little criticism' (House of Commons Commission 1991: 7). The commission also commended the structural changes made by the House of Lords Offices Committee that reflected the Ibbs proposals and looked forward to 'better decision making and accountability in the provision of services for Parliament as a whole' (House of Commons Commission 1991: 10).

In 1998, the House of Commons Commission called for what was in effect a post-implementation review of Ibbs, albeit almost a decade later. The Braithwaite report (1999) began by noting the contextual complexity of parliamentary administration:

> Resourcing a Parliament effectively is of vital constitutional importance, but extremely difficult. The business is complex, the environment reactive and unpredictable. Expectations of public bodies have increased, but the problems are no less. There must be strategic planning, effective management and financial control; but also sensitivity to the needs of the House and its Members. (Braithwaite 1999: 9)

Braithwaite was a management consultant from the private sector. He commended the Ibbs 'settlement' as a 'remarkable piece of work [resulting] in an integrated plan for the planning and delivery of services, and the House's control over its own expenditure' (Braithwaite 1999: 9–10). However, he concluded that much remained to be done in terms of strategic planning, political governance, better financial management and control, separation of political advice and decision-making and a 'corporate' method of operation among the house departments. Although the rise in levels of satisfaction with accommodation was striking, satisfaction with the management of emerging information technology was low. The commission had not taken a strategic view and members were still insufficiently knowledgeable about the House's administration and services. Braithwaite acknowledged that the clerk had assumed the role of chief executive to a greater extent over the previous few years; however, he noted a lack of formal authority over other heads of department and their performance.[7] While Braithwaite's willingness to acknowledge and build on earlier work was notable, he made it clear the status quo was not an option. Rush (2005: 47) recognised the achievements of Bottomley, Ibbs and Braithwaite, not just in organisational and managerial reform, with departments of the House becoming increasingly professionalised, but also as 'a means to the end of improving the ability of MPs and the House as a whole to fulfil [their] functions by providing appropriate and adequate resources'. He noted, however, that 'institutional professionalisation' had yet to be achieved.

In 2006, the House of Commons Commission initiated the third in its series of major management reviews, the Tebbit review. The terms of reference included whether the benefits of the Braithwaite review had been realised, whether further actions were required to achieve strategic plans and whether 'the organisational and staffing arrangements … are adequate to realise the objectives laid down in the Resolution of the House of 26 January 2005 relating to Connecting Parliament with the Public' (House of Commons Commission 2007a: i). A link was thus made between the management reform agenda and the outcomes of the Modernisation Committee established in 1997 as part of the incoming Labour government's commitment to modernisation and renewal (Kelso 2007a).[8] Tebbit was at pains to point out that his review was not intended to contribute primarily to reforming parliamentary procedure and constitutional policy prescriptions but was concerned with

> the more prosaic issue of how the services to support the institution of the House of Commons and members of parliament are governed, managed and delivered—vital in itself, given the importance of a well-functioning parliament in the affairs of the nation. (House of Commons Commission 2007a: 3)

Nonetheless, the review acknowledged a connection that cannot be dismissed between the need for effective management of both the procedural and the management functions within a highly political context.

---

7   David Limon was appointed clerk in 1994 and was the clerk to whom Braithwaite's comments were directed. As clerk assistant, he was part of the Ibbs review team and, from 1990, acted as implementation manager.
8   The Modernisation Committee's influence on procedural and constitutional reform and its apparent sidelining of the Procedure Committee, which traditionally has jurisdiction in procedural reform, is discussed by Kelso (2007a).

Tebbit (House of Commons Commission 2007a: 4), like Braithwaite (1999), acknowledged the work of his predecessor and the reputation of the House of Commons for its effective service delivery (barring estates and works, which required remedial action). His review highlighted, however, the changing role of members, including their constituency work, and pointed to a need to replace the semi-autonomous federal nature of the House of Commons Service with a more corporate direction to achieve greater levels of performance and efficiency. Tebbit questioned the assertion that the House of Commons was a unique institution unsuited to the application of modern management techniques and the impossibility of quantifying outputs and performance given the all-pervasive influence of politics. He referred to several unique public institutions facing similar complexities; to him, the special character of the House of Commons did not preclude the need to build organisational capacity and promote effectiveness, accountability and value for money. A major recommendation, while not seeking to replace the Clerk of the House as its principal officer, aimed to bolster the chief executive officer aspects of the role and lend greater support from below to carry out procedural duties. Tebbit was careful in balancing the need for radical management reform with longstanding parliamentary traditions and beliefs.

There is a clear trajectory in these reviews of the House of Commons Service towards the need for greater professional managerial influence in service provision and the establishment of a management culture within the service. But this did not prevent a massive deterioration in the public's trust in parliament following revelations in 2009 of dubious expenses claims by members (and their counterparts in the House of Lords). Nor did it resolve the longstanding tensions between the respective priorities accorded to procedural and management roles, as reflected in 2014 in the breakdown in the relationship between the House of Commons Speaker, John Bercow, and Robert Rogers, then Clerk/CEO of the House of Commons, giving rise to a further governance review, chaired by Jack Straw, a former Leader of the House (HOCGC 2014). Whether this was precipitated by a continuing deficiency in professional management skills, despite review after review through the decades, or whether it was driven by the 'caprice' of an independently minded and progressive Speaker anxious to leave his mark on the role he had occupied for some years is a matter of conjecture; there was much speculation at the time in media reports in both the United Kingdom and Australia.[9] Chapter 4 provides a full account of the events surrounding the HOCGC and its implications.

House of Lords administration

The reform process in the House of Lords administration appears to have been heavily influenced by repeated House of Commons reviews, but peers shied away from adopting to the same extent the managerial practices introduced in the Commons (Torrance 2017). Following the 1990 Ibbs review, the House of Lords streamlined its administrative arrangements by reducing the number of subcommittees and delegating responsibility for decision-making. However, as these committees had no terms of reference or ability to report to the House, matters still had to be handled by the Offices Committee, resulting in an overlap of responsibilities. When the Offices Committee resolved in 2000 to engage Michael Braithwaite, who was responsible for the 1999 review of the House of Commons administration, to conduct a similar review, some peers baulked at the prospect of introducing a management consultant and instead a steering group was appointed, headed by Lord Grenfell (Crewe 2010). In 2002, a further working group, under the chairmanship of Lord Tordoff, developed proposals including replacing the Offices Committee with a much smaller house committee and appointing a principal finance officer. The review took place in a climate of uncertainty surrounding possible House of Lords reform as part of the Blair government's modernisation agenda, but it was expected the review would lead to the House of Lords being able to better assert itself in its relations with the House of Commons regarding the provision of joint services, and most of the recommendations were agreed to (Torrance 2017).

Another review of the management arrangements in the House of Lords took place in 2007, at the same time as the Tebbit review of the House of Commons Service. The reviewers, Parker and Mahy, two senior officeholders in the energy industry, were given only five days to conduct their review and they apologised in advance for any misinterpretation of key issues. They recommended a greater focus on strategic planning and the appointment of external directors, and suggested the role of the clerk might be split to incorporate additional management capacity

---

9   See, for instance, Cooper (2014); D'Arcy (2014); Towell (2014).

rather than continuing to take a business-as-usual approach. A further report, based on the Parker–Mahy review, and taking account of Tebbit's recommendations for the House of Commons, concluded that only a tweaking of the House and domestic committees' membership and terms of reference was required. A subsequent report by the House Committee proposing new terms of reference was agreed to by the House (House of Lords Debates 2007; Torrance 2017). In 2011, a principal clerk in the House of Lords administration, together with an external consultant, conducted a 'light-touch' review of the structure of the administration and the operation of its management board. Interestingly, the only one of its recommendations not adopted was the recurring proposal to appoint a professionally qualified finance director[10] or head of corporate services to improve oversight of major programs and projects. Finally, in 2016, the House of Lords established its own commission, replicating the 2015 House of Commons administrative reforms (Torrance 2017).

Administrative reform in the Australian Parliament

In a research paper prepared for the then Parliamentary Service Commissioner, Andrew Podger, as part of a review of aspects of parliamentary administration, Adams (2002) documented at least 20 attempts over the previous century to change the administration of the Australian Parliament.[11] Podger described those attempts:

> It is a history of claims and counter-claims about bicameralism and the independence of Parliament from the Executive arm of Government and about costs, efficiency and improving services to Members. In terms of responsibility for services to Parliamentarians the history also illustrates administrative structures based essentially on history and sometimes on chance, rather than a careful consideration of good management. (2002: 5)

---

10   This was eventually achieved in 2017.

11   The principal functions of the Parliamentary Service Commissioner (PSC) are to advise the presiding officers on the management of policies and practices of the Parliamentary Service and to conduct any inquiries about the Parliamentary Service at the request of the presiding officers. The commissioner's annual reports since 2015–16 have noted the role is important; however, the involvement of the PSC is intermittent (Parliamentary Service Commissioner 2018). The commissioner also holds the office of Public Service Commissioner.

For decades, the debate had centred on parliamentary independence: whether parliament should control its own budget and whether that budget should cover the whole parliament; whether parliament's staff were different from those in the wider public service; and how the administration of parliament could be made more efficient without impinging on its independence. Governments and their central agencies were the main proponents for change, with the presiding officers becoming involved in the latter half of the past century. Key resistance to change had come from the presiding officers (in the first half of the past century), the clerks and senior departmental staff throughout the period, senators and individual backbenchers in the past 30 years and all those concerned about the diminishing role of parliament and a weakening of the separation of powers (Adams 2002: 7).

The resistance in some cases had centred on where the authority for staffing resided. Adams cited Robert Garran, a former solicitor-general, in asserting that primary responsibility for the parliamentary departments had always been in the hands of the presiding officers, but the role of senators had been strengthened by the Senate Standing Committee on Staffing and Appropriations, established in 1982, and a 1987 senate resolution requiring that the committee examine and report to the Senate on any proposed changes to the structure and responsibilities of the parliamentary departments. In 2011, the House of Representatives established its own Committee on Appropriations and Administration to consider, among other things, any changes to administrative arrangements. Both committees may confer with each other on appropriations for the DPS.

The principal focus of the reform proposals in the Australian Parliament was structural; they appeared to pay little attention to governance or strategy. Table 3.1 provides a chronology of key structural proposals from 1910 to 2004 (Adams 2002).

Table 3.1 Australian Parliament: Key structural proposals, 1910–2004

1910–12: Prime minister and presiding officers (in response)	Amalgamation of departments: Five into one. Amalgamation of departments: Five into two (including a separate Hansard department). No action taken.
1920–22: Presiding officer, McLachlan Royal Commission and senators	Divergence of opinion on absorption of parliamentary departments into public service; parliamentary offices included in *Public Service Act 1922*. Presiding officers retained control over staffing matters but were under pressure to conform to public service conditions.
1930: Executive	A further attempt to incorporate parliamentary departments into the public service failed; however, discretion afforded by rhetoric of parliamentary independence was limited.
1933: Pinner inquiry	Amalgamation of departments: Five into one. Rationalisation of common services; reclassification of positions; reorganisation of work. Report criticised for lack of understanding of parliament and rejected.
1953; 1975–76: Public Service Board	Amalgamation of departments: Five into one. Separate parliamentary service proposed. Proposals rejected.
1977: House of Representatives officials	Amalgamation of service departments: Three into one. Separate Department of Parliament proposed. Proposals rejected on grounds of autonomy of houses.
1977–79; 1980–82; 1987: Presiding officers	Separation of administrative from procedural services. Amalgamation of service departments: three into one. Interhouse rivalries prevented comprehensive examination of parliamentary administration; proposals did not proceed.
1988–96: Presiding officers and officials	Amalgamation of service departments. Various attempts did not pass the Senate.
1996–97: National Commission of Audit; presiding officers	Amalgamation of departments: Five into one. Presiding officers respond by proposing amalgamation of service departments into chamber departments. Not supported by the Senate.
1999: John Templeton, Department of the Parliamentary Reporting Staff Secretary; legislative change	Internal restructure of the Department of the Parliamentary Reporting Staff: 'One-stop shop' service support. *Parliamentary Service Act 1999* established.
2002–04: Presiding officers	Amalgamation of service departments: Three into one. Department of Parliamentary Services established on 1 February 2004.

Adams called on the observations of Broinowski, a former senate clerk, to encapsulate the essence of the entrenched resistance to change within the parliament, recited below:

> A succession of clerks, often with the connivance or tacit approval of the Presiding Officers, successfully and repeatedly used the principle of parliamentary independence to maintain autonomy from the general public service in matters in which they thought it advantageous to do so ... whilst maintaining the benefits of common standards in matters such as salary scales ...
>
> The members of the five departments thus withstood all early efforts to rationalise them. They became a self-contained and insular enclave, a priesthood, in which the status quo, the established order, and the importance of apprenticeship were heavily emphasised during the steady, often glacially slow progression officials would make through the hierarchy. Promotion depended primarily on seniority, and secondarily on profound knowledge of parliamentary practice. (Broinowski 2001: 60–61)

Adams (2002) and Reid and Forrest (1989) recounted the opprobrium from parliamentary staff towards those who would threaten the status quo that followed the 1933 report by Pinner, an inspector from the Public Service Board, at a time when the government of the day was fixed on economies in the public service. Aside from recommending a single department led by a single clerk, Pinner proposed staff cuts and a reduction in salaries and suggested that officers from the two chamber departments could help with stocktaking in the library during parliamentary recesses. Pinner was reviled for his lack of understanding of parliamentary practice, just as Compton would later be in the House of Commons.

Another radical five-into-one proposal came from the Howard government's National Commission of Audit (NCA 1996), which was established to review the operations of government. This proposal aroused significant controversy (particularly for its purported efficiency claims), yet it serves as a powerful illustration of the resistance to change within the parliament. According to a current issues brief written by a Parliamentary Library researcher:

> The Commission has attempted to highlight the cost of support services to the Parliament by calculating that the cost of operations by the five parliamentary departments works out to $600,000 for each Parliamentarian. This statistic is, however, quite misleading.

The operations performed by the parliamentary departments are not directed solely at Parliamentarians, but contribute to the functioning of a democratic system, benefiting all Australians, of which Parliamentarians themselves are a part. For example, the Parliamentary Committee system, whose costs are included in the above average, has played an important role in investigating and recommending action on a range of issues of economic and social importance, both within the private and public sectors.

Contrary to assertions in the Report, efforts to amalgamate parliamentary departments have been pursued in the past but failed for want of parliamentary support. Institutional changes in the Parliamentary Departments must have regard to the continued capacity of the Parliament to function independently and effectively. Were such changes to be seen as being dictated by the Executive Government, the preservation of parliamentary independence and the constitutional separation of functions performed in the two Chambers could also be an issue. (James 1996: 26)

James did concede that the existence of five separate departments of the parliament, with their own structures and hierarchies, could be anachronistic, particularly as each department was responsible on average for only 282 staff, compared with an average of 6,031 staff in executive departments, and that the amalgamation of routine corporate functions or the outsourcing of some tasks should be examined. This library researcher was not alone in expressing disquiet about the NCA proposal; it was vehemently opposed by the then Clerk of the Senate (Harry Evans) and the presiding officers, unsurprisingly, decided not to support it, although they did seek advice from a former secretary of the Department of Administrative Services, who concluded that the proposal *was* justifiable and *did* offer potential savings but may not have been *politically* achievable (Adams 2002). The proposal for a single parliamentary department has not resurfaced.

As we can see, the trajectory of administrative changes in the Australian Parliament was centred on attempts to increase efficiency by amalgamating departments. In the early years, there were inadequacies in the accommodation and facilities in the temporary Parliament House, but a proposed replacement was being planned as early as 1954. Indeed, as I have noted, following the 1988 move to the new Parliament House, concerns were expressed about the impersonal nature of the increased space and the distances between functional areas. The magnificent new building was a catalyst for a renewed approach to managing what was described as 'the equivalent of running a large industrial plant containing a five-star hotel in which two hundred and twenty-four major shareholders are staying at the same time' (JHD 1988: 6). Until the amalgamation of the three service departments, the Joint House Department had operated relatively autonomously and its annual reports reflected a private sector management approach, including adopting techniques of 'best practice' and 'total quality management'. Catering services were first contracted out in 1989. The recording and televising of parliamentary proceedings were aided enormously by the new facilities available. However, failures in the delivery of Hansard services, due to perceived ineffective management and the slow uptake of technology, and serious accountability issues in the then Parliamentary Information Systems Office, led to the departure of the heads of the Parliamentary Library and the Department of the Parliamentary Reporting Staff, following two critical audit reports.[12] In 1990, the Speaker of the House of Representatives appointed John Templeton, an 'outsider' from the Department of the Prime Minister and Cabinet, to head the Department of the Parliamentary Reporting Staff and subsequently the Parliamentary Library, arguably adding to the reported hostilities between the parliamentary departments.

In 2002, Podger recommended the three service departments be amalgamated. His review was also focused largely on cost savings and its terms of reference offered little encouragement to set a strategic direction for a restructured parliamentary administration, unlike the more farsighted observations of Ibbs (House of Commons Commission 1990), Braithwaite (1999) and Tebbit (House of Commons Commission 2007a) in the United Kingdom. Some of my interviewees expressed reservations about the effectiveness of the Podger review and Podger conceded he could have more actively addressed the poor relationships between the heads of the parliamentary departments:

> In relation to internal relationships at the top, if I had my time again I would probably be a bit more active as a Parliamentary Service Commissioner ... I chaired meetings once every three months of the heads of departments, but they were a bit perfunctory ... [I]f I had been clearer about agendas and what we should be getting out of them I could have teased these things out more. In hindsight, I was new to the Parliamentary Service and maybe I didn't take the role as substantially as I should have. That

---

12   See ANAO (1990a, 1990b).

might have forced a bit more dialogue. It would not have been a magic answer but if you handled the agenda and the meetings right you would ensure that different perspectives were put in the right way. And if you have papers around the agenda, you can tease the issues out very clearly, allowing discussion.[13]

The review did, however, secure the support of at least some parliamentary officials and both presiding officers, and the long sought-after amalgamation of the service departments was finally achieved, resulting in the establishment of the Department of Parliamentary Services in 2004.

The utility of this administrative reform was short-lived, at least initially, subsequent performance deficiencies were well publicised and hostilities were not resolved (SFPALC 2012a, 2012b, 2015a, 2015b; Mulgan 2014). Accounts of dysfunctional relationships or dissensus in Australia's parliamentary departments demonstrate the influence of individual parliamentary actors on the processes of administrative change that could otherwise be masked by a 'central analytic notion of "path dependency"' in historical institutionalism (Peters et al. 2005).

Conclusion

This chapter has depicted the specialised and insular environment in which parliamentary actors operate, using examples of the slow pace of reform and a culture of preservation and self-interest. It is not exhaustive—further accounts are developed in later chapters—but we are left with a dawning impression of hostile relationships between parliamentary actors, the influence of traditions and beliefs on parliamentary effectiveness and an ethos centred on parliamentary supremacy over the executive.

The UK Parliament has a long history of punctuated management reform that has the appearance of a planned, if glacier-like, approach, with a series of reviews recommending improved management processes, leadership and structures. Reform in the Australian Parliament has focused on the restructuring of departments to reduce duplication and increase efficiency, fostering a history of rhetorically based resistance and internal hostility to change that belies the extent of administrative reform resulting from a legislative framework that mirrors that of the wider Australian

---

13   A. Podger, pers. comm., 4 August 2015.

Public Service. There appears to be little difference in either parliament, however, in the perception by parliamentary actors that parliamentary administration is unique and, by implication, unsuited to wider public management reforms. Having established the historical context for administrative reform, I will analyse in the next chapter management issues in a more contemporary context, as well as the events that have contributed to continuing public dissatisfaction and internal discord.

4

Contemporary parliamentary management: How has it measured up?

Overview

In the preceding chapters, I have established the context for the underpinning tenet in this book—namely, that parliamentary management, while inherently complex and problematic, is not widely understood and remains undervalued. Issues range from parliament's ability to win the public's confidence, executive–legislative relations and a lack of overall authority and weak governance, to limited interest by many of parliament's members in administrative matters, lack of capacity and resources, and problems both practical and symbolic with the buildings in which the parliament is housed. Parliaments have displayed a resistance to external calls for reform, with parliamentary actors sticking to a widely held belief that parliament is unique, further embedding traditions of insularity and specialisation. Nevertheless, parliaments have not remained static; they have evolved inexorably as the world around them has changed. Notably, we have seen an expansion of the resources available to members to carry out their representative, legislative and scrutiny roles, including new and extended accommodation, and significant technological advancements in parliament's capacity for public engagement. Yet, the complaints about parliamentary effectiveness continue and, increasingly, they are directed towards parliament's management capacity. Also increasingly, the complaints are coming from within; members are identifying management shortcomings, yet few appear to see themselves as part of the solution.

In this chapter, I examine the parliament's management problems in a contemporary political context, addressing events to which I alluded earlier that have spurred a wider public interest in parliamentary governance. They go to the heart of the tensions that exist among the roles and priorities of parliament's many actors.

The view from the Australian Parliament

Department of Parliamentary Services

The starting point for this review of contemporary management within the Australian Parliament is the 2004 amalgamation of the three parliamentary service departments. It was designed to increase structural efficiency and reduce duplication but with little apparent regard for the difficulties of merging many distinct roles and cultures—from gardeners, mechanics, chefs and engineers to shorthand writers, librarians, security guards and IT and broadcasting experts—or to enhancing historically poor relationships between the procedural and management departments. Despite the best intentions, in some quarters, resentment and suspicion remained.

The heads of the three Australian parliamentary departments, writing in the overviews to their annual reports, looked towards their post-amalgamation futures with mixed levels of enthusiasm. Then Clerk of the Senate Harry Evans described his department's role as a 'sceptical questioner' of the amalgamation. He left no one in doubt about his department's approach:

> This administrative and financial rearrangement leaves the Senate Department much smaller in terms of budget and staff, but no less dedicated to its central functions of providing advice and support services to the Senate and its committees. It is hoped that the safeguards put in place by the Senate, the Appropriations and Staffing Committee and the President will ensure that the greatly enlarged joint department does not become a 'black hole', sucking resources out of the key legislative functions which remain the responsibility of the Senate Department. (Evans 2004: 5)

The Senate Clerk's counterpart in the Department of the House of Representatives, Ian Harris, presented a more positive view of the new joint department:

The establishment of the Department of Parliamentary Services (DPS) … was a major development in the administration of the Parliament. I welcomed this administrative change and worked with my departmental colleagues to help ensure the success of the new structure. Initially, as far as our department was concerned, the most pressing issue was the establishment of the centralised security arrangements, but the department commenced working constructively with the new department and the Department of the Senate on other issues of common interest, such as streamlined and consistent finance and personnel systems and procurement processes. (Harris 2004: 8–9)

The new department's first annual report (DPS 2004) revealed that savings from staff reductions were shaping up to be considerably less than those predicted in the Podger review (2002); the costs of managing Parliament House had increased disproportionately to past increases in budget funding and the divergence between costs and funding was likely to increase. The new department was forced into negotiations with the Department of Finance to seek a reversal of the funding cuts imposed for 2004–05 and the forward estimate years. Finance recommended careful analysis of the new department's activities in a search for further efficiencies—whether or not related to the amalgamation. In return, DPS claimed that identifying the services for which it had been notionally funded in the past would be difficult and it might need to 'start from first principles' in determining what level of services it could continue to provide and where service reductions could be made (DPS 2004: 68). The predicted outlook for DPS by its new departmental secretary, Hilary Penfold, only five months after its establishment, was gloomy:

> Having regard to our financial position, DPS will need to use this year to explore ways of providing our services more efficiently or renegotiating the provision of, or the service levels for, some of our services … At a departmental level, our focus will be on a number of areas that should provide efficiencies over the longer term … However, it is unlikely that these improvements will provide enough savings in the next two or three years to deal with our funding cuts and cost increases. (Penfold 2004: 14)

Penfold predicted reductions in standards of building maintenance, reduced service levels for Hansard and broadcasting, more efficient library services and the setting of priorities for IT and communications services.

The focus in the first full year of DPS, 2005, was almost exclusively on spending less money. External clients appeared to have found the transition fairly seamless, as far as the department was able to judge, but forthcoming efficiency reviews and a proposed departmental restructure left many staff uncertain of their futures and that of the department. Progress reported in 2005–06 included a major departmental restructure;[1] a performance audit by the Australian National Audit Office (ANAO 2006) into whether the objectives of the Podger review had been met; the appointment of a parliamentary librarian under the provisions of the amended *Parliamentary Service Act 1999* (which included a separate resources agreement for the library); the conclusion of the security enhancement project (about which the two chamber departments had been so concerned); and a call by the presiding officers for expressions of interest to operate a childcare centre in Parliament House.[2]

The ANAO performance audit concluded that improvements to physical security had been achieved but was ambiguous about the success of the amalgamation of the three service departments. It found that while 'not all the efficiencies envisaged by the Podger review had been realised', DPS had been able to absorb reductions of $6 million per annum with only 'minor changes to its services', while noting also that the department lacked objective measures of client satisfaction or an avenue for consultation on the types and levels of services required (ANAO 2006: 13–15). It also noted that decisions by the three parliamentary departments to pursue different human resource and financial information systems had not provided a foundation for efficiently moving towards the shared services model also envisaged in the Podger review (2002).

In 2007–08, then Parliamentary Service Commissioner Lynelle Briggs undertook a further review of the amalgamation of the service departments, finding that although significant savings had been delivered, it was not clear whether the savings were a result of the amalgamation itself or of direct management intervention. A sceptical questioner would likely

---

1   The rationale given was that DPS was structured entirely by reference to the skills and activities of its expert staff, not by reference to what its managers should be doing, leaving the amalgamated department with a lack of strategic planning capacity and 'several characteristics' that reduced its ability to provide the right service to clients in the long term. The restructure caused 'some upheaval' across the department; of the 11 officers who now made up the departmental executive, only one had been a Senior Executive Service officer in one of the former joint departments (DPS 2006).
2   Early planning for the provision of childcare in Parliament House was reported by the former Joint House Department in 2002 (JHD 2002).

conclude that the Department of Finance's imposition of a $6 million budget reduction immediately after the amalgamation was a form of 'direct management intervention'. DPS itself estimated that only $2 million in savings were directly attributable to the amalgamation and this amount was offset by its estimated $1.6 million cost. Briggs also recommended that the three departments develop a strategy to promote whole-of-parliamentary work and cooperation and embed the Parliamentary Service's values into governance arrangements (Parliamentary Service Commissioner 2008).

The financial pressures on DPS were again acknowledged when a new secretary, Alan Thompson, was appointed. He reported that DPS operated in 2007–08 within a budget (of $116 million) that was only slightly larger than the combined budgets of its three predecessor departments ($115 million) in 2000–01, even though the consumer price index had increased by more than 30 per cent in the intervening period. He did not, however, allude to cutting services or reducing service levels but undertook to continue 'normal' service delivery, albeit 'very frugally' (Thompson 2008: 5–6). The pressures continued in 2008–09 (Thompson 2009) and the need to 'progressively adjust' services was raised with a commitment to prioritising support for the chambers and committees. DPS and the departments of the Senate and House of Representatives all presented submissions to an inquiry into the efficiency dividend by the Joint Committee of Public Accounts and Audit (JCPAA 2008),[3] following which the committee recommended a 'parliamentary commission' co-chaired by the presiding officers to recommend funding levels for the parliamentary departments—common practice in other Westminster parliaments, including the United Kingdom. The government did not support the recommendation and subsequent attempts at greater collaboration between the parliament and the Australian Public Service appear to have been limited.[4]

---

3   Commonwealth entities are subject to an annual efficiency dividend that reduces operational budgets each year in anticipation of efficiencies being found.
4   For example, Stephen Sedgwick, Briggs' successor as Parliamentary Services Commissioner, discussed with parliamentary department heads the relevance to the Parliamentary Service of reforms to government administration proposed by an advisory group led by Terry Moran, then Secretary to the Department of the Prime Minister and Cabinet (Moran 2010; Parliamentary Service Commissioner 2010). It is not clear whether this discussion engendered any interest from the Parliamentary Service in learning from the wider public service. Sedgwick's successor, John Lloyd, offered no explanation in a letter to the author as to why the parliamentary departments were excluded from a subsequent Australian Public Service review by David Thodey (J. Lloyd, pers. comm., 4 June 2018; Independent Review of the APS 2019).

Table 4.1 Senate Finance and Public Administration Legislation Committee: The performance of the Department of Parliamentary Services — Background and interim findings

Date	Event
23 May 2011	Matters raised at budget estimates hearings and in answers to questions taken on notice relating to disposal of two billiard tables with possible heritage value.
23 June 2011	Senate reference to the Finance and Public Administration Legislation Committee (SFPALC 2012a) to inquire into and report on the performance of the Department of Parliamentary Services with wide terms of reference relating to asset management, heritage values, services and efficiencies following amalgamation, IT and any related matter.
16 November 2011	Public hearing — witnesses appearing: Romaldo Giurgola, Pamille Berg and Hal Guida, architects.
2 May 2012	Public hearing — witnesses appearing: National Trust of Australia (ACT); Walter Burley Griffin Society; Community and Public Sector Union; and Department of Parliamentary Services.
27 June 2012	Interim report published (SFPALC 2012a) — key comments and conclusions: Major weaknesses in DPS's stewardship of assets in Parliament House; the actions of the department in providing a senate committee with misleading information were unprecedented and unacceptable (p. 16). Disposal of billiard tables from Parliament House in 2010 resulted in significant expense for DPS and brought to light questionable practices in a parliamentary department where 'only the highest levels of conduct should be maintained and only the best example set' (p. 21). Committee acknowledged concerns of presiding officers regarding heritage listing of Parliament House and 'possible executive government interference in parliamentary decision making processes' (p. 31). Committee noted 'foresight of the [former] Joint House Department [JHD] in commissioning the Central Reference Document, the appointment of a Design Integrity Officer and the use of a building consultant to undertake annual audits', but was unable to judge the success or otherwise of the JHD's regime to protect the heritage of the building (p. 34). Matters for further consideration included the need to improve the accountability and transparency of DPS in relation to heritage matters; the role of presiding officers and parliament in relation to heritage matters; the role of outside experts in guiding change in the building; and what constitutes a 'significant change' to the building (p. 54).

Despite continuing reports of the financial, technological and political challenges to DPS's role in supporting the parliament, it appears to have been only by accident that MPs turned their attention to the parlous state of DPS and then only under the auspices of the Senate Finance and Public Administration Legislation Committee (SFPALC). The disposal of two billiard tables was questioned at estimates hearings in February and May 2011, where it transpired that a DPS official had misled the committee about the timing and status of an assessment of the heritage value of the tables (SFPALC 2012a). A wide-ranging inquiry ensued, including into the effects of the amalgamation on DPS's performance. The committee's hearings and interim findings are summarised in Table 4.1.

In 2012, a new secretary, Carol Mills, was appointed following the retirement of Alan Thompson amid the fallout from the 'billiard tables affair'. Mills began her own investigation of the circumstances surrounding the disposal of the billiard tables before the SFPALC's interim report was tabled in June 2012, resulting in more robust asset disposal policies and a 'strategic approach to heritage assessment' (DPS 2012: 17). But further cuts to the DPS budget, following an increase to the efficiency dividend, would lead to another 'reprioritisation' (Mills 2012: 2) and the financial year 2012–13 brought a 'transformational change agenda to reshape DPS into a more professional, outward-looking and service focused department', including changes in senior management and functional realignment (Mills 2013: 1). DPS was also required to respond to the final report of SFPALC (2012b) (see Table 4.2). Among other things, the committee called for greater accountability and transparency and a revision of performance measures that were considered to be not sufficiently informative. In the interim, Mills continued to develop the department's role in meeting the rapidly changing technology requirements of members, following a 'whole-of-parliament' external review of information and communication technology (ICT) services. A new ICT service delivery model was recommended and responsibility for all parliamentary ICT was transferred from the chamber departments and the Department of Finance to DPS (Roche 2012).[5] The role of independent external advice was strengthened by establishing a new audit committee with two independent members and creating an expert advisory panel to assist in developing a conservation management plan for Parliament House. The financial situation still presented a major challenge and substantial changes to services were forecast (Mills 2013).

---

5   The review noted a history of unsupported recommendations relating to greater coordination and strategic oversight of IT from Podger (2002); ANAO (2006); and Briggs (2008).

Table 4.2 Senate Finance and Public Administration Legislation Committee: The performance of the Department of Parliamentary Services — Final report

Date	Event
30 October 2012	Public hearing — witnesses appearing: Carol Mills, Secretary, DPS; Diane Heriot, Acting Parliamentary Librarian, DPS.
28 November 2012	Final report published (SFPALC 2012b) — key comments and conclusions:
	Lack of clear information (p. 56), strong leadership and vision (p. 207) and strategic planning for maintaining building (p. 57); reduced spending (p. 188).
	Major deficiencies in engagement with moral rightsholders, project management and design integrity (p. 90); poor asset disposal practices (p. 110).
	Poor and expensive security management and planning (pp. 148, 219).
	Deficiencies in ICT provision, including fragmented service delivery and poor project management (p. 174).
	Amalgamation savings not achieved; poor resource management leading to increased costs; ineffectiveness in securing adequate funding for new projects (p. 188).
	Poor contract development and management (p. 196).
	Lack of administrative responsibility by presiding officers (p. 197).
	Deficiencies in annual reporting (p. 201).
	Poor employment culture (p. 207).

The final SFPALC report (2012b) made 23 recommendations to address the identified shortcomings in DPS's performance, 20 of which were accepted by the department. But the committee also pointed to the failure to achieve the amalgamation efficiencies despite many attempts by DPS; a decline in DPS's purchasing power combined with increasing costs; the impact of further decreases on building maintenance and services to support parliamentary processes; and the ineffectiveness of administrators to ensure adequate funding. It declared:

> The requirement to seek funding from Government for funding the Parliament, in the committee's view is a matter which requires further consideration. There is a need to ensure that the budget for DPS is such that services required by the Parliament are sustainable in the long term and the committee considers that it is time for further deliberations on the appropriate model of funding for DPS. (SFPALC 2012b: 189)

Its first and key recommendation was for DPS's 'funding and administration to be overseen by the Senate Appropriations and Staffing Committee and the House Appropriations and Administration Committee meeting jointly for that purpose, and that *Standing Orders* be amended as necessary' (SFPALC 2012b: 208). Responses were equivocal. DPS officials supported an appropriate level of scrutiny *and advocacy* for its role and noted there was no single entity to advocate for its needs, unlike the chamber departments, each of which had a specific parliamentary committee. But they also suggested that existing levels of accountability were sufficient. The President of the Senate (who had appointed Mills to 'fix' the department) undertook to discuss this recommendation with the Senate appropriations committee and advised that the Senate House Committee would be an appropriate mechanism for raising concerns about services and facilities, which could then be forwarded to the Joint House Committee (both house committees meeting together). The Senate House Committee received briefings from DPS on two occasions, 10 months apart, including on the financial difficulties it was experiencing, but it appears no formal steps were taken to implement the SFPALC's recommendation on the oversight of DPS's funding and administration (SFPALC 2015b). On the contrary, there is little evidence of an ongoing interest in an *ex ante* governance or advocacy role for anyone in relation to DPS.[6] The recommendation that DPS be exempted from any future one-off additional efficiency dividends was also not supported by the government.

In 2013–14, Mills reported 'a cautious, but brighter view of the financial outlook for the year ahead' following her successful attempts, with the support of the presiding officers, to secure additional funding of $15 million with a one-off supplementation of $5.5 million. Savings in contract management and other costs, such as external cleaning, were also reported (Mills 2014: 6). An increasing emphasis was placed on visitors to Parliament House in collaboration with Canberra's cultural institutions and the tourism sector. The Parliamentary Budget Office (PBO 2013) became the fourth parliamentary department, on 23 July 2012, after significant discussion about its structure and location within the parliamentary administration.[7]

---

6   This claim is discussed further in Chapter 6.
7   The PBO was established as part of the agreement between the Gillard government and independent members during the 2010–13 parliament when that government had no majority in the House of Representatives. The presiding officers have only a broad administrative oversight of the PBO, which in practice does not include day-to-day engagement. The PBO is not subject to the direction of the presiding officers in carrying out its functions and prepares its work plan in consultation with the Joint Committee of Public Accounts and Audit (*Parliamentary Service Act 1999*).

Table 4.3 Further inquiries into DPS's performance

Date	Event
February 2014	CCTV images of a DPS staff member putting an envelope under the door of Senator John Faulkner's Parliament House office are used in the investigation of a staff management issue.
26 May 2014	Senator Faulkner raises concerns during estimates hearings about a breach of the CCTV Code of Practice and improper monitoring of interactions between his office and a DPS employee. DPS Secretary refers to 'inadvertent conflict' between staff management issues and protection of members' and senators' rights (SFPALC 2014: 31–42).
18 June 2014	On joint motion of senators Cory Bernardi and Faulkner, matter is referred to Senate Committee of Privileges (2014: 1) to investigate whether there was improper interference, whether disciplinary action was taken and whether a contempt was committed.
5 December 2014	Committee finds no contempt; rather, the CCTV Code of Practice had 'accountability gaps' and use of CCTV was not authorised. It refers to 'misleading evidence' given at estimates committee hearing on 26 May 2014 to SFPALC and recommends review of Code of Practice and training for senior officers 'to acquaint themselves with the principles of privilege' (Senate Committee of Privileges 2014: 38).
26 June 2014	Senate refers further inquiry into performance of DPS to SFPALC with multiple terms of reference.
26 February 2015	Following SFPALC's 2012 inquiry, ANAO publishes audit report that concludes that DPS's processes 'do not exhibit the discipline required to provide assurance that assets and contracts are being effectively managed' (ANAO 2015: 15).
21 April 2015	DPS Secretary's appointment terminated.
28 April 2015	SFPALC presents interim report covering asset and contract management, photography commission and inquiry into the use of CCTV material at Parliament House. Committee concludes that DPS is 'deeply dysfunctional' (SFPALC 2015a: 20) and announces intention to look broadly at role, functions and structure of DPS, in conjunction with presiding officers, to improve its management and operation.
25 June 2015	SFPALC presents second interim report (2015b), concluding it was misled by the DPS Secretary at the estimates hearing on 26 May 2014 and the misleading evidence had a substantive impact on its work. The report acknowledges the termination of the secretary's employment and reports it has pursued the matter as far as practicable.
27 August 2015	Senate President announces the presiding officers have requested the Parliamentary Service Commissioner arrange for an independent structural review of DPS (SFPALC 2015c: 3).

Date	Event
17 September 2015	SFPALC presents final report (2015c) with some terms of reference not addressed. Multiple recommendations related to:
	DPS updating committee on senior management structure; progress on conservation and design documentation; bullying and harassment complaints; Hansard; use of Parliament House facilities; and visitor experience review.
	Stocktakes and audits of assets and contracts.
	Joint meetings of relevant Senate and House of Representatives committees to oversee DPS's funding and administration.

After two years of financial deficits, DPS received significant investment in the 2014–15 budget, allowing it to begin to restore service levels because of Mills's efforts. But her tenure was marred by poor relations with her colleagues and alleged missteps and incompetence. In 2014, the attempted recruitment of Mills to serve as Clerk of the House of Commons by Speaker Bercow (discussed later in this chapter) became a major controversy in both parliaments, horrifying some members and senior officials. Following a House of Commons committee inquiry, her proposed appointment was terminated (HOCGC 2014). In April 2015, Mills's appointment in the Australian Parliamentary Service as DPS Secretary was also terminated by the presiding officers following critical findings by the Senate Committee of Privileges (2014), ANAO (2015) and a further review of DPS's performance by SFPALC (2015b). These further public inquiries and their outcomes are summarised in Table 4.3.

The independent review into DPS by the Parliamentary Service Commissioner was conducted by Ken Baxter, a former senior public servant in the NSW and Victorian governments (Baxter 2015). The commissioner forwarded Baxter's review to the presiding officers in December 2015 but it was not made public until April 2017, and then only in response to a question on notice from a member of the SFPALC. Baxter found a consistent view among officials that the objectives of the Podger review were not achieved and its implementation had not been particularly successful. Drawing on the highly critical reviews of DPS and discussions with members and parliamentary officials in the Australian, UK and Canadian national parliaments and the NSW and Victorian state parliaments, Baxter identified four key areas in which management was deficient: communications within parliament and between senators and members, the presiding officers and DPS; the absence of credible long-term strategic and financial planning on a whole-of-parliament basis; inadequate planning and funding for the ongoing maintenance of Parliament House; and administrative and financial inefficiencies resulting from a trifurcation of funding. Baxter attempted to address these deficiencies through several recommendations, including whole-of-parliament strategic planning and funding; a governance body, with external directors, like those operating in the UK and other parliaments; targeted funding of the building; and changes to organisational structures and nomenclature. In common with the HOCGC (2014), he made many observations that are germane to the questions raised and arguments promulgated in this book. Examples of these are incorporated in Table 4.4; they are indicative of the lack of priority afforded to strategic management and governance issues, and a lack of support for DPS.

Table 4.4 Relevant observations from Baxter (2015): Australian Parliament

Question (i): How do competing beliefs about the relative value of procedural and management skills influence effective parliamentary management? Question (ii): Do MPs engage constructively in managing their parliament?
'The Building' ... should dominate the debate about funding and ... will require ... greater supervision and control by the Parliament through the presiding officers (p. 10).
The current funding flows, associated administrative arrangements, and the management structure of DPS diminishes [sic] the ability of the department to prepare for implementation of a meaningful, measurable, medium to long term strategic plan for the whole of parliament and to gain acceptance of that plan from the presiding officers (p. 10).
There is a need for frequent, regular and well planned consistent communications within the whole of parliament and in particular between senators and members and their services provider DPS (p. 12).
The relationship and communication channels between the presiding officers and the Clerks of the two Houses are working well. The working relationship between the presiding officers and the parliamentary departments as a whole has been problematic ... [M]easures must be put in place to ensure that effective professional working relationships are reinforced and do not rely solely on personality and goodwill (p. 11).
[H]ad there been focussed, adequate, consistent and continuing oversight of the formation of DPS and its internal relationships, very different and far more positive results would have been achieved (p. 18).
[T]he major elephant in the room is that there is not an appropriate organisational structure to deal with major maintenance and renovation of 'The Building' ... [T]he Parliament ... should move as quickly as possible to establishing accounting and financial management systems associated with the 'global' or whole of parliament funding. This would require a single annual appropriation (p. 13).

The presiding officers were advised by then Parliamentary Service Commissioner John Lloyd that several of the recommendations required further thought and consultation (Lloyd 2015). In the end, not all were accepted, including the establishment of an advisory board and whole-of-parliament funding arrangements. In further correspondence with the presiding officers, Lloyd (2016) advised that he had discussed the report with the new DPS Secretary, Rob Stefanic, who was implementing important changes, some of which had been canvassed by Baxter. The letter included non-specific language, such as 'options are being explored to introduce a more strategic approach', 'senior executive roles have been reviewed to realise improved role clarity and better performance measurement' and 'DPS will work towards becoming a learning and forward thinking organisation' (Lloyd 2016: 2). Governance arrangements were left on an informal basis, leaving them open to being dependent on personalities and goodwill, and funding arrangements were not streamlined. It appears Baxter's recommendations to introduce formal governance and whole-of-parliament funding were unpalatable. Evidence from some interviewees confirmed that the Baxter report was not much more than a device to satisfy the SFPALC and followed the longstanding and familiar parliamentary practice of having 'to be seen to be doing something'. It was also suggested that Baxter's proposal to rename the titles of principal officeholders was not well received and he did not sufficiently understand the parliamentary context.

In the years following Mills's termination in 2015, DPS has continued to travel 'a path of transformation' designed to make it 'fit for purpose'. The three-stage, five-year process has included reforming core policies, processes and governance to increase accountability and coherence, strengthening capability across DPS to serve parliament effectively and moving DPS to a 'more agile and high-performance operational model', to meet its strategic priorities of 'innovation, quality service delivery and improving our corporate culture' (DPS 2020: 5).

From this detailed illustration of the troubled history of DPS during its short existence (in parliamentary terms), one could conclude that its problems were caused by poor management on the part of successive secretaries, and critics could point to evidence of a lack of judgement, foresight and management capability at senior levels of the new department. However, it is also evident that the performance problems were deep-seated and exacerbated by the design and implementation of DPS, subsequent funding decisions, an absence of constructive governance arrangements at the outset and a lack of support from members and senators, including successive presiding officers. Criticism of the department's performance has continued: in September 2020, the SFPALC announced a further broad-ranging inquiry into DPS's management and operations, which then collided with several investigations into an alleged sexual assault within a minister's office in Parliament House (the outcome of these investigations is addressed in the Epilogue). DPS management mounted a spirited defence to this inquiry and questioned the legitimacy of evidence submitted by some of its critics. One can only speculate as to the political intent of the inquiry; as it turned out, the committee distanced itself from related investigations into the alleged assault and DPS's handling of its security role. Its report was largely confined to acknowledging DPS's efforts towards improving workplace culture and ICT security. Nevertheless, additional comments by non-government senators suggest serious management problems, whether real or perceived, remain within DPS and the level of political scrutiny is likely to continue (SFPALC 2021). I turn now to a brief review of the two chamber departments from 2004 to 2021 to compare the extent and complexity of management challenges within the three departments.

Department of the House of Representatives

There is little evidence of serious challenge to or complaints about House of Representatives services following the amalgamation of the service departments—it has appeared to be largely a case of business as usual—although the House of Representatives has no estimates committees to regularly scrutinise departmental performance and its Standing Committee on Appropriations and Administration, which primarily considers the department's funding estimate, was not established until 2011. Annual reports pointed to high levels of satisfaction from clients and staff, while referring to the need to improve departmental culture, reduce barriers across the department and ensure the department's specialised working environment would not obscure its external view (Department of the House of Representatives 2006, 2007).

The 2010 election, which led to a minority government, posed procedural challenges for the House of Representatives departmental staff, but these were welcomed by the clerk (Wright 2011). In providing technical advice to multiple members on issues that may not have arisen before, the clerk took the unusual step of publishing detailed procedural notes, even on politically sensitive subjects, to ensure house practices were consistently explained. Under reform agreements negotiated by the minority government, the Appropriations and Administration Committee was established to consider, among other things, departmental funding. The committee was able to secure supplementary funding to meet the additional costs incurred by the new parliamentary arrangements and it was seen as an important conduit between members and departmental staff.

In 2016, the department acknowledged the importance of maintaining effective relationships with the other parliamentary departments (Department of the House of Representatives 2016).[8] The financial outlook for the department was positive: the report noted that public service agencies were continually being challenged to work more efficiently and deliver the best value for money and the Department of the House of Representatives was no exception. A collaboration theme was evident in the following year's annual report when the *Strategic Plan for Parliamentary Administration*, first mooted in 2013, was endorsed in 2017 (Department of the House of Representatives 2017; Parliament of Australia 2017b)— at least one outcome that appears to have been influenced by the Baxter review. The department also received a positive government response to its request for additional funding to enhance procedural capacity.

Continuing management themes for the Department of the House of Representatives in the twenty-first century appear to have been dominated by a highly specialised focus (particularly in responding to ongoing procedural challenges), both internally and in its interparliamentary and outreach work; a strong focus on staff development, departmental leadership and services to members, resulting in high satisfaction rates on both counts; and an acknowledgement of the need for cooperative relations with the other parliamentary departments. The department's annual reports reveal the hallmarks of a well-run, well-supported department providing high-quality services but apparently with few complex management challenges. Exceptions include the 43rd Parliament when the absence of a majority-elected government resulted in several unusual practices and reforms and a significant upsurge in chamber and committee activity, questions relating to dual citizenship under Section 44(i) of the

---

8   No doubt in response to the highly publicised fallout between the head of DPS and the Department of the Senate (see Box 4.1).

Australian Constitution and the ineligibility of certain members to sit, and the parliament's response to the Covid-19 pandemic (Department of the House of Representatives 2018a, 2020).

Department of the Senate

The value of the specialised work of the Department of the Senate was very much to the fore in its twenty-first-century annual reports. Senate Clerk Evans, until his retirement in 2009, consistently defended the Senate's constitutional and independent status. Before the 2004 amalgamation, the clerk defended a budget surplus in the Senate Department as resulting from a low level of legislative activity caused by the sidelining of the legislature by a 'rampant' executive and a 'cramming' of legislation designed to reduce sitting days and lessen the Senate's scrutiny of government activities. A budget surplus was 'not a matter for apology' (Evans 2003: 4); it could be justified on the basis that expenditure might arise in the future, notwithstanding that the number and scope of inquiries were limited by the available time of senators. This theme was repeated in subsequent reports: a fluctuating workload, combined with increased internal technological efficiency, requiring a continuing high level of resources in anticipation of future committee workload, notwithstanding that the time constraints of senators tended to militate against potential increases. The inevitable consequence was that after more than a decade of accumulating cash surpluses by 'efficient' use of its appropriations, the Senate in 2008 was required to return half its cash surplus (more than $10 million) to the government (Evans 2005, 2006, 2007, 2008).[9]

I have already touched on the self-proclaimed role of the Senate as the parliamentary service's sceptical questioner in relation to Podger's proposals for reorganisation of the parliamentary departments. Evans claimed there was a great deal to be sceptical about in the process and implementation of the Podger review, and there is evidence to support this claim, including from Podger himself (see Chapter 3). There are many references to the Senate, acting through its officials, playing a sceptical questioner role on matters of politics and management—for example:

---

9   One could speculate on the parliamentary uses to which these surplus funds could have been allocated had a whole-of-parliament funding arrangement applied.

A demand for public sector departments and agencies to look and sound like private commercial corporations has long been in evidence, and continues despite its poor conceptual basis and institutional inappropriateness. If regard were to be had to that demand, the most prominent feature of this report would be the considerable reduction in size of the Senate Department and its budget as a result of the transfer of the security function, equipment and staff to the joint department … Perhaps in commerce-speak it might be said that the department has downsized and is concentrating on its core business. That sort of conceptualisation only leads to even more inappropriate analogies: small bodies are ripe for takeover by larger organisations with more functions and money. No doubt there are some who see the change in those terms. The rationale of the department, however, is constitutional and institutional, not economic, and is related to the proper conduct of the public affairs of the body politic. (Evans 2005: 5)

The exhortations of the Senate Clerk forcefully staking a claim for more resources in anticipation of additional workload, combined with his vigorous defence of the Senate's institutional role, contrasted with the more understated reports of other parliamentary heads. They reflected a greater assertiveness on the part of the Senate that has pervaded administrative outcomes in the Australian Parliament through the years.

The successor to Evans as Clerk of the Senate, Dr Rosemary Laing, continued his formidable defence of the institution along the same lines: continuing financial pressures and the intellectual skills of senate staff with a strong emphasis on their professional development. Generational change and the need to retain ongoing corporate knowledge were tackled by developing a new learning framework, establishing the Senate Public Information Office and using new technologies, including Twitter (Department of the Senate 2011, 2012). Deviations from a business-as-usual approach included a strategic review of ICT across the parliamentary departments, commissioned by the presiding officers. The result was the establishment of a central ICT division within DPS—a 'one-stop shop' for the computing requirements of parliamentarians and staff—and staff in the parliamentary departments bringing a strategic overview to formerly unsatisfactory arrangements (Department of the Senate 2013). The limited effectiveness of the Senate Appropriations and Staffing Committee in seeking to influence the appropriations for the Senate Department and resolving disagreements with the government was reportedly enhanced by a new consultative process between the Minister for Finance, the Expenditure Review Committee and the Senate President. This was seen as 'an important step forward in recognising the constitutional independence of the Senate and the correct application of parliamentary procedure in the budget process' (Department of the Senate 2013: 6). A continued focus on financial independence for the Senate and institutional continuity was reported in 2014, together with updated coordination arrangements between the parliamentary departments and a modest surplus in the department's financial results. A third review of the scope for achieving efficiencies through shared services concluded the cost of system upgrades would outweigh potential efficiencies, although the discussion appeared to be ongoing (Department of the Senate 2014, 2019). In 2015, the department reported a continuing deterioration in its budget after years of efficiency dividends, and an unprecedented level of committee activity. The previous year's modest surplus had now become a small deficit with a similar outcome budgeted for the following year, notwithstanding a one-off injection of additional funding (Department of the Senate 2015).

The effects of the well-publicised differences between the Senate Clerk and the Secretary of the DPS in 2014 were tempered by a positive framing of the cooperation across the parliamentary departments following the centralisation of ICT and changed security arrangements. Indeed, collaboration between parliamentary departments and other parliaments was a key theme of the clerk's 2015–16 review (Laing 2016a). The debate on financial independence continued and, despite the efforts of the President of the Senate and the renamed Appropriations, Staffing and Security Committee, little changed regarding the budget setting.

The appointment of a new clerk, Richard Pye, in 2017 did not appear to change the Senate rhetoric; the key themes explored in his first review included institutional continuity, the need to raise awareness of the Senate's work, the capacity of its staff and the workload—again acknowledging that the demand for the Senate Department's services was 'directly influenced by the composition and dynamics of the Senate' and that senators themselves determined workload. Following the 2016 dissolution, referrals to committees increased to record rates as the number of parties in the Senate sought to pursue their policy and political interests (Department of the Senate 2017). The increased activity brought budget supplementation and the Appropriations, Staffing and Security Committee was able to secure an ongoing increase in following years (Department of the Senate 2018a). Institutional continuity, meeting the demand for procedural, legislative and committee support, and supporting staff and collegiality among parliamentary departments were key themes in subsequent reporting periods (Department of the Senate 2019, 2020).[10] The reported evidence over almost two decades indicates the Senate Department is managed well in terms of achieving its outcomes and securing sufficient funding; the same evidence also suggests an institutional outlook that could be interpreted as defensive and self-serving.

Externally, however, the reputation of the whole parliament was damaged by a series of allegations of misuse of parliamentary entitlements, particularly those relating to travel, and a publicly funded helicopter ride in 2014 led to the resignation of then Speaker Bronwyn Bishop (Grattan 2015). While the surrounding public disclosures were less dramatic than those in the United Kingdom some years earlier (detailed later in this chapter), numerous reviews led to the establishment in 2017 of the Independent Parliamentary Expenses Authority (IPEA) under the auspices of the Department of Finance. Although the public view portrayed by the media was inclined to see individual MPs who did not follow the rules as self-serving, the 2016 review of the entitlements system confirmed the conclusions of previous reviews that the system was complex, confusing, incomplete, contradictory and immensely difficult to follow and administer (Committee for the Review of Parliamentary Entitlements 2016). These issues are discussed further in Chapter 6.

The view from the UK Parliament

House of Commons Service

The previous chapter documented a series of management reforms conducted by the House of Commons Service, including in the early part of this century. A triumphant review of the 2007 Tebbit inquiry by an external member of the House of Commons Management Board concluded:

> [V]ictory can be declared on the major part of Tebbit with major improvements implemented across a wide range of activities ranging from transformation of a dysfunctional board of management to an effective management board to major improvements in service delivery and business management processes. (Jablonowski 2010: 4)

---

10   New approaches were required to support senate sittings and committee hearings during the Covid-19 pandemic.

But this positive evaluation of management performance—repeated in annual reports in following years—contrasted starkly with the fallout from two seemingly separate but related incidents that caught the public's attention and exerted considerable pressure on members of both the House of Commons and the House of Lords and parliamentary officials.

The first was an investigation in 2009 by *Telegraph* journalists that revealed systemic abuse of the system of allowances. Although most expense claims were found to be 'within the rules', the public could now see the extent to which the regime could be manipulated to maximise personal gain and the intentional lack of transparency and accountability that governed it (Winnett and Rayner 2009). The fact that members had deliberately sought to keep the details of their expense claims from being publicly disclosed reinforced a widely held belief that politicians were subject to a different set of rules and standards and were increasingly out of touch with the lives of ordinary British citizens (vanHeerde-Hudson and Ward 2014). The consequences of the scandal for the whole institution were far-reaching. They included the resignation of the Speaker, Michael Martin, who had fought strongly to prevent the release of the expenses details, a severe dent in the reputation of the Commons officials who had administered the expenses system and a major change to the House's future governance and administration (Gammell 2009; Wright 2014). Although the 'expenses scandal' was a significant political event, there were mixed views about its long-term impact, including on election outcomes.[11] VanHeerde-Hudson and Ward (2014) found that the most significant consequences were administrative. The 2019 release of a documentary by *The Telegraph* and an account by Crewe and Walker (2019) of why the scandal still mattered suggested the reputational damage was ongoing. Ten years on, Flinders and Anderson (2021) claimed subsequent reforms were more widespread than was commonly recognised yet the scandal had failed to stimulate discussion about the inevitable cost of politicians.

As a result of the 'scandal', the expenses system was taken out of the hands of the House of Commons Department of Resources (formerly the Fees Office) and an independent body, the Independent Parliamentary Standards Authority (IPSA), was set up to regulate and administer a new regime. IPSA itself did not escape criticism for its 'conflicted' role as both

---

11 For example, Pattie and Johnston (2014) found that although voters in the 2010 general election were disturbed by the expenses scandal, prospects for MPs standing for re-election were unlikely to have been damaged by their involvement in it.

regulator and administrator, its focus on the public interest rather than as a service provider to MPs and its treatment of members who found it to be bureaucratic and unhelpful (Gay 2014). Although parliament had to be seen to be doing something to appease public concern, the introduction, through IPSA, of complex rules and procedures rather than a risk-based approach appeared hasty and not well thought through (Fisher and vanHeerde-Hudson 2014; Gay 2014; Norton 2017). The response highlighted the dangers of legislating according to 'the something must be done syndrome' (Parpworth 2010).

The chair of the Select Committee on the Reform of the House of Commons established in response to the expenses scandal also pointed to regulatory overreaction and suggested that enforced transparency with tighter rules and audit would have been sufficient to improve the system had not political demands required political detoxification and public reassurance (Wright 2014). Wright was also frank about the reasons for the scandal in the first place: the problem was a lack of machinery to safeguard propriety or sound the alarm. Members controlled their own financial affairs and defended their parliamentary sovereignty against external intrusions. The officials administering the system believed their primary duty was to assist members to make claims. Importantly, from the perspective of this book, Wright (2014: 58) claimed the level of attention devoted by officials to ensuring the proper conduct of parliamentary proceedings did not extend to the administration of expenses and allowances and, as a consequence, parliament paid a high price for such laxity. It seems no one thought it was important enough.[12]

The Wright Committee recommendations were an enduring and positive consequence of the scandal; unlike earlier modernisation proposals, they addressed the relationship between the parliament and the executive by proposing the election of select committee members and allowing backbench members to control more of parliament's business (Russell 2011b). The expenses scandal also prompted the Institute for Government (Nicholls 2010: 3) to argue for a reinterpretation of the principle of self-regulation and a move away from an 'insular model of governance of MPs, by MPs and for MPs'. It made several recommendations to

12 In defence of parliamentary officials, Andrew Walker, former head of the Fees Office, recounted his attempts to win agreement from members for changes to the system but found no political appetite existed (A. Walker, pers. comm., 23 September 2015). His story was published in *An Extraordinary Scandal: The Westminster expenses crisis and why it still matters* (Crewe and Walker 2019).

improve transparency and accountability, capacity and capability, and risk management, including value-for-money audits by the National Audit Office,[13] the inclusion of more non-executives on the House of Commons Commission and the management board, and public committee hearings on the House's administration.

The second significant event in bringing the governance of the UK Parliament to public attention was precipitated by the election of John Bercow as Speaker, following the forced resignation of Speaker Martin as a consequence of the expenses scandal.[14] It was also a catalyst for reform, both procedural and administrative (HC Debates 2009; Wheeler 2009). Bercow, although a Conservative Party member, was seen as more progressive than his predecessors and keenly supported the Wright reforms, particularly those strengthening the role of the backbench. His ambitions, though, led to clashes with his principal official, the Clerk of the House Robert Rogers.[15] Rogers' subsequent resignation triggered a bizarre recruitment controversy—the aforementioned 'Mills affair'— which highlighted the relationship between the Speaker and the Clerk of the House of Commons and the roles of clerk and chief executive and culminated in the establishment of the House of Commons Governance Committee (HOCGC), chaired by a former Leader of the House, Jack Straw. The HOCGC (2014) recommended sweeping changes to the House of Commons Service's governance and administration, including the appointment of a new position of director-general. As we have seen, the recruitment controversy also involved the Australian Parliament and contributed to an unusual level of media interest in that parliament's administration. The HOCGC inquiry and its report are summarised in Box 4.1.

---

13   The Comptroller and Auditor-General (C&AG) and the National Audit Office (NAO) audit the financial statements of the House of Commons and the House of Lords and provide an opinion on whether the accounts are true and fair, and whether the income and expenditure have been applied to the purposes intended by parliament. In addition, the C&AG may perform value-for-money work on certain topics. The NAO also provides support to parliament through secondments to the House and supporting committees and projects with NAO representatives—for example, in areas such as joint working and change programs (P. Ryan, National Audit Office UK, pers. comm., 1 August 2017).

14   Speaker Martin was also criticised for his role in the 2008 arrest of Damian Green for allegedly 'aiding, abetting, counselling or procuring' misconduct in public office by a Home Office civil servant, following which serious weaknesses in accountability at the top of the internal organisation in the House of Commons were revealed and the Speaker was criticised for failing to exercise control (House of Commons Committee on Issue of Privilege 2010; Bradley 2012).

15   For example, he allegedly swore at the clerk, precipitating his early departure—an allegation that was later denied (HC Debates 2014a; Wintour 2014).

Box 4.1 The Mills affair

Highlighting the relationship between the Speaker and the Clerk of the House of Commons and the roles of clerk and chief executive

On 16 July 2014, the House of Commons acknowledged the early retirement of then clerk Sir Robert Rogers (HC Debates 2014a). Members commended his role in steering reform and his contribution to improving the House's procedures and the public's understanding and appreciation of its work, as well as his achievements as chief executive.

Media reports (Cooper 2014; D'Arcy 2014; Wintour 2014) discussed persistent rumours that the clerk's early retirement resulted from his working relationship with Speaker Bercow. The relationship was said to be untenable and highlighted conflict between clerkly conservatism and the Speaker's frustration at the slow pace of implementation of his push to reform the workings of the Commons. In the recruitment process for a new clerk, Speaker Bercow was said to have emphasised the executive side of the job and downplayed the procedural advice side, so that the job description that once required a 'detailed knowledge' of parliamentary procedure now called only for 'awareness', allowing for a much deeper recruitment pool (D'Arcy 2014).

On 30 July 2015, a selection panel of five members and one independent person, appointed by the Speaker, recommended the appointment of Carol Mills to the role of clerk. (Ms Mills was at the time the Secretary of the Department of Parliamentary Services in the Australian Parliament, having assumed the role in 2012.) When knowledge of the proposed appointment emerged, a furore ensued. Several House of Commons members were concerned about both the process and the outcome (HC Debates 2014b). The Clerk of the Senate in the Australian Parliament, Dr Rosemary Laing, in an email to the retiring Commons Clerk, Rogers, launched a 'stinging attack' on Ms Mills and her professional abilities. According to Dr Laing, staff in Canberra's Parliament House were 'utterly taken aback' that someone with no understanding of parliamentary procedures could be under consideration for such a role (Towell 2014). Mills was disparaged in the United Kingdom as the 'Canberra caterer' (Doyle 2014; Guido Fawkes 2014).

Acknowledging the level of disquiet among members about the suitability of the proposed appointment, on 1 September 2014, the Speaker announced a 'modest pause' in the recruitment process (HC Debates 2014b). On 10 September 2014, the House agreed to the appointment of the House of Commons Governance Committee, to consider the governance of the House of Commons, including the future allocation of the responsibilities for house services currently exercised by the single office of Clerk of the House and chief executive (HC Debates 2014c). The committee reported on 17 December 2014 (HOCGC 2014). It recommended, among other things, the appointment of a new director-general to run the delivery of services, under the authority of the clerk, who was to remain as head of the House Service.

Unlike the SFPALC management inquiries in the Australian Parliament, the HOCGC did not arise directly out of concern for a systemic failure in the management of services to the House, and its report noted that not all the individual failings brought to its attention resulted from poor management.[16] Some were the consequence of the inherent complexity of a bicameral parliament, while others resulted from different perspectives or experiences (HOCGC 2014: 35). The report was muted in its criticism of inconsistencies in the recruitment of a new clerk/chief executive and proposed an organisational framework in which the House could operate more efficiently and effectively, reinforcing the development of a unified House Service. It noted that governance of the House had developed over time, often in response to issues or events. Inherent complexities had been compounded by layers of interventions, building on and adapting what went before rather than rationalising or restructuring arrangements (HOCGC 2014: 13).[17] An academic interpretation might construe this finding as a veiled criticism of a path-dependent approach to parliamentary administration, although the committee did commend earlier reforms, noting the increased emphasis on the CEO part of the clerk/CEO role and a more efficient and unified service following the Tebbit review. But it acknowledged longstanding concerns about the relationship between management board officials and members of the commission; inadequate decision-making and implementation; a culture that placed the clerk's procedural role above that of the management role, with sharply divided views on which should prevail in any new structure; a lack of focus on strategic management issues; and insufficient attention to the development and recruitment of senior staff.

Evidence given to the HOCGC (2014) directly relates to questions raised in Chapter 1: first, the persistence of the perception that the procedural role is superior to the management role (whether embodied in the same person or not); and second, the level of constructive engagement by members in managing their parliaments. Table 4.5 provides extracts from evidence to the committee; it contains some illuminating and sometimes colourful descriptions.

---

16 However, many members had complained that the House was poorly managed (HOCGC 2014), and this book commenced with comments lamenting the shambolic state of the House's management and the absence of clear chains of command for many of its functions and its organisational and management structures. The expenses scandal also played a part.

17 Recalling Mahoney and Thelen's 'layering' approach to incremental institutional change leading to the 'introduction of new rules on top of or alongside' existing ones (2010: 15–16).

Table 4.5 Relevant evidence taken by HOCGC, UK Parliament

Question (i): How do competing beliefs about the relative value of procedural and management skills influence effective parliamentary management?	
A. Spicer and J. Silvester, psychologists, Cass Business School	We think in some quarters there is a deeply held but maybe unexpressed concern that the rise of a more thorough-going managerial approach will lead to these [deeply held] traditions being replaced by a more generic corporate culture which could be found in any workplace (p. 33).
David Blunkett MP	It does not follow that those with legal training and constitutional expertise should have primacy over those running the personnel and services of the House of Commons ... It strikes me that the objections raised to anything that does not give the Clerk complete primacy over all other personnel (and therefore functions), fall into the category of William Blake's 'mind-forged manacles' (GOV0009, p. 94).
Sir Peter Luff MP	I am becoming more and more concerned that the House of Commons is becoming a tourist attraction, catering facility and visitor centre rather than a place of democratic debate, scrutiny, and legislation. We are in danger of losing sight of the purpose for which this place exists. I am therefore clear that the Clerk's role must be the predominant one in the new arrangement. He or she must be the custodian of our procedure and the guarantor of our freedoms (GOV0005, p. 95).
Andrew McDonald, CEO, IPSA	Does one want to reinforce the existing culture, which prizes procedural expertise above all else? Or does one recognise that the quality of its leadership and management are fundamentally important? The choice is an important one. Important to the future direction and culture of the whole House administration (GOV0073, p. 95).
Baroness Royall	[T]o have a chief executive officer or a chief operating officer for Parliament as a whole would be a very sensible way forward.
	The public see us as Parliament, and for Parliament to be managed as a whole would be very sensible. But that should not impinge on the role of the Clerks in their constitutional duties: advice to whatever is happening in the Chamber. That is my personal view (EV, Q487).
Question (ii): Do MPs engage constructively in managing their parliaments?	
Nigel Mills MP	Probably no one came to Parliament to spend a lot of time considering the price of a bottle of Coke in a vending machine. Clearly people's priorities will be proper priorities of Parliament, not running the internal House service. Some people are press-ganged, rather than choosing to be there, and obviously people are promoted out of the way and therefore can't stay on the Committee. I don't think it is a sign that the [Administration] Committee is dysfunctional, it's probably a sign that we can't actually make fundamental decisions. That is the way it is (EV, Q303).

Robert Flello MP	My experience over almost ten years is that the bureaucracy of the Commons is self-serving. Decisions are taken that suit the wishes of those running the House and, too often with the acceptance of House Committee chairs, they are nodded through with no real scrutiny and yet with the fig leaf of acceptability as having been agreed by one or more of the various committees.
	Reports or papers are brought to House Committees where the select few MPs have been asked to attend. Some MPs don't attend because of the demands on their time of other parliamentary matters whilst others, and I include myself in this, refuse to lend credibility to a system that is believed to be a fig leaf for House officers running things for their own purposes (GOV054, p. 94).

The HOCGC inquiry could be considered a defining influence on management of the House of Commons Service—characterised by some as a masterful compromise by its chair—particularly in its decision to 'split' the clerk/CEO role and establish a new role of director-general.[18] It is not clear, however, that a public management culture has become ingrained within the parliamentary institution. Not all of those affected by the outcomes of the inquiry were unanimous in their assessment of its utility.[19] The inquiry itself may also have been seen as the creature of former Speaker Bercow, about whom opinions were sharply divided. Indeed, following Bercow's departure, the election of the new Speaker, Sir Lindsay Hoyle, and the appointment of the new Clerk of the House of Commons, Dr John Benger, we can discern subtle but important differences in the influence and standing of the director-general's office. From 2018 to 2019, the administration's annual reports contained joint rather than separate introductions by the clerk and the director-general; in 2021, opening remarks by the director-general disappeared altogether (House of Commons 2019, 2020, 2021). The 2021 report revealed changes arising from a review undertaken by the clerk 'to consider whether the House of Commons Service teams and departments were structured in the best way to deliver key parliamentary functions and services' (House of Commons 2021: 11). The changes had the overall effect of strengthening the influence and status of three categories of 'core' parliamentary functions: chamber and legislative-focused activities, select committee-focused activities, and supporting members in their

---

18 Whether the role was 'split' was also contested; one argument was that some functions had merely been delegated.
19 Their reactions are comparable with those following the amalgamation of service departments in the Australian Parliament.

constituency work through research and information services. Greater 'circulation' between committee staff and chamber staff was designed to improve career paths for those staff and offer greater potential to attract external candidates and internal candidates at more senior levels. The bulk of the participation/engagement function was brought within the purview of the clerk assistant, with its managing director no longer represented on the Commons Executive Board. The review also flagged some dissatisfaction with the current House of Commons strategy and foreshadowed an improved approach to strategy development (Benger 2020). The changes reflect the observations of Silvester and Spicer that the closer one's role is to the legislative process, the higher are the status and importance accorded to that role (HOCGC 2014).

Following the review, the inaugural incumbent of the position of director-general, Ian Ailles, left the service of the House. The functions of a newly described position of Director-General (Operations) are now more narrowly specified, and the former *ex officio* role of the director-general as chair of the Commons Executive Board (above the clerk) has been removed. We may have witnessed the end of the *primus inter pares* experiment, a gradual rewinding of the clock and a restoration of the old order—according to Ailles, the changes represent a 'dilution and regression' in management reform[20]—or perhaps the latest restructure is a necessary refocusing of the arrangements embedded in the Bercow era. In either case, we can detect ongoing tensions between the procedural and management roles and the forging of new internal alliances. The structure of the House of Commons Commission itself has also not escaped recent criticism, with a former Leader of the House, Andrea Leadsom, suggesting its members should be elected and officials and non-executive members should be entitled to vote (Haddon and Thimont Jack 2020).

House of Lords Administration

The House of Lords has taken a hesitant but mainly positive approach to elevating the management role, falling broadly into line with the House of Commons while maintaining its commitment to self-regulation and maintaining the House of Lords 'voice' (HOCGC 2014). It, too, was affected by significant external events, including the expenses scandal, and repeated attempts (or threats) by successive governments to reform it.

---

20   I. Ailles, pers. comm., 27 October 2021.

The Lords' response to the expenses scandal, in which a number of peers were embroiled, differed from that adopted in the House of Commons, with the Lords preferring to keep matters largely within their own control. The code of conduct was strengthened and the position of the Independent Commissioner for Standards was established to investigate any breaches. The Review Body on Senior Salaries, an advisory non-departmental public body, reviewed the financial support provided to peers and the Lords agreed to new 'flat rate' allowances, tighter arrangements for the designation of principal residences and more frequent publication of information relating to peers' expenses (SSRB 2009).

Both peers and House of Lords administration officials contributed to the HOCGC inquiry, emphasising their willingness to engage in providing joint services, and even highlighting the potential for one chief executive officer for the whole parliament. Lord Laming, then a member of the House of Lords House Committee, argued that the danger was in drift; it was healthy to pause from time to time and reflect on changed circumstances and key values (HOCGC 2014). There was evidence of good working relationships between the two houses with occasional meetings of their respective governance committees. The House of Lords Leader's Group on Governance (House of Lords 2016a) examined governance of the services and facilities provided to members of the House. Its report acknowledged increasing scrutiny of the House of Lords, closer public interest in how the House worked and how peers conducted themselves, and the growing need for cohesion and shared purpose between the two houses. It recommended the establishment of a House of Lords Commission, with two external members and two supporting committees—a structure very similar to that in place in the House of Commons. Of note is the report's concentration on productive relationships between members and staff, including informal settings for meetings; the need for routine and effective communication; and a focus on improving the governance of shared and joint services with the House of Commons. It went so far as suggesting an annual 'away day' for members of the commission and management board to discuss strategy, priorities and business and financial plans.[21] It also called for regular joint meetings with the equivalent Commons committees to discuss and decide on issues of common concern.

---

21 A suggestion eventually taken up (House of Lords 2021).

The House of Lords' annual reports provide some evidence of a constructive approach to management, giving a richer context for the changes resulting from formal governance reviews. Like the House of Commons, the House of Lords has moved slowly towards adopting a stronger focus on management and appears to have followed the reform path without too much outward resistance but with limited apparent effectiveness. The Lords governance reviews I have recounted reinforced a desire to involve peers more closely in administrative matters, but, as later chapters will reveal, officials in both houses have expressed cynicism about the extent of members' interest in administration—except when things go wrong—and further external reviews have been critical of management effectiveness, particularly the Ellenbogen review of workplace culture in 2019 (see Chapter 7 for a detailed account). The most recent annual reports I have examined (House of Lords 2017–18 to 2020–21) reference a continuing 'professionalisation' of senior staff with the appointment of new finance and human resources directors; strategic priorities that emphasise adaptation and innovation, excellence in service delivery, working together and embracing diversity; and an innovative response to the Covid-19 pandemic.[22] In 2020, the House of Lords Commission ordered an external management review (EMR) of the governance, management and organisation of the House of Lords (one of Ellenbogen's recommendations). The EMR uncovered continuing organisational issues of concern stemming from unclear accountabilities, insufficient professional capabilities, insufficient general management capacity, tentative leadership behaviours (including slow progress in tackling the perceived 'clerk privilege' highlighted by Ellenbogen) and outdated systems and processes (Leslie and Mohr 2021). It proposed 'a new approach to governance, management and people development', favouring a 'step-change' over incremental improvement and with new leaders in senior management roles 'who can make the change happen' (Leslie and Mohr 2021: 5). However, the review stopped short of supporting a key recommendation from Ellenbogen (2019), which itself went a step further than the HOCGC (2014). Ellenbogen recommended the appointment of a director-general who would have ultimate authority within the House administration. Instead, having considered 'insights from current and former leaders in the House of Commons' and the risk of 'conflict between two centres of power', Leslie and Mohr's review (2021: 87) recommended

---

22   David Beamish, former clerk of the parliaments, suggested some effects would have lasting significance—in particular, experience with virtual and hybrid proceedings would provide alternatives to current restoration and renewal options (Beamish 2021).

the appointment of a chief operating officer. At first glance, the proposed chief operating officer's functions and authority appear to emulate the 'diluted' version of the House of Commons Director-General; however, as deputy chief executive reporting to the Clerk of the Parliaments, the chief operating officer would have 'oversight of major change programmes and all non-procedural services to the House' as well as responsibility for 'most of the House's approximately 600 employees', the 'bulk of the resource and capital budgets' and providing 'visible and inclusive leadership to the whole organisation' (Leslie and Mohr 2021: 113–27). This sounds like a broad and complex remit with the risk it could lead to the new occupant becoming the 'fall-guy' for the next crisis. The EMR also sought, inter alia, to address a lack of management capacity and interest within the commission by recommending a small panel to assist the commission's oversight of the management board and establishing a statutory basis for House of Lords governance like the *House of Commons (Administration) Act 1978*.

Although embracing change, prima facie, the traditional custodians of practice and procedure continue to be concerned about ceding control to management newcomers. Further work to consider and implement EMR recommendations was due to take place in the financial year 2021–22 (House of Lords 2021). Time will tell whether the EMR's 'wide-ranging and radical' recommendations (if adopted) will herald another 'new era' of effective management in the House of Lords.

Factors influencing management effectiveness in two parliaments

In Chapter 1, I questioned how structural and other differences between the two parliaments inhibited or facilitated effective management and governance. I have provided examples in Table 4.6. An obvious effect arises from differences in the way procedural and support functions are organised. In the Australian Parliament, most of the non-procedural support functions have been located in separate departments and now reside within the DPS, which has lacked political support and shouldered the burden of financial efficiencies since its formation in 2004. A high turnover of senior executive staff within the DPS and the missteps exposed by senate committees have led to perceptions of a lack of deference towards parliamentary procedure and culture (see later chapters) and suggestions of 'reckless ignorance or indifference' on the part of officials whose job it is to serve the parliament (Laing 2014: 8). Latterly, the DPS has been accused of mismanagement, abuse of process and perpetuating a dysfunctional organisational culture (SFPALC 2021). In the UK Parliament, each house is responsible for its own management services—a factor that might be expected to have generated more support from members and clerks for the management function; however, repeated management reviews in the UK Parliament have demonstrated that this is not necessarily the case. Organisational structure alone is no panacea for effective management.

A second factor is the resources available to each parliament through their respective funding arrangements. Chapter 5 discusses these in more depth; for now, it is apparent that the power of the executive in appropriating the Australian Parliament's funds is a significant driver of efficiencies while a lack of executive control may have, at least in the past, reduced the incentive for the UK Parliament to commit to more radical efficiency reforms. In this respect, the size of each parliament is also significant: the Australian Parliament, as a small agency, is disproportionately affected by the efficiency dividend imposed by the executive (JCPAA 2008). But this difference belies the expenditure constraints that are placed on both parliaments by public expectations, particularly when new expenditures or budget overruns attract media publicity. Alleged misuses of parliamentary expenses by members, whether deliberate or inadvertent, can also be seen as failures of parliamentary management, particularly in the UK Parliament.

A third factor is the constitutional differences between the two parliaments, which are reflected in the relative powers of the Senate and the House of Lords to influence administrative reform, including through joint departments, and this might explain to some extent the reluctant adoption of modern management principles by the House of Lords.

A fourth factor is the different governance environments in the two parliaments. The legislative framework from which the Australian Parliamentary Service draws its authority mirrors that of the Australian Public Service, which serves the executive government of the day, and the presiding officers do not enjoy the same independence as those in the UK Parliament. On the one hand, this may have contributed to a more efficient and accountable parliament; on the other, the Australian Parliament has no overarching governance body that simultaneously oversees and advocates for the effective funding of procedural and management services across the parliament.

Table 4.6 Factors influencing management effectiveness in the two parliaments

Question 3: How do structural and other differences between the two parliaments inhibit or facilitate effective management and governance?		
Influencing factors	UK Parliament	Australian Parliament
Location of management support services	Procedural and management support services collocated with House of Lords and House of Commons administration. Slow pace of reform reflects lower management priorities. Repeated reviews have led to incremental change with some changes prompted by critical events.	Procedural and management support services located in separate parliamentary department. With less political support, reduced funding and shorter tenure for senior officials, DPS has become a target for extensive criticism.
Funding, authorisation and efficiency	House of Commons sets out its own estimate; House of Lords budget rarely challenged.	Australian Parliament is funded by executive, subject to efficiency dividend.
Constitutional limitations or freedoms	The House of Lords is an unelected chamber with limited powers and little capacity to influence administrative reform sponsored by the House of Commons, although it strives to retain its 'voice' in joint arrangements.	The Senate, as an elected chamber, usually with a non-government majority, claims greater legitimacy and has greater powers to influence or oppose administrative reforms initiated in the other house.
Governance	The two houses are not governed by an executive-driven legislative framework and the presiding officers function independently of government. The *House of Commons (Administration) Act 1978* is not prescriptive. Presiding officers are independent.	The *Parliamentary Service Act 1999* mirrors the *Public Service Act 1999*, and the parliament is a Commonwealth agency under the *Public Governance, Performance and Accountability Act 2013*. Presiding officers are not independent. There is no overarching governance body.

Conclusion

We have seen from this account of contemporary parliamentary management that despite the differences in the way each parliament is structured and governed, there are many similarities in their management approaches. Both parliaments have been slow to reform, insular and self-interested. Administrative reforms have been influenced by the need to preserve parliamentary sovereignty; procedural expertise has traditionally been prioritised over management expertise; and MPs, while eager to protect their privileges and immunities, appear less willing to engage in constructive management reform, lacking time, expertise or interest. In the following chapters, I analyse specific examples of governance, management and procedural and cultural reforms, using Bevir and Rhodes' (2006) concept of dilemma to explore how the beliefs and practices of parliamentary actors can be both explained and modified. I also discuss more closely differences between the two parliaments' organisational structures, strategic planning and public engagement activities.

5

Who *is* responsible for governing parliament?

Introduction

The UK Parliament has embedded arrangements for governing its support services in its two houses by establishing formalised governance structures to provide greater focus and continuity in planning and decision-making rather than concentrating only on the narrower perspective of oversight and scrutiny. The Australian Parliament has not formally adopted encompassing governance arrangements and relies on informal collaboration and consultation between the separate procedural and service departments without an established role for parliament's members in strategic planning. Former DPS officials and advisers to presiding officers have suggested that governance tends to occur in a vacuum.[1] Even where formal structures exist, in the form of advisory and scrutiny bodies, there is little evidence of strategic planning and clarity of decision-making or of a 'strategic conversation' at the interface between politicians and administrators (Shergold 1997; Alford, Hartley et al. 2017).

In this chapter, I provide an overview of the governance arrangements in each parliament before examining three dilemmas confronting parliamentary actors. The first concerns who has legitimate authority for

---

1   C. Mills, pers. comm., 11 May 2017; M. Croke, pers. comm., 19 May 2017; C. Paterson, pers. comm., 17 August 2017; Q. Clements, pers. comm., 7 July 2017.

parliamentary administration and who can advocate for its reform; the second relates to financial autonomy and control; and the third discusses the concept of collective responsibility for outcomes.

How the UK Parliament is governed

> Governance arrangements ... must enable an organisation to meet its primary purposes ... They must deliver clear decision-making, with a high degree of transparency and clarity, whilst incorporating appropriate levels of oversight, challenge and effective personal accountability. They must be practicable and resilient under pressure, taking account of how people behave. They must also have the support and confidence of those who operate within them. Good governance distinguishes between strategic and operational decision making, and has mechanisms in place to ensure that those decisions are then delivered and the objectives met. Central to all governance arrangements is a focus on the achievement of the main objectives of the organisation. (HOCGC 2014: 8)

The House of Commons Commission sets the strategic framework for the provision of services to the House. It meets monthly and is supported by domestic parliamentary committees including the Finance Committee, Administration Committee and Administration Estimate Audit and Risk Assurance Committee. The Commons Executive Board is accountable to the commission for delivering strategy and managing day-to-day operations. The Clerk of the House is accounting officer. The House of Lords Commission is supported by the Services Committee and Finance Committee, a management board takes strategic and corporate decisions within a framework set by the commission and the Clerk of the Parliaments is accounting officer. Several 'sub-boards' deal with bicameral issues, including digital strategy and joint investment. External members serve on both commissions, which also determine the annual estimate (or appropriations) for each house. Table 5.1 depicts the governance, financial and oversight arrangements in the UK Parliament.[2]

---

2   A full description of governance arrangements for the House of Commons and House of Lords can be found at House of Commons (2021) and House of Lords (2021).

Table 5.1 Overview of governance, financial and oversight arrangements in the UK Parliament

House of Commons	House of Lords
House of Commons (Administration) Act 1978, Parliamentary Corporate Bodies Act 1992 Formal governance body is the House of Commons Commission, consisting of members, senior officials and external members, supported by the Commons Executive Board and domestic committees. It sets the strategic framework for services. Meeting agendas and minutes are publicly available. House of Commons Commission presents for the House's approval the estimate for House of Commons Administration each financial year. Commission is advised by the Finance Committee (expenditure and budgets) and Administration Committee (improvements to services). Internal audit provides independent evaluation of governance, risk management and control. Administration Estimate Audit and Risk Assurance Committee, which includes MPs and external experts, advises commission and accounting officer, oversees internal audit and work of NAO and produces annual reports.	*Clerk of the Parliaments Act 1824, Parliamentary Corporate Bodies Act 1992* Formal governance body is the House of Lords Commission, consisting of peers and external members, supported by management board and two domestic committees. Meeting decisions and minutes publicly available. House of Lords funded by Supply Estimates, expenditure authorised and voted by parliament. House of Lords Commission agrees to annual estimate, oversees financial support for members, works with management board on development and oversight of strategic, business and financial plans, including monitoring performance. Audit Committee advises accounting officer on effectiveness of internal controls, risk management, financial practice and governance; reviews financial statements and accounts. Also meets jointly with House of Commons Administration Estimate Audit and Risk Assurance Committee.
By agreement with the accounting officers in both houses, the National Audit Office audits financial statements and may perform value-for-money work on certain topics, at the request of parliament.[3]	

How the Australian Parliament is governed

With the passage of the *Parliamentary Service Act 1999*, governance of the Australian Parliament was formally separated from the Australian Public Service, ending a long-disputed connection between the two institutions that had failed to sufficiently recognise the independence of the parliament

---

3　P. Ryan, National Audit Office UK, pers. comm., 1 August 2017.

and its presiding officers (Reid and Forrest 1989). The Act is more prescriptive than the *House of Commons (Administration) Act 1978*, the *Clerk of the Parliaments Act 1824* or the *Parliamentary Corporate Bodies Act 1992*. It defines the constitution and role of the Australian Parliamentary Service and its independence from executive government, prescribes the powers of the presiding officers and heads of department and establishes parliamentary values, employment principles and a Parliamentary Service code of conduct. The Act makes specific provisions to protect the independence of the Parliamentary Library and the Parliamentary Budget Office as well as the advice provided to the Senate and the House of Representatives, and their members, by their clerks. The clerks are appointed by their respective presiding officer and have limited tenure of a single, non-renewable term of 10 years. Their appointments can be terminated only by a resolution of their respective house. The secretary of the joint department, the DPS, on the other hand, is appointed by both presiding officers, with advice from the Parliamentary Service Commissioner, for up to five years initially. Parliamentary departments, as Commonwealth entities, are subject to the provisions of the *Public Governance, Performance and Accountability Act 2013* (*PGPA Act*) and the *Fair Work Act 2009* with their heads being the accountable authority for their respective departments.[4] The presiding officers have formal control of the parliamentary precincts under the *Parliamentary Precincts Act 1988*.

The Australian Parliament's first parliament-wide governance framework is set out in the *Strategic Framework: The Parliamentary Service* (Parliament of Australia 2020), but it does not specify a formal role for the presiding officers or other members and does not invite formal external input to governance. Meetings of departmental heads are held quarterly, a parliamentary administration advisory group of senior departmental staff supports department heads and the Parliamentary ICT Advisory Board meets quarterly to guide strategic elements of ICT service delivery. Formal joint meetings of the two house committees, where members of both houses used to meet to discuss corporate matters, were seen to be ineffective and these meetings no longer take place.[5] Two bodies one would expect to be influential in the provision of key services, the Joint Standing Committee on the Parliamentary Library and the Security Management Board, are not mentioned in the framework.

---

4   The main objective of the *PGPA Act* is to ensure that Commonwealth entities can meet high standards of governance, performance and accountability.

5   C. Mills, pers. comm., 11 May 2017; R. Stefanic, pers. comm., 24 January 2018.

All parliamentary expenditure is funded under separate appropriation Acts for the parliamentary departments. Table 5.2 provides an overview of the governance, financial and oversight arrangements in the four departments making up the Australian Parliamentary Service.[6]

Table 5.2 Overview of governance, financial and oversight arrangements in the Australian Parliament

Parliamentary department	Governance feature
Parliamentary Service Act 1999; *Parliamentary Precincts Act 1988*; *Public Governance, Performance and Accountability Act 2013*; *Fair Work Act 2009*; senate estimates committees (Senate, DPS and PBO); ANAO	
Whole-of-parliament: Presiding officers	Advisory committees to the presiding officers and parliamentary departments include the Security Management Board, Parliamentary ICT Advisory Board, Parliamentary Administration Advisory Group, Joint Standing Committee on the Parliamentary Library.
Department of the House of Representatives	Speaker of the House, as presiding officer; Clerk of the House, as accounting authority; Executive Management Committee and Audit Committee.
	House of Representatives Standing Committee on Appropriations and Administration determines amounts for inclusion in appropriation bills and considers proposals for changes to the department's administration.
	Standing Order 222 provides for committee to confer with senate committee on estimates of funding for DPS.
Department of the Senate	President of the Senate, as presiding officer; Clerk of the Senate, as accounting authority; Program Managers Group and Audit Committee.
	Senate Standing Committee on Appropriations, Staffing and Security determines amounts for inclusion in appropriation bills and can inquire into proposals for senate estimates and variations to staffing structures and policies.
	Standing Order 19 provides for committee to confer with House of Representatives committee on funding for ICT services.
	Senate Finance and Public Administration Committee may evaluate departmental performance.

6   A full description of the governance of the departments making up the Australian Parliamentary Service can be found at Department of the Senate (2021a); Department of the House of Representatives (2021a); DPS (2021a).

Parliamentary department	Governance feature
Department of Parliamentary Services (DPS)	Presiding officers (jointly responsible), Secretary, Executive Committee and Audit Committee. (See Senate Standing Order 19.) (See House of Representatives Standing Order 222.) Senate Finance and Public Administration Committee may evaluate departmental performance.
Parliamentary Budget Office (PBO)	Presiding officers (jointly responsible), Secretary, Executive Committee and Audit Committee. Senate Finance and Public Administration Committee may evaluate departmental performance (but not the Department of the House of Representatives).

Discussion of governance arrangements in the Australian Parliament appears to have been limited to a focus on the efficiencies that might be achieved by a reduction in the number of departments rather than on clarity of decision-making, appropriate oversight or effective personal accountability, as emphasised by the HOCGC (2014), or on the simplicity of planning and implementation and clarity of objectives—the basic principles of the Baxter review (2015).

While there does not appear to be a consistent view of governance in the Australian Parliament, it is not devoid of governance mechanisms. Each house of parliament has a House Standing Committee (the House of Representatives Standing Committee on Appropriations and Administration and the Senate Standing Committee on Appropriations, Staffing and Security) looking at resources (broadly defined) and, as noted, the presiding officers are advised by the Joint Standing Committee on the Parliamentary Library and a number of bodies related to the joint services for which they are responsible. The parliamentary departments have their own departmental management structures. But as far as can be publicly discerned, there is an absence of *ex ante* engagement by members and senators in strategic governance issues, as opposed to *ex post* criticism of performance, and the governance framework lacks the formalised transparency and clarity of decision-making, delivery mechanisms and strategic intent highlighted by the HOCGC (2014) and the House of Lords Leader's Group on Governance (House of Lords 2016a).

The dilemma of who speaks for parliament

The first governance dilemma relates to authority and advocacy. I have questioned whether MPs are constructively engaged in managing and governing their own parliaments. Key elements of constructive engagement are the extent to which members exercise authority or accept responsibility for parliamentary administration, and whether they are willing to advocate for management reforms (see also Norton 2017; Judge and Leston-Bandeira 2018). In this context, I contrast advocacy with scrutiny—a willingness to engage with and publicly support improvement and reform rather than a narrow focus on critiquing operational performance. Notwithstanding that we expect public managers to be greatly concerned with the lawful and efficient operation of their respective functional areas, there is little evidence of a collective responsibility among members for ensuring parliamentary effectiveness. Advocacy remains in short supply.

The concept in public management theory of engaging with an 'authorising environment', or a coalition of stakeholders, whose support is critical to achieve valued objectives proposed by public managers, has been hotly contested (Moore 1995; Rhodes and Wanna 2007, 2008, 2009; Alford and Hughes 2008; Alford and O'Flynn 2009; Benington and Moore 2010). Wanna equated the term with a 'disarticulated negotiated environment'.[7] It is unlikely the theoretical concept of an authorising environment has been seriously considered or applied in the parliamentary context, yet the idea lends itself to an environment in which there is an institutionalised blurring of the divide between political and administrative authority. In Lynn's (2006) public management dimension of 'structure', there is (or should be) a clear line of authority between a minister and a departmental secretary. However, examination of the governance structures and processes in the UK and Australian parliaments, recent academic literature on parliamentary authority (Norton 2017; Judge and Leston-Bandeira 2018), the views of some interviewees aired in this chapter and other empirical evidence, including from the HOCGC (2014), shows that this normative relationship does not exist in the parliamentary environment. Paradoxically, Moore's concept of a loosely described authorising environment, especially when conceived of as a coalition of stakeholders, may provide some value in navigating the complexities of parliamentary governance.

---

7   J. Wanna, pers. comm., 30 April 2018.

Even where legislated mandates or formal structures exist, the sources of administrative power and authority in the UK and Australian parliaments are not clearly delineated in practice, unlike in those countries' respective civil and public services, and this was made apparent by many interviewees. A senior clerk in the House of Lords described the UK system as a 'nice platter of different cheeses'; there is no final source of authority; everything must be negotiated.[8] At a University College London (UCL) Constitution Unit lecture in the UK Parliament on 16 March 2015, Lord Lisvane, former clerk of the House of Commons, reinforced a point made in the HOCGC (2014: 9) report: the House of Commons is run by 650 members, all of whom are skilled at articulating concerns and making an argument. He observed later that members were not always sufficiently consistent or well-enough informed to be supportive of the role he was trying to discharge as clerk, but also they were not enthusiastic about handing too much power to one individual. The inevitable unpredictability of parliaments and rapid shifts of focus posed additional difficulties.[9] Historically, the Speaker derives authority from the *collective* members of the House. The HOCGC (2014: 17), at the urging of then Leader of the House William Hague, reiterated that there should *not* be any *sole figure* in charge in the same way that a secretary of state is accountable for his or her department. Herein lies the dilemma of the 'authorising environment' (Moore 1995).

In the Australian Parliament, the observations are similar: in strict terms, the presiding officers have legal authority over their respective departments (except over employment matters) and the heads of department have strong powers and responsibilities to exercise their roles (see *Parliamentary Service Act 1999*). In practice, according to then Clerk of the House of Representatives David Elder, 'parliaments do muddle along a bit without anybody in charge … it is a bit of a moveable feast'.[10] One former president of the Senate did not believe it was the role of the president to become involved in the day-to-day management of the Department of the Senate or the co-management of DPS.[11] His successor believed that parliamentary administration was entrusted to the two presiding officers to jointly administer the parliamentary departments. He noted that while the two clerks have autonomous roles, under broad policy

---

8   Clerk, pers. comm., 14 April 2015.
9   Lord Lisvane, pers. comm., 11 May 2016.
10   D. Elder, pers. comm., 7 April 2017.
11   Former president, pers. comm., 20 June 2017.

direction, administration of DPS was more at the whim of the presiding officers, with the departmental secretary having more of a direct reporting responsibility without the security of tenure.[12] One might expect that less autonomy would equate to more engagement with the presiding officers, but evidence from interviewees did not bear this out.[13] Indeed, former DPS secretary Carol Mills claimed that when she arrived at DPS, her biggest problem was that it was 'friendless':

> I kept saying, 'We've got no friends. We've got no advocates. We've got no one in the positions of importance who put us as a priority.' Our friends [should be] the presiding officers, but we're not their best friends; their main friends are the clerks, and that's understandable. There was no committee or anything that I could go to that was responsible for supporting us … There was no one that you could build a rapport with who would be held responsible for supporting you and making sure that you were doing a good job … It cuts both ways. I thought that was a really big problem. We just didn't have any way to build friendships.[14]

In a joint submission to the SFPALC (2015d), then presiding officers Bronwyn Bishop and Stephen Parry claimed the role of the presiding officers in respect of DPS *was* similar to that of a minister overseeing a department of state, but the evidence did not support the presence of an advocacy role; instead, it suggested a blurred accountability in the context of limited 'ministerial' management skills and a reluctance to drive improvement (see Di Francesco 2012; Rhodes 2016). At worst, there appeared to be an abdication of the management or governance role of the presiding officers; at best, as we have seen in earlier chapters, it suggested a siloed approach towards 'departmental' rather than 'parliamentary' management. As Norton (2017) and Judge and Leston-Bandeira (2018) concluded regarding the UK Parliament, it appears there is no clear authority for promoting the Australian Parliament as a holistic institution or seeking to engage its members or the general community in thinking strategically about its future role.

---

12 Former president, pers. comm., 15 June 2017.
13 A. Podger, pers. comm., 4 August 2015; R. Stefanic, pers. comm., 10 April 2017; C. Mills, pers. comm., 11 May 2017; A. Thompson, pers. comm., 13 July 2017; C. Paterson, pers. comm., 17 August 2017; A. Smith, pers. comm., 27 October 2017.
14 C. Mills, pers. comm., 11 May 2017.

The level of constructive engagement by members in exercising authority for administrative decision-making appears to be a differentiating factor between the two parliaments. Although in both there is no clear line of ministerial-type authority and accountability for their administration, the establishment of formal governance structures in the House of Commons and House of Lords administrations indicates a greater acceptance of the need for members to be involved. How effective that engagement has been remains arguable.

The tradition of independence of the office of Speaker of the House of Commons is also a contributing factor in the extent of engagement, including advocacy for reform.[15] The incumbent is less fettered by any real or perceived allegiance to the executive and at greater liberty to argue for reforms that might be viewed as privileging the parliament over the executive, particularly in terms of reforming parliamentary procedures (see Chapter 7). According to the Institute for Government's first *Parliamentary Monitor 2018*:

> The current Speaker's [Bercow] willingness to grant more of these [backbench] requests than his predecessors has renewed many of these procedures. Reforms to other mechanisms, such as petitions, have also offered greater scope for backbench involvement. Many of these changes have made Parliament appear more accessible, and relevant, to the public. (Lilley et al. 2018: 77)

It is unlikely, however, that the UK Speaker's independence from the executive is the only factor explaining his or her engagement in administrative or procedural reform. The strong enthusiasm for engagement with administrative issues exercised by former Speaker Bercow stands in contrast with his immediate predecessors, Michael Martin and Betty Boothroyd (Boothroyd 2001; vanHeerde-Hudson 2014).[16] Indeed, Martin's incapacity to manage the unfolding crisis of the members' expenses scandal and its effect on the UK Parliament's reputation led to his resignation in 2009.[17]

---

15   On election, a new Speaker must resign from their political party and remain separate from political issues even in retirement. If a Speaker wishes to remain in office following a general election, they will not campaign on any political issues but will simply stand as 'the Speaker seeking re-election'. Incumbent Speakers are generally, but not always, unopposed by the major political parties, who will not field a candidate in the Speaker's constituency, including the party of which they were originally a member.

16   See also A. Walker, pers. comm., 23 September 2015.

17   See discussion of the expenses scandal in Winnett and Rayner (2009).

According to many interviewees, Bercow's strong engagement in administrative and procedural reform was driven by his personality.[18] In adopting new beliefs and performing new actions, he would appear to be a classic example of a 'situated agent' (Bevir and Rhodes 2006), exercising his ability to transform practices embedded in tradition. Not all his parliamentary colleagues considered his engagement constructive, as is evident from the 'Mills affair' recounted in Chapter 4 (see also Geddes and Meakin 2018; Leston-Bandeira and Thompson 2018). Some have suggested that Bercow's election to the speakership and his motivation for reform were designed to upset his former Conservative colleagues (see, for instance, Wheeler 2009; Wintour 2014). Many others believed he overstepped the role of Speaker (Hope and Krol 2017; Walker et al. 2017). But it must be remembered that he still required the support of a majority of his colleagues in the House to be re-elected, and his willingness to act as an advocate for institutional reform can also be associated with outcomes that are widely regarded as positive for the parliament in its three broad roles of enabling, scrutiny and deliberation, including his support for a greater role for backbenchers and his advocacy for greater diversity within the House Service.[19] Bercow described his role thus:

> I'm not always 'cruising for a bruising', always wanting to have a fight about everything—absolutely not—there is much to be said for periods of stability. But I have always said that you can either be a reforming Speaker or you can be an uncontroversial Speaker, you can't really be both. If you choose to try to make reforms—some of your own initiative, others that require the support of colleagues—there will be opposition, there always is, that's life. People, either because of their vested interests, because they are wary of change, they are comfortable with the status quo or they are people who have always been against you anyway and they see a chance to cause some trouble—they will oppose. My view is that it is not worth having an argument about everything, but where you think there is an enduring and significant worthwhile change that can be achieved it is worth going for it. If there is a bit of flak or a few people complain or there ends up being a bit of an

---

18   O. Gay, pers. comm., 16 September 2015; L. Sutherland, pers. comm., 15 September 2015; Lord Lisvane, pers. comm., 11 May 2016; Clerk of the House of Commons, pers. comm., 23 September 2015.
19   J. Bercow, pers. comm., 11 May 2016. Bercow's advocacy for greater diversity appears to have become embedded within House of Commons management (HC Debates 2021).

argument or you get some criticism either from colleagues in the newspapers or whatever, so what? What is that old expression 'one in five people is against everything all the time'.[20]

In the House of Lords, the Lord Speaker and senior Deputy Speaker are also required to put aside their party affiliations for the period they are in office, thus removing the constraints of party allegiance on reforms that might affect the status of the institution. There is some evidence that they are taking a strong position on governance matters, partly to try to retain the Lords' voice on issues of joint governance and to secure greater public regard (House of Lords House Committee 2016; Russell 2017b).[21]

The 'independence' tradition plays out differently in the Australian Parliament and in its two houses. Former Speaker of the House of Representatives Tony Smith pointed out that he was required to be 'impartial' rather than 'independent'—the latter being an impossibility in a parliament where neither house could afford to relinquish seats.[22] He did not demonstrate the strong advocacy role for parliamentary administrative reform displayed by Bercow; rather, he took the Lenthall view that this was a role for the House and not the Speaker, although his attempts to improve standards of behaviour in the House of Representatives chamber have been widely praised, particularly following his resignation as Speaker in late 2021.[23] The Senate President also is not independent of his or her party, although the ability to act independently is likely to have greater force in a house that is rarely controlled by an executive government.

The paradox of who speaks for the parliamentary institution is articulated by Judge and Leston-Bandeira (2018: 154), who claim that 'those who "speak for" (most loudly and most persistently) and "act for" parliaments as institutions are not primarily elected representatives but rather non-elected officials'. They suggest that at a time when elected representatives are 'cowed by populist claim-makers' and confronted routinely by claims

---

20   J. Bercow, pers. comm., 11 May 2016. Adding to the controversy, in 2022, the Independent Expert Panel that investigated an appeal by former Speaker Bercow against allegations of bullying, which had been upheld by the Parliamentary Commissioner for Standards, concluded that Bercow was a serial bully. The chair of the panel observed: 'It is for historians to judge whether the respondent was a successful reforming Speaker of the House of Commons. However, there was no need to act as a bully in order to achieve that aim. A great office can be filled forcefully and effectively without descending to such behaviour' (Independent Expert Panel 2022). Bercow continues to deny bullying claims (Dale 2022).

21   A. Makower, pers. comm., 15 June 2016; F. D'Souza, pers. comm., 9 June 2016.

22   T. Smith, pers. comm., 19 April 2017.

23   T. Pasin, pers. comm., 10 May 2017; Australian House of Representatives (2021a).

that are 'intrinsically anti-parliamentary and anti-elitist', this should be a concern in terms of representative democracy (Judge and Leston-Bandeira 2018: 169). Norton (2017) also addressed the problem of a declining public trust in parliamentarians, arising not just from recent scandals and perceptions of poor behaviour but also from broader societal and technological changes. In part, he ascribed the problem to parliament's unique constitutional nature by which no individual can claim to speak for parliament. The solution, he claimed, lies not in adopting defensive responses to crises, such as the 'rushed and flawed' creation of the Independent Parliamentary Standards Authority, but in the members in each house adopting an outward-looking, proactive rather than reactive approach: '[I]t is important that members come out of the bunker, guns firing' to meet public expectations and convey a sense of public service (Norton 2017: 200–1). These viewpoints from established academics, one of whom is also a parliamentarian, help to clarify the representational problem of who speaks for parliament. On the one hand, they champion a greater understanding of institutional and representative claim-making; on the other, they urge members to become more engaged in addressing the relationship between themselves and the public. I argue, too, that institutional advocacy and claim-making, as well as accountability and responsibility, might be enhanced by members exercising collective authority for decisions affecting the administration of their parliaments through formal, transparent and engaged governance structures.

The shibboleth of financial independence: A dilemma that may need reframing

Few would suggest that parliamentary sovereignty justifies unlimited public funding. However, the parliamentary funding dilemma, particularly the question of financial independence from the executive, has emerged as a significant influence on beliefs and actions within the two parliaments. In the Australian Parliament, chiefly within the Senate, the dilemma has been framed as a threat to its ability to carry out its scrutiny role, but it is not clear how much of the argument is driven by government-enforced efficiencies (Verrier 2007). Breukel et al. (2017) reviewed key reports and literature on parliamentary independence and provided a jurisdictional comparison of Australian and other parliaments regarding parliamentary funding. They suggested that, in Australia, and particularly in the State of Victoria, 'executive creep' or encroachment had weakened parliamentary independence (see also Donaldson 2017)—

a suggestion that resonated strongly with the documented views of former Senate Clerk Evans. Governance of the funding arrangements and the role the executive government plays in appropriating funds—who is in control of the purse strings—have long been a sore point, but many of the officials I interviewed felt the concern had been overplayed.

The arguments for an independent appropriation—where the parliament, not the executive, determines the level and direction of funding—stem from the belief that when the executive controls the amount of money appropriated to the parliament, it will exercise its power to limit the extent to which parliament can hold the executive to account or provide sufficient support to opposition parties. The UK Parliament has more control over its funding than the Australian federal and state parliaments (CPA 2005; Verrier 2007) and it is unsurprising, therefore, that concerns about financial independence are more prominent in Australia, particularly among clerks and Parliamentary Library staff (Evans 2005; Verrier 2007; Laing 2016a, 2016b; Breukel et al. 2017). Several mechanisms for resolving the issue have been proposed, such as an independent funding model, greater collaboration between the parliament and the Treasury and establishing a parliamentary corporate body (CPA 2005; Verrier 2007; Baxter 2015; Breukel et al. 2017), but there is no utopia of total parliamentary control. Sloane (2014) explained why financial independence is unachievable under Australia's Constitution and its proponents have also conceded that true financial independence is not achievable in any publicly funded organisation. Even the much-vaunted financial independence of the UK Parliament is itself constrained at least in part by public opinion and this is prominently reflected in the establishment of the Independent Parliamentary Standards Authority (IPSA), which controls and authorises members' remuneration and most of their allowances (Gay 2014). The Commonwealth Parliamentary Association (CPA 2005) has acknowledged that public opinion is the 'real counterweight' to budgetary autonomy. The drawn-out debate on options for the restoration and renewal of the Palace of Westminster is also testimony to the power of public opinion.

One former Senate president did not think it appropriate that the Senate should have to be a supplicant to the Cabinet's Expenditure Review Committee during budget discussions, refusing to appear before it and instead insisting that the Treasurer and finance minister should visit him.[24] Some officials considered such a view to be illogical or ineffective.[25]

---

24 Former president of the Senate, pers. comm., 15 June 2017.
25 D. Kenny, pers. comm., 27 June 2017; A. Smith, pers. comm., 27 October 2017.

Parliament's funding model was also taken up by the independent review of the DPS (Baxter 2015), which was set up apparently to satisfy the Senate Finance and Public Administration Legislation Committee that 'something was being done' about the department's performance failures. As noted in Chapter 4, Baxter recommended inter alia that the funding arrangements for the parliament be consolidated into a 'global' or 'whole-of-parliament' model based on long-term strategic and annual operating plans, providing adequate coverage of essential modernisation and renovation of Parliament House; and that relevant parts of the ministerial and parliamentary services branch of the Department of Finance be transferred to the presiding officers. The review also reported that several senators and members had considered that it might be appropriate to establish a Joint Standing House Committee with appropriate terms of reference to oversee DPS, and its recommendations included establishing an overarching advisory board that would complement existing statutory and administrative arrangements. The proposals were not taken up.[26] Baxter suggested one reason was the potential reduction of staff numbers in the Department of Finance: 'There are still those within the bureaucracy who regard the number of people they have in the department as a significant indicator of their power. And it exists here in this parliament.'[27]

We can detect here a case of self-interest or public-choice theory at work and the purported sentiment is not too far from some of the thinking expressed in senate annual reports. According to Baxter, another opportunity to improve governance was missed:

> I came back, after very lengthy discussions, not only with the Speaker of the House of Commons but also with members of the House of Lords and the House of Commons, with a very strong view that it [a governance body] would overcome a lot of the problems and issues we've got, particularly in the next 10 years when they're going to have to deal with, if our population continues to grow, under the constitution, increased numbers of parliamentarians, which means in turn dealing with internal design within the parliament. They're going to have to think about how they maintain the public's view of the parliament as an important institution in our democratic framework. It is about how they try and rebuild the trust in the institution per se, as against whether

---

26 Q. Clements, pers. comm., 7 July 2017; K. Baxter, pers. comm., 21 August 2017.
27 K. Baxter, pers. comm., 21 August 2017.

you like the current incumbents of the ministries. I certainly would strongly argue for a role that's similar to what they've got in the Speaker of the House of Commons in the UK.[28]

In Australia, there has been a strong push for efficiencies in line with public expenditure constraints generally and earlier chapters have documented this increasing focus. The evidence suggested that parliamentary departments were traditionally seen as 'hollow logs' carrying over large surpluses and arguing for their retention to mitigate the potential problem of increased future expenditure (Evans 2003).[29] In the DPS—the department hit hardest by the executive government's quest for efficiencies—the financial independence argument was not widely proselytised. David Kenny, DPS deputy secretary from 2005 to 2012, expressed no concern about being required to apply to the government for funding improvement through the Expenditure Review Committee; he did not think the existing funding model had worked badly:

> No matter what you do, the parliament is not going to be raising its own money. So the money is always going to be coming from government. Wherever the decisions are taken as to how much money is provided to parliament, it's still going to be getting it from the Finance Department.[30]

Hilary Penfold, the first DPS secretary, said she had not seen a proposed independent funding model that would give her confidence that the parliament would not be squeezed in subsequent years in the light of unforeseen events, once it was given control of its own budget.[31] Andrew Smith, a former Joint House Department senior executive, suggested that at the time of DPS's formation, the presiding officers should not have allowed the Department of Finance to reduce its budget; they should have pushed back:

> Because the presiding officers' influence is fairly weak, it's very hard for DPS or any of the parliamentary departments to get any innovative things up and running or to get increases in budgets or to stave off attacks on their budgets by the central agencies at any stage.[32]

---

28 ibid.
29 Also C. Paterson, pers. comm., 17 August 2017; former senior adviser, pers. comm., 23 August 2017.
30 D. Kenny, pers. comm., 27 June 2017.
31 H. Penfold, pers. comm., 19 July 2017.
32 A. Smith, pers. comm., 27 October 2017.

These arguments suggest that rather than gaining agreement from the executive that a budget prepared by the parliament should go unchallenged, which might even bring unintended consequences, a preferable outcome would be for the parliament to develop a stronger ability to argue for effective funding on a case-by-case basis. Smith argued that these skills were not prevalent within the parliamentary service.[33] Recent annual reports show that both houses have successfully negotiated additional funds for chamber and committee support (see Elder 2017; Pye 2017); it appears more difficult to secure funding for non-procedural activities.

As we know, in the United Kingdom the budget for the House of Commons administration is not limited by the Treasury, and it is conventional for the vote for the House of Lords administration estimate to go unchallenged (Breukel et al. 2017). But this does not mean the UK Parliament's expenditure on its administration goes unchecked, as is evidenced by the austerity program after the 2010 election and the decision to limit the growth in expenditure in both houses;[34] the setting up of IPSA following the expenses scandal (Winnett and Rayner 2009; vanHeerde-Hudson 2011; Gay 2014); and the deep concerns about the costs of restoring the Palace of Westminster, which have continued to delay critical decisions (House of Commons–House of Lords Joint Committee on the Palace of Westminster 2017; Meakin 2017b; Meakin and Anderson 2019; Meakin et al. 2020; Engel 2020). Notwithstanding that the House of Commons Commission can determine its own funding without going cap in hand to the Treasury, efficiencies have still been regarded in some quarters as politically driven. This view was strongly articulated by Ken Gall, a long-serving House of Commons Hansard official who also served as a member of the Trade Union Side, which represents key industrial organisations within the parliament:

> In my view, one of the biggest mistakes that has been made by the administration here has been an acceptance of a very politically driven narrative which involves efficiencies. It involves value for money, it involves savings and austerity. I'm not saying that there is a bucket of money that, once it is emptied, can immediately be filled up again and can be thrown at parliaments … But this constant fixation with efficiencies, value for money, the need to generate savings, has been bought into hook, line and sinker by the administration of the House and has caused … a blurring of what parliament is about.[35]

---

33   ibid.
34   M. Barrett, pers. comm., 15 September 2015.
35   K. Gall, pers. comm., 20 May 2016.

But many other interviewees, particularly those more recently appointed, agreed on the need for restraint in the UK Parliament's administrative funding, as evidenced by the following comments from Myfanwy Barrett, then finance director:

> My view is that we are quite well resourced. There are relatively few areas that are under serious pressure. This is quite an important point because I think that if you've been here for 40 years since you left university and you've never worked anywhere else and you've seen us gradually become more critical, more scrutinising of the deployment of our resources and with tighter budgets, it feels to you like we have got far too much going on and we haven't got enough resources and we are all under too much pressure. If that person went to work for a health authority for a fortnight, I think their view would be completely different.[36]

Overall, there was a strong sense from across the spectrum of interviewees of the need for efficiency and reduced wastage accompanied by some scepticism about the extent of efficiencies that could be harvested from initiatives such as joint working.[37] Difficulties with deciding from where efficiencies should be sourced and how outcomes could be measured were also raised.[38] As well, strong views were put forward that finding efficiencies should not preclude spending on worthwhile initiatives such as public engagement.[39] There was little doubt, however, that without external pressure, the drive towards efficiency was tempered, even in seemingly harvestable areas like catering. As a former Clerk of the House put it:

> The Lords wouldn't want [their catering arrangements] to be taken over. They have a particular house style and if they can make money selling it, good luck to them with their spotted dicks and funny old puddings. A lot of people obviously like it because they buy it. They can always go somewhere else.[40]

36   M. Barrett, pers. comm., 15 September 2015.
37   ibid.; L. Sutherland, pers. comm., 15 September 2015; D. Natzler, pers. comm., 25 May 2016.
38   O. Gay, pers. comm., 16 September 2015; J. Silvester, pers. comm., 22 September 2015; I. Ailles, pers. comm., 9 May 2016.
39   E. Crewe, pers. comm., 21 September 2015.
40   D. Natzler, pers. comm., 25 May 2016.

The catering services often came to the fore in terms of complaints, both internal and external,[41] and there was an obvious frustration with the failure of the joint working program to make savings in this area. According to the former House of Commons director-general, the prospect of an imminent decant from the building appears to have served as an excuse not to rationalise the separate catering services and he conceded that the joint working program had become a matter of spending money without any outcome. However, he remained

> utterly convinced that if you put the two caterings together, you could have at least as good a service, and probably a better service, and you could save a million or two pounds a year easily enough, and almost without breaking into a sweat. If we had the will, we could bring these two catering services together by next Easter, and we'd have 6½ years, even if we move out in 2025—a £2 million saving a year. Again it's a really good indicator of glacial speed and glacial thought. So we're walking away from £13 million in savings to the taxpayer.[42]

Following his departure, Ailles reiterated a lack of resolve within the commission to drive down costs; members who seek to withdraw or adjust services for other members become unpopular.[43]

We can see a difference between attitudes in the drive for efficiencies in parliamentary administration in both countries, which appears to be related to who governs those efficiencies. In Australia, from the Senate's point of view, the issue is essentially the ability of the Senate to carry out its scrutiny role effectively. Similar arguments have come from the Parliamentary Library and its supporters about the importance of their ability to provide unrestricted research services to members, particularly opposition members (see especially Verrier 2008). We cannot downplay the need for either parliament to be effectively resourced to achieve its key purposes and it appears that the drive for efficiencies, particularly following the imposition of the efficiency dividend, has been greater in Australia than in the UK Parliament, where the two houses are somewhat ambivalent about the potential efficiency gains from joint services. Despite this, one could argue that the separation of powers argument

---

41   It was surprising how often the catering arrangements were emphasised in an examination of annual reports from 1980.

42   I. Ailles, pers. comm., 18 September 2018.

43   I. Ailles, pers. comm., 27 October 2021.

in Australia, focusing on parliament's need to assert its supremacy over the executive in terms of control of the proportion of public funds it receives, is unhelpful. The arguments have also been influenced by disagreements over the share of resources each department receives, which can manifest as an internal power struggle about the supremacy of the two house departments over the separate services department (see Reid and Forrest 1989; Adams 2002; Department of the Senate annual reports). Even strong advocates of financial independence for parliaments have conceded that true independence is not achievable; the parliament cannot appropriate its own resources independently of government. There are opportunities, however, to strengthen a parliament's financial capacity through its governance arrangements, as demonstrated in the UK and other parliaments.[44] There appears to be little appetite for such a formal governance body in the Australian Parliament, or for closer financial collaboration between the two houses.

The governance dilemma: Are members of parliament missing in action?

I have discussed the differences in the two parliaments between their governance arrangements and the extent to which they galvanise the authority and advocacy of the presiding officers and other members and officials in 'speaking for parliament' (Norton 2017). For the Australian Parliament, a significant contrast lies in securing financial resources and the ability of its presiding officers to act independently. But to return to a key concern in this book—the constructive engagement of members in parliamentary governance and management—I draw on Verrier's (2007: 73) acknowledgement that even a statutory underpinning would not be sufficient to ensure a parliament's independence 'in the absence of ongoing, consistent stakeholder interest in parliamentary administration'. The same sentiment applies to effective governance. The JCPAA (2008), SFPALC (2015c) and the Baxter review (2015) recommended seemingly sensible changes to the Australian Parliament's governance, including joint meetings of the respective houses' administration committees and

---

44   For instance, the newest of Australia's parliaments, the Legislative Assembly for the Australian Capital Territory, has established the Office of the Legislative Assembly as a parliamentary corporate body and endorsed budget protocols to be observed in developing and considering its budget appropriations (Breukel et al. 2017; Skinner 2017).

the establishment of an overarching governance body. But, according to Quinton Clements, former senior adviser to then president Parry, the presiding officers believed there was 'enough meat to the governance structure already' and there was no need to add another body that might take away their authority. The potential dilution of authority was also given as the reason for resisting joint meetings of the appropriations and administration committees.[45] The Australian Parliament appears to have suffered from not just an indifference to proposals for strengthening governance, but also active resistance.

When Norton (2000, 2017) argued the case for greater agency for parliamentarians, he was also concerned with restoring public trust in parliament. Most recently, he saw the relationship between the parliament and the public as being under more significant challenge than at any time over the past century while parliament's effectiveness in performing its scrutiny role was, in fact, 'greater than at any time in modern political history' (Norton 2017: 191; see also Russell et al. 2016; Russell and Gover 2017; Russell 2019a, 2019b).[46] Norton (2000) argued that achieving reform in parliament, whatever its nature, needs a window of opportunity, a coherent reform agenda and political will or leadership (see also Kelso 2009; Geddes and Meakin 2018; Meakin and Geddes 2020). Acknowledging the difficulty of achieving any change within parliament, the dilemma I have posed here is that of engaging members' interest in parliamentary administration and reform at a time when they are also increasingly under pressure to meet the expectations of their parties, their constituents and the public at large. Advocating for a particular reform is likely to be controversial in terms of its influence on a member's ability to fulfil conflicting expectations.

In my research, I sought the views of members who might be expected to contribute to their parliament's governance through their membership of internal governance or procedure committees. Among those in the Australian Parliament who agreed to be interviewed, enthusiasm for advocating for administrative reform was mixed. Some strongly defended the status quo. Then Chief Government Whip in the House of Representatives Nola Marino was a member of both the House Procedure Committee and the House Appropriations and Administration

---

45   Q. Clements, pers. comm., 7 July 2017.
46   It must be noted that Norton was speaking during a period of minority government at the height of the national debate on Brexit.

Committee. Her key consideration in her procedural role was the 'smooth management of government business to make sure that the government achieves its legislative aims' and, on administrative matters, 'in a similar way, just ensuring the smooth management and also that the appropriate level of scrutiny is applied'—a business-as-usual approach by a Government Chief Whip committed to achieving the executive agenda. She declined to comment on whether any joint discussion had occurred between the houses on an appropriate parliamentary funding model.[47]

The Senate's established response to administrative reform has been to safeguard its financial interests and constrain the power of other parliamentary departments. The senators I interviewed by virtue of their membership of the Appropriations, Staffing and Security Committee and/or the Senate Procedure Committee offered little to suggest a coherent reform agenda. Then Deputy President, Senator Sue Lines, gave priority to ensuring that procedural rules are fit for purpose in allowing the Senate to continue to play a strong scrutiny role.[48] Senator Katy Gallagher saw her then associated roles as Opposition Business Manager and member of the Procedure, Appropriations, Staffing and Security, and Finance and Public Administration committees (roles she was given, rather than aspired to) as facilitating or advocating the Labor Party's interests.[49] So, is it up to the clerks in both houses and other senior officials to play a role in governance or institutional representation, as Judge and Leston-Bandeira (2018) claim to be the case in the UK Parliament? Should they be entering the 'purple zone' (Shergold 1997; Alford, Hartley et al. 2017) and, if so, at what stage of the reform process? Then deputy clerk, now Clerk of the House of Representatives, Claressa Surtees, suggested that departmental officials had been 'a little bit coy in talking about the stewardship issue' and they might be perceived as 'stuck in the past'. She said: 'We have to make sure that the narrative we've got around stewardship is a very modern and open one, so that people understand what it means. It doesn't mean doing what you've always done and not changing anything.'[50]

She advocated a more collaborative relationship between the parliamentary departments—'you need to bring your partners on board'—and between officials and those members who, while insisting on a well-oiled

---

47 N. Marino, pers. comm., 14 June 2017.
48 S. Lines, pers. comm., 15 August 2017.
49 K. Gallagher, pers. comm., 14 June 2017.
50 C. Surtees, pers. comm., 6 June 2017.

administration, were not sufficiently interested in administrative issues. Several current and former senior clerks were supportive of a House of Commons–style commission or board, where members would actively engage with governance issues.[51] The caveat was that their engagement would need to be at the highest level, rather than becoming involved in the 'nitty-gritty' or day-to-day operations—a theme that was consistent in both parliaments. Surtees advocated for greater unity among parliamentary officials:

> I want people to think of themselves as servants of the parliament or supporters for the parliament rather than of this department or that department, and trying to promote the interests of one department against another department. I don't actually think that's very helpful for anybody, it isn't going to deliver a better service, and it will make us look like we can't get along. That's not very professional. The rest of the countryside probably thinks it's one organisation. And we are; we're one parliamentary service. So let's act like it.[52]

Julie Owens, then a shadow assistant minister and Deputy Chair of the House Appropriations and Administration Committee, said she could not imagine the clerks would ever speak out on management issues, particularly funding, and would need to rely on members to do so. She thought members of the Appropriations Committee had done a good job but acknowledged that there had been increasing budgetary pressure over some years.[53] On the other hand, Senator Gallagher did see a role for the clerks, as the 'best thinkers and experts in their field', in promoting reform, in partnership with the parties and the crossbench.[54] The Clerk of the Senate, Richard Pye, and former deputy Maureen Weeks were more circumspect. Weeks described herself as an 'old-school' senate officer and did not consider herself an advocate for reform; rather, her role was to work with the president or deputy president to resolve problems or confusion in the chamber:

---

51   D. Elder, pers. comm., 7 April 2017; C. Surtees, pers. comm., 6 June 2017; B. Wright, pers. comm., 25 May 2017.
52   C. Surtees, pers. comm., 6 June 2017.
53   J. Owens, pers. comm., 30 May 2017.
54   K. Gallagher, pers. comm., 14 June 2017.

I see it as a very organic thing that evolves. To have it work, you can't have someone taking a hard line and saying, 'We must not do this,' or 'We must do that' … It's a very organic thing, and to try and place more rigid theories of management over it just creates difficulties and avoids possibilities.[55]

Pye recognised the increasing governance responsibilities of the clerk's position, particularly in terms of satisfying the requirements of the *PGPA Act*. Although very conscious of his role in negotiating resources and cooperation to provide the best possible level of services to senators, he also appeared less inclined than previous clerks to 'jealously guard' resources and functions within the Senate and recognised the potential benefits of a parliament-wide approach. Of particular interest given the discussion in the previous chapter, he questioned the effectiveness of senators continuing to demand more and more senate committee inquiries despite their lack of time to contribute effectively to them. The lengthy quotation below presents an alternative view of the Senate's scrutiny role and the responsibility of the clerk:

We need to make sure that senators are constantly aware of how much work they have generated for themselves and how much work they have generated for senate committees, and how effective senate committee processes are being in achieving the aims of particular inquiries … There is lots of criticism of senate committee reports at the moment on that basis, that the time isn't there for anybody to sit down and do that analytical stuff, and to come to agreement between the different political parties and independents who are sitting on committees. Instead, we get party policy positions stapled together, with some reference to the evidence that's been taken. That's not desirable, in my view. Part of it is desirable; it's always desirable to get evidence from people, particularly people who are affected or people who are experts. But if you don't round that out with a consideration among senators themselves of the possibility of compromise or the possibility of understanding each other's perspectives, that is a real lost opportunity … Senators need to see for themselves that they need to step back from the number of inquiries so that they can give themselves the time to do it right. But they have to come up with the criteria for doing that. We can't say to them, 'This one's worthy and this one isn't', because that's not our role … What we can do is make sure that every agenda lists every reference that

---

55   M. Weeks, pers. comm., 23 May 2017.

is before that committee at the time … to make it more visible. As I say, it's not for us to arbitrarily determine where the line should be drawn, but we can help people to make that decision for themselves, which I think is a proper role for us.[56]

It is possible these comments from the then recently appointed clerk represented a change in senate thinking from scrutiny and inquiry at all costs to a focus that included considerations of value. Pye's approach was acknowledged by other senate interviewees.[57] But although he was positive about the 'upswing of cooperation' and the 'partnership vibe' across the parliamentary departments, particularly in the provision of IT services, he left little doubt that he, too, remained a 'sceptical questioner' in relation to governance issues.

In the UK Parliament, notwithstanding the existence of formal governance structures, views were mixed about the level of engagement in governance by members. Then Clerk of the Parliaments[58] David Beamish said:

> [T]here are a number of areas where one wants to do what members want. And members want one to do what members want but it's not easy to discern what members want. We have a committee structure, and members who aren't part of that complain that they weren't consulted. On anything controversial there is a variety of views. So you will probably find members who will complain that the clerks are running the show and things happen the way they want … I am hoping that the new structure will get the members of the relevant bodies behaving more like a board where they have a shared responsibility on behalf of other members for coming to a sensible conclusion.[59]

Other House of Lords interviewees, including a former adviser to the Leader of the House and the Chairman of Committees, affirmed the difficulties in engaging members in governance matters: administrative decisions did not always reflect the views of the majority; a single spokesperson for the House of Lords was not practical in a self-regulating house; issues moved between shades of the political and the administrative.[60] The House of Lords was also concerned about losing its voice in arrangements for joint

---

56   R. Pye, pers. comm., 12 April 2017.
57   Q. Clements, pers. comm., 7 July 2017; M. Weeks, pers. comm., 24 May 2017.
58   As the Clerk of the House of Lords is known.
59   D. Beamish, pers. comm., 24 May 2016.
60   Clerk, pers. comm., 14 June 2017; Lord Laming, pers. comm., 13 June 2017.

working; one example given was a controversial decision by former House of Commons Speaker Bercow to establish a parliamentary education centre within the parliamentary precincts.[61]

In the House of Commons, one senior clerk felt the new governance arrangements expected too much of members in asking them to set a strategic direction for staff, having seen little evidence of member engagement to the level of detail required to run a complex organisation.[62] Others noted a lack of trust; still others were concerned about the involvement of members in the more important governance and management challenges and some claimed members were interested only in getting into government.

Views from members of the House of Commons Commission themselves about their roles and purposes were mixed, although mainly positive. Members of the commission were frank about the continuing need to reinforce the importance of strategic change and collaboration, including across the houses. Prominent Labour member and former commission member Chris Bryant was sceptical about the quality of parliamentary governance. He advocated a whole-of-parliament approach by suggesting a single committee of the parliament responsible for the running of all 'management-type' functions, leaving the Standing Orders and ways and means of doing business within each house.[63] For that to succeed, and for the parliament to run more efficiently and to create greater public value, he was adamant that the House of Lords and House of Commons would have to work together, with the Lords focusing less on its own identity and self-regulation. Labour member Nick Brown, then chair of the Finance Committee and member of the commission, was pragmatic about the difficulties, not only of getting the Lords and Commons to work effectively together, but also of actively engaging Commons members in reform and in reconciling the plurality of stakeholder interests. He was positive, however, about the role of advisers and the external members of the commission in providing assurance about the advice that the Finance Committee would provide to the commission, particularly on administration estimates and major capital projects.[64]

---

61 The decision was approved by the House of Commons on 21 November 2013 (HC Debates 2013) and the education centre opened on 15 July 2015 (UK Parliament 2015). Bercow commented on the House of Lords' resistance in a speech to Policy Exchange (Bercow 2015).
62 Clerk, pers. comm., 23 September 2015.
63 C. Bryant, pers. comm., 23 May 2016.
64 N. Brown, pers. comm., 7 June 2016.

His attitude contrasted with what we have seen from members involved in administration in the Australian Parliament, which suggested a culture of critical rather than supportive engagement.

Sir Paul Beresford, also a (Conservative) member of the House of Commons Commission in its former and reincarnated forms, and then chair of the new Administration Committee, displayed no concerns about lack of trust between members and officials, nor was he disparaging of the requirement for effective governance. He, too, was positive about the benefits of having external members on the commission. He challenged the view of members being interested only in getting into government, no doubt because, as a former minister, he had 'been there, done that', but he made a very good case for careful selection (or election) of members to their governance bodies. It is, perhaps, unsurprising that the chairs of the two supporting committees to the commission would be positive about the commission's effectiveness—there is undoubtedly an element of 'they would say that, wouldn't they?'—and we can also look at evidence to the contrary (see later chapters).

Although the UK Parliament (as evidenced in both houses) appears to have established a greater potential for effective governance and management by virtue of formalised governance arrangements, and regular reflection on their adequacy and appropriateness, it is by no means assured of success.[65]

Conclusion: A case of 'not me, guv'[66] or benign neglect?

In this chapter, I have addressed the extent to which MPs are constructively engaged in the governance and management of their institutions, and how structural and other differences between the two parliaments inhibit or facilitate effective outcomes. To answer the provocative question heading this section, I do not conclude that either the UK or the Australian parliaments are bereft of responsible governance, but the evidence does show that members collectively seem to be missing in action and, in particular, both parliaments suffer from a lack of administrative advocacy

---

65   The external management review of the House of Lords sets out a powerful case for change (Leslie and Mohr 2021); House of Commons annual reports indicate a weakening of the governance role.
66   Relevant uses of this metaphor for avoiding responsibility in the United Kingdom and Australia include Taxpayers' Alliance (2007) and Pelling (2017).

and authority. Differing views have been presented of where the line falls between the responsibility of parliamentary officials and members for delivering effective governance and management and the oft-cited argument for parliamentary control over its appropriations.

The UK Parliament, in both houses, has established formal governance mechanisms, but many parliamentary actors were not confident of their current or likely success. However, there is greater potential, at least in the House of Commons, for the Speaker to exercise his or her independence and authority, and former Speaker John Bercow was an exemplar in this regard as I will further demonstrate (while also acknowledging his subsequent excoriation on leaving office; Independent Expert Panel 2022). In Australia, factors including the political strength of the Senate and a lack of agency from presiding officers have in the past influenced the extent to which parliamentary departments collaborate with each other, even though the Senate and the House of Representatives are served by a single services department. I have also argued that repeated calls for Australia's parliamentary budgets to be developed independently of the executive could be better proselytised through more holistic, whole-of-parliament governance mechanisms. In the next two chapters, I explore the challenges of managing in the parliamentary environment and outline the case for continuity *and* reform in the institutionalised procedures and cultures of the two parliaments.

6

The challenges of managing in the parliamentary environment

Introduction

In both parliaments, the concept of 'management' appears to have been relegated to secondary importance after traditional and specialised parliamentary services. For many years, the approach to management in the United Kingdom was that of the 'gentleman amateur' (HOCGC 2014),[1] and this approach was also reflected in the Australian Parliament when administration was 'something to be done on a Friday afternoon at the end of a sitting week'.[2] Management was viewed with suspicion—something for others to be concerned about. Administration was uninteresting and unnoticed—until something went wrong. Senior officials usually focused narrowly on their areas of expertise. But the early years of the twenty-first century have been marked by an accelerating pace of change. Both parliaments have faced significant management challenges while more public exposure has simultaneously ushered in a new age of public cynicism and loss of respect for, or deference towards, members of parliament. Among the challenges is the need for those in the management box seat to overcome resistance from those favouring the status quo—an 'embedded political elite' consistently rejecting or diluting reform agendas that threaten their privileged position; in other words,

---

1   Noted also by C. Bryant, pers. comm., 23 May 2016.
2   Noted also by D. Elder, pers. comm., 7 April 2018.

a clash between 'aversive and aspirational constitutionalism' (Flinders et al. 2018a). This challenge can also be seen as a clash between a historical institutional and path-dependent perspective, where change occurs only as a result of a crisis or accident (Kelso 2009; Russell 2011b; Flinders et al. 2018a; Petit and Yong 2018), and the strategically planned collaborative management approach that public management experts would advocate.

This chapter highlights issues of structural identity and institutional divides before examining three associated management dilemmas: multiple stakeholders and competing roles, balancing operational and strategic management, and coping with necessary but sometimes counterproductive scrutiny mechanisms.

Structural identity and institutional divides

> When the organizational structure is well conceived ... the process of identification permits the broad organizational arrangements to govern the decisions of the persons who participate in the structure. Thereby, it permits human rationality to transcend the limitations imposed upon it by the narrow span of attention. (Simon 1977: 288–89)

Fledderus et al. (2014) claim that identification-based trust forms when parties identify each other's goals and understand and value each other's wants. Such trust is not essentially cognitive but emotional. The UK and Australian parliaments have different organisational structures, but it is not evident whether either is conceived well enough to contribute to a shared parliamentary identity. Both parliaments have grappled with establishing joint working arrangements, as outlined below, but neither appears to have transcended the limitations imposed by narrow spans of attention or addressed an inherent hierarchy between the procedural and the managerial.

In the United Kingdom, the clerks of the two houses retain ultimate control over all non-procedural services, either separately or under a shared services arrangement where costs are split between them, generally under a 40:60 or 30:70 ratio. In 2007, the *Parliament (Joint Departments) Act* was passed to allow the corporate officers (the clerks) in both houses to establish joint departments, subject to the approval of their respective governance bodies. The only joint department is the Parliamentary Security Department, but more than 60 per cent of services are shared between the two houses, including digital services, procurement, archives, maintenance and outreach (HOCGC 2014; Torrance 2017). An outcome from the HOCGC (2014) was a commitment to review joint working in other services, including Hansard, the library and catering; however, this was later abandoned, despite its potential to offer significant savings, particularly in the catering function, as noted in Chapter 5. The *Parliamentary Buildings (Restoration and Renewal) Act 2019* established joint management and governance arrangements for the restoration and renewal program. These included the Sponsor Body, acting as a single client accountable to parliament, overseeing the Delivery Authority, which was responsible for the scope, budget and timescale of the program. The relationship between the Sponsor Body and the two house administrations was defined under a Parliamentary Relationship Agreement (Houses of Parliament Restoration and Renewal 2020).

In the Australian Parliament, the procedural and management functions were clearly delineated on its establishment in 1901, as set out in Chapter 3. The 'personal fiefdoms' comprising the clerks of the Senate and House of Representatives and the heads of Hansard, library and building management services were jealously guarded (Reid and Forrest 1989). The eventual amalgamation in 2004 of the three joint service departments following the Podger review (2002) disrupted the fiefdoms in one department only and left intact the structural division between the 'procedural' and the 'managerial'. The ongoing structural delineation between the two 'professions' or skill sets could be seen as a catalyst or explanation for poor relationships between the clerks and other parliamentary service managers in Australia (see, for instance, Reid and Forrest 1989; Towell 2014, 2015).[3] It is unclear, however, whether the evolution of management services under the authority of the Clerk of the House of Commons and the Clerk of the Parliaments (House of Lords) has led to a more unified service in either house of the UK Parliament. Indeed, evidence provided to the Governance Committee and observations made by scholars and practitioners suggest the hierarchy between clerking and managing has always been a strong feature of the parliamentary institution, with procedural services highly valued and

---

3   Also, Q. Clements, pers. comm., 7 July 2017; C. Paterson, pers. comm., 17 August 2017; former senate adviser, pers. comm., 23 August 2017.

support services less so (Crewe 2005, 2010; Silvester and Spicer 2014; Gay 2017).[4] In both houses, the providers of longstanding traditional support services, such as library researchers and Hansard reporters, have fallen somewhere between the 'procedural' and the 'managerial' cleavage while arguing strongly for their recognition among the higher echelons (Weatherston 1975; Reid and Forrest 1989; Verrier 1995; Gay 2017).

In the face of such a hierarchy, Oonagh Gay, a former House of Commons Library official, was sceptical about the capacity to develop a unified, corporate House of Commons Service, while conceding that things could be changing:

> If you work for DCCS [the Department of Chamber and Committee Services,] you are perceived to have higher status than other staff in the parliamentary administration … And that has been perceived for many years as a problem when we are trying to create a unitary corporate service. One answer to that is to do away with departments altogether and simply develop functional units … [T]here is no easy answer. But I think there is a real inheritance of dislike of the clerks as seeing themselves as different and superior to the rest of parliamentary staff and that is felt very keenly by many parliamentary staff. It may not be fair anymore but because so many parliamentary staff started their careers 15 or 20 years ago old feelings linger.[5]

Lorraine Sutherland, former head of the House of Commons Hansard service, was of a similar opinion. While she was extremely complimentary about the clerks' knowledge and procedural skills, she lamented:

> They have in the past just been too aloof and too hierarchical in their approach and they haven't fully respected or appreciated anybody else who works for parliament. It is going to take a long time for people to get over that. It is going to take a long time for all the clerks to stop behaving like that. It is going to take a long time for the non-clerks to accept that they have changed and to feel that they are properly valued.[6]

Professors Jo Silvester and Andre Spicer, psychologists from Cass Business School, studied the working relationships between a small group of House of Commons staff and members. They found that if one took

4   Also, L. Sutherland, pers. comm., 15 September 2015.
5   O. Gay, pers. comm., 16 September 2016.
6   L. Sutherland, pers. comm., 15 September 2016.

the view that parliament should have a 'somewhat limited purpose of improving legislation and holding the executive to account', the legislative process was the 'core' and all other services were there strictly to support that process:

> The closer you are to this process, the higher the status and importance that is accorded to your role. The Clerks are seen to be at the core, the library service at some remove, with services like IT and catering at an extreme distance. (Silvester and Spicer, Cass Business School, in HOCGC 2014: 94)

The effects of differences in the management structures in the two parliaments can be interpreted in several ways. On the one hand, there might have been a greater opportunity, within a unified service, for staff at all levels with multiple functions to identify with the purpose, strategies and goals of the organisation, and this opportunity was, arguably, strengthened by the changes made by the incoming Director-General of the House of Commons (House of Commons 2016). These changes were likely, in turn, to have influenced the acceptance of change within the House of Lords administration based on its adoption of practices similar to those recommended by the HOCGC (2014). On the other hand, the accretion of responsibility by the clerks over decades for the panoply of increasingly complex managerial—on top of procedural—services has inevitably led to a prioritisation of the procedural over the managerial[7] and this was borne out in the evidence taken by the HOCGC (2014) and in comments from interviewees.

Conversely, a separate services department might be expected to be more efficient and responsive than a hybrid department, provided there is a strong connection with the parliament's purposes, strategies and goals. The concept of a unified service in the Australian Parliament was encapsulated at least in theory by the implementation of the *Parliamentary Service Act 1999*, but in the case of DPS, many interviewees saw the absence of a strong cultural identity as the harbinger of many performance problems after its creation in 2004.[8] Since 2004, the clerks have also experienced a 'hollowing out' of their management responsibilities other than the more routine management and governance of their own

---

7   J. Bercow, pers. comm., 11 May 2016.
8   C. Surtees, pers. comm., 6 June 2017; C. Paterson, pers. comm., 17 August 2017; R. Pye, pers. comm., 12 April 2017; R. Laing, pers. comm., 7 September 2017; C. Mills, pers. comm., 11 May 2017; D. Heriot, pers. comm., 10 April 2017; R. Stefanic, pers. comm., 1 August 2018.

departments. They have lost responsibility for the security function and, subsequently, IT responsibilities following a review of parliament-wide services (Roche 2012). As noted in Chapter 4, former Senate Clerk Evans saw the loss of functions as an institutionally inappropriate acceptance of private commercial concepts and, according to senate adviser Quinton Clements, communications between the Senate Department and DPS were at a very low ebb when the consolidation of IT services within DPS was first proposed by former Senate president John Hogg in 2012.[9] Senate officials had been clearly of the view that they should not have to deal with DPS. According to Clements, they saw the department as a 'usurper' that should never have been created and the departments did not really communicate. The relationship between the Senate and DPS deteriorated further during the tenure of Carol Mills as secretary and the subsequent performance reviews by SFPALC, and these events have been well documented. Clements also noted, however, that successive clerks in the House of Representatives and Senate had brought a new form of pragmatism to their roles, realising they had 'to just get on with it' and concentrate on providing services to members and senators, and this was also evident from their interviews.[10] Chris Paterson, senior adviser to the Speaker in the years after DPS's establishment, doubted whether the model of a separately constituted services mega-department, responsible to two authorities, was appropriate. There were problems with the model, and the structure had never been accepted by those affected; it was something that had been imposed on them.[11] To Paterson:

> It was an implementation issue. The problem is that the presiding officers change; with the new ones, it takes them a long time to get their heads around it. You may very well have a change of staff ... As soon as you get a change, we're all back to square one ... I've always felt that the three departments really need to work in a more collegial fashion ... [W]here they've created a DPS ... in New South Wales [they] have regular meetings, with agendas, papers and decisions recorded ... with both presiding officers ... [Y]ou can get away from a 'this is our turf' type situation.[12]

---

9   Q. Clements, pers. comm., 7 July 2017.
10   D. Elder, pers. comm., 7 April 2017; R. Pye, pers. comm., 12 April 2017.
11   Q. Clements, pers. comm., 7 July 2017; C. Paterson, pers. comm., 17 August 2017.
12   C. Paterson, pers. comm., 17 August 2017.

In Australia, the continuing rivalries between departments have not been confined to disdain from the house departments towards the services department. Officials recounted the ongoing feud between former clerks of the Senate and the House of Representatives, even to the extent of refusing to be in the same room together.[13] The examples I have recounted might be attributed to personality differences were it not for corroborating evidence of longstanding differences (Reid and Forrest 1989; Adams 2002). Even so, governance arrangements should transcend such differences or at least allow for their accommodation, but the forums in the Australian Parliament for discussing and enhancing parliamentary administration are limited. The evidence does not point to one best organisational structure in terms of management effectiveness. Instead, it appears that both parliaments have suffered from a lack of a common identity and purpose.

The governance structures in the UK Parliament, where members and peers are formally engaged in governance processes, appear to provide a greater potential for collaboration. Some members and officials in the House of Lords were also actively engaged in the HOCGC review (2014)[14] and there are arrangements in place for the audit committees and commissions of the two houses to meet. But these governance arrangements are not without their shortcomings and do not guarantee collective responsibility or engagement in management decisions. Often there appears to be little common ground among members and non-elected officials on administrative reform. Silvester and Spicer (2014) noted that staff can tend to 'mirror politicians' behaviour' by focusing on 'handling' the discussion rather than presenting options to resolve a problem, resulting in confused or no decision-making. The Ellenbogen inquiry into bullying and harassment in the House of Lords (see Chapter 7) described the relationship between peers and administrators as 'transactional and paternalistic' (Ellenbogen 2019: 74).

---

13 Former senate adviser, pers. comm., 23 August 2017; H. Penfold, pers. comm., 19 July 2017; C. Paterson, pers. comm., 17 August 2017. The former clerks' professional disagreement also extended to their individual interpretations of Section 53 of the Constitution and the powers of their respective houses (Appleby and Williams 2009).
14 David Beamish, then Clerk of the Parliaments (House of Lords), Lord Browne of Madingley, Lord Laming and Baroness Royall of Blaisdon gave evidence to the HOCGC. Written evidence was also provided by David Beamish, Lord Blencathra, Lord Cormack, Lord Kirkwood of Kirkhope and Lord Martin of Springburn.

Members of the UK Parliament expressed a variety of views about the level of engagement and interest in management. Chris Bryant, former Shadow Leader of the House and member of the House of Commons Commission, was not confident that either the procedural or the management roles were being carried out effectively.[15] He cited shortcomings in both political management ('We are glorious amateurs; we love being amateurs and I dislike that. I would prefer us to be more professional') and in the operation of the House of Commons Commission ('It should be a management team … and it's not run as a team in any sense at all … this is a place full of silos'). He claimed the whole parliament was 'devoid of management techniques' such as 'away days' to promote team cohesion.[16] He was joined in this observation by Baroness D'Souza, then Lord Speaker, who spoke of the hostility she encountered when she suggested an 'away day' for fellow peers.[17] Lord Laming, then Convenor of the Cross Bench in the House of Lords, thought serving on the administrative committees 'ought to be seen as a privilege and a responsibility' by peers and 'something really important' in their day-to-day lives, thereby implying that it was not.[18]

Bernard Jenkin, then chair of the Public Administration and Constitutional Affairs Committee, was not a member of the commission but claimed to have been instrumental in laying the ground for the HOCGC. He was emphatic about the need for a corporate structure—a board with non-executive and elected MPs to provide governance and leadership—arguing that a lack of leadership had been a more fundamental problem than whether to split the role of clerk and CEO.[19] In the context of this book, that is a useful observation; it implies criticism of the lack of engagement of members themselves in the governance and management of the House of Commons. The difficulties of engaging members in management issues, as well as the value of so doing, were echoed by members of the commission.[20]

---

15   Chris Bryant is also author of a biography of parliament in which he notes that in terms of political reform 'an obsessive respect for the past and a dedication to constitutional evolution rather than revolution [have] led to piecemeal reform and a fudged constitution perilously dependent on custom, convention and gentlemen's agreements' (2015: 5).
16   C. Bryant, pers. comm., 23 May 2016.
17   F. D'Souza, pers. comm., 9 June 2016.
18   Lord Laming, pers. comm., 13 June 2016.
19   B. Jenkin, pers. comm., 25 May 2016.
20   P. Beresford, pers. comm., 2 June 2016; N. Brown, pers. comm., 7 June 2016; T. Brake, pers. comm., 8 June 2016.

Some members of the House of Commons Commission were also critical of a perceived disinterest in management in some quarters and a tendency for the commission to focus on the trivial rather than the strategic, which was attributed partly to the highly charged political environment and also to a constant concern with external perceptions: 'What would the members think?' or 'What would the man or woman on the Clapham omnibus say about this?' Some spoke frankly about the need for a greater appreciation of business processes and project management skills and suggested some of the 'unique' characteristics of the UK Parliament could be overplayed and there was scope for greater collaboration between the two houses. Others were confident that the organisation was moving away from its silo mentality while also being conscious of a culture of limited engagement that viewed change as doing the same thing in a slightly different way. Some were bemused by the way common services were provided by separate bodies and saw opportunities for joint working and collaboration. Speaker Bercow anticipated 'more and more pressure over time to identify things that can be done together, more efficiently'.[21] Along with Chris Bryant and Ian Ailles, he was one of a minority of those interviewed to see potential in an administrative structure that crossed both houses. Other, perhaps more 'constitutionally averse', interviewees saw the provision of joint services as flawed, and some were reluctant to adopt the 'Australian model' of a joint services department in the light of the well-publicised criticism of its performance. Indeed, more than one senior official stated off the record that the UK Parliament had managed a narrow escape with the termination of the recruitment process for Speaker Bercow's choice of clerk.

In the Australian Parliament, officials have attempted more recently to limit the degrees of separation and enhance internal collaboration. The first whole-of-parliament strategic plan was published in 2017 following a thawing of relations between the Senate and DPS. Former Senate Clerk Laing was a driver of the plan and she welcomed the arrival in 2015 of a new head of DPS, who had, in fact, once been a senior clerk in the NSW Parliament.[22] Her successor as Clerk of the Senate spoke of a new era of 'rampant cooperation'.[23] But relations between members and officials, particularly management officials, have not been formalised to the same extent as they have in the United Kingdom. Officials are not

---

21   J. Bercow, pers. comm., 8 June 2016.
22   R. Stefanic, pers. comm., 10 April 2017.
23   R. Pye, pers. comm., 12 April 2017.

members of either the Senate Standing Committee on Appropriations, Staffing and Security or the House of Representatives Standing Committee on Appropriations and Administration, and there is no published record of the two committees meeting, despite a change to Standing Orders that would have facilitated such administrative collaboration. Instead, some senators were opposed to joint administration either through these forums or through the Joint House Committee, which was also considered ineffective.[24] The SFPALC inquiries (2012a, 2012b, 2015a, 2015b) reflected a greater reliance on scrutiny and criticism than on engagement and collaboration—a dilemma that is discussed at greater length later in this chapter. Although there are moves to ameliorate conflicts in both parliaments, in the Australian Parliament there appears to be less evidence of a commitment to a broader parliamentary identity, a limited ability to 'transcend limitations imposed by a narrow span of attention' (Simon 1977) and less opportunity for members and officials to exercise collective agency.

The relationships between clerks and management officials, between members and officials and between the two houses in each parliament can be problematic. They have been influenced to some extent by structure, particularly in the Australian Parliament, as we have seen from repeated attempts at structural change and repeated criticisms of management effectiveness. For both parliaments to achieve their strategic aims—including 'supporting a thriving parliamentary democracy' and 'securing Parliament's future' (House of Commons 2020: 13), 'to support and strengthen the House of Lords' (House of Lords 2020: 4) or in 'serving, supporting and upholding the institution of the Parliament' (Parliament of Australia 2020)—it might be expected that parliamentary administrators would display the public management skills of the future, including negotiating interests among an array of different groups, working more productively with citizens, enhancing communication and emotional skills and working across boundaries (OECD 2017). However, as I have suggested, parliamentary administrators' agency is also situated within a web of beliefs and traditions (Bevir and Rhodes 2006), and parliamentary reform can be seen as dependent on actors' beliefs and is 'often wrapped up in power relationships between different actors' (Geddes and Meakin 2018: 22).

---

24   Q. Clements, pers. comm., 7 July 2017; C. Paterson, pers. comm., 17 August 2017.

The dilemma of multiple roles, multiple stakeholders and multiple relationships

The challenge of fostering a unified parliamentary service identity that encourages collaboration across houses and departmental or functional boundaries is compounded by a lack of unanimity about the roles and functions of parliamentary administrators and the stakeholders they are serving (Silvester and Spicer 2014). This dilemma is compounded by a diffusion in the 'authorising environment' (Moore 1995; HOCGC 2014; Silvester and Spicer 2014). Public managers have a public service ethos; they are serving the needs of the public, but they usually do so through the auspices of their minister, who is accountable for the performance of their department or agency. Parliamentary administration is seen by its practitioners as more complex: at senior levels in the two parliaments, there is not always a clear line of sight between service providers and their stakeholders, particularly in the Australian Parliament with its separate services department.

This observation might appear to be somewhat simplistic: public servants, too, are faced with dilemmas in terms of crossing the administrative–political divide and entering the purple zone, and when facing exhortations to be more innovative, strategic, responsive and accountable (Moore 1995; Shergold 1997; Alford, Hartley et al. 2017; OECD 2017). However, at least in theory, they identify strongly with their minister and his or her goals, and the value of the public advice, product or service they are providing is more readily articulated. The goals of 650 members and more than 800 peers in the UK Parliament and 150 members and 76 senators in the Australian Parliament are less discernible and the value to the public of an efficient and effective democracy is not easily captured. Given these issues, the questions 'Who are the stakeholders?' and 'Whom do we serve?' are presented here as a dilemma for parliamentary actors. In general, parliamentary administrators seem to identify very strongly with their particular roles, rather than with their organisation; they are role-oriented and task driven rather than goal driven. This can lead to conflicting priorities among different actors: managers, presiding officers and other members, clerks and other advisers.

In the Australian Parliament, senior officials in the DPS generally held outward-looking views of serving the public, as demonstrated by the following extracts from interviews with the then DPS chief information officer, chief operating officer and secretary:

> I guess it comes down to our real customers or clients being the general public and the parliamentarians and their staff ... [W]e are here to facilitate the work of parliament, and that includes members, senators and the staff ... Then obviously there is the way that the general public interacts with that. They can read *Hansard*, they watch broadcasts and they visit the building. Those, to me, are our real customers.[25]

> In my mind, it's primarily about supporting the operations of the parliament. But a big part of that goes then on to that visitor group that's coming through and engaging with parliament. We've had to modify and adapt that a little bit with the security issues, but we still get a huge volume of visitors, a huge number of school children coming through each year, and we're hoping to increase both of those.[26]

> My service priority is obviously to the presiding officers (as my ministerial equivalent), the parliamentarians, their staff and then parliamentary department staff who support the parliament. Because we are also a tourist attraction, there is the public value element in terms of visitors who are citizens of Australia and international visitors who come to Parliament House to learn about parliamentary democracy.[27]

There also appeared to be a strong understanding of the need to manage the relationships between different actors with a view to accommodating conflicting needs, as recognised by Luke Hickey, Assistant Secretary of the Parliamentary Experience Branch:

> I knew that there were some tensions in and around the different departments, between DPS and the Department of the Senate and the Department of the House of Representatives. My first objective ... was to ... repair and rebuild those relationships. For us, as a visitor-facing function, it is so important that we are telling [a story about] the work of the parliament as a whole, and for

---

25 I. McKenzie, pers. comm., 6 June 2017.
26 M. Croke, pers. comm., 19 May 2017.
27 R. Stefanic, pers. comm., 10 April 2017.

us to be able to tell that, we have to be able to understand what the Senate and the House of Representatives actually see as the important part of that story and how we can bring that over.

The other really challenging part to juggling this building is that it is a working parliament, a working building. What I might like to achieve from a pure visitor and tourism point of view in bringing people in and around the building the whole time simply does not work ... particularly in a sitting week. So it is about juggling the tensions between attracting as many visitors as we can and helping to connect them not only with the building itself but with the parliament and to leave with a better understanding of the parliament and how it works. That is a really important part of DPS's role. But how do I do that without disrupting people who are working in and around offices, who are trying to access the building and who have their own visitors and guests coming to meet with them on work-related topics as well? ... [W]e have a really big advocacy role. Then there is a really important strategic job that we need to get to and spend more time on that often gets drowned out by the sheer volume of the operational work. It is a challenge. I'd love to be able to just go off and have autonomy in making decisions and coming up with great ideas, rather than having to go through and negotiate on everything. But it wouldn't work. It would end up in the kind of issues that the department has had in the past.[28]

These observations are telling given comments by the former departmental secretary Carol Mills, who was brought in to fix the department's shortcomings after the 'billiard tables affair' and the first excoriating reports on the department's performance discussed in Chapter 4 (SFPALC 2012a, 2012b). Mills was quite clear in her discussion with me as to what she had been brought in to achieve:

I made that really clear at all of my interviews. I said, 'It seems to me that the distance between politicians and the community is getting greater. And when you think that DPS has the library, media recording, the IT systems, the building itself, the whole public side of parliament, there's a real opportunity for us to more strategically help the community and parliament get closer.'

To my way of thinking, that was an interesting part of the job. So there was the change management aspect and the bigger picture about the parliament—not necessarily just the department but, through the department, the parliament ... That whole culture of who does parliament belong to and so on seemed to me to be a significant issue. Because both of them [the then presiding officers, former Senator Hogg and former MP Peter Slipper] were very receptive to that sort of direction and were keen themselves to drive change and made it clear they were looking for a different way of both receiving services and engaging, I decided to give it a crack. I read a lot of the material about Parliament House, the building, and what it was designed to try and achieve. I thought those were all absolutely meritorious ambitions—pride in the building, Australian workmanship, access to the building, displaying for visitors, either official or tourists, the best of the country—and I thought lots of people were contributing well to that, but it wasn't seen as important. One of the things I wanted to do was raise the profile of those people, to show the value of what they were contributing ... [and] give a lot more information about what we did, and be much more on the front foot about it so that people could recognise the skills and efforts that went into things. When the new presiding officers came [former Senator Parry and former MP Bishop,] they weren't interested in the kind of bigger picture stuff. They weren't very interested in the fact that I was only just starting a change program.[29]

Mills's account suggests a disconnect between her beliefs as head of a multifunction services department and the beliefs of those to whom she was immediately accountable. When I interviewed former Speaker Tony Smith, I did not find that he was 'keen to drive change and look for a different way of both receiving services and engaging', as recounted by Mills. Reform was a role for parliaments; he saw the Speaker's role as an umpire and his focus was very much on managing the business of the chamber, for which he received many plaudits after his resignation. In his public role, he placed a strong emphasis on his visits to schools. His approach was borne out by his colleague, Tony Pasin, the Chair of the Procedure Committee, whose comments on improving the public reputation of the parliament were directed at maintaining order in the House and using the Standing Orders to improve members' behaviour. While these endeavours obviously have merit, neither the Speaker nor the Procedure Committee chair emphasised other activities that might have the effect of creating value for members of the public.

---

29   C. Mills, pers. comm., 11 May 2017.

Former president Parry claimed to be a reforming president, saying: '[T]he simple thing would be for me to turn up here, do the same old, same old and have an easier life.' In administrative terms, he appeared determined to wrest control over the Senate's resources from the Department of Finance.[30] The clerks, as we have learnt, tended in the past to hold to a view of their roles as procedural curators, guardians and advisers with management seen as a peripheral function. Their stakeholders are predominantly the presiding officers and their deputies and other members, with the public receiving the end product. David Elder, former clerk of the House of Representatives, was keen not to overemphasise his role as a guardian of the institution, preferring to see himself 'as the humble servant of the most meagre backbencher'. He and the Clerk of the Senate confirmed the hollowing out of management responsibilities in their respective departments, reflecting that their principal role now was to provide a 'secretariat' to their respective houses—a term that clearly delineates the very specialised nature of the role of the house departments.[31] These two clerks did not appear to feel threatened by this loss of function or see it as 'institutionally inappropriate' (Evans 2005); on the contrary, the Senate Clerk particularly relished the prospect of devoting more resources to his primary function of advising the Senate and its committees, throwing open the possibility of ceding more responsibility in the IT space to DPS.

Elder remarked that the only 'joint' responsibilities of either house were to administer the Parliamentary Relations Office (from the House of Representatives) and the Parliamentary Education Office (from the Senate). To Pye, the purpose of public engagement appeared to be largely a function of presenting information about the work of the Senate; to Elder, the emphasis was on school visits, either of schoolchildren to parliament or of members (including the Speaker) to schools.[32] The attention by each parliament to engaging with the public stands out as one of the significant differences between them and, in the case of the Australian Parliament, was acknowledged by the then Deputy Clerk of the House of Representatives as a missed opportunity, due mainly to a lack of resources.[33] This important distinction is discussed in more detail in Chapter 7.

---

30   S. Parry, pers. comm., 15 June 2017.
31   D. Elder, pers. comm., 7 April 2017; R. Pye, pers. comm., 12 April 2017.
32   D. Elder, pers. comm., 7 April 2017; R. Pye, pers. comm., 12 April 2017.
33   I acknowledge the body of work undertaken by the Parliamentary Relations Office in the Australian Parliament and its UK counterpart, the Overseas Office. The important interparliamentary work of the two parliaments is not discussed in this volume, which emphasises public, rather than parliamentary, engagement.

Some of the frankest, but also pragmatic, views about the tensions within the UK Parliament among parliamentary officials, members and staff in their beliefs about their roles and purposes came from Paul Evans, long-serving House of Commons clerk and author on parliament. According to him, tensions exist between members and officials and between government and opposition members: first, in preserving institutional continuity while making the parliament more accessible to the public; and second, in a government being able to achieve its political aims without jeopardising its continuing ability to do so when in opposition—in effect, the maintenance of intraparliamentary comity. He emphasised the essentiality of a central parliamentary purpose, rather than a set of cultural values, while acknowledging the difficulties of achieving such an outcome:

> You don't expect everyone in an institution as large as this, even though it's not very large, to be signed up to its cultural values. That's a kind of hegemonic, fascist ideology that wouldn't be desirable anyway. It's good to have grit in the oyster. So we don't want everybody getting up every morning and singing the parliamentary anthem and doing the parliamentary dance. We want people who don't give two hoots about it as long as they are good at adding up sums or putting in toilets—that's fine. I don't think we have to make everybody sign up to the institution in that sort of vocational way. But you do want a culture in which you understand that the central purpose of the institution is to enable democracy to work and that includes people who hoover the floors and look after the plumbing and look after the finances. The central purpose is not to have an efficient financial system; it is to have an efficient and effective parliament and that message has to be very clearly communicated and enforced, to use a slightly coercive word. The risk is the more you managerialise, the fewer people who are conscious of the importance of that message and the means of communicating it.[34]

The 'doing sums, putting in toilets, plumbing and hoovering [vacuuming]' view of management echoes a clerkly disdain for the management role; an analogy from the former clerk of the House and now Lord Lisvane was 'keeping the lights on and emptying the bins'.[35] But in conforming with

---

34   P. Evans, pers. comm., 17 September 2016.
35   Lord Lisvane, pers. comm., 11 May 2016. As Clerk of the House, Rogers was widely recognised for his approach to procedural reform and outreach (see Rogers and Gay 2009).

Crewe's account of the 'sympathetic yet cynical' parliamentary servant, Evans also did not spare the procedural function in his frank assessment of reforms following the expenses scandal:

> That's the way we went because everybody was in a flat spin about the expenses scandal and that gave a window of opportunity for a particular MP in the shape of Tony Wright, who is one of the small handful—10 per cent, 5 per cent, 3 per cent—who are very interested in how the place works, to forward his own agenda with the help of some clerks and people like Meg [Russell].[36] There have been changes; I'm not saying they are changes for the better, they are just changes. They are changes in the direction that these people think are positive. What I had hoped would come out of the creation of the backbenchers' business committee was a real focus for backbench culture—the government, the opposition and the backbenchers who would become somehow an across-party identity. I don't think that's really happened. They are the ones who would preserve parliament against the degradations of the executive, the front-benchers on either side. All they are interested in is being in government and doing things. Parliament is really just a blocker, not an enabler.[37]

Other interviewees were frustrated with the plurality of the roles they were sometimes expected to play as head of a hybridised house service. David Beamish, then Clerk of the Parliaments, stated that he was 'here to run a parliament, not to sweat the assets of the Palace of Westminster' when describing a conflict over whether the House of Lords' catering facilities should be operated on a commercial basis:

> I'm running a legislative chamber and not a club. Although the place has some of the appearance of a club with its smart, historic[al] décor, banqueting facilities and so forth, I don't see my skills as running that sort of thing … It is a bit different from being a chief executive where you are actually engaged in the business. To that extent it is a slightly unusual position, exacerbated perhaps by the fact that members sometimes have strong views on these things.[38]

---

36 Professor in Comparative Politics at the Constitution Unit, University College London.
37 P. Evans, pers. comm., 17 September 2015.
38 D. Beamish, pers. comm., 24 May 2016.

Unsurprisingly, more recently appointed officials on the management side appeared more enthusiastic about their public management roles, particularly after the appointment of the new director-general, Ian Ailles. They were oriented towards the general public, particularly in terms of participation, engagement and the digital service, and the director-general's review introduced a range of initiatives that included a greater focus on the customer and working across boundaries and balancing customer service with stewardship—defined as a 'continuing responsibility we have on behalf of the public for the good order, the effective running and the reputation of the House of Commons' (House of Commons 2016: 12). Penny Young, librarian and Managing Director, Participation and Research and Information, displayed a strong public values approach to her role:

> [T]hrough research, engagement and participation, we have a real opportunity—not by ourselves—to help to shift the reputation of the House through encouraging MPs to do certain things and through providing them with great information that they use and through reaching out to the public to explain and involve more. I think where we have got to with 'supporting a thriving parliamentary democracy' is wonderful ... because there was a really boring draft one when I arrived, which basically could have been translated into 'lie down and do whatever the MPs want'—not as simple as that.[39]

Rob Greig, then director of the Digital Service, echoed this enthusiastic, outward-looking, public-facing approach:

> There is a disconnect, or sometimes a disagreement, about who the customer is. If you talk to different subsets and groups of members, some will say the officials of parliament are here to serve members. That is it. They are not interested in us doing anything else. It's about serving members. They will say to you, 'You do not exist without us.' I am not so sure about that actually ... Just like there is diversity in the value sets of members—the opinions, the politics—there is exactly the same when it comes to digital. So there are those who think, absolutely we should be doing the public thing and there are others—a loud minority—who think, 'You are here to service us.' I firmly believe that digital has a responsibility for reaching out to the public, supporting democracy and telling the story of Parliament.[40]

---

39   P. Young, pers. comm., 9 June 2016.
40   R. Greig, pers. comm., 27 May 2016.

The continuing dilemma of multiple perspectives was insightfully explained by Ruth Fox, Director of the Hansard Society and a long-time advocate of reform, in relation to public engagement and working practices in both houses (2009, 2012a, 2012b). She was somewhat alarmed that a shift of power to new parliamentary actors after the director-general's review represented a loss of 'political capital'. People just 'didn't get it', she said:

> You have to engage with members; you have to bring them in; you've got to make them part of the process. You can't stand apart and say 'we are doing this anyway'. What worries me is people coming from outside who think that because of everything that's happened in terms of expenses, reputation and so on they are going to come in, reorganise and clean up and they owe their responsibilities to the public more than to members and therefore they dismiss members as part of the equation. That's what worries me ... [I]f you take that approach, you won't get it done. And, the services of this House are designed to enable it to run as a legislature. Of course, it's got to have accountability to the public and so on, but it's got to function as a legislature and that means you've got to work with members. I'm not sure some of the people I'm dealing with who've been brought in from outside in the last year clearly understand that.[41]

The evidence I have presented of the tensions between the more traditional procedural view and the newer management view suggests the dilemma has been more significant for the UK Parliament than for the Australian Parliament, particularly in the latter's new era of 'rampant cooperation'. But many observations about the UK Parliament would have been salient during Mills's tenure in the Australian Parliament and could again be relevant in any return of the hostile relationships of the past. The evidence also suggests the UK Parliament has reflected more closely on its engagement with a whole range of stakeholders and placed a higher priority on its public-facing role than has the Australian Parliament, without dismissing the need to continue to provide an effective service to members. The scale of reflection and inquiry the UK Parliament has afforded to its governance and management has also allowed it to engage more collaboratively and strategically in planning for its future. But in later chapters, we will see there are still significant problems.

---

41   R. Fox, pers. comm., 10 June 2016.

The dilemma of business as usual or designing the future: Balancing operational and strategic management

The case for improvement

The bias towards efficiency—at least in terms of spending less money—is stronger in the Australian Parliament, where it is the likely product of the blunt instrument of the executive-imposed efficiency dividend introduced in 1987, which has constrained expenditure in a parliament that does not set its own budget. The UK Parliament has not been subject to the same degree of external pressure (except in the aftermath of the expenses scandal) but has weathered continuing calls for efficiency through numerous management reviews over several decades in both houses. In 2010, following the then Conservative government's austerity program, the House of Commons voluntarily imposed its own internal savings program, reaping a budget saving of 17.5 per cent over the next four years (Petit and Yong 2018). Rather than trying to compare the relative efficiency of each parliament, it is more useful to examine the priorities and actor relationships governing the allocation of scarce publicly funded parliamentary resources.[42] As Geddes and Mulley (2018) point out, there are unanswered questions in terms of institutional support for MPs and the purposes and interests to which resources are directed, and these issues go to the heart of the dilemma I have discussed above. To these questions, I have added an emphasis on determining the broader public value of parliamentary administration.

---

42 To put the efficiency question into context, I draw on the Institute for Government's *Parliamentary Monitor 2018* (Lilley et al. 2018), which noted that in 2017–18, the combined cost of running both houses of parliament, including members' salaries, allowances and expenses (and net of income generated through catering and retail outlets), was £527.1 million—the cost of running a medium-sized Whitehall department. A comparable statistic for the Australian Parliament was not available; however, Uhr and Wanna (2000) cited a figure of $550 million, or 0.09 per cent of gross domestic product, as the cost of running the parliament, including related expenditures. Former Independent Member of the House of Representatives Peter Andren (1999) claimed the Australian Parliament was one of the most expensive legislatures in the world, at $19 per head per annum, while Harry Evans (1999) noted that the annual budgets of the parliamentary departments amounted to 0.062 per cent of Australian Government expenditure while total expenditure on parliament, including expenditure on members' remuneration and entitlements and services provided by other departments, was 0.16 per cent of all government expenditure. These statistics suggest the relative cost of parliament is low from a total public expenditure perspective, but see Dickinson (2019) on ratio bias and Malcolmson (1999: 104), whose comparison of cost-effectiveness between the UK and Australian parliaments concluded the Australian Parliament was overstaffed and far from international best practice.

There are continuing concerns about administrative effectiveness in the two parliaments. Petit and Yong (2018)—more than three years after the report of the HOCGC (2014) was published—predicted a key element of future governance and administration would be joint working, particularly on the restoration and renewal of the Palace of Westminster, but they also noted that the joint working program aimed at gaining efficiencies across the two houses had 'fallen off the political radar'. (I have already discussed the lack of political will to join up the two catering services.) As Ian Ailles, the former director-general, surmised:

> You can only do joint working if both sides want to do joint working. I always think of myself as being employed by the parliament, not by the Commons. But that view is not shared with people who have been here for a long time.[43]

The former clerk of the House of Commons and now Lord Lisvane was credited with attempting to reform and modernise the management of the House, notwithstanding his well-publicised falling out with the Speaker. But he was 'constantly haunted' by the fear of a 'catastrophic failure' of the building's services and was continually firefighting to head off adverse media publicity.[44] There is a long history of avoidance and delay in the restoration and renewal of the Palace of Westminster (see Crick Centre 2018; Flinders et al. 2018a; Meakin 2018, 2020; R. Kelly 2022; and later chapters of this volume). As we saw in the opening chapter and from the HOCGC (2014) report, there has been much criticism of waste and inefficiency directed towards building operations and facilities. The management and preservation of the parliamentary building, both as a functional workplace and a symbol of parliamentary democracy, are key elements of parliamentary administration. They provide a useful example of the challenges presented by multiple stakeholder perspectives and the emphasis placed on operational versus strategic management. As the former clerk of the House of Commons, David Natzler, put it:

> We've had this concentration on R&R [restoration and renewal] over the last two or three years. It has become an almost overwhelming, almost obsessive priority, to the point where one forgets that we're trying to run a parliament, whatever the

---

43 I. Ailles, pers. comm., 18 September 2018.
44 Lord Lisvane, pers. comm., 11 May 2016. His fears were justified when, for example, a significant water leak caused the Deputy Speaker to suspend a House of Commons sitting. The House subsequently adjourned for the day (see Walker 2019).

building is. It has become an obsession and it has absorbed a lot of resources, including not just money but management time and resources, and political effort.[45]

The HOCGC (2014: 35) may have reiterated that its inquiry was not the result of any failure in services to members, but it also emphasised that 'good performance in the past is no guarantee of good performance in the future'. Notwithstanding the increases over time in the resources and facilities provided to members, a report provided to the House of Commons Administration Committee on the success of new members' induction and their use of house services after the 2017 general election (Kenny 2018) indicated there is no guarantee that perceptions of good performance are universal among members and their staff. Concerns were expressed about 'alien' parliamentary procedures, information overload, office accommodation, digital services, catering and unclear communications. Many of the concerns had been highlighted previously and there was a perception that further action was required.

In the Australian Parliament, the Podger review (2002) was principally concerned with security administration and financial savings and offered little by way of a strategic path. Its author acknowledged that the parliament does not tend to look at its administration in a systematic way and that, as the Parliamentary Service Commissioner, he could have played a more substantial role in facilitating dialogue between departmental heads. He was annoyed that the implementation of the review was also compromised by an associated Department of Finance–imposed funding cut.[46] The Australian National Audit Office (ANAO 2006: 13) reported that eight of the nine Podger resolutions had been partly or fully implemented and DPS had absorbed the Finance-imposed reductions with 'only minor changes to its services'. Nevertheless, it called for an improvement in the measurement and reporting of DPS service levels and concluded that the parliament's administration could benefit from greater strategic planning for security and ICT and more formal processes for planning major initiatives.

A submission by another former Parliamentary Service Commissioner, Stephen Sedgwick, to the ongoing inquiry by the SFPALC into the performance of DPS noted that a 2009 review by his predecessor, Lynelle Briggs, had inter alia emphasised the 'desirability of looking

---

45 D. Natzler, pers. comm., 12 September 2018.
46 A. Podger, pers. comm., 4 August 2014.

for better ways for the parliamentary departments to continue to work together to take advantage of strategic opportunities and achieve economies of scale not available to smaller organisations' (Sedgwick 2011: 3). He concluded his submission by noting that he had not been approached by the presiding officers, either 'to inquire further into these matters, or [to] undertake any further review' (Sedgwick 2011: 4). As noted, the inquiries conducted by SFPALC (2012a, 2012b) into the performance of DPS strongly criticised its long-term approach to the management of Parliament House, lack of leadership and strategic planning, threats to design integrity and heritage values and poor employment practices. In 2015, it reported that it found it hard to identify anything positive coming from the many recommendations made in its 2012 interim and final reports (SFPALC 2015c).

This snapshot of management performance challenges in each parliament suggests a different tenor in the calls for a more strategic approach. In the United Kingdom, the establishment of and outcomes from the HOCGC (2014) were predominantly an acknowledgement of many competing views about the adequacy and relative importance of management skills; they also represented the extent of frustration in some quarters with the lack of 'professional' management. The committee made thoughtful recommendations for delivering effective strategic management. The senate committee inquiries into DPS's performance were, on the other hand, excoriating and seemingly made little effort to restore a more cooperative relationship between the houses and between members and officials. In the context of the conflicting beliefs of institutional actors and consequent dilemmas I have identified, these inquiries appear to have been concerned with highlighting failures rather than encouraging success. The SFPALC has remained highly critical of DPS's performance in relation to building works, security and IT, notwithstanding the progress on these fronts reported by DPS (SFPALC 2018, 2019a, 2019b, 2021; Stefanic 2018: 1–9).

Designing for future performance

My study compared each parliament's strategic planning framework given calls for more effective strategic planning. Comparisons were made from planning documents viewed in 2018 and 2019, when much of the research took place and when many of the events recorded occurred. Strategic plans have since been updated in the two parliaments with minor changes in emphasis.

As noted, the Australian Parliament is included as a Commonwealth entity under Section 10 of the *PGPA Act*. A key focus of the Act is to 'improve the standard of planning and reporting for Commonwealth entities'; good-quality performance information can, at the highest level, 'help us all to judge whether Australians' quality of life is being enhanced and whether public policy goals are being achieved' (Department of Finance 2014: 6). Some parliamentary stakeholders saw the Act as having the potential to engender more productive, informed and less adversarial relationships between agencies and parliamentary committees, although others questioned whether better linkages between performance documents and the elevation of non-financial performance information would succeed in making the performance cycle more transparent (Barrett 2014). The former House of Representatives Clerk and his colleagues did not appear fazed by their responsibilities to manage efficiently and effectively under the Act.[47] The Senate Clerk was also sanguine, claiming to be happy with where the Senate had landed in terms of the Act's requirements, although he did think it odd that his department should be describing what it does according to a system put together by 'Finance boffins', and he was not keen about throwing more people than he needed to at corporate tasks. He also noted that this type of governance expertise was more likely to reside within the DPS.[48]

Tables 6.1–6.3 compare the planning frameworks between and within the two parliaments during the study period. Table 6.1 depicts characteristics in the strategies prepared by the UK House of Commons and House of Lords. Table 6.2 depicts the strategic plan for the whole Australian Parliamentary Service, while Table 6.3 sets out the main features of the corporate plans of the principal parliamentary departments. Inferences can be drawn from the different emphases placed on functions, including whether they indicate future-oriented action or business as usual, and internal versus external engagement. All the parliamentary services were committed to providing effective support for members—a business-as-usual outcome. The evidence also pointed to the House of Commons Service exhibiting a more aspirational, collaborative and outward-facing approach than the other services, including through expressions such as 'supporting a thriving parliamentary democracy', 'facilitating' effective scrutiny (with connotations of an enabling rather than a blocking motivation), 'involving and inspiring the public' and 'securing Parliament's

---

47   D. Elder, pers. comm., 7 April 2017; C. Surtees, pers. comm., 6 June 2017; C. Cornish, pers. comm., 26 May 2017.
48   R. Pye, pers. comm., 12 April 2017.

future'. Officials were encouraged to be ambitious, collaborative, helpful and proactive (House of Commons Commission 2016). The House of Lords administration adopted a more conservative view, focused on services but also with an eye to improving the public's perception of the House. Officials were expected to display values of impartiality, integrity, diversity, inclusion and respect (House of Lords 2016b).

Table 6.1 Strategic planning and reporting in the UK Parliament

Features of the Strategy for the House of Commons Service, 2016–21				
Document	Business as usual	Internal facing	Future oriented	Outward facing
Strategic plan			Supporting a thriving parliamentary democracy.	
Objectives	Facilitating effective scrutiny and debate: outstanding professional expertise, advice, research, facilities, technology.		Involving and inspiring the public: Changing for the better, facilitating representation, relevant and accessible, challenging misconceptions; securing parliament's future, steering the House through challenges, preparing for the future.	
Behaviours	Ambitious, collaborative, helpful, proactive.			
Values	Skilled, united and diverse workforce, customer at centre, spending money wisely.		Maximising digital potential, working impartially, inclusively and in partnership.	
Delivery plan	Actions, success factors, team, deadline.			

Features of the Strategy for the House of Lords administration, 2016–21				
Document	Business as usual	Internal facing	Future oriented	Outward facing
Strategic plan	Support and strengthen the House and its members in carrying out their parliamentary functions.			
Objective	Effective services to facilitate work of the House.		Promote public understanding of House of Lords; make the House safer, more secure and sustainable.	
Values	Respect for role of the House, impartiality, integrity, diversity, inclusion, respect.		Responsibility to taxpayers, society and the environment.	
Measurement	Regular surveys of members, staff and public.	Evaluate impact and effectiveness.	Take account of best practice.	Improve performance-monitoring tools.

Table 6.2 Strategic planning and reporting in the Australian Parliamentary Service

Features of the Strategic Plan for the Australian Parliamentary Service				
Document	Business as usual	Internal facing	Future oriented	Outward facing
Strategic plan	Serving and supporting the parliament.		Community access and engagement.	
Purpose	Parliament and committees function effectively. Senators and members supported.			
	Parliament House sustained as workplace and national institution.			
	Independent, non-partisan parliamentary service enhanced.			
Strategies	Continue to provide, deliver and manage advice and support; office accommodation; security, maintenance and accessibility of Parliament House; values, learning and collaboration across Parliamentary Service.		Develop, implement and explore innovative services and technology; support engagement, promote parliament.	

Table 6.3 Strategic planning and reporting in the Australian parliamentary departments

Features of the Department of the House of Representatives Corporate Plan, 2017–18				
Document	Business as usual	Internal facing	Future oriented	Outward facing
Corporate Plan Purpose	Support House of Representatives, advice and services.		Wider parliament, community and other parliaments.	
Activities	Advice, support to chambers, committees.			
	Community awareness.			Publications, seminars
	Schools and school visits.		Interparliamentary relations, capacity-building.	
	Members' and corporate support.			
Capabilities	Workforce, information, community, asset management, stewardship, collaboration.			
Performance	Subscription data, client and staff satisfaction surveys.			

Features of the Department of the Senate Corporate Plan, 2017–18				
Document	Business as usual	Internal facing	Future oriented	Outward facing
Corporate plan	Secretariat to Senate.	Serving whole parliament.		
Purpose				
Objectives	Continued expertise, support committees, publish records.			
	Education programs.			Community engagement.
Capability	Institutional continuity, IT governance, risk management.			
Performance	Accuracy, timeliness, satisfaction surveys.			

Features of the Department of Parliamentary Services Corporate Plan, 2017–18				
Document	Business as usual	Internal facing	Future oriented	Outward facing
Corporate plan	Supports functions of Parliament House, work of parliamentarians through professional services, advice and facilities.			
Purpose				
Strategic themes	Effective stewardship of Parliament House; delivery of works program.		Respond to changing needs	Enhance community engagement.
Capabilities	Communication, innovation, customer focus, accountability leadership.			
Contributing outputs/ targets				

The Australian Parliamentary Service is guided by legislated values; its officials are expected to be committed, ethical, respectful, accountable and impartial (*Parliamentary Service Act 1999*). The values were not reproduced in its first *Strategic Plan for Parliamentary Administration* (Parliament of Australia 2017b), which was developed in the period of 'rampant cooperation' that followed the Mills affair.[49] It appeared to be an acknowledgement of the Australian Parliamentary Service itself; it was descriptive rather than performative and included no associated performance outcomes or links to other planning documents. Collectively, the outward-facing elements of the planning documents across the three

---

49   ibid.

main Australian parliamentary departments (Department of the House of Representatives 2018b; Department of the Senate 2018b; DPS 2018)[50] indicated a commitment to community access and engagement, innovation in technology and a renewed focus on the preservation of Parliament House after SFPALC's (2012a, 2012b, 2015a, 2015b) extensive criticisms.

As the tables show, each parliament is committed to formally documenting its plans and performance outcomes. (It was beyond the scope of the study to attempt to evaluate and compare their success.) However, the comparison of strategic planning frameworks indicates that in the Australian Parliament a greater emphasis is placed on 'core' business as usual, particularly in the chamber departments but also in the whole-of-parliament strategic plan, rather than on taking a more reflective and strategic approach. The public engagement role is expressed in terms of physical access to Parliament House, including school visits, access to publications and engagement with other parliaments. In contrast, the UK Parliament's planning framework, particularly in the House of Commons Service, demonstrated a greater focus on outreach and dialectic engagement.

Examination of the latest planning documents in the two parliaments, however, revealed some changes in emphasis (apart from those relating to the Covid-19 pandemic and its effects on parliamentary operations, about which I say more in the final chapter).[51] In the Australian Parliament in 2021–22, the focus by DPS on managing relationships was extensive, including with many customers and stakeholders external to the Parliament. Also to the fore was organisational innovation and capability, particularly digital capability. The Senate and House of Representatives departments expressed a commitment to digital technology as well, while recognising that the greater responsibility resided within DPS, and their commitment to engagement with other parliaments was reflected in the latest strategic framework. All departments emphasised the need to maintain productive or collaborative working relationships, focus on staff wellbeing and enhance policies to prevent bullying and harassment, acknowledging the Jenkins review (AHRC 2021).

---

50 The Parliamentary Budget Office, which has a singular purpose, is not included.
51   See DPS (2021b); Department of the House of Representatives (2021b); Department of the Senate (2021b); Parliament of Australia (2020).

Changes in emphasis have also occurred in the UK Parliament. The House of Commons' strategy has been 'refreshed' and, at least until March 2023, its strategic goals now include creating a diverse and inclusive working environment. 'Ambitious, collaborative, helpful and proactive behaviours' became 'collaborative, courageous, inclusive and trusted values' (no doubt in response to inquiries into bullying and harassment, detailed in the next chapter). Interestingly, an earlier objective of involving and 'inspiring' the public changed to 'informing' the public (House of Commons 2019, 2021), perhaps reflecting a less ambitious approach to public engagement.[52] In the House of Lords' updated strategy, respect, collaboration, adaptation and innovation are priorities, reflecting in particular the inquiries into bullying and the need to work closely with the House of Commons administration on restoration and renewal (House of Lords 2022).

By exploring the planning frameworks of each parliament in some detail and observing gradual changes in focus, I have sought to demonstrate the difficult path both parliaments tread in balancing the present and future requirements of their internal actors while responding to the external environment, including changing public expectations.

The dilemma of party politics: An abundance of scrutiny or an excess of criticism?

Parliamentary scrutiny of government

To begin, I briefly address the scrutiny function ascribed *to* rather than *of* parliament—that of scrutinising the executive government of the day, including through deliberating on its legislative program, holding its ministers to account and examining the day-to-day operations of government departments and agencies. In theory, one could expect effective parliamentary scrutiny of the government to play an essential part in enabling the passage of government policy through careful deliberation and thoughtful amendment where appropriate, in both chambers of a bicameral parliament, thus avoiding the potential excesses of majority rule

---

52   This was confirmed in later conversations (in 2022) with some interviewees.

and protecting minority interests.[53] But this ideal is often at odds with the conflicting political goals of government and opposition: on the one hand, to pass legislation as quickly and efficiently as possible; on the other, to ensure the capacity of opposition parties or individual members to thwart those parts of a government's legislative program that do not coincide with a particular set of interests. Parliamentary scrutiny can be directed to the pursuit of political advantage rather than effective policymaking or deliberation and I noted in Chapter 5 the Senate Clerk's comments on 'stapled together party policy positions'. In the context of select committee inquiries—generally considered effective forums for scrutiny and deliberation—committee chairs and members are also sometimes at odds in the way in which they exercise their individual styles.[54] Even the most staunch defender of the Senate's scrutiny role, Harry Evans, conceded that to the average observer parliamentary scrutiny would appear to be 'patchy, messy, inconsistent and of dubious effectiveness', mostly carried out along partisan lines following issues raised first by the media or particular interest groups. He opined that question time was universally derided as a useless scrutiny tool (Evans n.d.). A longitudinal study of the attitudes of ministerial officeholders in the Australian Parliament towards executive accountability also found that high-achieving Cabinet ministers thought their accountability was primarily to the party rather than to the parliament and even less to public opinion (Walter 2012). I have also noted the scepticism from House of Commons Clerk Paul Evans about the willingness of most backbenchers to work across party lines in the interests of effective parliamentary scrutiny.[55] These issues are discussed at greater length in Chapter 7; for now, my purpose is to bring to the fore the challenges facing parliamentary administrators in responding to scrutiny of their activities by the media and by internal and external official scrutiny mechanisms.

---

53 There is considerable debate about the effectiveness of parliamentary scrutiny and its capacity to influence policy development, which is beyond the scope of this book, but see Russell and Gover (2017) for a comprehensive analysis of the influence of parliamentary actors in the Westminster legislative process.

54 Geddes (2016) identified different styles among committee chairs: catalysts, who enable and build on the work of other members, and chieftains, who insert their own expertise and priorities into the agenda. See also Geddes (2019a) for a fuller explanation of how committee chairs, members and officials perform their scrutiny roles.

55 Norton (2017) suggested that parliamentary scrutiny in the United Kingdom has never been more effective, but this was no doubt influenced by the fact of minority government.

Scrutiny of parliament by the media

> Parliaments are trophy organisations for the media ... [T]hat is the nature of parliaments, they are constantly in the public eye.[56]

Scrutiny of parliamentary administration is not confined to regulatory mechanisms, audit oversight or parliamentary committee oversight. One of the great challenges to parliamentary administration is the risk of adverse media reporting.[57] A heightened and intrusive awareness by the media often promote distrust and suspicion from the general public.[58] Lord Lisvane spoke about the capacity of the media, including the 'FOI brigade' to influence management behaviours and decision-making within the House of Commons Service.[59] He saw it as an unavoidable frustration and, notwithstanding some regret about the original decision to include the UK Parliament in the provisions of the *Freedom of Information Act 2000*, he was not an advocate for its reversion. A former secretary to the House of Commons Commission also pointed to the inclusion of both houses of parliament under the *Freedom of Information Act* as making a huge difference to the level of transparency and openness in the twenty-first century. He saw this as having led, on the one hand, to a more proactive communication of issues by the parliament but, on the other, to a greater public distrust of parliament, particularly when other issues are brought to light, as evidenced by the 2009 expenses scandal and the havoc it wreaked on parliament's reputation. Members themselves have no hesitation in airing in the House or to the whips their complaints about service[60] even though the House of Commons Commission does in fact have a nominated spokesperson in the House of Commons to deal with questions about its administration. In the absence of a political target, the media will often turn to criticising a parliament's administration, particularly in a 'fallow news period'.[61] On a more positive note, Mark D'Arcy, the BBC's parliamentary correspondent, dismissed the 'familiar lament' that the reporting of parliament continues to decline by pointing to a new golden age of public access provided by non-traditional media,

---

56 Lord Lisvane, pers. comm., 11 May 2016.
57 ibid.; R. Stefanic, pers. comm., 10 April 2017; A. Thompson, pers. comm., 13 July 2017; H. Penfold, pers. comm., 19 July 2017; S. Lines, pers. comm., 15 August 2017.
58 Former secretary, pers. comm., 12 May 2016.
59 Lord Lisvane (pers. comm., 11 May 2016) was referring to the practice of some journalists of making repeated requests for information on which to base media stories.
60 Former commission secretary, pers. comm., 12 May 2016; P. Beresford, pers. comm., 2 June 2016.
61 J. Bercow, pers. comm., 11 May 2016.

and he noted that key actors recognise the need to engage with the media to avoid adverse publicity and enhance public understanding (D'Arcy 2018: 207).[62]

Uhr and Wanna (2000) cited an absence of media commitment to mobilising positive public interest in the Australian Parliament and saw little prospect of subsequent parliamentary reform. The Australian Parliament is not covered by Australia's *Freedom of Information Act 1982*[63] and there is no Australian parliamentary 'FOI brigade', but even the most minor issues of parliamentary management are similarly in the public eye.[64] Within the parliamentary environment, it is generally accepted as futile to rail against the media and its relentless pursuit of politicians— particularly those who behave inappropriately—and associated administrative issues, whether significant or trivial. Media reports of the expenses scandal in the United Kingdom and rows over parliamentary entitlements in Australia did nothing to enhance the reputation of MPs or parliamentary administration—quite the contrary—but they have led to notable reforms in both parliaments in the provision and oversight of parliamentary expenses. In the United Kingdom, the media disclosures also precipitated significant business reforms in the House of Commons (Russell 2011b). Recent television productions designed to enhance public understanding of how each parliament works have been generally well received, but even these did not escape criticism.[65]

---

62   Noted also by R. Stefanic, pers. comm., 10 April 2017; L. Hickey, pers. comm., 26 May 2017; Lord Lisvane, pers. comm., 11 May 2016.

63   Under Section 68A, departments and officeholders in the Parliamentary Service are not prescribed authorities for *Freedom of Information Act* purposes; a review of the *Freedom of Information Act* tabled on 2 August 2013 recommended the Act should not apply to the Parliamentary Librarian but should apply to documents of an administrative nature in the possession of parliamentary departments (see OAIC 2019).

64   For instance, an AAP story about Hilary Penfold, former DPS secretary, taking home her banana skins led to questions about the lack of composting facilities in Parliament House (H. Penfold, pers. comm., 19 July 2017). Alan Thompson, former DPS secretary, claimed that 'B' and 'C'-grade journalists in Parliament House maintained a personal interest in housekeeping in the building (A. Thompson, pers. comm., 13 July 2017). Rob Stefanic, current DPS Secretary, noted a *Sydney Morning Herald* article on the furore around renewing the lease for Parliament House's well-known Aussie's café, which, unusually, defended the DPS position (Public Eye 2017; R. Stefanic, pers. comm., 10 April 2017).

65   In the United Kingdom, see the BBC Two series *Inside the Commons* (BBC 2015) and *Meet the Lords* (BBC 2017). Both series attracted criticism from some quarters (see, for instance, Wollaston 2015; Collins 2017). In Australia, see the ABC TV series *The House with Annabel Crabb* (ABC 2017), which was widely acclaimed (see, for instance, Peatlin 2017), although some concern was expressed within DPS that the program failed to provide a comprehensive factual account of its work.

Promoting parliament to the public as an institution to be valued is evidently problematic, particularly in the face of public concern over the behaviour of individual politicians—a concern that is exacerbated by largely negative media coverage. Media scrutiny was cited by the Speaker of the House of Representatives as a key distinction between parliamentary administration and public management.[66] Simply disseminating information publicly about the work of the parliament, while probably necessary, is not sufficient to restore parliament's reputation. Nevertheless, the UK Parliament directs considerable effort to its public engagement and participation function and the public engagement role could be strengthened within the Australian Parliament, including by taking a whole-of-parliament approach.

Official scrutiny mechanisms of parliament

Highly visible as it is, media scrutiny is not the way in which parliaments are officially held to account even though it may be a catalyst. Table 6.4 depicts the official scrutiny mechanisms that complement the governance arrangements in each parliament described earlier.

Table 6.4 Official scrutiny mechanisms in the UK Parliament and the Australian Parliament

Scrutiny mechanism	UK Parliament	Australian Parliament
Internal audit	✓	✓
	House of Commons Administration Estimate Audit and Risk Assurance Committee; Members Estimate Audit Committee; House of Lords Audit Committee oversees internal audit's objective evaluation, advice and assurance.	Each parliamentary department has an internal audit committee to provide advice, oversight and assurance.
External audit	✓	✓
	National Audit Office audits financial accounts, may undertake value-for-money audits at parliament's request.	Australian National Audit Office audits financial accounts; may also undertake performance audits.

---

66   T. Smith, pers. comm., 19 April 2017.

Scrutiny mechanism	UK Parliament	Australian Parliament
Independent review of salaries and expenses	✓ Independent Parliamentary Standards Authority (IPSA) sets and administers salaries and expenses; operates within a 'stronger integrity regime' than the Australian Independent Parliamentary Expenses Authority (IPEA) (Madden and McKeown 2018).	✓ Independent Parliamentary Expenses Authority (IPEA) monitors MPs' travel and allowances, Senate and House of Representatives pay members' salaries, which are determined by Remuneration Tribunal.
Members code of conduct	✓ House of Commons Code of Conduct upheld by Committee on Standards and Parliamentary Commissioner for Standards; Code of Conduct for members of the House of Lords (and members' staff).	✗ No similar provision (but see AHRC 2021). Members and senators are required to register interests and the Parliamentary Service Values and Code of Conduct apply to all parliamentary staff.
Internal committee scrutiny (for example, estimates committees)	✗ No similar provision but the House of Commons and House of Lords commissions together with their associated domestic committees provide financial and administrative oversight and authority.	✓ Senate Appropriations, Staffing and Security Committee; House of Representatives Appropriations and Administration Committee oversees house budgets; Senate Finance and Public Administration Estimates Committee examines annual appropriations of the Department of the Senate, DPS and PBO.
Questions in parliament about administration	✓ House of Commons Commission spokesperson answers questions in House of Commons chamber and written questions. Both House of Lords and House of Commons commissions publish decisions.	? Speaker and president may (rarely) be asked questions about administration during question time in each house.

Sources: UK Parliament website and House of Commons and House of Lords annual reports (2018); annual reports of Australian parliamentary departments (2017); Madden and McKeown (2018).

Perceptions of the lack of effective scrutiny of parliament's members and its administration are widespread.[67] To illustrate the dilemma of determining when too much scrutiny can become an excess of criticism, I will return to two events I have already introduced. The first are the expenses/entitlements scandals (in each parliament) and the second is the performance of the DPS in the Australian Parliament. I have pointed to the consequences of the expenses/entitlements exposure for parliament's reputation and its future administration.[68] In the United Kingdom, according to Andrew Walker, the former head of the Fees Office to whom much of the blame for the expenses scandal was attributed, appropriate systems were proposed before the scandal broke, following the implementation of the *Freedom of Information Act 2000*.[69] But the proposals were rejected by politicians who believed in 'self-government' and who raised spurious arguments about constitutional sovereignty. They doubted—erroneously as it turned out—the public would be much interested in members' expenses, failing to anticipate the consequences of the *Freedom of Information Act*. Members of the House of Commons were not enamoured of the independent regulatory authority set up in response to the scandal, IPSA, citing its failure to comprehend the intricacies of members' representational duties (Gay 2014). It was seen as overly complex, bureaucratic and uncommunicative and members no longer received the 'friendly guidance' they had been used to from inhouse officials (Gay 2014: 181). Several interviewees confirmed this assessment:

> The members don't like it. It wasn't created in a vacuum or in an atmosphere where all other things were equal. It was created at speed as a result of a crisis, not least a crisis of confidence between the public and their elected representatives.[70]

> [A]ll MPs hate IPSA. IPSA was given a dual role, which I think is difficult for it to fulfil: 1) to enable MPs to do their job and 2) to regulate MPs. I think those are mutually exclusive and that's quite difficult for them.[71]

---

67 For a useful exposition on parliamentary investigations and their capacity to reform the parliamentary workplace, see Dickinson (2018).
68 But note Dickinson (2019), who suggests the correlation between the expenses scandal and the current level of trust in the UK Parliament is misguided; that trust in parliament has always been low and this may reflect a structural gap between expectations and reality and ratio bias—an inability to put 'large-sounding' numbers into context.
69 A. Walker, pers. comm., 23 September 2015; see also Crewe and Walker (2019).
70 N. Brown, pers. comm., 7 June 2016.
71 C. Bryant, pers. comm., 23 May 2016.

IPSA has been brought in for all the right reasons, it is independent and that sort of thing, but its officials' understanding of what MPs do is sadly lacking and you can get some quite obtuse decisions from them.[72]

In a public lecture in Australia, the inaugural head of IPSA, Andrew McDonald, recounted the 'unrelenting' hostility with which IPSA was initially regarded (quoted in Easton 2017). He observed that the expenses scandal in the UK Parliament inflicted more damage to its reputation than the parliamentary entitlements episodes have to the Australian Parliament; nevertheless, both are examples of how appropriate and timely intervention could have avoided public opprobrium.

In Australia, the Independent Parliamentary Expenses Authority (IPEA) was established in 2017, following numerous (and, by inference, ineffective) attempts to rein in the misuse of parliamentary entitlements.[73] In its early stages, some commentators questioned its independence, describing it as a 'confidential advisory service designed to help [parliamentarians] avoid expense scandals' rather than a way of restoring public trust (Easton 2017, 2018). But this response throws up further questions: Why should the chief purpose of the IPEA not be to guide politicians through the time-consuming, intricate process of claiming workplace expenses, avoiding errors and thereby reducing the potential for the further erosion of public trust? Or is public trust engendered by further examples of opprobrium and punishment? The IPEA's corporate plan appears to suggest the former, presenting its twin goals as providing support to parliamentarians in exercising their functions as well as creating a culture of accountability and transparency, including through education and awareness. A statement to a senate estimates committee by the IPEA's CEO confirms this positive approach (IPEA 2019; Godwin 2019). McDonald has suggested that to help restore trust in the Australian Parliament, the IPEA might need to 'gently educate' members to coax them 'towards a better way of behaving', where there is less risk of rorting (Easton 2017). He also stressed that the massive damage done to the UK Parliament would not be 'made good' by the IPSA (or, by inference, the IPEA); rather, MPs themselves would have to make it good—in essence, calling on the constructive engagement with which this book is concerned.

---

72 P. Beresford, pers. comm., 2 June 2016.
73 See ANAO (2009); Committee for the Review of Parliamentary Entitlements (2010); Remuneration Tribunal (2011).

The second example—the management performance of DPS—illustrates how easily an abundance of scrutiny can also manifest as excessive criticism. The department has been subjected to continuing *ex post* scrutiny of its administration at the hands of the SFPALC, which has undoubtedly adversely affected its reputation, not just in the public domain, but also in the resulting damage to relationships between its officials and senators and members (SFPALC 2012a, 2012b, 2015a, 2015b, 2015c, 2021). Not all interviewees, however, considered the level of scrutiny by estimates committees excessive. To one former secretary, it was a 'really useful accountability model' and an opportunity to fix up 'things that were embarrassing for the department' that might be raised.[74] But to other managers, the intensity of scrutiny at the parliamentary coalface was greater than they had experienced in other public organisations and could be seen as contributing to a culture of risk aversion.[75]

Reactions from interviewees to the SFPALC performance inquiries were mixed. Senator Katy Gallagher joined the committee between its 2012 and 2015 inquiries into DPS. She was critical of the perceived lack of responsiveness of the incoming DPS executive team to fix past shortcomings and what she saw as 'hostile engagement' with SFPALC:

> I was surprised on a number of fronts. One was the clear inadequacies that existed within DPS. Whilst I had come quite late to that saga, it was clear to me that even though they'd been under a fair bit of scrutiny, to keep presenting to the finance and admin committee as though 'there's nothing to see here and we're not ready to answer your questions' or 'we don't have that policy' or 'it's taken five years and we still haven't done something', they didn't present as a professional outfit at all … It spoke to me of a lack of leadership and a lack of direction to senior staff, which was flowing right through the organisation. That was pretty clear, I thought, from even the first hearing, without reading the back story.
>
> The other thing that surprised me was the hostile kind of engagement [between the committee and DPS] due to years of frustration … The department hadn't noticed that or hadn't picked up on that or didn't care about it … [A]gain, it didn't speak well for DPS. You've got your key stakeholders: in DPS,

---

74 Former secretary, pers. comm., 19 July 2017.
75 There was sensitivity among interviewees towards commenting negatively on the level of scrutiny through estimates committees.

you've got the President and the Speaker, you've got executive government hanging around. They fund you. You've also got the actual members and senators. To be so disrespectful of that was a surprise, and something I hadn't really seen so blatantly before.[76]

On the other hand, Carol Mills, the then secretary, told me:

I knew that I either had to get money or difficult decisions had to be made. But I was also aware of the reports and things, and I thought … 'let's take the positive out of that. Instead of working in a vacuum, we're actually going to get a report with recommendations that we can hang our hat off, if we're given the time to do it.' When I went there, I thought it was a three-year task, to make the change. Within about six months, I realised it would be five years, because it's just much more conservative, and change is slower than I would have ideally liked. But I thought it was a five-year transformation and, even if we didn't have full parliamentary cooperation across all the agencies, we could actually transform DPS in a way that would become a role model for parliamentary services. I think we got some way down that track, and then we got another inquiry, plus the Auditor-General decided to do one, and I always wonder why that happened.[77]

Gallagher also suggested that, after scrutiny, DPS management presented as 'a more professional outfit' and took a 'more positive' approach to estimates committee hearings. She acknowledged—perhaps somewhat contradictorily—that 'you've got to give people the opportunity to improve, under new leadership. It's not something that will happen overnight.'[78] As we have seen in earlier chapters, there was little sympathy for Mills, either internally or in the public domain, and her statement to the SFPALC at the time of her termination was perceived as an excuse for incompetent management.

To put these views into context, before Mills's appointment was terminated, she was given two and a half years to rectify the management problems of a department already judged by Senator John Faulkner as the worst administered department he had ever seen (Australia, Senate 2012). The 2015 ANAO report on managing contracts and assets in Parliament House found there was scope for DPS to improve aspects of its strategic

---

76   K. Gallagher, pers. comm., 14 June 2017.
77   C. Mills, pers. comm., 11 May 2017.
78   K. Gallagher, pers. comm., 14 June 2017.

planning, risk management and performance reporting, and was critical of the lack of progress by DPS in responding to recommendations from the 2012 SFPALC inquiry. However, it also acknowledged that DPS had faced a substantial change agenda over the previous four years, which had 'a significant impact' on staff morale and turnover and more work was required to 'build cohesion and engagement between DPS management and staff to encourage constructive working relations within an environment of ongoing external scrutiny' (ANAO 2015: 119–20). The ANAO report also acknowledged that results from a joint ANAO–DPS survey indicated that parliamentarians were largely satisfied with DPS's activities to support the operation of Parliament House. The greatest level of dissatisfaction (30 per cent) was with the Parliament House catering and food and beverage outlets—complaints unlikely to engender much public sympathy. Even more tellingly, only 33 of the parliament's 225 members and senators responded to the survey—a response rate of less than 15 per cent.[79]

It is unsurprising that Mills presented a defensive account of the change program in contrast to the conclusions of the SFPALC. She claimed that once she arrived at DPS, she realised it would take five years to transform it, citing as key inhibitors hostility from other parliamentary departments, an insular and 'separate' parliamentary culture that was resistant to change and a lack of interest in and support for administration from a series of presiding officers.[80] I have thoroughly examined the evidence relating to the unsatisfactory performance of DPS, which came to a critical juncture with the 2015 SFPALC inquiry and the subsequent termination of Mills (see Chapter 4). The validity of the evidence of poor performance has been largely accepted in parliamentary circles and by numerous commentators (including Mulgan 2014; Senate Committee of Privileges 2014; Lewis 2015; Peatling 2015). I have sought to add to the analysis of the Australian Parliament's management performance by presenting factors that interviewees and other sources have identified that could have contributed to DPS's perceived poor performance—many pre-dating Mills. They include poor implementation of the amalgamation of its predecessor departments; a lack of collaboration bordering on hostility between the parliamentary departments; the decision by the Department of Finance to impose a pre-emptive budget cut of $6 million in anticipation

79 One can only assume that non-respondents were either satisfied or not sufficiently concerned about the quality of support services to comment.
80 C. Mills, pers. comm., 11 May 2017.

165

of poorly justified predicted savings from the amalgamation; a disregard for the cultural challenges involved in amalgamating disparate functions, notwithstanding a 100-year history of insularity and defensiveness; a lack of institutional continuity in the management rather than the procedural area; and an apparent shortfall in administrative leadership by successive presiding officers. These could be considered as mitigating factors in a period of relentless scrutiny from a small cohort of parliamentary actors and from the media.

Conclusion: Competing perspectives of effective management

In this chapter, I have addressed competing beliefs about the relative value of procedural and management skills, the extent to which MPs engage constructively in management issues and how structural differences between the two parliaments inhibit or facilitate effective management. In both parliaments, notwithstanding their different organisational structures, a higher priority has traditionally been placed by parliamentarians on procedural rather than managerial skills and functions. The UK Parliament has displayed more signs of an outward-facing and strategic approach to its management functions, particularly public engagement, and the Australian Parliament has had a greater (externally enforced) focus on efficiency. However, the absence of a cohesive parliamentary identity or vision, sustained leadership and authority, and poor relationships between procedural and managerial officials have emerged in both parliaments as explanatory factors in their effective management. Interviewees have pointed to tensions arising from different beliefs about the primary duty of parliamentary actors, whether this be to members, to individual constituents, to political parties, to the institution itself or to the public as a whole. But it also appears that these tensions can be at least partly explained by a relatively narrow interpretation of what effective management means. When it is concerned only with delivering ancillary support services such as facilities management, catering, ICT, human resources and financial systems, the challenges appear to be routine, operational and plebeian, if manifold. When effective 'management' of a parliament is seen as encompassing the achievement of all its principal purposes and maintaining its relevance, reputation and position of trust in a country's system of democratic governance, the challenges become more complex, strategic and intellectually challenging. For MPs (principally in the House of Commons and House of Representatives) whose main focus is on serving their constituents (thereby securing re-election) and their party (thereby securing promotion and/or ongoing preselection), it is perhaps understandable that their interest in management relates narrowly to their own partisan interests in obtaining advice and resources that will help them to achieve these objectives, while simultaneously performing their representational and influencing roles. But a disregard for sustaining the reputation of the wider institution in an era of increasingly cynical media and public scrutiny and perceived shortcomings in parliamentary self-regulation have had repercussions. In the next chapter, I discuss the challenges of procedural and cultural reform to meet changing societal expectations.

7

Guarding the institution: The case for procedural and cultural reform

Introduction

In this wide-ranging chapter, I conceptualise effective parliamentary administration from a viewpoint that elevates the broad concept of public management without necessarily subordinating effective procedural management. Procedural and management functions should be seen not as opposites, working in competition, but as part of a continuum of effective parliamentary administration. Managing the rules is crucial to performing parliament's role of scrutinising the executive while also enabling the executive to implement its programs and, in the following sections, I seek to engender an appreciation of the purpose, complexity and evolution of procedural rules and the need for their careful stewardship. But I also examine three procedural and cultural dilemmas that go to the heart of balancing continuity and reform: changing rules and behaviours to meet public expectations; the need for public engagement strategies that are representative and not merely informative; and the danger of consigning reforms to the too-difficult box. Procedural and cultural reform are crucial components of good public management; however, sustaining and enhancing a parliament's effectiveness encompass more than managing and playing by the existing rules, as important as these may be.

The case for defending the rules

> It is more material that there should be a rule to go by than
> what that rule is, in order that there may be a uniformity of
> proceeding in the business of the House, not subject to the
> momentary caprice of the Speaker or to the captious disputes of
> any Members ... [I]t is not so material that the rule should be
> established on the foundation of sound reason and argument as it
> is that order, decency and regularity should be preserved in a large,
> numerous and consequently sometimes tumultuous assembly.
> (Hatsell c. 1796, quoted in Evans 2014)

For an insightful history and analysis of the origins and purposes of
the procedural rules of the House of Commons, which the House
of Representatives has largely followed, Paul Evans's Open Lecture
to Aberystwyth University provided a valuable and occasionally
self-deprecating source.[1] An early canon of procedural law was Hatsell's
Precedents of Proceedings in the House of Commons with Observations,
published between 1776 and 1796, and later incorporated in Thomas
Jefferson's *Manual of Parliamentary Procedure*, which continues to hold
some sway in the US Congress as a final authority on procedure. Hatsell's
work was overtaken by Erskine May's 1844 *Treatise on the Law, Privilege,
Proceedings and Usage of Parliament*, which has become the 'bible of
parliamentary procedure' (Evans 2014). The House of Lords is guided
by the *Companion to the Standing Orders and Guide to the Proceedings
of the House of Lords* (2013), the first edition of which was compiled
in 1862 by the Clerk of the Parliaments. In Australia, both houses
have also developed their own 'bibles': *House of Representatives Practice*
and *Senate Practice*, the latter being strongly associated with its original
author and known as 'Odgers' in the 'Erskine May' tradition. Both
parliaments have voluminous Standing Orders that govern conduct in
their respective chambers.

Evans (2014, 2017) put forward two dichotomous views about the
purpose of procedural rules: the Platonic/Methuselan view, representing
the minority against the inroads of the executive, and the Aristotelian/

---

1   For instance, in his wry account of the work of Hatsell, Clerk of the House of Commons for
52 years in the eighteenth century, Evans observed that his predecessor's 'work–life balance' saw him
sending a deputy to work for 24 of those years; and, in lieu of a salary, he received income from the fees
for taking private bills through the House, thereby 'reaping the profits of the House's legislative activity
on behalf of enclosers, canal-cutters, railway undertakers, corporations and their like' (2014: 2–3).

Modernist view, ensuring that good governance is achieved by taking a more consensual approach to passing legislation. He doubted, however, that each could be so discretely encapsulated. Both philosophical camps (however characterised) would agree that parliament is about the struggle of ideas; one prioritises 'actions and outcomes', while the other prefers 'deliberation and caution' (Evans 2017: 13–14). Attempts to reform house business and procedure in the UK Parliament have reflected the changing balance between the two camps: the efficient delivery of the government's program against greater opportunities for scrutiny and deliberation. Evans credited the House of Commons Reform Committee (2009, the 'Wright Committee'), in the aftermath of the 'accidental' expenses scandal and the election of a coalition government in 2015, with the beginning of a reversal of the drift of control of the House of Commons' agenda to the government that had occurred through the previous century and a half. He noted that select committees were now the principal locus of scrutiny efforts. His views are supported by those of Ryle (2005), Kelso (2009) and Russell and Benton (2011).[2] Russell and Paun (2007), in a comparative study of procedural rules and their influence on parliamentary autonomy, provided strong arguments for electing a Speaker prepared to be an outspoken public defender of parliament and for backbenchers to be given more control over managing house business—both of which were realised in the House of Commons during Speaker Bercow's term.[3] They noted that the procedure committees in both the Australian House of Representatives and the UK House of Commons[4] were more transparent and open than in the Australian Senate, where procedural reform was dominated by covert dealings between the whips and frontbenchers, and this observation was reflected in my interviews with clerks and members.

Russell and Cowley (2018), in a revision of King's (1976) modes of executive–legislature relations, acknowledged a reduction in the whips' patronage power, greater status for committee chairs, including an ability to speak for parliament, and a greater cross-party ethos. They also found that substantial reform to the House of Lords' membership, including

2   But see an alternative view by Philip Aylett, House of Commons Clerk, that the introduction of select committees in 1979 was just one part of a sustained process of committee strengthening that started in 1965 (Aylett 2018).
3   However, the full effects on executive control of the re-election of the Johnson government with a large majority and the Covid-19 pandemic remain to be seen.
4   The House of Commons Modernisation Committee also played a significant role in parliamentary reform; however, it was chaired by the Leader of the House and was generally regarded as being concerned with 'efficiency' reforms that favoured the executive. For further reading, see Kelso (2009).

the virtual abolition of hereditary peers, has increased its influence and that management of the House of Commons has become more complex, particularly when there is no single party majority (Russell and Cowley 2018: 21). In fact, before the election of the Johnson government in 2019, the dominance of the executive in the UK Parliament had decreased to such an extent that some parliamentarians questioned whether the House of Commons was becoming too powerful.[5] In the context of Brexit, Norton (2018a) contrasted the best of times—the strength of parliament in relation to the executive—with the worst of times: parliament's relationship with the public, whose members exhibited little trust in parliament as an institution. In the latter respect, media headlines have even invoked outrage against the tyranny of parliament (Hartigan 2019).

In the Australian Parliament, the House of Representatives has been largely under the control of the executive since 1940, with the exception of the 2010–13 parliament when procedural reform tended to favour the House over the executive.[6] After the 2016 election, the government's numeric hold further decreased and, by late 2018, its majority had disappeared, with Independent members and the government's own backbench gaining influence over government policy.[7] The Australian Senate has stronger powers than most upper houses (Russell 2000) and, since 1949, the executive has rarely controlled the Senate. Procedure has tended to be viewed by senate officials very much from a Platonist/Methuselan perspective in guaranteeing the rights of elected minority parties and individual senators against the ravages of government (Evans, H. 2002; Laing 2013; Evans, P. 2014, 2017).[8]

---

5   After the 2017 election, when the Conservative government lost its majority, executive control was further diminished (see Russell 2019a).

6   During this period, significant procedural reform was negotiated between the minority Gillard government, the Greens and Independents, including parliamentary processes favouring private members, greater independence for the Speaker, the conduct of question time, the establishment of a House Committee on Appropriations and Staffing and the establishment of the Parliamentary Budget Office (see agreements between the Australian Greens and the Australian Labor Party, 1 September 2010; the Hon. Julia Gillard and Andrew Wilkie, 2 September 2010; the Australian Labor Party and Independent members Tony Windsor and Rob Oakeshott, 7 September 2010, in Parliamentary Library 2013).

7   In 2018, the House of Representatives was close to the end of its term and was not marked by its contribution to procedural reform. The Morrison government was elected in its own right in 2019; however, its majority was slim.

8   Also noted by M. Weeks, pers. comm., 24 May 2017.

We can see that defending procedures against 'momentary caprice' or 'captious disputes', while important, does not mean that nothing should change; indeed, the balance of power between the parliament and the executive is influenced by many factors other than procedural continuity. The approach to procedural practice articulated by Evans (2014, 2017)— namely, 'if you can't ride two horses, you shouldn't be in the circus'[9]— must balance efficiency and effectiveness by allowing a parliament to *enable* as well as to *scrutinise* (see also Norton 2000; Kelso 2009). But, in the words of former Clerk of the House of Commons Sir Courtenay Ilbert (1902–21) parliamentary procedure 'remains a mystery, unintelligible except to the initiated, and the officials who [formulate] the rules [are] not anxious that their knowledge should be too widely shared' (quoted in Evans 2014: 10). That summation remains the case today (Williamson and Fallon 2011; DDC 2015; Leston-Bandeira 2015; Crewe 2017). If the purpose of procedural rules is to 'demonstrate fair play and to win the assent of the people to the exercise of sovereign power' (Evans 2014), logic dictates and reformers agree that the rules should also be relevant and publicly accessible, just as should be the physical embodiments of parliament, including access to its building and proceedings. Taking a broad view, managing the procedural function involves more than just preserving 'order, decency and regularity in a tumultuous assembly', more even than riding the two horses of efficient government and effective scrutiny. I return to Crick's view expressed in Chapter 2 that

> the purpose of any institution, or the operative ideals of any group of men are only realizable through procedures; and so existing procedures must constantly be examined in light of the great radical question: 'Do they serve the public interest?' (Crick 1968: 12)

Thus, procedural management extends beyond the close management of Standing Orders and business processes (important as these are; see Russell and Paun 2007) towards placing a greater focus on public value and cultural change in the way parliaments go about their business. Seen in this light, effective procedural management requires exercising control over two different horses while also negotiating the terrain beyond the circus ring to better serve the public interest.

---

9   Attributed by Evans to Thomas Makin; see also Speake (2015).

The stewardship role

In arguing the case for both stewardship *and* procedural and cultural reform, in pursuit of Crick's public interest test, I look first at 'stewardship' and the belief that it occurs where managers' motives are aligned with their organisation and its principals. Stewards are understood to act not as self-serving utility maximisers but to display pro-organisational, collective (rather than self-interested) behaviours (see Donaldson and Davis 1991; Davis et al. 1997). The director-general's review in the UK House of Commons defined parliamentary stewardship as a 'continuing responsibility we have *on behalf of the public* for the good order, the effective running and the reputation of the House of Commons' (House of Commons 2016: 12n.1; emphasis added; see also Chapter 5, this volume). In the Australian *Parliamentary Service Act 1999*, the term 'stewardship' is legislated but not defined.[10] Although some Australian interviewees displayed pragmatism towards stewardship, advocating a 'modern and open' approach,[11] others were more cautious about change.[12] Stewardship was viewed more from a protectionist and conservative perspective than a reforming or anticipatory one.

As demonstrated in Chapter 6, impediments to management reform are institutional divisions, multiple stakeholders and multiple roles of parliamentary administration. From a theoretical perspective, it might be difficult to determine precisely who are the owners or principals of the parliamentary institution and on whom the responsibility for stewardship rests. Nevertheless, there is sufficient evidence to put ownership of the parliament in public hands, albeit through the collective agency of its members (see Rogers and Walters 2015), and to argue that stewardship of procedure (in its broadest sense) should also favour the interests of the public (or owners) through facilitative structures and procedures even if there is room for doubt as to who has authority or responsibility over a particular matter (see Donaldson and Davis 1991). This brief discussion of stewardship and how it might be interpreted by parliamentary actors is important to an understanding of the need for, and processes of, both

---

10   Other than requiring it to be practised 'within the Department and, in partnership with other Secretaries, across the Parliamentary Service' (Section 57). In the *Australian Public Service Act 1999*, it is coupled with developing and implementing strategies to improve the Australian Public Service.
11   C. Surtees, pers. comm., 6 June 2017.
12   K. Gallagher, pers. comm., 14 June 2017; N. Marino, pers. comm., 14 June 2017; S. Lines, pers. comm., 17 August 2017.

procedural and cultural reform. Put simply, it illustrates the tensions that can exist between changing traditions and practices or preserving them; between the interests of those advocating or opposing reform; and between differing perceptions of the public interest (Ringeling 2015).[13] And here I re-emphasise the dual purposes of parliament's public engagement role: first, to engender a wider, more sophisticated and less divisive understanding—if not wholehearted appreciation—of parliament's competing roles in both enabling and scrutinising government; and second, to encourage greater public participation in its deliberative processes. These align closely with two of this book's stated purposes. More aspirational is the potential for parliament, represented by its members and officials, to join with other public institutions in seeking broader democratic reform—a third stated purpose for this book.

Achieving procedural reform: Challenges and limits

Norton (2000) elaborated on the purposes of procedural reform: to expedite government business, to improve the working environment for members, to eliminate archaic procedures that have little meaning and to strengthen parliament's scrutiny role. He prescribed three conditions for reform: a window of opportunity, usually at the beginning of a parliament; a coherent reform agenda; and political leadership, whether from the backbench, the incumbent government through the Leader of the House or a combination of both. Kelso (2009) characterised the dilemma of procedural reform as a contest between those who would seek to ensure that an elected majority can successfully secure their legislative program unencumbered by procedural complexities (efficiency reforms) and those who would encourage parliament to take a more proactive role (effectiveness reforms). But, as she also points out, the two categories are not necessarily mutually exclusive and both might be viewed as either advancing or detracting from the public interest.

---

13   See Ringeling (2015: 305) for a useful discussion of determining the 'elusive concept' of public interest, the competing roles of politicians and officials and the role of citizens in the public sphere.

As noted in Chapter 4, Harry Evans, former clerk of the Senate, was a staunch supporter of the Senate and a self-described 'sceptical questioner'. His views on reform have been well publicised.[14] Even though he conceded that traditional procedures and practices may have had no substantial legislative value and, in some cases, bore 'the taint of colonialism', he pointed out the dangers of losing useful procedures through the hostility of radical denouncers 'jettisoning everything bearing the cursed mark of real or supposed antiquity' (Evans 2009: 147–49). Reform of procedures and practices should be 'careful and rigorous' (p. 150). Parliament needed not reform but 'reformation' to return the institution to its original purpose (Evans 2002: 5).

Table 7.1 displays examples of procedural reforms in both parliaments designed to increase the effectiveness of scrutiny and/or deliberation, increase efficiency in transacting government business or increase public participation and/or representation. Many reforms, such as the establishment of committees, have more than one purpose. Efficiency reforms usually originate from government and are designed to smooth the passage of its legislative program. Effectiveness reforms are more likely to follow a criticism or crisis that can be exploited by willing actors, such as the Wright reforms in the United Kingdom (Norton 2000; Kelso 2009; Russell 2011b). The parliamentary agreements made during the 2010–13 parliament in Australia also fall into this category. The hybrid arrangements adopted in both parliaments in response to the Covid-19 pandemic are not easily categorised, although they have been criticised for diminishing parliament's influence.

---

14   See Evans (2002). Evans believed that most reform proposals of major institutions did not ask (or answer) fundamental questions about the purpose and effectiveness of the institutions they sought to reform, but, rather, reflected government orthodoxy in its second or third term. Government orthodoxy relating to parliament saw it as no more than a 'rubber stamp' enabling government to govern with total power between elections (Evans 2002: 1).

Table 7.1 An illustration of types of procedural reforms in the Australian and UK parliaments

Reform type	Australian Parliament	UK Parliament
Effectiveness (scrutiny)	**1970 Senate Legislative and Standing Committees:** Substantial contribution to parliamentary control and scrutiny, particularly estimates committees.	**1979 select committees:** Widely regarded as most effective form of scrutiny.
	1979–81 House of Representatives Legislation and Estimates Standing Committees: Abandoned, having failed to add to parliamentary control, partly through lack of backbench support.	**2000 Royal Commission (Wakeham report):** Recognised scrutiny role and self-regulation; led to review of working practices to achieve 'constructive engagement' between houses.
	2003 House of Representatives consideration of estimates: Including joint/concurrent hearings with Senate not pursued.	**2009 Select Committee on Reform of the House of Commons (Wright Committee):** Recommended greater control of parliamentary agenda; election of committee chairs; greater public participation, deemed partially successful.
Efficiency (business)	**1993 Procedure Committee report *About Time:*** Established Main Committee (renamed Federation Chamber in 2004) to facilitate legislation; also revised sitting hours.	**1997 Select Committee on Modernisation of the House of Commons:** Criticised as facilitating government business and neglecting parliament.
	2016 House of Representatives Procedure Committee report *Division Required?:* Recommended electronic voting within chamber; not considered in Senate since 1990.	**2001–04 House of Lords Leader's Group review:** Review of working practices to sustain efficient scrutiny. Trial practices agreed by Procedure Committee.
Effectiveness (deliberation, participation, inclusion, representation)	**1993 Main Committee/ Federation Chamber (see above):** Facilitating backbench participation; more amenable to consensus or collaborative decision-making.	**1979 select committees:** Few considered 'agenda-setting' but could influence policy process and contribute to debate; possible improvements include better attendance, follow-up and ability to commission research.

Reform type	Australian Parliament	UK Parliament
	1999 Procedure Committee report *It's Your House*: Proposals for greater community involvement received lukewarm government response.	**1997 Select Committee on Modernisation of the House of Commons:** Established parallel debating chamber, Westminster Hall.
	2008 Proxy voting: This was introduced for nursing mothers in House of Representatives chamber; not permitted in Senate as arguably unconstitutional (*Odgers' Australian Senate Practice*).	
	2010–13 minority government: Significant reforms negotiated with Independent members, favouring parliament.	**2009 Wright Committee (see above):** Recommended greater public participation. Needed follow-up.
	2016 House of Representatives e-petitions: Introduced in House of Representatives 'within existing resources'. Deemed successful; however, system made no provision for response or debate.	**2015 House of Commons e-petitions:** Successful collaboration with government on public engagement enabling responses and debates on social issues.
	2017 House of Representatives Procedure Committee Inquiry into Disorder: Found lukewarm support for increasing sanctions.	**2016** *The Good Parliament* **(Childs 2016):** A blueprint for representation and inclusion; to enhance effectiveness and legitimacy of House of Commons; cross-party support for standards of behaviour. Commons Reference Group on Representation and Inclusion established by House of Commons Commission to respond to report.
	2018 Senate Standing Committee on Procedure *Disorder Outside Formal Proceedings* **report:** Warned against personal abuse but changes to Standing Orders considered 'undesirable' (p. 2).	
	2019 Senate Procedure Committee: Did not recommend code of conduct for senators.	**2019 Proxy voting:** Pilot system introduced into House of Commons chamber.
	2020–21 House of Representatives: Periods of hybrid participation in proceedings; informal pairing during divisions during Covid-19 pandemic.	**2020–21 House of Commons:** Periods of temporary arrangements for hybrid participation, remote and proxy voting for members during Covid-19 pandemic.

Reform type	Australian Parliament	UK Parliament
	2020–21 Senate: Adopted rules for remote participation in proceedings for senators affected by travel restrictions, quarantine requirements or personal health advice during Covid-19 pandemic.	**2020–21 House of Lords:** Periods of virtual and hybrid arrangements including remote voting for peers during Covid-19 pandemic.

Sources: For Australia, Reid and Forrest (1989); House of Representatives Standing Committee on Procedure (1999, 2005, 2016, 2017, 2020); Wright and Fowler (2012); Laing (2016b); Elder and Fowler (2017); House of Representatives Standing Committee on Petitions (2018); Senate Standing Committee on Procedure (2018, 2019, 2021). For the United Kingdom, Norton (2002); House of Commons Reform Committee (2009); Kelso (2009); Russell and Benton (2011); Newson (2012); House of Commons Political and Constitutional Reform Committee (2013); Childs (2016); House of Commons Procedure Committee (2014, 2017, 2020); HC Debates (2019b). A summary of attempts at institutional reform of the House of Lords until 2014 can be found on the UK Parliament's website (www.parliament.uk/business/lords/lords-history/lords-reform/) and a comprehensive account of earlier reforms is in Russell 2000 (see also Russell 2011a, 2013, 2017a, 2017b; Russell and Sandford 2002).

In Australia, I detected resignation among interviewees about their ability to achieve procedural reform. Then House of Representatives Clerk David Elder, while recognising that he was not a political player, thought there was a role for clerks in promoting reform by working with MPs and making suggestions. But, as he said, 'sometimes you get sick of sticking your head up and having it shot off'.[15] In his experience, the knowledge and ability of members to advocate and implement procedural reforms were variable and not currently strong, partly due to the rapid turnover of members and the loss of many years of parliamentary experience. Then Deputy Senate Clerk Maureen Weeks confirmed that most senators 'come unwillingly to the table' and rely heavily on the whips for the information they need.[16] She saw her own role as one of anticipation rather than advocacy. Chris Paterson, former House of Representatives adviser, conceded that even sensible suggestions could only be 'around the edges' or during a minority government, claiming:

> You're not going to change the procedures. Procedures are there because the government and the opposition want them that way … Really, procedures will only change [if] the Leader of the

---

15 D. Elder, pers. comm., 7 April 2017.
16 M. Weeks, pers. comm., 24 May 2017.

House and the Manager of Opposition Business can sit down and figure out what they want to change, and if they want to change it, they'll change it.[17]

Even the Wright reforms in the UK Parliament, while partly satisfying two of Norton's conditions for reform—taking advantage of a window of opportunity and an established reform agenda—met the third condition of political will or leadership only with caveats. The Backbench Business Committee would not have been established without the support of outside groups (Russell 2011b).

I interviewed the then chairs of the Procedure Committee in both the House of Representatives and the House of Commons. Tony Pasin, from the House of Representatives, stated his commitment to reform of the Standing Orders in pursuit of the efficiency goal. He talked of shorter speaking times,[18] allowing members more time to spend in their constituencies, and electronic voting, which he conceded had been on the agenda for an 'embarrassingly long time'. He also identified an intrinsic relationship between 'efficient' and 'effective' reforms in his suggestion that making it easier to suspend members would not only increase efficiency, particularly during question time, but could also improve the public perception of parliamentary conduct. However, his tongue-in-cheek suggestion that question time should not even be broadcast, to improve the public's perception of parliamentary behaviour, would hardly be seen as an effective response even among those who deride question time as a form of effective scrutiny. Like the clerk, Pasin confirmed there was little sense of ownership of the Standing Orders and the Procedure Committee was no longer the 'warehouse of longstanding members like the Sinclairs and the Ruddocks'.[19] He suggested a new world view that focused on technology and was not wedded to the rules could be an opportunity, but, as a backbencher, his main goal was government efficiency rather than parliamentary effectiveness.[20]

---

17   C. Paterson, pers. comm., 17 August 2018.
18   An objective also advocated by Senator Katy Gallagher, member of the Senate Procedure Committee (K. Gallagher, pers. comm., 14 June 2017).
19   Former House of Representative members Ian Sinclair and Philip Ruddock.
20   T. Pasin, pers. comm., 10 May 2017.

On the other hand, Charles Walker, then Chair of the House of Commons Procedure Committee in the United Kingdom, was greatly concerned with the need for procedural reform, citing the reluctance of the executive to give back powers ceded to it by the parliament over the past 120 years. He described the need for parliament's members to seek the permission of the executive to achieve reform as an 'irritant'. He differentiated between types of reform attempts—for example, introducing the House of Commons Petitions Committee to replace a 'botched, government-only system' was part of the government's reform agenda and therefore presented fewer challenges than other reforms. Walker's committee was able to 'skilfully' steer it 'much more towards parliament than government' and 'without the goose hissing too much as we plucked it'.[21] He also recounted a well-publicised event in which he was blindsided by the government, which sought, without notice, to introduce a procedural reform that would have threatened the re-election of controversial and independently minded Speaker Bercow.[22] The attempt by the executive to manipulate a suggested 'effectiveness' reform to remove a perceived impediment to its own efficiency was defeated and Walker's reputation for independence and political will was roundly applauded in the House of Commons and elsewhere (Hardman 2015; HC Debates 2015; Simons 2015). The political will required to advocate for the role of parliament appears more prevalent in the UK House of Commons than in Australia's House of Representatives—perhaps encouraged by a larger backbench. This claim is diminished, however, by the controversial resolution by the former Leader of the House Jacob Rees-Mogg against the wishes of the Procedure Committee, many members and external commentators to discontinue the acclaimed virtual parliament, including remote voting, introduced at the peak of the Covid-19 pandemic (White 2020a). A large majority and a three-line whip will usually win the day for a government determined to have its way. And, despite commitment by successive Procedure Committee chairs to introduce effective procedural

21 C. Walker, pers. comm., 14 June 2016.
22 A new Speaker is elected by secret ballot; however, after a general election, the process of re-electing a former speaker who wishes to remain in the position is considered a formality and a secret ballot is not required. In 2010, the Procedure Committee recommended that the House consider requiring a secret ballot for the re-election of the Speaker. No debate on the recommendation occurred. In March 2015, in an attempt to oust Speaker Bercow, whose reformist agenda had alienated some of his Conservative colleagues, then Leader of the House William Hague introduced a motion to require a secret ballot to re-elect the Speaker, without informing the Chair of the Procedure Committee. Charles Walker gave an emotional speech in the House against the motion, declaring that he had 'been played for a fool' and the motion was defeated (see R. Kelly 2020).

reform, we cannot assume an ongoing interest by the House of Commons itself; we saw in Chapter 6 Paul Evans's dismissive assessment. There is also a continuing problem of inconsistent and archaic Standing Orders and a lack of interest from the government in reviewing and redrafting them.[23] Progress has been slow due in part to the effects of devolution and the early election in 2017 (House of Commons Procedure Committee 2017). In the House of Lords, procedural reform is strongly influenced by its culture of self-regulation and attempted large reforms to the composition of the House have a long history.[24] But the Lords themselves are recognising the need to 'self-regulate' towards a more contemporary and efficient advisory chamber.[25]

Effective procedural management requires procedural experts, elected or not, to combine their expertise and judgement and exercise collective agency in fulfilling Norton's conditions for procedural reform—not least by exploiting opportunities or crises, but perhaps more enduringly by establishing a coherent reform agenda and amassing the necessary political will to make considered improvements to parliamentary practice. But success is by no means assured. Before completing this section, I will outline two controversial procedural events that unfolded in the UK Parliament in January 2019, which go to the heart of the dilemmas highlighted in my study: the question of who speaks for parliament; the use of authority amid calls for impartiality; continuity versus change, efficiency versus effectiveness (or government versus parliament); and meeting public expectations (see Boxes 7.1 and 7.2). The events concern Speaker Bercow's decision to override an established procedure during the Brexit withdrawal Bill (Box 7.1) and the actions of a senior clerk in advising a member on procedural tactics (Box 7.2).

---

23 M. Evans, pers. comm., 14 June 2016; see also C. Leston-Bandeira, pers. comm., 10 September 2018, on accessibility, but note also the recent online publication of Erskine May (Natzler 2019b).
24 See, for example, Russell (2000).
25 Baroness D'Souza, former Lord Speaker, cited her biggest achievement as articulating concerns about the way the House works—its size and its recruitment processes and in strengthening its scrutiny role (F. D'Souza, pers. comm., 9 June 2016); see also Lord Speaker (2017, 2018) on the size of the House of Lords; and the Act of Union Bill 2017–19 introduced to the House of Lords by Lord Lisvane, a former clerk of the House of Commons, which proposed options for radical reform of the UK Parliament.

Box 7.1 A voice for parliament or a danger to democracy?

On 9 January 2019, Speaker John Bercow decided to accept an amendment tabled by a conservative member of the House, Dominic Grieve (also known as a rebel Tory and a Brexit 'Remainer'), to a government business motion relating to Section 13(1)(b) of the *European Union (Withdrawal) Act 2018*, despite a precedent that only a Minister of the Crown could move a motion to vary the order of government business. The amendment had the effect of requiring the prime minister to table an alternative plan within three days of any defeat of the government's withdrawal motion (the Brexit deal).

Support for the Speaker's decision was divided, with some claiming it was an exercise in sophistry; some as lacking in impartiality (Bercow having previously declared himself a Remainer); or a refutation of the advice of the Clerk of the House of Commons. Others welcomed the Speaker's decision to act on behalf of a significant grouping within the House (HC Debates 2019a). Press commentary was also divided between outrage and support. An article in *The Economist* (Bagehot 2019), while noting the Speaker's job was an extraordinarily difficult one, requiring 'subtle choices between lots of different rulebooks ... produced over the centuries', also warned that Bercow 'will have to make far more complicated and delicate decisions than he has ever made before' and that to lean too far in one direction 'risks damaging not just himself but the House of Commons' and, potentially, the whole institution. Bercow himself appeared to be aware of the perils of exercising his authority. He justified his decision to his colleagues in the House thus:

> If we were guided only by precedent, manifestly nothing in our procedures would ever change. Things do change. I have made an honest judgment. If people want to vote against the amendment, they can; and if they want to vote for it, they can. (HC Debates 2019a)

In an interview with the author, on 17 September 2018, well before the controversial decision and after giving due recognition to both sides of the Brexit debate, Bercow offered this foresight:

> What's my role in all this? As you know, it's not to speak, and not to vote unless there's a tie, but it is for me to decide, 'If there are amendments to be selected, which amendments do I select, and how many different votes are allowed?' and so on. These are matters that can't really be discussed in the abstract. They can only be discussed in the particular, and they can only be decided at the time. So, when anybody asks me about it, I always say: 'These are the considerations, but I will have to make a judgement about it at the time.' Of course, I will consult the clerk, but in the end I'll have to do what I think is right.

The debate was put into context by a former clerk, Andrew Kennon, who opined that the government 'must now be regretting the opportunity missed in 2010 to put the planning of Commons business on to a firmer footing' by supporting a unified House Business Committee comprising representatives of all parts of the House (Kennon 2019).

Sources: BBC News (2019); Boulton (2019); Perkins (2019).

Box 7.2 A Commons coup or merely advice?

On 20 January 2019, *The Sunday Times* reported that the 'rebel MP' Dominic Grieve had been 'in secret communications with Colin Lee, the Clerk of Bills, with the explicit intention of suspending Britain's departure from the EU' (Shipman 2019). According to the report, the clerk drew up three versions of advice, each of which would overturn 'centuries of parliamentary precedent'. Apparently, the official was effectively overturning the normal rules of parliament. Brexiteers were appalled. However, according to the Commons Press Office (2019): 'It is common practice for Clerks to provide advice to members on the drafting of many items of Parliamentary business, such as bills, motions and amendments. This advice is done on a rigorously impartial basis.' And David Natzler, then Clerk of the House of Commons, subsequently called *The Sunday Times*'s 'insinuations' a 'gross misrepresentation of the nature of the relationship between Clerks and Members of Parliament' and called for a correction and apology (Natzler 2019a).

Having established a context for procedural reform, including the difficulties inherent in achieving it, I now present three dilemmas that highlight the case for change over continuity.

The dilemma of changing behaviours to meet public expectations

The Inter-Parliamentary Union's report *Parliament and Democracy in the Twenty-First Century* suggested that, for parliament, the key dialogue is one that runs through all policy and legislation debates—that is, how to shape the future by 'treating the past as a source for creative change rather than merely as an obstacle to progress' (Beetham 2006: 183). In these terms, I suggest, institutional change can no longer be path-dependent, slow, reluctant and incremental if parliament is to meet the expectations of society. Recent literature supports the contention that effective procedural management (again, using procedure in its broadest sense) requires an approach that goes beyond the goals of effective scrutiny and efficient government and includes issues of public interest, representation or 'ownership'. First, an academic–practitioner collaboration between Martyn Atkins (senior House of Commons committee clerk) and Mark Goodwin (from Birmingham University) claimed the processes of modernisation in the UK Parliament have generally been internal and directed much more at the relationship between parliament and government than towards the external environment in terms of adapting to societal change or sharing power more widely among citizens. They argued:

The endeavours of the Modernisation Committee, and subsequently the Wright Committee, have produced a fair amount of parliamentary reform, albeit with a limited scope, but only slow, reluctant and incremental modernization as that term would usually be understood outside the House: that is to say, a reflection of the norms of the society which Parliament is meant to serve. (Goodwin and Atkins 2018: 301)

Professor Meg Russell, Director of the UCL Constitution Unit, suggested that more innovative parliamentary procedures were required to break the Brexit deadlock and avoid 'procedural tricks' that risk undermining public legitimacy—a particularly pertinent observation given the controversial procedural decisions outlined above (Russell 2019b).

Goodwin and Atkins' 'societal norms' argument was also reflected in Sarah Childs' (2016) work on *The Good Parliament*, a report designed to achieve a more representative House of Commons, thereby enhancing the effectiveness and legitimacy of the House. To address the 'institutional deficiency' identified by Childs and the report's numerous recommendations, Speaker Bercow (himself a champion of encompassing societal norms) convened the Commons Reference Group on Representation and Inclusion to progress the report's recommendations, working collaboratively with other parliamentary bodies (UK Parliament 2018a).[26] As well as highlighting concerns about gender equality and representation, *The Good Parliament* traversed issues of behavioural and cultural reform, calling on the Speaker to secure cross-party support for a concord regarding 'unacceptable and unprofessional behaviour in the Chamber and more widely in the House' (Childs 2016: 11).

---

26   After a lengthy process involving the Speaker, the clerks and the Procedure Committee, and publicity surrounding voting difficulties for MPs on maternity leave, a pilot proxy voting or 'baby leave' scheme was agreed to by the House of Commons on 28 January 2019, with the first proxy vote cast on 29 January 2019 (see Childs 2019a). The debate included calls to extend proxy voting to other necessary absences (HC Debates 2019b). However, Childs also condemned a Commons decision to cancel the half-term break as 'going against' *The Good Parliament* report's recommendations on scheduling parliamentary business (Childs 2019b). Following the decision to extend the Brexit withdrawal date, Childs wrote of the serious implications of the Brexit debate for the institutionalisation of a diversity-sensitive House of Commons. She argued that much remains to be done in relation to working hours, 'masculinised' politics, representation and inclusion (Childs 2019c). In 2020, proxy voting was extended to include at-risk MPs who were shielding during the Covid-19 pandemic.

The Childs report and the reference group appear to have had a positive effect across the parliament,[27] but the Speaker's advocacy was overshadowed by a series of well-publicised allegations about bullying and harassment of Commons staff by some members, bringing to light a deep-seated culture that has survived many previous attempts at reform.[28] The allegations engulfed the House of Commons and the House of Lords and led to an independent inquiry by Dame Laura Cox (2018) and subsequent inquiries that have also had significant implications for parliamentary management in the United Kingdom.[29] From the perspective of this study, the bullying allegations have important ramifications for parliamentary management and public perceptions of the UK Parliament's performance. The Cox inquiry reported in October 2018 and was scathing about the ability of the House of Commons Commission to provide an effective response to the bullying allegations, and the media was swift to call for the head of Speaker Bercow.[30] The report highlighted a reactive management culture that was ill equipped, even disinclined, to adopt policies and procedures that were commonplace in other workplaces. As Cox concluded:

> This cycle of repeatedly reacting to crises only after they have developed into crises, and sometimes only after unwelcome publicity, is a perilous approach to adopt for any organisation, but it is completely hopeless for a place of work. And the House of Commons, for all its unusual features, is ultimately a place of work for everyone, including MPs, their staff, and all the House staff appointed by the Commission.

27 For example, the Women and Equalities Select Committee was permanently established in 2017 (Childs 2019d); the UK Gender-Sensitive Parliament Audit was published in November 2018 (UK Parliament 2018c), with the two house commissions publishing a combined response in June 2019 (UK Parliament 2019b); in 2018, the Fabian Society published proposals for a series of parliamentary reforms based on insights from new Labour members (Frith 2018); and the House of Commons debated making parliament a more modern, family-friendly and accessible workplace on 13 June 2019 (HC Debates 2019c).

28 See, in particular, the debate on sexual harassment in parliament (HC Debates 2017b); debate on the Independent Complaints and Grievance Policy (HC Debates 2018a, 2018b; R. Kelly 2021); BBC reports on bullying and harassment (Cook 2018; Cook and Day 2018); and the subsequent response to staff by the Clerk of the House of Commons (Natzler 2018).

29 In the House of Commons, an inquiry by Gemma White QC into historical claims of bullying and harassment was announced on 6 November 2018 following a resolution of the House; the House of Commons Commission agreed to the appointment of Alison Stanley on 28 January 2019 to review the first six months of operation of the ICGS (she reported on 31 May 2019); the House of Commons appointed an independent director for cultural change to set a 'transformation strategy'; the House of Lords Commission agreed to an independent inquiry into the workplace culture of the House of Lords and appointed Naomi Ellenbogen QC; a new House of Lords Conduct Committee including external members with full voting rights was proposed in April 2019 (for a full account, see R. Kelly 2021). An external management review of the House of Lords was conducted in 2020–21 (Leslie and Mohr 2021).

30 See, for instance, Elgot (2018); Maguire (2018); Pierce (2018).

The problems of bullying, harassment and sexual harassment in the workplace have been well documented and well understood for decades. The law reports bear testimony to the development of the jurisprudence in these areas, much of it the result of legislation by Parliament, the irony of which was not lost on many contributors to this inquiry. At common law a duty of care is owed to members of staff by those who employ them, to ensure their safety and dignity at work, and most employers have long had policies, procedures and training programmes in place to tackle this kind of behaviour. (Cox 2018: 25)

Cox (2018: 28) noted the HOCGC's references to 'complexities compounded by layers of interventions which have built on and adapted what went before rather than rationalising or restructuring it'.[31] She suggested that little had changed culturally since. Striking a chord with the research questions posed in Chapter 1, she noted tensions between the traditional approach of the 'guardians of the procedural' and those seeking to introduce a more 'corporate management culture' as well as tensions between a customer service approach, emphasising the needs of individuals and groups, and stewardship or protection of the wider good (Cox 2018: 29). Management remained occasional and hierarchical, with a 'calculated aloofness and a kind of sniffiness' at anything external—part of the template for sustaining the institution and concealing its problems. Cox declared that the doctrine of 'exclusive cognisance' had historically been interpreted too broadly by senior administrators to resist change and avoid external scrutiny, with a chilling effect, and that parliamentary privilege should not put a member's own conduct above the law.

The Ellenbogen inquiry into bullying and harassment in the House of Lords reported during the final stages of this study. Its findings had significant implications for the relationship between procedural and management expertise, as the extracted quotes from the report below highlight:

> 'All positions of power within the administration are filled by clerks and, as a consequence, clerks are favoured in every aspect …'

> 'I cannot overestimate the embeddedness of the culture that the clerk is supreme and everyone else is superfluous. Everything comes round to protect the clerk.'

---

31   Again, recalling Mahoney and Thelen's 'layering' approach (2010: 15–16; see Chapter 4, this volume).

'There is a snobbery around intellect and education. Most people who work here are incredibly bright—you just have to find and tap into it.'

'Nobody will challenge the clerks and they most definitely recruit in their own image.'

Outside the clerking structure, many senior employees considered that they were not viewed as being of equivalent rank, or importance to the organisation. (Ellenbogen 2019: 70–72)

In fact, Ellenbogen went beyond a narrow interpretation of the problems that pre-empted the inquiry to propose a radical restructure of the House of Lords administration:

[T]he knowledge and skill set required of an excellent clerk does not necessarily correlate with the knowledge and skill set required of an excellent Chief Executive Officer or Chief Operations Officer …

I recommend that, on the expiry of the Clerk of the Parliaments' current tenure (that is, with effect from 16 April 2020), a Director General of the House of Lords be appointed. That person should be able to demonstrate considerable experience and expertise in running other complex organisations, including in the private sector. He or she should have overarching responsibility for delivery of services to Members of the House and the public, serve as Accounting Officer and be the person to whom all staff in the Administration, including the Clerk of the Parliaments, should ultimately report. (The reporting structure adopted in the House of Commons, as between the Director General and the Clerk of the House, is, in my view, apt to create problematic and conflicting reporting lines and is over-reliant on the willingness of the particular incumbents of each role in order to work effectively. I do not recommend the adoption of that model in the House of Lords.) Under the system that I do recommend, clerks would retain their highly specialist, procedural roles, for which they are rightly respected, and would continue to have management responsibilities, but would have no special status as a group …

I recommend that no clerk should be eligible to apply for, or be appointed to, any one of the three most senior clerking posts, without first having spent a significant period of time working outside Parliament and the Civil Service, gaining fresh perspectives, expertise and experience. I make the same recommendation in relation to the most senior management posts elsewhere in the Administration. (Ellenbogen 2019: 124–25)

Despite the many good intentions revealed in the Childs report and accompanying efforts towards procedural and cultural change across both houses following the Cox and Ellenbogen reports, the lasting public impression is of a parliament unable to manage its culture. The impression is only amplified by the 2020–21 external management review of the House of Lords (Leslie and Mohr 2021).

No less significant, given later developments, were allegations of bullying, harassment, sexual misconduct and poor behaviour raised against members in the Australian Parliament. An independent investigation in 2018 into complaints against a female MP, Emma Husar, by her staff was conducted by barrister John Whelan, through the member's political party, and was not made public, although its findings were reported in the media.[32] The Barnaby Joyce affair[33] was seen as an example of poor judgement and a possible misuse of parliamentary entitlements[34] and did nothing to improve the reputation of parliamentarians. Neither, it seems, did the consequent knee-jerk amendments to the ministerial code of conduct— the 'bonking ban' (Murphy 2018a; Remeikis 2018a). A further example of poor workplace culture and behaviour was the claim by one of the Liberal Party's few women MPs, Julia Banks, that she had been harassed by her own colleagues during the Turnbull leadership challenge (Australia, House of Representatives 2018; Crowe 2018). Her decision to see out the rest of the parliamentary term as an Independent member cost the then new Morrison government its majority in parliament. At the same time, Banks took the opportunity to call out both parties on women's representation in parliament, the lack of an independent whistleblower system and a workplace culture 'years behind' the business world:

> Equal representation of men and women in this parliament is an urgent imperative which will create a culture change. There's the blinkered rejection of quotas and support of the merit myth, but this is more than a numbers game. Across both major parties, the level of regard and respect for women in politics is years behind the business world. There is also a clear need for an independent whistleblower system, as found in many workplaces, to enable reporting of misconduct of those in power without fear of reprisal or retribution. (Australia, House of Representatives 2018: 11571)

---

32   See, for instance, O'Malley (2018); Remeikis (2018b); Warhurst (2018).
33   In which the former deputy prime minister admitted to a long-term affair with a former staff member.
34   The Independent Parliamentary Expenses Authority subsequently found that Joyce's travel claims during the relevant period met the required legislative thresholds (IPEA 2018).

Accusations of unparliamentary behaviour in the Senate also led to a rare intervention by Senate President Ryan—described as 'a one-man operation against intensifying political insanity'—to curtail the use of senate procedures to facilitate 'unedifying' behaviour following Senator Matt O'Sullivan's offensive remarks and insinuations allegedly directed towards Senator Sarah Hanson-Young (Murphy 2018c; Australia, Senate 2018: 8775).[35] Staff working for MPs in Australia are employed by members or ministers on behalf of the Commonwealth under the *Members of Parliament (Staff) Act 1984*, on terms and conditions established in accordance with the *Fair Work Act 2009*, but these legislative provisions have not prevented cultural shortcomings in the parliamentary workplace, confusion about authority and practice and a shortage of management skills. O'Malley (2018) described the parliamentary workplace thus:

> There is one thing, though, that all staff agree upon. Parliamentary staff work in a terrible environment and have been failed not just by individual MPs, not just by political parties, and not just by the exhausting, needlessly adversarial nature of our political process, but also by Parliament itself. Even in the best of circumstances, Parliament House has a special way of making staffers miserable.

O'Malley reported on a former member and doctor, Mal Washer, who described Parliament House as a prison, exacerbated by high stress, intense competition and long working days. He claimed political staff and MPs had 'nowhere to go when things go wrong' and 'the parties are determined to hide any hint of scandal'. To most staff, it is not clear who the employer really is—the individual MP (as is the case in the United Kingdom) or the Department of Finance. Neither appears to take responsibility for staff wellbeing. The national parliament is isolated from the voters outside and the occupants are disconnected from each other (Murphy 2018d; Warhurst 2018). The then shadow leader of the House of Representatives (now prime minister), Anthony Albanese, pointed to features of the parliamentary building itself that contribute to members' loneliness and isolation and an intolerance of opposing views. Returning to the Husar allegations, a *Sydney Morning Herald* editorial (SMH 2018) laid primary responsibility at the feet of the senior ranks of her party, raising a further dichotomy between what constitutes party politics and what constitutes

---

35   Senate President Ryan also used the Turnbull leadership spill as a catalyst to float procedural reforms that would accord with the changing nature of the Senate's role, including adopting an Australian version of the Salisbury Convention in the House of Lords to secure a government's legislative mandate (Murphy 2018b).

parliamentary business. The unpublished Whelan report recommended the Ministerial and Parliamentary Services Branch of the Department of Finance review processes for resolving staff complaints, and there are continuing calls for a code of conduct for all MPs (Brien 1998; Senate Committee of Senators' Interests 2012; Ng 2018; AHRC 2021). These insights into cultural and behavioural issues are not new: there have been many previous calls for training and assistance for members (see Coghill et al. 2007, 2012; Lewis 2012) and a greater appreciation of what they do (Crewe 2010, 2015). Weinberg (2013) and Flinders et al. (2018b) call for greater scholarly attention to MPs' mental wellbeing and a study published in *The British Medical Journal* highlighted the growing incidence of mental health problems among MPs (Poulter et al. 2019).

Turning to public expectations of the Australian Parliament, on 26 November 2018, then Independent MP for Indi Cathy McGowan introduced the National Integrity Commission Bill 2018, accompanied by the National Integrity (Parliamentary Standards) Bill 2018, with the objective of promoting public trust and confidence in parliament and parliamentarians and ensuring their responsibilities reflected community expectations. Comparisons can be drawn with UK reforms—in particular, the establishment of the Committee on Standards in Public Life (the Nolan Committee), which led to a code of conduct for members and the creation of the Office of Parliamentary Commissioner for Standards (CSPL 2002). Under pressure, on 13 December 2018, the Morrison government finally announced its own version of a Commonwealth integrity commission (CIC), after dismissing the need for one as a fringe issue, but it was widely criticised for being limited in scope and power and without transparency (see, for instance, Coorey 2018). From a reading of the discussion paper issued by the Attorney-General's Department (2018), its proposals were not as encompassing as those included in the McGowan Bill, which aimed to 'boost public confidence in the … parliament by equipping it to prevent, manage and resolve *its own* integrity issues wherever possible' (McGowan 2018: 4; emphasis added). McGowan's proposal eschewed a culture of public naming and shaming, preferring to create a 'national culture of integrity, where the expectation is that "we [parliamentarians] be our best selves"' (p. 2). McGowan seized a window of opportunity (increased crossbench influence) and engaged constructively with the problem of public perception. Although her successor as an Independent member, Helen Haines, indicated that she would continue McGowan's advocacy and subsequently introduced the Australian Federal Integrity

Commission Bill 2020, as of December 2021, the government had not agreed to bring it on for debate nor had it introduced its own bill (Australia, House of Representatives 2021b). (The Albanese Labor Government introduced the *National Anti-Corruption Commission Bill 2022* on 28 September 2022.)

The aggressive nature of parliamentary relationships is fuelled by party politics, as we have seen from the broad-ranging Jenkins inquiry into the culture of Commonwealth parliamentary workplaces following allegations of a sexual assault in a minister's office and a subsequent alleged political coverup (AHRC 2021). Unfortunately, the public impression of parliamentary behaviour belies the extent of cooperation and collaboration behind the scenes, including in committee work, all-party groups and on national and parliamentary ceremonial occasions.

It is worth observing, in terms of minimising the differences between parliaments and other public organisations, that a culture that allows bullying and harassment and sanctions poor behaviour is not unique to the parliamentary institution; one has only to note the findings of investigations into other institutions.[36] This is not to absolve parliaments of their responsibility to stamp out such behaviour; rather, it is to draw attention to the opportunity for them to learn from the experiences of other non-parliamentary institutions and provide leadership in return. Arguably, for parliaments, a further challenge is that even if they do set up processes for overseeing workplace culture, an absence of authority or collective will for tackling problems may render them less than effective, as appears to be the case in both the United Kingdom and Australia. By taking a broad view of procedural change to include behaviour and culture, I have sought to establish that necessary reform goes beyond conserving traditions or concepts of exclusivity, independence and sovereignty. It also needs to balance the tensions between efficiency and effective scrutiny with meeting public expectations in an increasingly complex environment. Achieving an acceptable workplace culture does not come without significant effort and cost, as both parliaments have demonstrated.

---

36   See, for instance, the royal commission into misconduct in the banking industry (Hayne 2019); the House of Commons inquiry into sexual abuse in the aid sector (House of Commons International Development Committee 2018); and the Defence Abuse Response Taskforce (2016).

The dilemma of speaking or listening? How should our parliaments engage with the public?

Public engagement has become a key priority for many institutions and parliament is no exception (Leston-Bandeira and Walker 2018). In this respect, the UK Parliament seems to be more adventurous than its Australian counterpart. It is difficult to measure the effectiveness of public engagement outputs and one could argue that the higher level of activity in the United Kingdom is driven by a poorer public perception of democracy, but this assumption is not borne out by the evidence. According to a global survey conducted by the Pew Research Center (Wike et al. 2017), only 52 per cent of people in the United Kingdom were satisfied with the way democracy was working; for Australia, the figure was slightly higher at 58 per cent. However, the *Trust and democracy in Australia* report, compiled by the Museum of Australian Democracy (MoAD) and the University of Canberra (Stoker et al. 2018), found that satisfaction with how democracy works in Australia had fallen from 71 per cent in 2013 to 41 per cent, suggesting a much starker picture comparatively. This report also canvassed citizen satisfaction with political institutions; unfortunately, it did not include parliament itself as a political institution, thus making it more difficult to measure the Australian Parliament's public standing. Similar concerns with democracy in Australia have been identified by the Lowy Institute (Oliver 2018; Kassam 2019)[37] and the Australian Election Study (Cameron and McAllister 2016).

The Hansard Society monitors perceptions and knowledge of the UK Parliament in its annual audits of political engagement (2017, 2018, 2019). Its 2017 audit found that satisfaction with parliament was on a shallow downward trajectory; in 2017, only 30 per cent of people were at least 'fairly satisfied' with the way parliament worked. Seventy-three per cent felt that parliament was essential to democracy and consistent support, averaging 88 per cent, was shown for the importance of its core functions; however, only 33 per cent felt that parliament had done a good job in carrying them out (Hansard Society 2017: 27–30). In 2018, it found

---

37   The Lowy Institute 2018 poll found a surprising ambivalence about democracy as a system of government. However, its 2019 poll, which posed a different question, found that 70 per cent of respondents were satisfied with the way democracy worked, which was similar to the MoAD 2013 result.

that although knowledge of parliament and politics had risen over the life of the audit (since 2004), most people remained political bystanders rather than active citizens and 'too often, the political reform agenda had been driven not by constitutional principle but by the requirements of party or media management'. It called for a 'comprehensive examination of electoral and constitutional arrangements, and the culture and practice of politics' (Hansard Society 2018: 11). Alarmingly for advocates of democracy, the 2019 audit found that 42 per cent of respondents thought the government could deal with the United Kingdom's problems more effectively if it did not have to worry about votes in parliament. In an interesting twist, the National Centre for Social Research in its latest survey of British political attitudes found that claims the Brexit stalemate would stimulate disenchantment among voters and discourage them from political involvement could be overdrawn. Although there were signs that trust and confidence in how the country was being governed fell to a record low, it appears the Brexit debate has increased voters' interest in politics rather than fostered disengagement (Curtice et al. 2020). The implications of this finding for public understanding of and engagement with parliament remain unclear.

There are also numerous reports and studies on enhancing public engagement, such as those published by the Hansard Society, the Australasian Study of Parliament Group and parliamentary committees. Significant among these was the 2005 Puttnam Commission (Hansard Society 2005), which found that the UK Parliament had consistently failed to present itself as the sum of its parts and stay abreast of developments and opportunities. It cautioned that the level of 'informed, transparent and engaged democracy' that citizens had come to expect was comparatively expensive but 'cut-price democracy will never represent much of a bargain' (Hansard Society 2005: vii). The House of Representatives Standing Committee on Procedure (1999), inquiring into community involvement, also recommended more resources for engagement as well as greater power to self-refer and greater media coverage for committees, but it received a negative response from the government. Interviewees in both parliaments highlighted difficulties in managing public engagement activities, both in prioritising expenditure and in evaluating its effectiveness.[38] The dilemma here, even if a consensus can be reached on resourcing parliamentary

38   C. Surtees, pers. comm., 6 June 2017; R. Laing, pers. comm., 7 September 2017; I. Ailles, pers. comm., 9 May 2016; P. Young, pers. comm., 9 June 2016.

communications, is the consistent evidence that citizens are turning their backs on democratic engagement while appearing to agree that democracy is important. According to Stoker et al. (2018), they are challenging the allegiant model of democratic culture, with its features of deference and trust, while valuing stability in the political system. But they are not turning to new and more critical forms of participation as envisaged by an assertive model; rather, they are reflecting a culture of disengagement, cynicism and divergence from political elites. Indeed, as we have seen in the United Kingdom, a significant proportion of voters have suggested that democracy is now becoming less important. We have already noted the public's tendency to conflate parliament, politicians and government, and this further complicates any evaluation of the effectiveness of a parliament's public engagement activities. Effective public engagement appears to be a 'wicked' or intractable problem (Rittel and Webber 1973; Head and Alford 2015).[39] Parliamentary actors see themselves as promoters and preservers of democracy while remaining divided about how best to exercise their roles and evaluate their effectiveness. Meanwhile, members of the public appear to be increasingly disparaging about parliamentary effectiveness and display little interest in understanding how parliament works within the democratic system, even if they are at times stimulated by the political process.

Communications professionals Weerasinghe and Ramshaw (2018) claim that diffuse lines of authority make parliamentary communications a more challenging prospect than political communication generally; the messages communicated by impartial officials on behalf of parliamentary institutions must balance the competing narratives and priorities of all members. Again, officials emphasise the differences between parliament and other public activities. However, a reading of a major report on government communications with citizens worldwide (WPP Government & Public Sector Practice 2019) suggests the challenges are equally daunting, including increasingly fragmented audiences, an overreliance on one-way 'broadcast' communication and a lack of communication and influencing skills.

---

39   Rittel and Webber (1973) describe wicked problems as 'planning problems' that are neither tame nor benign, are not definable and separable and do not have findable solutions. They rely on elusive political judgement for resolution. (Head and Alford 2015: 733) propose new strategies to partially resolve wicked policy problems through shared understandings of their nature. They argue that these must 'coexist with "business as usual" obligations and call for broad managerial capabilities'.

Public engagement, or outreach, has multiple dimensions and this book cannot provide an in-depth analysis of its development over time. The UK and Australian parliaments do play a valuable public education role, particularly in activities directed at young people, and information about these activities can be readily found on each parliament's website. In this account, I discuss three types of engagement: the institutional representation of parliament and its work to the public, encouraging public participation and facilitating members' individual constituency roles. Acknowledging Head and Alford's (2015) approach, I argue that these are all functions that require a public management approach (rather than a routine or procedural one) with an emphasis on collaboration across organisational structures.

Institutional representation of parliament to the public

Judge and Leston-Bandeira (2018: 155) cite the growing significance of institutional representation when 'basic assumptions about the legitimacy of parliamentary institutions come under sustained critical questioning'. They point to evidence showing that the public does not view politicians as parliamentarians and that parliament itself struggles with its identity as a holistic institution (see also Kelso 2007b; Leston-Bandeira 2014; Walker 2019). Members do not as a rule engage in institutional representation and this role falls to presiding officers and, increasingly, to non-elected parliamentary officials (Judge and Leston-Bandeira 2018). This 'hollowing out' of parliament's institutional representation is compounded by political leaders (amplified by the media) seeking to gain an electoral advantage by referring to the Westminster or Canberra 'bubble' (Cadwalladr 2016; Cowley 2015; Hayne 2018)—a less than constructive representation of their respective institutions that does nothing to enhance their reputations. Leston-Bandeira confirmed her views on institutional representation in our interview:

> [T]here is, increasingly, a role for officials to be that public face, almost like defending an institution, or at least presenting an institution. I usually call clerks and officials the guardian angels of parliament because they're very much about trying to show what the institution is for, despite all the politics. The fact that they were not doing that role explicitly for a long time didn't really matter, because politics wasn't so antagonised, and you got on with things, even if you didn't like a particular party or a particular

government. But as politics has become so corrosive, what's left is just the bones of it, the structures, and that's the institution. It's almost like a reminder: why do we have this system? And it's because we can't have 60 million people making the decisions all the time. We need representatives to do that.[40]

The question of parliamentary representation and overcoming the 'trust gap' is complicated at the outset by diffused authority, competing messages and internal disengagement by MPs from their *collective* institutional representational role even if they are committed to representing their *individual* constituents. The role falls, as Judge and Leston-Bandeira (2018) suggest, to presiding officers and officials, but not without controversy.

Reformist Speaker Bercow set up the Digital Democracy Commission with the aim, among other things, of counteracting the alienating jargon and practices of the House and taking a constructive approach to ameliorating the insularity of parliament. He saw the weight of information about politics acting as a wall, 'keeping the citizen out of the mysterious world of Westminster' (DDC 2015). Williamson and Fallon (2011: 790) researched the influence of technology on parliaments' internal processes and relationships with the public in the United Kingdom, Canada, Chile and Australia, finding that 'going digital' allowed parliaments to escape from traditional practices, supplement archaic language with accessible information and provide better tools for members to understand the legislative process. Both the UK and the Australian parliaments have published digital strategies, but they reflect different emphases. The UK Parliament appears to recognise the potential for digital technology to transform the way parliament works; it includes a culture of collaboration and openness in its guiding principles. The Australian Parliament appears to privilege more technical outcomes; its principles include a focus on user experience and partnership with other parliamentary departments (Parliament of Australia 2019; UK Parliament 2019a).

There are pitfalls to greater public engagement, notwithstanding digital innovation. A major impediment is resourcing and, even if we agree with Puttnam that cut-price democracy is not the answer, the public appears to have little appetite for more spending by parliaments, as is evidenced by the debate over the restoration and renewal of the Palace of Westminster

---

40   C. Leston-Bandeira, pers. comm., 10 September 2018.

(Flinders et al. 2019). Another factor, reported by the Hansard Society (2018), is that digital and online technologies are still far from overtaking traditional sources of information and almost half of respondents to its annual audit thought social media made political debate more divisive or superficial. Weerasinghe and Ramshaw (2018) argued that the public is simply not interested in engaging with parliament or being involved in decision-making. Flinders et al. (2018b: 258) argued that efforts to open parliament to the public may have made its members even 'more vulnerable to popular cynicism, a disinterested and hyper-critical commercial media, and the immediacy of snap online reprimands'. Nevertheless, not to engage with the public would be a false economy that could further threaten confidence in parliament. The pitfalls of public engagement should not diminish its value, including efforts in both parliaments to promote their parliamentary buildings as representative democratic symbols by improving visitor access and experiences and even providing opportunities for reshaping politics (Flinders et al. 2019). But as we saw in Chapter 6, there are internal dilemmas in both parliaments about the priority accorded to these activities by different actors.[41]

Participatory approaches to engagement

I turn now to the second public engagement challenge I have identified. In a comprehensive House of Commons Library Briefing Paper, Uberoi (2017) noted the growth of public engagement activities in response to declining trust and political engagement.[42] The paper drew attention to calls for change, from traditional forms of engagement to a more participatory approach—in other words, from 'representational' or 'speaking' to 'participatory' or 'listening'. But this change also has its challenges. According to Kelso (2007b), it is not clear whether parliament really *wants* to foster participation as a new form of political involvement; it was never an intrinsically democratic institution; neither, as I have noted, is either parliament a united institution with a corporate identity.[43]

---

41   The Australian Parliament's structural arrangements whereby 'management' functions are separated from 'procedural' functions appear to work against a collaborative approach to public engagement in all its forms. In the United Kingdom, the restoration and renewal debate has exposed a reluctance to confront public cynicism and seize new opportunities (HC Debates 2017a; see also House of Commons Modernisation Committee 2004).
42   This paper provides a publicly accessible and very useful overview of the evolution of the public engagement function in the UK Parliament, highlighting recent innovations and current activities.
43   See also Walker (2019).

Parliamentary committees are increasingly viewed as a key component of parliamentary activity, not only for holding the executive to account—sometimes in adversarial and partisan forums—but also in allowing wider input to policy development. We can look to this area for new approaches to improving public participation and increasing parliamentary effectiveness. Writing about the Australian Parliament in the twenty-first century, Halligan et al. (2007) provided an in-depth analysis of the policy roles of committees—scrutiny, legislative appraisal, review and strategic investigation—and cited public interaction and communication as a further responsibility. They concluded that the most important effect of decades of growth in parliamentary committee work was the opportunity it offered for broader participation in policy development. They suggested 'outside engagement may come to be of the highest significance for the functioning of the parliament as the leading institution of representative democracy in Australia' (Halligan et al. 2007: 238). Marsh and Miller (2012), Marsh (2016), Forkert (2017), Gaines et al. (2019) and Hendriks and Kay (2019) acknowledged the role parliamentary committees can play in democratic renewal and citizen participation in the political system. The current and potential roles of committees in enhancing parliamentary effectiveness have until recently been understudied, particularly in Australia (Russell and Benton 2011; Marsh and Halpin 2015). The impact of parliamentary policy is also 'notoriously difficult to assess, as it can take many forms, some of which are largely invisible' (Russell and Benton 2011: 7).

A comprehensive comparison of the work of committees in both houses of the UK and Australian parliaments and their influence on policy debate and outcomes was beyond the scope of this study, but it is apparent the UK Parliament has advanced further and more reflexively in developing ways to increase the influence of committees on parliamentary effectiveness and policy outcomes, and the committee structure itself is more conducive to achieving greater influence.[44] For example, House of Commons select committees decide their own topics of inquiry and most undertake a mix of inquiries into ongoing government actions and those that are likely to be 'agenda-setting'. Following recommendations from the Wright Committee on House of Commons reform, most select committee chairs are elected (on a party proportional basis) by a secret

44   For further insights into committee influence and effectiveness in both parliaments, see Halligan et al. (2007); Hindmoor et al. (2009); Monk (2009a, 2009b); Russell and Benton (2011); Marsh and Halpin (2015); White (2015); Hendriks et al. (2019).

199

ballot of all members, with committee members then elected by secret ballot within their parties (Russell and Benton 2011).[45] Committees themselves seem more willing to evaluate their own effectiveness. While acknowledging the risk of drawing subjective conclusions, Russell and Benton found that House of Commons select committees were taken seriously by government and 'have become an established and respected part of the system'. Nevertheless, they noted that factors such as poor follow-through on recommendations, a lack of original research, poor attendance by members and a lack of focus all contributed to the ongoing problem of committee work *not* being taken seriously enough.

In the foreword to a 2015 Institute of Government study into the impact of parliamentary committee inquiries on government, Tony Wright, former chair of the House of Commons Reform Committee, pointed to systemic problems with the organisation and leadership of House of Commons select committees. He articulated what might be achieved

> if the select committee system set about the task of making itself as effective as it might be. Committees are not good at evaluating what they do and working out how they might do things better. They are often unclear about the outcomes they want to achieve and the sort of impact they want to make. There is a difference between making a headline and making an impact. An individual committee may not work collectively enough to maximise its effectiveness; and committees may be more concerned with protecting their own territory than exploring how they might work together … There is also an issue about the leadership and organisation of the select committee system as a whole, with the capacity to drive improvement and performance … [C]ommittees are good at asking questions of others, but they need to be as good at asking questions of themselves. (Wright, in White 2015: i)

Like Russell and Benton, White's study found an absence of feedback processes and she also noted a tendency for committees to operate in silos, suggesting that committee chairs should work together to drive crosscutting work by actively identifying emerging issues within the remit of several committees.

---

45   See Hansard Society (2021) for an updated guide on how select committees operate.

Lately, however, in the United Kingdom, the focus on committee influence has shifted to public input. Russell and Cowley (2016) pointed to evidence-taking by select committees as an important means of parliamentary engagement with pressure groups and bureaucrats. Rogers and Walters (2015) highlight the 'delayed drop' effect of select committee reports, which can change the nature of public debate. Leston-Bandeira and Thompson (2017) noted calls to integrate public participation directly into parliament's processes and highlighted the potential of mechanisms such as the public reading stage of a bill to incorporate alternative viewpoints. Former House of Commons select committee chairs Clive Betts and Sarah Wollaston used a citizens' assembly to find consensus within their committees (Health and Social Care and Housing, Communities and Local Government) for the long-term funding of adult social care (Betts and Wollaston 2018).[46] Gaines et al. (2019) suggest the United Kingdom's select committees may be increasingly useful in mobilising public opinion.

In 2019, commemorating 40 years in operation of the departmental select committee system in the United Kingdom, the House of Commons Liaison Committee inquired into the effectiveness and influence of the select committee system.[47] It agreed with Professor Leston-Bandeira's evidence that the assumption behind 'making work accessible to the parliament', created in 2012 as a core public engagement task for committees, implied a broadcasting mode designed to inform the public about parliament's work. Instead, Leston-Bandeira submitted, public engagement is also about listening to the public and reflecting the public view in parliamentary business. The committee devoted a chapter of its report to public engagement and the need 'to listen to those with lived experience'. It made a number of suggestions for improving current public engagement practice, including taking a more strategic or purposeful approach, increasing accessibility, monitoring and recording engagement practice across committees, consistently presenting information obtained through public engagement in committee reports, providing feedback to participants and facilitating dialogue through the use of digital tools.

---

46 Following its success, the Climate Assembly UK was commissioned by six House of Commons select committees to examine how the country should meet its target of net zero greenhouse gas emissions by 2050. The assembly met for six weekends between January and May 2020 and produced a comprehensive report in September 2020 (Climate Assembly UK 2020).
47 See also *Parliamentary Affairs* (vol. 72, no. 4, 2019), devoted to the effectiveness of select committees—in particular, Beswick and Elstub (2019) and Walker et al. (2019) on participation and engagement.

It noted, too, the success of the abovementioned Citizens' Assembly on Social Care, while acknowledging that public engagement of this type is resource intensive and would require further consideration by the House. Perhaps of greatest relevance to the themes contained within this book were the committee's recommendations targeted at gaining access to a diverse range of research information, as reflected in the chapter's concluding comments:

> The impact that committees have is crucially dependent on the information and evidence that they have access to. We must continue to widen and diversify the range of voices we hear from, and we should listen carefully to those who have a professional commitment to impartiality. Our conclusions and recommendations would benefit from access to the rich body of knowledge held by the academic and third sectors and membership bodies, as well as those with lived experience. We must endeavour to create the conditions which enable us to have access to the best research evidence available. We must be flexible and imaginative in tailoring the style and pace of our interactions to those we are communicating with. We must welcome and encourage those who might not otherwise be heard to come forward. The wider the range of voices we hear, the more effective and influential our findings are likely to be. And the more we work in partnership with others, the more likely we are to be heard. (HCLC 2019: 67–68)

As with most factors related to committee effectiveness, it will take time to determine the success of these public participation initiatives.

The Australian Parliament appears not to have benefited from similar comprehensive and collaborative evaluations of its committee systems since the analysis provided by Halligan et al. (2007). Monk (2009a) offered a framework based on surveys of stakeholders followed by a statistical analysis of government responses to committee reports (Monk 2009b). In 2010, the House of Representatives Standing Committee on Procedure recommended additional resources and greater use of emerging digital technologies to enhance parliament's relationship with the public. It received a lukewarm government response in 2015, which noted that a review by parliamentary departments was under way. Marsh and Halpin (2015) quantified participation in parliamentary committee work based on committee activity in senate committees between 2010 and 2012, finding that most hearings attracted very little interest and evidence-giving could be considered a one-way attempt by pressure groups to exercise influence. They concluded that a comprehensive assessment was overdue and asked whether committees could 'occupy a more prominent role in outreach or more inclusive policy analysis and development' (Marsh and Halpin 2015: 147).

Hendriks et al. (2019) also noted that specific empirical studies of public engagement in parliamentary studies are rare. Their assessment of participatory adaptation in contemporary parliamentary committees in Australia is therefore illuminating. Although their study included insights from the committee systems within six Australian parliaments, and not just the federal parliament, the findings can be related to all. While some committees were found to be adapting conventional public engagement practices, changes were modest, variable, cautious and ad hoc. Four main types of adaptation included new ways to promote and publicise committee work, managing public input through digital interfaces, increasing accessibility to affected publics and building participatory capacity. Drivers of adaptation included changing public expectations and preferences, increased complexity of issues and the changing roles of politicians and political parties. Barriers included a lack of resources, participation disinterest, fatigue or lack of knowledge of parliamentary procedures, including privilege issues.

Hendriks et al. (2019) found inter alia that adaptation was rarely the result of strategic initiatives in Australian parliaments. Arguably, this makes it unlikely that committees will take on the task of 'agenda-setting' or 'strategic review' in response to a weakened advocacy of policy agendas by political parties. Nor does it suggest they will respond proactively to an increased citizen preference to engage in politics via specific issues about which they care. In this respect, the UK Parliament certainly appears to be ahead, particularly in the willingness of committees to work collaboratively with each other and with outside bodies, including charities, on initiatives such as establishing citizens' assemblies to advise on key policy issues. We should note also that committees in the House of Representatives and the Senate require references from their respective houses and are not able to self-identify and inquire into contemporary policy issues as are House of Commons select committees. This factor may also act as a barrier to increasing public participation through committees. It may require other forms of deliberative democracy or alternative spaces for reflection and listening, particularly in an era when a plethora of communication means can fragment and distort debate (Ercan et al. 2019).[48]

A study by Hendriks and Kay (2019) also presented a strong case for public engagement to play a more central role in the deliberative work of parliaments, especially through committees, and argued for more inclusive forms of engagement. They, too, suggested different approaches to engaging with the public, such as providing new spaces for engagement, integrating citizen deliberation, connecting with informal public activities and actively seeking out places where communities might gather to engage with them on their own terms, while noting that this would require new skills, revised procedures and greater resources. More fundamentally, it would require a cultural shift in how members see their roles in representative democracy; no longer could parliament justify its existence by 'presenting a window to the public, allowing citizens to peer in as spectators whilst its practices remain steadfastly unchanged' (Hendriks and Kay 2019: 43); no longer could committee members resort to standard partisan politics, blame games and media management.

Public input to the task of making the parliament and its members function more effectively is rare. Public attention to parliament usually follows a crisis in governance, as demonstrated by the expenses/entitlements and bullying/harassment scandals outlined earlier, and media exposure of alleged administrative shortcomings. Consequently, public reaction tends to be exceptionally critical—of the 'a plague a'both your houses'[49] variety—perpetuating the myths surrounding the parliamentary decline thesis (Flinders and Kelso 2011).[50] Poor public perceptions of parliamentary effectiveness will not disappear easily. As the 2019 audit by the Hansard Society (2019) revealed, amid great concern, such perceptions increase the potential for citizens to shun parliament, with consequential implications for the future of representative democracy (Fox and Blackwell 2019).

---

48 Note also Dryzek's sponsorship of the Citizens' Parliament, which assembled in Old Parliament House, Canberra (Dryzek 2009).

49 See Mercutio in Shakespeare's *Romeo and Juliet*, available from: www.enotes.com/shakespeare-quotes/plague-o-both-your-houses.

50 Flinders and Kelso (2011) address the problem of closing the expectations gap between what the public expects parliament to deliver and what it can realistically deliver given its resources and the prevailing socioeconomic conditions. They argue that parliamentary scholars have a public duty to correct rather than propagate the myths that surround their chosen subject matter.

Practitioners and academics in the United Kingdom have at least tried to grasp the nettle in terms of exploring new ways of engaging with the public, including through narratives and storytelling (Prior 2018). David Clark, head of the UK Parliament's outreach program, said:

> You can't talk about parliament in just a procedural, factual way because it is an emotional thing that people need to interact with. And that's when people get excited about it. You need to help them connect with parliament on an emotional level, otherwise they will never get it.[51]

Penny Young, House of Commons Librarian and Director-General of Information Services, claimed to spend much of her time telling stories with data:

> We don't really produce our content for a time-poor, mobile audience of members ... [We are] encouraging people not to lose quality, not to lose relevance, not to lose impartiality but to be hugely more accessible ... [I]t's about being more compelling in the way we write.[52]

Both parliaments and their members invest in traditional forms of engagement, including school visits, visits by members to constituency events, petitioning and, lately, e-petitioning. When interviewed, the presiding officers emphasised their public representational roles. In comparative terms, the UK Parliament directs more resources towards encouraging academics and the public to contribute to and engage with its work; the Australian Parliament's activities are focused more on explaining what it does. Table 7.2 provides examples of public engagement activities in each parliament. On the face of it, the activities are broadly similar but differences in emphasis are noticeable.

---

51 D. Clark, pers. comm., 3 June 2016.
52 P. Young, pers. comm., 9 June 2016.

Table 7.2 Examples of public engagement activities in each parliament

Type of engagement	Australian Parliament	UK Parliament
Institutional	**Website:** www.aph.gov. au (5.2 million visits in 2016–17); separate social media accounts, wide variety of information, live streaming of proceedings, search facilities.	**Website:** www.parliament.uk (15 million visits in 2016–17), invites followers to engage on numerous social media sites, including @UK ParlEducation, *Parliament Explained* podcast, wide variety of information, live streaming of proceedings, search facilities, House of Lords 'digital chamber'.
	Ceremonial activities, including Welcome to Country at opening of parliament.	**Ceremonial activities,** including State procession and opening of parliament.
	Parliamentary Education Office: Publishes resources for schools and facilitates school visits.	**UK Parliament Education:** Publishes resources for schools and facilitates school visits and tours, teacher training, in-class workshops.
	Museum of Australian Democracy: Parallel organisation promoting democracy, housed in Old Parliament House.	**Education Centre:** Workshops, immersive technology.
	Senate/House of Representatives: Fee-paying seminars for graduates and public servants on work in respective houses; annual lectures; publications and briefing notes; Senate and House practice.	*How parliament works* (Rogers and Walters 2015) joint publication in 'straightforward language' designed for public consumption, including by journalists, civil servants, academics and researchers.
Participatory and outreach	**Public petitions:** Presented in respective chamber, printed in *Hansard*, may receive response.	**Public petitions:** Presented in respective chamber, prescribed number of signatories guarantees response or opportunity for debate.
	Parliamentary Education Office: Interactive website for schools, school visits.	**Education Centre:** Immersive technology, themed learning spaces.
		Massive open online courses, including introduction to parliament.
	Senate occasional public lectures: On topics of current interest.	**Parliamentary Office of Science and Technology:** Seminars and events for parliamentarians and public.
		Public talks and events

Type of engagement	Australian Parliament	UK Parliament
	Parliament House: Visits, tours, exhibitions and events.	**Houses of Parliament:** Visits, tours, exhibitions and events.
	Parliamentary Library: Some research briefings, blogs, periodic fellowship program and summer scholarship award.	**House of Commons Research and Information team:** Services to members and public research briefings. **Participation team:** Includes bicameral public outreach, engagement and education, public information and resources.
	Members of parliament: Meeting individual constituents and visiting local organisations. Speaker and president external visits (no comparable statistics).	**Members of parliament:** Meeting individual constituents and visiting local organisations. Speaker and Lord Speaker (900 external engagements in 2016, with 46,000 participants).
	Joint Reconciliation Action Plan: Also Parliamentary Service Indigenous Employee Network.	**Black and ethnic minorities (BAME):** Targeted in engagement activities. **Equality networks:** ParliAble, Parligender, ParliREACH, ParliOUT.
	Committees: Taking public evidence; focus on explaining committee experience and procedure.	**Committees:** Taking public evidence; focus on encouraging involvement from public and academics, reporting on witness diversity.
	Engagement with external (non-parliamentary) organisations: ABC documentary; Australasian Study of Parliament Group.	**Engagement with external (non-parliamentary) organisations:** Including Hansard Society, Institute for Government, UCL Constitution Unit, BBC documentaries, Study of Parliament Group. 'Your story, our history' partnerships in films showing legislative impacts on people's lives. Academic/practitioner publications — for example, *Exploring parliament* (Leston-Bandeira and Thompson 2018).
	Parliamentary Law Practice and Procedure course: For practitioners only, delivered through a contracted university.	**Parliamentary Studies module:** Delivered through more than 20 universities.

Type of engagement	Australian Parliament	UK Parliament
	Graduate placements	**Policy internships:** Parliamentary Office of Science and Technology.
		Apprenticeships and placements: Multiple, including Speaker's scheme for those from disadvantaged backgrounds and House of Lords apprenticeships.
		Academic research: Encourages specialist academic research within research excellence framework; offers a range of academic fellowships.
	Media communications: Individual departments and committees.	**Media communications:** House of Lords Press Office promotes work of House and committees and handles media inquiries.
		House of Commons Media Relations Team handles procedural and corporate inquiries.

Sources: For Australia, Australian Parliament website (www.aph.gov.au); for United Kingdom, parliament website (www.parliament.uk); Uberoi (2017).

The increasing efforts at public participation in the UK Parliament do not appear to require a constant injection of additional resources, according to the former clerk of the House of Commons. Most 'fresh' money is now going to the digital service, which is where it is most needed, to stay up to date and make the parliament transparent and accessible—a 'deliberate strategic decision'.[53] The UK Parliament also appears to be more open than its Australian counterpart to working with third parties, including universities, in its promotional activities, and there is greater academic input into the public engagement space (Leston-Bandeira and Thompson 2018; Kelly and Bochel 2018; Prior 2018; Asher et al. 2019). However, recent discussions with some interviewees have suggested the focus on public engagement may be waning.

Conversely, a report into Australia's cultural institutions by the Joint Standing Committee on the National Capital and External Territories (JSCNCET 2019: viii) expressed concern that 'relevant institutions

---

53 D. Natzler, pers. comm., 12 September 2018. It appears these activities are driven by a coherent reform agenda, drawing on political (and official) will, meeting Norton's second and third conditions of parliamentary reform (Norton 2000).

may not be presenting a shared and consistent vision about Australian democracy, nor is there a clear delineation of the programs and activities conducted'. It recommended, inter alia, that the Parliamentary Education Office's student programs be made accessible to the general public, not just schoolchildren, and the functions of the MoAD, the National Electoral Education Centre and the visitor and education services at Parliament House be more closely aligned, or even brought under the auspices of the presiding officers, with Old Parliament House becoming a 'working extension of Parliament House ... in relation to educational, support and visitor services' (JSCNCET 2019: 59). The committee clearly believed there is an opportunity for greater collaboration and resource efficiency, even if the functions are presently fiercely protected by their administrators. The report was critical of the MoAD,[54] suggesting a disconnect between MoAD's strategic role and its public engagement direction (JSCNCET 2019: viii–ix). As I noted earlier, MoAD appears to have sidelined parliament altogether in its regular surveys of trust in Australia's democratic institutions. The JSCNCET's recommendations contain elements of a coherent reform agenda; they await a government response.

The 2022 global report of the Inter-Parliamentary Union and UN Development Programme could not be more persuasive about the benefits of public engagement to parliaments, parliamentarians and the wider community, validating many of the points raised above. For example, it confirms a growing reliance by parliaments on digital tools; suggests that listening, and not just informing, is an essential element of engagement; highlights difficulties in overcoming a 'blizzard of information'; and urges greater attention by parliaments to the growing public demand to influence decision-making. The report predicts that the attention by incumbent governments to key public demands has the potential to emerge as a key element of parliamentary scrutiny. It would be disappointing if current efforts to achieve effective engagement, especially in the UK Parliament, were allowed to regress through a lack of commitment or ambition, or under the cover of insufficient resources.

---

54 A corporate Commonwealth entity under the *PGPA Act*, accountable to the Minister for the Arts.

Members' engagement with constituents

Finally, in terms of public engagement, I turn to the relationship between members and their constituents. Much has been written about members' constituency roles, and this book does not provide a comprehensive account (but see Norton and Wood 1993; Rush and Giddings 2011; Lewis 2012). It is here that one might have the most sympathy for MPs when contemplating increasing workload pressures and threats to their physical security from the rapid expansion of social media and voters' rising, often divisive, expectations of their representatives.[55] Paul Beresford, Chair of the House of Commons Administration Committee, spoke of the need to protect members from difficult constituents and incidents in their constituency offices or elsewhere.[56] One member of the House of Commons Commission raised the inherent problem of an overly critical focus on members' expenditure. For example, although supportive of the level of transparency provided by the Independent Parliamentary Standards Authority, he remarked that he had not made a mileage claim since its establishment:

> because if you do actually put up a mileage claim, you're likely to have someone going around with a tape measure and checking whether what you claimed [to be] the distance between A and B wasn't 100 yards longer than was actually the case.[57]

Lindsay Tanner, a former Australian MP, bemoaned the changes to politicians' behaviour occasioned by relentless trivialisation in the media of complex social and economic issues (Tanner 2012). Speaker Bercow, shortly after his election to the speakership (and the expenses scandal), declared it a 'cruel paradox that at a time when MPs have never worked harder, their standing has rarely been lower' (UK Parliament 2009). As I have noted from numerous sources, MPs are not particularly interested in administrative or even procedural management and reform, and nor, it appears, are their constituents. This proposition is borne out by Campbell and Lovenduski (2014), who researched the views of MPs and those who

---

55   In 2016, Jo Cox was murdered outside her constituency office (HC Debates 2016) and the murder of Sir David Amess in a constituency surgery in 2021 led to a further review of security arrangements for MPs (Booth 2021). Members of the UK Parliament were subject to horrific verbal abuse, bordering on assault, for expressing views including in the ongoing Brexit debate (see HC Debates 2016, 2017c; Johnston and Dempsey 2017; Sylvester and Thomson 2019). For an Australian example, see Molloy (2019).

56   P. Beresford, pers. comm., 2 June 2016.

57   House of Commons Commission member, pers. comm., 8 June 2016.

voted for them as to the most important MP roles. A large and similar percentage of MPs and voters (65.4 and 54.9 per cent, respectively) reported that the most important role for an MP was as a local advocate, 'taking up and responding to issues and problems raised by constituents' rather than contributing to legislation and taking part in parliamentary debates (Campbell and Lovenduski 2014: 700). Voters' interest in politics and their social status had no significant impact on their preference for their MP to focus on local or national work, challenging assumptions that people more engaged with the political process will place a higher value on national policy work (and, presumably, representing the parliamentary institution). MPs are, in effect, social workers. Members of the House of Representatives in Australia also ranked their constituency priority highly in a study by Heitshusen et al. (2005), although the priorities varied depending on their length of service, the safety of their electorate and travel times. As my interviews with UK Parliament members Beresford and Brake revealed, constituents' expectations of their MPs are not matched by their perceptions of the levels of financial support and resources received by MPs—further evidence of an expectations gap in terms of parliamentary effectiveness (Flinders and Kelso 2011). Stringent rules about members' use of resources are changing the way they perform their constituency role, notwithstanding increasing demands. Lawrence McKay (2018), from the University of Manchester, summed up the dilemma when he outlined his concerns about the current state of constituency communications:

> The stringent limits placed on permissible communications outlawed staples of communication such as the newsletter. MPs may also use their resources too sparingly, given that, since the expenses scandal, they understand every penny is under media and IPSA scrutiny. Meanwhile, the precipitous decline of local media may cut MPs off more and more. While social media may point to a bright future, its limits as a tool for constituent communications have been repeatedly highlighted in the literature. Communications might, theoretically, serve to build the MP–constituent relationship, but are they reaching their potential, and will their effectiveness be maintained in the years to come? (McKay 2018)

Providing effective support for members' constituency roles requires a complex juggling of priorities, particularly within the rapidly expanding communications space, while working within the constraints of the entitlements regimes, the separation of parliamentary and political roles and new levels of security. This is particularly so in the Australian Parliament, which places a high priority on IT support for members (Roche 2012). Ian Mackenzie, then DPS chief information officer, spoke positively about the opportunities for collaborating with other parliaments in overcoming security threats while also highlighting the difficulties of managing political relationships:

> Where it gets a little bit greyer is around engagement with constituents. I believe part of a parliamentarian's job is to engage with constituents to get the sense of the electorate, because they're representing that electorate within the parliament, and that's important, to gain that understanding. The line can get a bit blurry where they engage with constituents for that but they also engage with constituents to get re-elected—in terms of party politics, campaigning and fundraising. We're very clear that we can't support anything that is around party political or around fundraising or campaigning … There has to be an element of trust and an understanding that sometimes the line is a little bit blurry.[58]

Evidence available for the UK Parliament suggested a stronger focus on digital engagement with the public (HOCGC 2014; DDC 2015).[59]

The foregoing discussion on managing three kinds of parliamentary engagement—institutional representation, public participation in the work of parliament and facilitating members' individual representational roles—has illuminated more of the challenges parliamentary actors face. When the public is seemingly turning away from parliament, they must find more effective ways of enhancing the multiplicity of roles parliament plays. This is easier said than done, particularly when appropriate resourcing of parliament is a major public concern (see also Flinders et al. 2019); but the challenges cannot be avoided without creating another dilemma, as the next section will reveal.

---

58   I. McKenzie, pers. comm., 6 June 2017.
59   Noted also by, R. Greig, pers. comm., 27 May 2016; T. Brake, pers. comm., 8 June 2016; P. Young, pers. comm., 9 June 2016.

The dilemma of consigning reforms to the too-difficult box

In the preceding sections, I have discussed parliamentary reform from several perspectives: procedural, behavioural and cultural, and public engagement. A common theme across these perspectives is public expectations. Kelso (2009) observed that calls for the UK Parliament to be reformed procedurally were commonplace in the life of British politics, and the same could be said about the Australian Parliament. But as noted in Chapter 1 of this book, calls for democratic reform from a variety of sources are becoming more numerous. Some are directed at government (see, for instance, Key 2017; Smith 2018; Richards 2019); others address both parliament and government, demonstrating once again the tendency to conflate parliament and government within the Westminster democratic system (see, for instance, Menadue 2019; Renwick and Palese 2019). Menadue (2019) provides a shopping list of potential parliamentary reforms in Australia, including four-year fixed terms; an independent Speaker to encourage more inclusive, open and less adversarial parliaments; regular audits of MPs' entitlements *and* performance; more conscience votes; greater discussion of key public issues; and enhanced resources for committees and the Parliamentary Library (although without evaluating the effectiveness of those already allocated). Patience (2019) argued that federal politicians should get out of the Canberra 'bubble' and the two houses should spend at least half their sitting times in different capital cities, meeting local organisations. Warhurst (2018) cited senate electoral reform, an anticorruption commission and changes to the parliamentary workplace as much-needed reforms. In the United Kingdom, Photiadou and Dunleavy (2018) list current weaknesses of the House of Commons, arguing that few parts of its legislative activities work well; MPs' behaviours are ritualistic, point-scoring and unproductive; modernisation remains stalled as a result of traditionalist objections and *ex ante* budget control is non-existent. In earlier chapters, I have cited longstanding attempts to reform the House of Lords' governance (House of Lords Debates 2016; House of Lords 2016a; House of Lords House Committee 2016) and the potential loss of opportunities to modernise provided by the restoration and renewal of the Palace of Westminster (Flinders et al. 2018a, 2019). These examples are not exhaustive; they are illustrations of the public perception of what is still wrong (or now wrong) with parliament, long after the question was posed by Hill and Whichelow in 1964 and following series after series of procedural and management reforms in the interim.

The examples I have presented raise further questions about Norton's conditions for reform: Where is the window of opportunity, the coherent set of proposals or the political leadership from the backbench or the incumbent government (or, as Judge and Leston-Bandeira 2018 have suggested, from parliamentary officials)? How can any reform process be effectively managed without being hijacked for political purposes by government; thwarted or resisted by the opposition, minority parties, officials or those parliamentarians who do not want change; or disregarded by the public? How does a parliament balance the need to preserve and protect its independence from the government at the same time as ensuring its relevance as the principal democratic institution in the Westminster system? Most importantly, in an era of mass public disaffection and cynicism, how can parliamentary actors effectively fulfil Crick's vision of a parliament that serves the public interest?

Charles Clarke, a former UK politician, developed the idea of the 'too-difficult box' in a lecture series as a visiting professor at the University of East Anglia: 'We all know what to do; we just don't know how to get re-elected after we've done it.'[60] Clarke (2014) recognised that all governments find it difficult to address important issues and often set aside some as too difficult to solve within any conceivable time frame. This, he said:

> creates an enormous challenge for democratic institutions and democratic politicians. They need to develop a long-term culture to deal with long-term problems. They need to promote genuine rational discussion and debate in place of populist sound bites. They need to find means of engaging politics far more directly with people. And they need to show that democratic politics really can make a difference and help people overcome the problems that they experience.

> The dark and dangerous flipside of this coin is that if democracy fails to find the solutions that people are looking for they will listen to other voices, as we now see in the rise of ultra-populist and nationalist political parties across Europe. People will be impatient

---

60   Clarke attributed the statement to Jean-Claude Juncker, then head of the European Commission (see The Telegraph 2014).

with possibly self-serving explanations of why problems could not be solved. The often false promises of those who peddle instant solutions will seem increasingly appealing. (Clarke 2014: 86)

Clarke may be addressing his remarks to government policymaking but they are equally relevant to sustaining the parliament. In Australia, Warhurst (2019) has also recognised the 'democratic disconnections between big ideas and election politics', pointing to the tendency for institutional reforms to be pushed from outside the system and noting the role of Independents in both houses 'whose presence is one direct outcome of the perceived failure of the *status quo*'. As Warhurst says: 'Business as usual is not nearly good enough.'

I have recounted numerous examples of where both parliaments have failed to develop a long-term culture to deal with long-term problems. In the United Kingdom, despite a long history of management reviews and attempts at modernisation and procedural reform, we saw continuing criticism of the inefficiency and waste highlighted by the HOCGC (2014), ineffective decision-making and widespread public contempt for members of both houses, directed particularly at their support from the public purse and manifested by regular media stories about dishonesty and venality. Long-running attempts at modernisation and procedural reform have come and gone with mixed effectiveness. The clash between the Platonists/Methuselahs and the Aristotelians/Modernists continues (Evans 2014, 2017). Perhaps still consigned to the too-difficult box are the restoration and renewal of the Palace of Westminster, reform of the House of Lords and changing the culture and behaviour of those enjoying the benefits of their 'gentlemen's club' within the Westminster 'bubble'. Members' behaviour is still (always) in the spotlight. In the meantime, questions about members' relationships with their constituents and parliament's relationship with the executive and the public continue to be raised without a clear strategy for determining what parliament might look like and how it might operate in the future.

The decision not to implement a key recommendation of the highly critical Ellenbogen review that the House of Lords administration should be headed by a newly appointed director-general may not signify a return to the status quo, but it still falls short of the radical change called for by many staff. The House of Commons administration has appeared to take a step backwards in terms of management authority and public engagement, while retaining some key elements of the Bercow legacy, including greater diversity.

The eagerness of members in both parliaments to return to pre-pandemic operations is also illustrative of the problem. The 2020 World e-Parliament report suggests ways in which parliaments worldwide can build on innovations developed during the pandemic such as making permanent changes to rules so that parliament can function remotely and virtually, integrating a more holistic parliament-wide view of digital innovation into the 'fabric and culture of parliament' and retaining already realised efficiencies (Williamson 2021).

In the Australian Parliament, management issues, including those raised at every estimates committee hearing, are often trivialised. The efficiency dividend is driving lower spending but is the Australian Parliament able to recover public trust and sustain its future? Recent demographic surveys, contemporary literature and interviews with parliamentary actors would suggest not. The Australian Parliament House is modern and is not facing catastrophic failure, as is the Palace of Westminster, but calls for a more strategic focus on its funding and sustainability appear to have been ignored, along with proposals for more formalised governance arrangements.[61] It is not clear whether perceptions of low morale and bullying in the DPS, particularly among security and Hansard staff, have been resolved following intensive scrutiny by a senate committee (SFPALC 2015b). Calls for an independent Speaker seem unlikely to take hold, despite external support (Menadue 2019). The President of the Senate is still a member of the majority party in that house. The prohibition on dual citizenship in Section 44 of the Australian Constitution— acknowledged as an out-of-date and restrictive concept—has not been resolved despite a recommendation by the Joint Standing Committee on Electoral Matters (2018) to propose a constitutional amendment. Ongoing management of the issue has been left with the parties.[62] The parliament does not effectively influence its own appropriations. Issues

---

61   Baxter (2015); K. Baxter, pers. comm., 21 August 2017.
62   The report by the Joint Standing Committee on Electoral Matters proposed that Sections 44 and 45 of the Constitution be repealed or amended to enable 'current, and future, generations to debate and set the expectations of their Parliamentarians'. According to evidence by Colebatch (JSCEM 2018), Section 44 was 'drafted in haste' in 1898 and 'accepted out of weariness', reflecting societal standards established in 1901. It seems the Turnbull government's refusal to accept the committee's recommendations in the face of anticipated public hostility to the proposal perpetuated this 'drafting accident' rather than achieving a constitutional redesign and the 'soap opera' will continue (see also Howard, in O'Brien 1993; House of Representatives Standing Committee on Legal and Constitutional Affairs 1997; Saunders 2017; Colebatch 2019). For the Australian Parliament, resolving the dilemma of changing the rules to meet public expectations is heightened by the difficulties of constitutional change; on the other hand, in the United Kingdom, the Brexit referendum has demonstrated the apparent ease of changing an unwritten constitution has not turned out to be at all easy and the lack of a formal constitution is not a panacea for political and institutional reform.

have been left in the too-difficult box (or the 'too-hard basket', to use the Australian vernacular), with the potential to become wicked problems. The recommendations of the Jenkins report into parliamentary workplace culture will be implemented only because of the public outrage resulting from the exposure of widespread allegations of bullying, sexual harassment and sexual assault (AHRC 2021).

In both parliaments, members work in an environment that is hazardous to their mental health and wellbeing (Weinberg 2013; Flinders et al. 2018b; Warhurst 2018; Prasser 2019; Baldwin et al. 2020; AHRC 2021). Weinberg (2013) found the prevalence of psychological strain among politicians was well above what could be expected in the working population and questioned whether the jobs of MPs should come with a government health warning. The aforementioned *British Medical Journal* study (Poulter et al. 2019) found that a higher proportion of members of the House of Commons had poor mental health than among the general population; they were unlikely to discuss mental health issues with their whips and were not aware of parliamentary wellbeing services (see also Baldwin et al. 2020). The potential for discussion of working practices is much less apparent in times of crisis, such as the expenses scandal in the UK Parliament (Weinberg 2013) and, by extension, the misuse of entitlements in the Australian Parliament. MPs inspire little sympathy or support from the public in carrying out their vital democratic role (Marr 2017). This is a problem that should in fact inspire them to 'develop a long-term culture to deal with long-term problems' and to acknowledge 'the perceived failure of the *status quo*' (Clarke 2014; Warhurst 2019).

Conclusion: 'Rules to go by' in serving the public interest

Procedure and management are not separate functions to be compartmentalised and prioritised. The ability to maintain procedural continuity and stability while simultaneously advocating, negotiating and implementing ongoing reform is a complex requirement for parliamentary effectiveness. It requires the retention of highly skilled procedural advisers. But it also involves a wide interpretation of procedural expertise to include a capacity to predict change and to identify and adopt parliament-wide cultural and behavioural reforms that cross internal boundaries. This discussion has, necessarily, covered a lot of ground. I have defended the need for robust procedural rules and the knowledge and expertise required to maintain, interpret and adapt them—essential components of effective parliamentary administration. I have acknowledged the challenges to and limits of procedural reform in the context of the tensions between government and opposition—a traditional approach for parliamentarians and parliamentary scholars. The principal purpose of the chapter, however, has been to demonstrate the pressing need for parliamentary reform to meet public expectations, address societal norms, better support MPs and their staff and improve policy outcomes (Baldwin et al. 2020). First, to change workplace culture requires significant management intervention, which is amply illustrated by the examination of incidents of bullying and harassment and alleged sexual assault in both parliaments, and a willingness to adopt, and be seen to adopt, behavioural change. Second, the concept of public engagement has become far more complex than merely broadcasting information about parliament and its proceedings to a largely disengaged public. More participatory approaches are required with implications for forms of direct and representative democracy; adequate resourcing of public engagement is likely to require greater internal and external collaboration to harness efficiencies. Third, parliamentary actors cannot avoid tackling difficult problems; they need to look outside the parliamentary box rather than recede within it.

In the next chapter, I relate the dilemmas I have described in the areas of governance, management and procedural/cultural reform to the questions posed in Chapter 1 and discuss the different perspectives on parliamentary management they have revealed. Parliamentary administration/management has never been easy and, as we have seen, it is becoming increasingly complex. I have sought to provide a new perspective on how these challenges might be resolved, or at least ameliorated, in the struggle to enhance parliamentary effectiveness. I suggest that an appreciation by parliamentary actors collectively of their overarching roles as public managers, accompanied by greater knowledge of and respect for public management approaches and skills, both in theory and in practice, could assist, including by increasing parliament's capacity to influence broader democratic reform.

8

A public management approach to parliamentary administration

The management of parliament: A reckoning

Despite ongoing attempts to strengthen governance arrangements in the UK Parliament, they do not yet enshrine a collective responsibility for ensuring parliamentary effectiveness, and the House of Commons and House of Lords commissions do not yet, in practice, provide an effective authorising environment or a source of advocacy and support. There remains an excessive concern—which is particularly evident in the House of Lords—with precedent, process and preservation, a prioritisation of rules, traditions and conventions and a preference for observing social niceties while avoiding difficult decisions. To some, the parliament remains determined to 'reclaim parliament for the parliamentarians'.[1] The lack of collective responsibility is institutionalised in the Australian Parliament, with the separation of procedural and management departments making it easier to find someone to blame when things appear to go wrong.[2] It has resisted adopting a whole-of-parliament governance structure with

---

1   I. Ailles, pers. comm., 27 October 2021. See also Cox (2018); Ellenbogen (2019); Leslie and Mohr (2021).
2   Increasing criticism of the Australian Parliament's management coincides with a rise in 'blame it on the manager' literature and critical assessments of management ideology from the turn of the century (Keulen and Kroeze 2014).

greater input from members. Although the UK Parliament has greater independence in its funding appropriations, neither parliament seems able to inspire public confidence in the benefits of securing funds for legitimate parliamentary purposes, including members' support, public engagement and the maintenance and preservation of parliamentary buildings, reflecting a deficit in institutional representation and claim-making (Norton 2017; Judge and Leston-Bandeira 2018).

Both parliaments have accorded a lower priority to the concept of 'management' than to 'procedural' functions. In one sense this is understandable, and self-fulfilling, when management is seen only as providing routine and ancillary support services rather than as pursuing the effectiveness and sustainability of parliamentary democracy, as envisaged in this book. This narrow view of management militates against taking a strategic and innovative approach to parliamentary management and embeds traditions of guardianship and preservation and a culture of exception and insularity. Institutional divisions and multiple roles, stakeholders and relationships have contributed to different beliefs, practices and priorities for parliamentary actors, heightening tensions among them. The media sees parliament as a trophy organisation, often leading to excessive criticism, which in turn fuels public disengagement. High levels of scrutiny, including from MPs, of the institution's administration, while often justified, are rarely accompanied by advocacy and/or support.

Procedural and cultural change are slow; parliamentary actors have been reluctant to change rituals and behaviours to meet changing societal expectations. While public engagement has enjoyed increasing levels of attention, opinions differ as to how and where engagement initiatives are directed and whether the intended audience is listening. Members' constituency roles are becoming more demanding and, as we have seen in the UK Parliament, increasingly unsafe, leading to further questions about their future. Encompassing all these dilemmas is the too-difficult box—a symbol of short-term thinking and avoidance. Arguably, the ongoing challenge of balancing the goals of efficiency, effectiveness and meeting public expectations has become parliament's 'wicked problem' (Rittel and Webber 1973).

The tendency for the public (and some practitioners in studies of democracy) to conflate perceptions of the parliamentary institution with government and politicians generally in itself is a sign that parliaments are less relevant than their place in their respective constitutions would imply. If trust in democracy is low, as the evidence I have cited would suggest, parliament is less likely to be able to effectively pursue its role in providing a forum for deliberation and the sharing of ideas, thus contributing to enhanced public policy. Without agency and innovation by parliamentary actors, parliament is in danger of being overlooked, sidelined or marginalised. An institution that heralds its independence and political importance is in danger of ceding to others its capacity for action.

Parliamentary administration and public management: The same or different?

Like all public organisations, parliaments have been forced to respond to waves of management reform requiring a shift from bureaucratic and entrenched rules-based practices towards efficiency, adaptability and results-led performance requiring external expertise. Operational management skills, including in the fields of human resources and financial management, have been emphasised and designated 'professionals' in these fields have been recruited to both parliaments at the same time as longstanding parliamentary officials have been encouraged to forsake 'amateurish' approaches. But public management has not remained static.[3] Newer approaches to public management have emerged in intersecting and overlapping streams (Lindquist and Wanna 2011). Their objectives have included creating public value, achieving greater collaboration with internal and external stakeholders and encouraging active participation by citizens in the democratic process. Like parliament, all public organisations have become ever more complex, facing increasing demands and requiring new skill sets to manage them. Issues including relevance, organisational culture, public engagement, collaboration, relationship-building and citizen participation affect all public and many private organisations. Shortly, I will relate these public management approaches to aspects of parliamentary management; before doing so, it is necessary to examine the oft-cited claim that parliament is unique. If the 'uniqueness' of parliamentary administration continues to be overemphasised, it is unlikely parliamentary actors will be attracted to wider concepts of public management.

---

3   For a summary of the history of management thinking, see Keulen and Kroeze (2014).

Table 8.1 Perceived similarities and differences between parliament and other public organisations

Feature	Characteristics
Similarities	
Accountability, governance	Leadership, generalists can be effective if context is understood, same decision parameters, different operating environment.
Capacity to change, internal and external review	Differences overplayed but 'guild' or 'club' approach makes change difficult;[4] change frustratingly slow, parliament has not kept pace. Comparisons with other institutions included the royal family, the English Football League, National Health Service, local government, hospitals and universities.[5]
Operational management	No difference in non-member-facing roles, but can be too much political meddling.
Differences	
More stakeholders, complex relationships	Need to support members, including in constituencies as well as public; no control over demand; accountable to whole nation — an 'abstract collective'.[6]
Historical, traditional, constitutional	Historical legacy, custodial relationship, need for independent funding; exclusive cognisance; status conscious, hierarchical; devotion to institution, impartiality, specialised knowledge.
Locus of authority, decision-making	No binary relationship or single authority as in government; self-regulating; no single agenda, each member equal.
Political context, divisions, interests	Different *dramatis personae*; some administrators 'don't get it',[7] capacity to interpret political context required; administrators can work across divides if they have political capital but evidence of a lack of trust.
Media and public scrutiny, sensitivity	Media scrutiny, very public; tensions between houses; risk of exposure; lack of visibility, conflation with government.

Most of the parliamentary actors who participated in my research, from across the spectrum in both parliaments, acknowledged the similarities between their own institution and all public organisations in terms of their common requirements, including good governance, accountability,

---

4   C. Mills, pers. comm., 11 May 2017.
5   R. Fox, pers. comm., 10 June 2016; I. Ailles, pers. comm., 9 May 2016; P. Beresford, pers. comm., 2 June 2016; R. Mulgan, pers. comm., 7 June 2017.
6   E. Crewe, pers. comm., 21 September 2016.
7   R. Fox, pers. comm., 10 June 2016.

professionalism and expertise. When interviewed, their principal focus was on operational management—'administration is administration', parliament is 'not fundamentally different' or 'not completely different'[8]— and several also cited capacity for change and a need for continuing internal and external review. Many actors noted that differences could be overplayed, that parliaments like to think they are unique when they have more in common with other organisations. Differences can be perceived as a protection and independence can be taken advantage of. In Table 8.1, I analyse responses to interview questions about the differences and similarities between parliament and other public organisations.

Most parliamentary actors, whether members, managers, clerks or observers, cited differences as well as similarities between parliament and other public organisations. An important distinction, however, is the way these differences were interpreted. To some interviewees, they reinforced the 'uniqueness' or 'independence' of the parliament. To many others, they represented public management challenges common to other public organisations within their own contexts; all organisations are different to some extent. The following quotations, taken from a range of parliamentary actors, support the argument that differences should not be barriers to effective public management reform within parliament. In fact, these views are indicative of a willingness to entertain it:

> [T]here are plenty of people with their own issues out there. They may not be quite the same because of the member angle but it's not as if they are all uniform elsewhere—they are also different.[9]

> I'm not sure that I would buy into the differences … In many ways, there is nothing that we do that is completely unique and different from any other organisation. I think those who argue that it is tend to use that as a blanket reason for not learning from outside … One of our weaknesses is that we don't learn enough from what happens in the real world. To a certain extent, we exchange with other Commonwealth parliaments and things but there is a reluctance to look at simple and best HR [human resources] practices in the public sector and to learn from them.[10]

---

8   S. Parry, pers. comm., 15 June 2017; A. Walker, pers. comm., 23 September 2015; I. Ailles, pers. comm., 9 May 2016.
9   D. Beamish, pers. comm., 24 May 2016.
10   A. Kennon, pers. comm., 24 May 2016.

I am much more [inclined] towards the line of similarities than differences. In the end, we are all human beings. We all behave, we all project, we all have our own inadequacies, we all like warm fuzzies, we don't like cold pricklies, and I don't think that's any different from anywhere else other than the fact that we have allegiance to parties.[11]

[T]oo often everyone says, 'Oh, it's completely different.' Actually, quite a lot of it is not completely different. There are not enough people inside the railings with experience outside the railings because there's a perception in here that it's so different that nobody could make the crossing. Having said that, some of the differences are startling, along the lines of how MPs operate or don't operate, the lack of organised activities, the fact that everyone is so individually distinct.[12]

It may be unique in a sense, but I don't know that it is the only kind of bureaucracy that is unique. I think all bureaucracies probably are unique in their own way, which does not detract from the proposition that they're also alike in a lot of ways.[13]

[I]n some ways the differences are perhaps not so great. Ninety-five per cent of my career was in the parliamentary service, but I know that the federal sphere is also characterised by a lot of very dedicated people in lots of executive departments who have great cultures of professional expertise and pride in all sorts of areas … Parliament is a special service, but there are lots of other services that are also characterised by a lot of idealism, professionalism and long-term traditions of neutral service.[14]

Acknowledgement of the many similarities between parliament and other public organisations, and an appreciation of the extent or context of perceived differences, affords an opportunity to look outwards from the parliamentary environment and learn from public management as well as parliamentary practice and scholarship.

A final point on 'uniqueness': my research has illustrated an inherent conflict in traditional beliefs around the concept of parliamentary 'independence' (or exclusive cognisance) and a parliament's capacity to meet societal expectations. I present five examples of this conflict:

11 C. Bryant, pers. comm., 23 May 2016.
12 I. Ailles, pers. comm., 9 May 2016.
13 H. Penfold, pers. comm., 19 July 2017.
14 B. Wright, pers. comm., 25 May 2017.

first, as in the aversive constitutionalism argument of Flinders et al. (2018a), the independence argument can be used to thwart reform to protect individual and political interests (we have seen evidence in earlier chapters of this occurring in the Australian Parliament). Such a use is not directed towards meeting Crick's (1968) or Reid and Forrest's (1989) test of parliament as a broker of ideas and deliberation with the assumed outcome of a better-informed and engaged public. Second, when the independence concept is considered in the scrutiny or investigative context, its use tends to encourage adversarial or pejorative perceptions of the 'we need to keep the bastards honest' type,[15] rather than collaborative or constructive outcomes. It does little to encourage public confidence.[16]

Third, advocates for the independence of presiding officers from their political parties typically mean to free incumbents from the constraints of political affiliation and allow them to always act impartially; however, this may be unachievable. When an independent Speaker exercises authority over a parliament's proceedings, their actions are not always considered impartial[17] and may even be seen as an abuse of their independence (see Chapter 7). Fourth, the constant call for the Australian Parliament to take control of its own finances in line with the somewhat misplaced doctrine of the separation of powers within Australia's 'Washminster' system is, to some, another myth to be dispelled. Fifth, the traditional belief that parliament is 'unique' could in fact bolster an inherent tendency for parliamentary actors to prefer not to rely on external influences, including those that could help to improve parliament's effectiveness. The concept of independence may militate against effective parliamentary administration when it is used to signify exclusion, rather than inclusion. However, when used in the context of authorised and legitimate agency directed to the interests of the parliament rather than party allegiance, it could engender a greater appreciation of public management concepts.

---

15 Attributed to Don Chipp (c. 1980), former leader of the Australian Democrats (Megarrity 2017).
16 This concept was usefully illustrated in the context of policy development by Wilkins and Phillimore (2019). In the context of the Hayne royal commission into the banking industry, they questioned how well suited royal commissions are to the dual roles of uncovering wrongdoing and contributing to policy reform.
17 See the discussion on Speaker Bercow's selection of amendments during the business debate on the *European Union (Withdrawal) Act 2018* (No. 2). But see also evidence given to the House of Commons Public Administration and Constitutional Affairs Committee (HCPACAC 2019), which discussed the concepts of 'neutrality' and 'impartiality' in the context of the 'unusual' circumstances of the House of Commons after the Brexit referendum.

Parliamentary administration in a public management framework

In calling for a rethinking by parliamentary actors of the concept of parliamentary administration, I am not suggesting that adopting a specific public management approach will provide an ideal model for parliaments. Although my research has highlighted many similarities between managing parliaments and public organisations generally, fundamental differences include the lack of a single authority, with no one wholly in charge, relentless public scrutiny and the seething tensions among members, officials and parliamentary observers about what an effective parliament really looks like—tensions that are exacerbated by the nature of the political contest in which the parliamentary institution is steeped. Nonetheless, a key challenge for managers in both parliaments, in an era of declining public trust, is how to place a greater focus on projecting and sustaining parliament into the future while also understanding, if not always preserving, the traditions of the past. This task would seem to require a greater reliance by all parliamentary actors on strategic and collaborative public management skills and expertise, practised across intra and interorganisational boundaries. A further challenge lies in engaging members more constructively and strategically in managing their parliaments, rather than simply criticising management activities or avoiding responsibility altogether, particularly when many do not see themselves as sharing a public management role. This would require both officials and members in key administrative roles, particularly the presiding officers, to exercise 'situated agency' working sensitively within the political/administrative zone.

A third management challenge is how to develop collaborative mechanisms with potential external contributors, and this is where the potential for broader democratic reform becomes apparent. This goes to my third purpose in writing this book and highlights the role parliament's managers can play in strengthening parliament's reputation and relevance, thus enhancing its capacity to engage with the public in the 'national conversation' on crucial policy issues (Leslie and Mohr 2021). This is not a novel suggestion; if anything, it is a reaffirmation of the views of revered parliamentary advocates, including Jennings and Crick.

This book has not set out to provide a comprehensive analysis of public management theory.[18] It is necessary, however, to provide some explanation of its various phases to support the book's contention that an appreciation of public management approaches by parliamentary actors would be beneficial. In the sections below, I outline some characteristics of public management that have a demonstrated or potential relevance to parliamentary management.

'Old' public administration

The evolution of public organisations from public administration to newer theories of public management is well researched (see Albrow 1970; Bourgon 2011; Lindquist and Wanna 2011; Christensen 2012; Bryson et al. 2014; Osborne et al. 2015; Esmark 2016), and I am in danger here of oversimplifying numerous and varied explanations. Nonetheless, I can draw from Albrow's (1970) critiques of Weber's rational bureaucracy to identify characteristics that have also typified the forms and structures of traditional parliamentary administration. These characteristics included lifelong salaried professional jobs, fixed career structures requiring specialised knowledge and the formation of social classes, assisted by higher education. Lifelong tenure, a fixed salary and inalienable pension rights in a Weberian bureaucracy presupposed that civil servants (or parliamentary officials) were shielded from undue political pressure and corruption and would refrain from acting out of personal interest (Christensen 2012). Structures were impersonal and hierarchical with clearly specified functions; officers were selected based on a professional qualification. Career promotion was typically governed by seniority. In common with other organisations, public administrators also had a symbolic function, as characterised by Mintzberg (1973) and Pfeffer and Salancik (1978).

Less positive features of bureaucracy included age and security, a stifling of administrative vitality and managerial creativity, an overdevotion to precedent, lack of initiative, procrastination, duplication of effort and departmentalism, inability to learn from errors, self-interested use of rules to preserve the status quo and uneven distribution of power (Albrow 1970). Early literature on the roles of parliamentary officials (Rydz 1979;

---

18 For a more comprehensive account of phases of public management reforms in the United Kingdom and Australia, see Barrett (2019). For more on the application of public management approaches to parliamentary administration, see Barrett (2021).

Reid and Forrest 1989) concurred with this perspective, and the self-interest element of parliamentary service is also reflected in discussions with parliamentary actors.

'New' public management

New public management (NPM) is customarily associated with neoliberal ideas of reinventing government so that it works better and costs less (Osborne and Gaebler 1993) or perceptions that bureaucracy is broken and needs fixing (Savoie 2006). It has numerous characterisations: competition and incentives (Dunleavy et al. 2006); a focus on outputs and outcomes rather than processes; more measurement and increased accountability; flatter structures and decentralised responsibility, allowing and encouraging management discretion; market-like strategies; the use of contracts; and an emphasis on service quality and customers (Pollitt 2003; Rainey 2012; de Vries and Nemec 2013; Esmark 2016). It has seen a shift in values towards efficiency and professional public sector management (Hood 1991; Pollitt 2003; Savoie 2006), leading to a more managerial and open senior leadership for whom roles have changed from those of traditional public administration to a greater emphasis on business planning and corporate governance principles.[19] Advice is contestable and political leaders have experienced heightened demands for performance and greater public expectations (Halligan 2012). Claims that NPM has achieved the holy grail of better performance outcomes are not universal (Moynihan 2012) and the same may be said about parliamentary administration (Barrett 1999; Aldons 2001a; Duncan 2004; Verrier 2008). But de Vries and Nemec (2013) claim that NPM is still alive and kicking even though its ideas may have been translated into different tools. While the ideologues of minimal intrusion by the state and privatisation of services are less dominant, the emphasis on internal efficiency remains, albeit with a renewed emphasis on improved effectiveness and good governance, and this appears to be the case also in the two parliaments.

Bevir and Rhodes (2003) questioned the whole conceptualisation of NPM as a 'global paradigm' and argued against an institutionalised approach to its analysis. They preferred an interpretative approach to public management reform focusing on historical traditions and individual agency, based on actors' beliefs, actions and practices, and this is the approach taken in this book. The influence of NPM on parliamentary

---

19 Evidence in earlier chapters points to where this has occurred within parliamentary administration.

administration appears to have brought a strong focus on structural efficiency, performance management and accountability, particularly in Australia, but with less emphasis on 'the market' and competition, although several services in the Australian Parliament—particularly facilities management, catering and parliamentary reporting—have been subjected over time to outbreaks of outsourcing.

Public value and associated post-NPM 'paradigms'

Moore's (1995) seminal work on public value introduced a new way of thinking about how public managers should think and act, and it is worth spending a little time exploring the concept here. It was apparently 'seized on' by public managers as a way of rediscovering themselves after the 'predations of new public management' (Rhodes and Wanna 2007: 407; see also O'Flynn 2007). (Moore's 2013 publication capitalised on the popularity of the public value concept and responded to criticisms relating to its measurement: Rhodes and Wanna 2007, 2009; Alford and Hughes 2008; Alford and O'Flynn 2009; Williams and Shearer 2011.) In one of a series of workshops facilitated by the Australia and New Zealand School of Government (ANZSOG) in 2016 (which I attended), Moore told managers he wanted them to engage intellectually with their public management roles, that they had a duty and obligation to think long term and look beyond the narrow and sometimes bureaucratic nature of those roles. As well as thinking of a system in terms of its efficiency, they should be looking to improve it to create new benefits for the direct recipients of the service, policy or regulation as well as the recipients of the greater social outcomes. According to Moore's thinking, if citizens are willing to pay for services with no immediate or tangible benefit for themselves, public managers need to make sure they are not wasting their money, but rather are maximising the value of the public good and providing transparency, fairness and justice. In parliamentary terms, this is a dilemma in itself: citizens are unwilling to pay too much for 'democracy' when the concept is strongly equated with the interests of politicians, as continuing expenses and entitlements 'scandals' in both parliaments have demonstrated.[20]

Moore saw his public value model working in public organisations of all kinds (although it is unlikely he was thinking specifically of parliamentary administration). Nor did he confine his definition of 'public manager' to

---

20 For a recent (at the time of writing) instalment, see Maguire and Ellery (2021).

unelected officials. He instead urged all public officials, including those elected to their roles, to carefully consider the opportunities for creating value and to account for the spending of public authority (or consent) as a cost to be borne against the intrusion of the state. At the risk of accusations of conceptual stretching, it is not difficult to argue in the same way for a balance between what citizens might perceive as intrusion—a parliament urging citizens to play a more informed, energetic and responsible role in the democratic system (the view of Jennings [1941])—against the resources required to achieve greater public engagement and deliberation. Indeed, Horner and Hutton (2010) promote the efficacy of public value concepts in tackling the democratic deficit (see also Horner et al. 2006).

The public value concept has many critics,[21] but we can apply three broad tests to it (and its usefulness in the parliamentary context): it must create something substantively valuable, be legitimate and politically sustainable and be operationally and administratively sustainable (Alford and O'Flynn 2009). These tests also equate with Lynn's (2012) dimensions of responsible public management, which must be constitutionally authorised, performed skilfully and efficiently and reflect the values of a wider society. To Bryson et al. (2015), public value management is a way of moving philosophically, theoretically and practically beyond older public interest debates towards public value governance across multiple sectors and stakeholders and involving multiple conflicting and contentious value judgements (see also Stoker 2006a; Talbot 2008; Bryson et al. 2014).[22]

In making a connection between Moore's public value and parliamentary administration, I do not ignore criticism of its perceived emphasis on managerialism. A pragmatic approach is required that is consistent with the important (institutionalised) values at stake (Alford and Hughes 2008), but that also reflects a long-recognised need for organisations to acquire and use resources in a way that responds to the prevailing social context (Pfeffer and Salancik 1978).[23] And while some critics have outlined drawbacks for public managers in adopting the public value concept,

---

21 See, for instance, Rhodes and Wanna (2007, 2009); Talbot (2008, 2009); Gains and Stoker (2009); Hartley et al. (2017); Brodsky (2014); Prebble (2018).

22 Further positive support comes from public practitioners in both the United Kingdom and Australia (R. Kelly et al. 2002; Coats and Passmore 2008; Bromell 2012; Alford, Douglas et al. 2017; Ballintyne and Mintrom 2018).

23 See also Hillman et al. (2009) for a review of Pfeffer and Salancik's (1978) resource-dependence theory and the opportunities it presents for further development and application by incorporating research from other areas. Pfeffer and Salancik's contention that all organisations are constrained by interdependencies with other organisations and must manage associated power imbalances would seem to apply to parliamentary administration.

including its implications for accountability and legitimacy (Rhodes and Wanna 2007, 2009; Gains and Stoker 2009), there is no broadly settled view about the real or desirable relationship between the political and administrative realms. The normal functioning of government requires public managers to engage with politics in various ways to create what they see as value for the public, with most seeing their interface with politicians as entering a zone—sometimes called the purple zone—rather than crossing a line between the administrative and political realms (Shergold 1997; Hartley et al. 2015; Alford, Hartley et al. 2017). Value conflict appears to be inherent in contemporary political and administrative life in liberal societies (Wagenaar 1999, 2014). Within parliaments, conflict between administration and politics is also a fact of life.

The 'pragmatic', 'non-ideological' or 'whatever works' approach to public value has contributed to a continuing scholarly discussion on 'new' governance relationships within the public realm (Alford and Hughes 2008; Coats and Passmore 2008). Bevir et al. (2003) argue that public governance changes emerge not solely from traditions and practices but also from the way these are interpreted by actors over time, emphasising the role of agency over institutional path-dependency. Stoker (2006a) argues that public value management is best situated in the systems of dialogue and exchange that characterise networked governance, relying for its motivation on *successful relationships rather than rules or incentives*. Osborne's (2010: 9–10) new public governance pointed to fragmentation and uncertainty as key features of twenty-first-century public management requiring a focus on 'the organisation within its environment' and the negotiation of values, meaning and relationships. Edwards (2002: 60) predicted that the public sector in Australia would need a different set of structures, principles and values to support collaborative arrangements within government and with external partners and citizens, while Flinders (2002) discussed attempts in the United Kingdom to foster a greater degree of interorganisational cooperation in its 'joined-up government' program. All these approaches suggest a new governance 'paradigm' with traditional hierarchical approaches becoming decentred and relational. Bryson et al. (2014, 2015) describe 'public value governance' as a new movement that responds to the challenges of a 'networked, multi-sector, no one-wholly-in-charge world' in which 'democratic values' beyond efficiency and effectiveness are prominent. We can make a connection between the evolving paradigms of NPM, public value management and new public governance to the dilemmas of parliamentary administration explored in earlier chapters while also taking account of related criticism.

Parliamentary actors also need to avoid 'the public service reform syndrome in which reform succeeds reform, with no time for the intended changes to take place, no evaluation, and no clear evidence of either success or failure' (Rhodes 2016: 638) and, as evidenced by the recent harsh reviews of workplace culture, they should not ignore issues of entrenched power and marginalisation (Dahl and Soss 2014).

On collaboration and co-production

Finally, I conflate two more evolving concepts of public management: collaboration and co-production. Collaborative public management was described by McGuire (2006: 33) as 'a process of facilitating and operating in multi-organisational arrangements in order to remedy problems that cannot be solved by single organizations'. It is not a fresh approach but one that has been occurring for decades with the realisation that wicked problems cannot be addressed through traditional bureaucracies (McGuire 2006; see also Rittel and Webber 1973; Head and Alford 2015). Similar definitions encompassing 'boundaries', 'civic spheres', 'public purposes', 'public problems', 'collective forums' and 'consensus-oriented decision-making', all of which formally distinguish collaboration from simple interaction and transactional relationships, are offered by Ansell and Gash (2008), O'Leary and Bingham (2009), Agranoff (2012), Emerson et al. (2012), Emerson and Nabatchi (2015) and Scott and Thomas (2017). Indeed, to Agranoff, management itself *means* collaboration. If parliaments are deemed to be 'single organisations', it is still difficult to determine where the boundaries lie (or should lie) between different organisational environments: members and their constituents; members and officials; governments and oppositions; clerks and managers; the Senate and the House of Representatives; the House of Lords and the House of Commons.

McGuire (2006) also argues that many of the skills required for successful collaboration—communication, strategic planning and management within existing rules and structures—are just as important in traditional hierarchical organisations; it is to the *behaviour* of public managers that he turned in distinguishing effective network management from the traditional command and control of a hierarchy. Scott and Thomas (2017) offered insights into why and how public managers (and potentially parliamentary administrators) might choose to use collaborative tools, while Sullivan et al. (2012) related leadership and collaboration to situated agency to explain why actors in the same context might form different interpretations of collaboration.

A broader and widely accepted view of collaboration involves the representation of key groups and joint problem-solving between agencies and concerned citizens (Reilly 1998; Connick and Innes 2003; Aschhoff 2018). Specifically, Emerson et al. (2012) suggested that collaborative arrangements could be used to inform participatory governance and civic engagement. Indeed, in terms of policymaking, parliamentary committees regularly call for evidence from key interest groups who contribute to consensus decision-making. A basis for collaboration is already in place and could be expanded; we saw in Chapter 8 the example of the citizens' assembly on adult social care in the United Kingdom (Betts and Wollaston 2018).[24] The UK Parliament's Liaison Committee inquiry into the effectiveness and influence of the select committee system was discussed in the previous chapter; it also flagged the possibility of more joint working and greater accountability to the electorate.[25] Using the already well-established forums of committees would seem an ideal way to build the parliament's citizen-centred collaborative capacity, as well as its organisational collaborative capacity to work across party lines (Aschhoff 2018).

Posited positive effects of collaboration that are relevant to the parliamentary context—particularly in terms of strengthening parliament's reputation and relevance and enhancing its capacity to engage with the public—include the claim that collaboration can operate in contrast to adversarial policymaking and enhance an organisation's legitimacy by including relevant stakeholders in public decision-making (Innes and Booher 1999; Lynn 2006; Ansell and Gash 2008, 2018; Hill and Lynn 2009; Torfing 2019). Crosby et al. (2017: 665) provide normative insights into the need for public managers to be better prepared for a 'new public governance paradigm' that involves collaborative innovation and public value creation, as opposed to a sole focus on responding to political needs and priorities and budgetary and media-fuelled accountability pressures in 'contemporary monitory democracies' (see also Keane 2010 on democracy and media).

---

24   Allen and McKee (2019) from the UCL Constitution Unit discuss the benefits and mechanisms of citizens' assemblies given evidence from the Brexit and social care experiences; see Taylor (2019) for an introductory guide to citizens' assemblies.
25   The final report (HCLC 2019) called for greater strategic planning, improved behaviour, greater engagement with research and public engagement centred on 'listening' rather than 'broadcasting'— themes that resonate with the evidence uncovered in this book (see Chapter 7).

The characteristics required for collaboration to succeed include strong structural relationships, clear objectives, shared commitment, mutual respect, and trust and governance mechanisms with decision-making authority, agreed rules and accountability. Good collaborators will exhibit bridging, mobilising, persuasive and adaptive skills and collaborative intelligence (Butcher et al. 2019). Bartelings et al. (2017) found that contemporary management activities still fell within the 10 traditional managerial roles identified by Mintzberg (1973) in his seminal study on managerial work: figurehead, liaison, leader, monitor, disseminator, spokesperson, entrepreneur, disturbance handler, resource allocator and negotiator. But they added a new role, orchestration, which emphasises the interorganisational aspects of management while focusing on the individual manager rather than the networks usually associated with collaboration. Whereas Mintzberg described the manager above all as a leader, Bartelings et al. defined the role as a spokesperson—an observation that resonates with the governance dilemmas considered earlier. Despite warnings about the pitfalls of collaboration from both sceptical questioners and outright detractors,[26] the potential exists for more collaborative approaches within public and parliamentary administration. Indeed, the emphasis on collaboration within the two parliaments' planning and reporting documents would suggest it has now become a byword for effective outcomes.

The foundational idea for the co-production of public services was that citizens could participate in producing public services and not just consuming them (Ostrom and Ostrom 1977, cited in Alford 2014). By extending this concept to the delivery of democracy, one could argue it is not far removed from Crick's (1968) view that parliament's most important function is to act as a broker of ideas and information so the electorate can sit in judgement. This view places as much emphasis on the role of parliamentary administrators in shaping and meeting public expectations as it does on supporting governance and management structures and practices. After all, the very act of placing an 'informed' vote (Jennings 1941)—or even voting at all in the case of the United Kingdom—would seem to require more urgently than ever the willing and informed involvement of citizens.

---

26   For example, Huxham (2003); Fels (2008); Wanna (2008); O'Flynn (2008, 2009); Prebble (2015); Wegrich (2019); Gruen (2019).

Support for co-production is extensive, including from those who see it as restoring trust in government (or parliament, by extension) in contrast to the distrust expressed by the compliance and control mechanisms of NPM (Kettl 2006; Van de Walle 2010; Fledderus et al. 2014). Empirical research by Thomsen and Jakobsen (2015) found that programs more extensive than simply sending out information might be required to encourage citizen co-production. Alford (2016) claims citizens value the institutions that enable *them* to discern what is valuable, including by facilitating public deliberation; and, increasingly, external organisations and scholars are calling for greater participation via citizens' juries, deliberative polls or 'mini-publics', claiming that contemporary representative democracy is ineffectual and an 'elitist and technocratic approach will not wash' (Breckon et al. 2019: 4; see also Flinders et al. 2020). Levy (2019) has suggested that deliberative or informed referendums could harness the populist trend in a more useful and benign direction.[27] Nabatchi et al. (2017) provided a sophisticated analysis of the public administration and services management implications for co-production and its variant forms and participants, arguing for a broad definition of the concept to maintain its generalisability and ensure its usefulness[28] (see also Osborne and Strokosch 2013). Again, the concept has its detractors. To Osborne et al. (2016) and Nabatchi et al. (2017), the concept of co-production remains 'woolly' or 'muddled' and, despite its normative appeal, the evidence base for its application is weak (see also Williams et al. 2016; Dewey et al. 2018). But we can turn to recent advocacy by a group of 15 distinguished scholars, drawing on Ostrom, for a positive approach to the theoretical study of public administration (Douglas et al. 2021). This requires 'a dedicated effort in learning how to learn from "what works" in public policy' (Douglas et al. 2021: 4), rather than a concentration on examining failures, negative performance, scandals and crises, which certainly reflects the path of administrative reform in parliaments.

From the above account, we can see similarities in the evolution of parliamentary and public management in the United Kingdom and Australia, starting with the classic public administration model, distinguished by respect for the rule of law and the separation of politics/administration; requiring merit, anonymity and political neutrality; being

---

27 For a useful perspective on populism, see Bryant and Moffitt (2019).

28 They defined co-production as 'an umbrella concept that captures a wide variety of activities that can occur in any phase of the public service cycle and in which state actors and lay actors work together to produce benefits' (Nabatchi et al. 2017: 769).

efficient, accountable, rules-based, stable and impartial; and allowing minimal discretion. Changes in public management approaches from the 1980s towards new neoliberal hybrid models of cooperation between public organisations and citizens; a focus on performance, efficiency, productivity and competition, greater use of ICT and enhanced public engagement and participation have driven administrative reform in both parliaments, with tangible results. These similarities were acknowledged by interviewees, when they were asked to compare parliament with public organisations, particularly in relation to accountability, operational management, the need for internal and external review, leadership and capacity for change, although some saw the pace of change within parliament as frustratingly slow (see Table 8.1). To others, parliament's historical and constitutional legacies enshrine characteristics of custodianship, independence, hierarchy, status and specialised knowledge, exacerbating the tensions that exist between the 'classic' parliamentary administrator and those who see themselves as generalist public managers.

It is in the 'newer' public management approaches where we can see both the explanatory and the normative potential for viewing parliamentary administration through a public management lens. This is where the argument that parliament is 'unique' and 'independent', and that its members and officials are somehow absolved from any responsibility to learn from well-researched and widely advocated public management approaches (or even to see themselves as public managers), is weak. Of course, parliaments face specific challenges in seeking to behave like other public organisations or to adapt for parliamentary purposes the theoretical management approaches advocated by academics, and these have been acknowledged throughout this book. Even if we set aside historical and constitutional factors, parliamentary actors still must address multiple stakeholders and complex relationships, diffused authority and decision-making, divisive political interests and relentless media and public scrutiny. But arguably, these additional challenges make it even more important for parliamentary actors to see themselves as public managers, to engage proactively with stakeholders (and each other) in the collective public interest, to seek new models of collaborative governance and alternative methods of service delivery and to encourage citizen and community engagement with democratic ideals.

Table 8.2 depicts how public management approaches, characteristics and skills can be related to key parliamentary functions.

Table 8.2 Relating public management approaches to parliament

Principal roles	Actors	Functions/forums	Issues	Management approaches/characteristics/skills	Outcomes/success criteria
Scrutiny/ oversight	Presiding officers Members Clerks Researchers Parliamentary Budget Office	Parliamentary debates Question time Standing committees Select committees Estimates committees Procedure committees Research outputs	Executive control: Resourcing, financial and programming Individual and collective agency	**Old public administration:** Respect for rules/hierarchy; separation of politics and administration; efficiency, accountability, impartiality; 'craft'; political astuteness. **New public management:** Performance, efficiency, discretion, citizen-centric, business and strategic planning.	Efficient, effective and impartial scrutiny and oversight mechanisms. Adequate resourcing and programming. Efficient, effective and accountable public/parliamentary administration. Citizen knowledge and engagement.
Governing/ legislating	Presiding officers Ministers Members Clerks	Parliamentary debates Question time Standing committees Select committees Public bill committees Procedure committees	Executive control: Resourcing, financial and programming Individual and collective agency	**Old public administration:** As above. **New public management:** As above.	'Order, decency and regularity' (Evans 2014). Efficient, effective and accountable public/parliamentary administration. Legislation and policy impact.

Principal roles	Actors	Functions/forums	Issues	Management approaches/characteristics/skills	Outcomes/success criteria
Deliberation/public engagement	Presiding officers, Ministers, Members, Clerks, Officials, Public, External organisations	Parliamentary debates, Standing committees	Authority and advocacy	**Old public administration:** As above.	As above.
Policy development		Select committees, Collaborative spaces, for example, citizens' assemblies, mini-publics	Public participation, Policy impact	**New public management:** As above. **Public value/governance:** Strategic leadership; legitimate authority/advocacy, feasibility and value; dialogue and exchange, negotiation, 'orchestration'; prioritising relationships over rules and incentives; transparency, fairness, justice; collective social outcomes; legitimate authority, feasibility and value.	As above. Reduced democratic deficit. Increased trust in parliament and other political institutions.
Parliamentary support and development		Procedure committees, Governance and domestic committees, Collaborative spaces	External and member participation, Authority and advocacy, Strategic planning	**Collaboration:** Facilitation, tackling intractable problems, interorganisational; non-adversarial; consensus-building. **Co-production:** Citizen efficacy, engagement and participation.	Public input to policy/parliamentary development, collaboration with external organisations. Reforms to workplace culture, representation, electoral systems, how parliament works. Efficient and effective support for parliamentary management.

Assumptions: Political partisanship, media and public scrutiny, budget limitations, public disengagement.

Risks: Perceived lack of impartiality arising from agency, public scepticism, cynicism, lack of political judgement, defining public interest/benefits, conflicting actor motivations, dominant traditional cultures.

A practical approach to parliamentary administration

My research has suggested that MPs with governance responsibilities could provide greater input, support and advocacy to decisions relating to the running of parliament, including its engagement with the public. Beyond that, a recognition of their public management roles would also strengthen their ability to form a strategic agenda for garnering greater parliamentary influence in wider democratic reform. Turning to practical solutions, and notwithstanding earlier comments rejecting a 'one best way' approach to organisational design, in the case of the Australian Parliament, an ability to balance the competing interests of multiple actors in parliamentary administration could be enhanced by an overarching governance structure—a parliament commission—which had a degree of political independence and whose decisions were publicly accessible. Such a body, designed along the lines of the House of Commons and House of Lords commissions, but more radically structured to operate across both houses, would, ideally, engage external members and provide not just assurance but also strategic advice and assistance towards restoring and strengthening the public perception of parliamentary effectiveness. In terms of efficiency, there is no reason the two existing appropriation and administration committees could not meet simultaneously (as envisaged in their respective governing Standing Orders, but not, apparently, currently practised). Their chairs—*ex officio*, the Speaker and the President of the Senate—could represent each house's interests on the commission and issues of priority funding could be addressed. These could include the maintenance, promotion and repurposing of the parliamentary building during the remainder of its 200-year life to avoid the pitfalls of decades, if not centuries, of neglect, as evidenced in the Palace of Westminster (see Baxter 2015), as well as seeking additional funding for intra-organisational collaborative innovation on citizen engagement.

A formal governance structure would help to provide legitimacy and authorisation for strategic, politically independent and decisive action on the management of the Australian Parliament. As with any other committee, its advice should be public even if its deliberations are conducted privately. It would give presiding officers and other parliamentary actors the authority to work more effectively in the purple zone between the administrative and the political, acting in the interests of the parliament while cognisant of the interests of their parties. Indeed, such a body may also have leverage in promoting party-based reform to meet societal expectations, such as addressing poor behaviour and effectively representing women and minority groups in the parliament. (As I emphasise in the Epilogue to this book, the consequences of not acting in this way have now been made remarkably clear in the Jenkins report on the independent review into Commonwealth parliamentary workplaces; AHRC 2021).

While a parliamentary commission's decisions would be open to scrutiny by the SFPALC in as much as they related to the Senate itself, the Speaker and members of the House of Representatives would not be answerable to that committee; on the other hand, greater transparency in decision-making could make estimates hearings more constructive and attract fewer 'shouty' media episodes (Wroe 2019), provided members refrained from political point-scoring. Of greater importance still, such a body would be in a position *as a whole* to argue for effective funding, including by departments preparing persuasive business cases and working in concert—an outcome that would mitigate any attempts by the Department of Finance to play off each department against the other (Reid and Forrest 1989). And in relation to a proposal that the Australian Public Service Commissioner should be head of the Public Service (Podger 2018), there is no reason the Parliamentary Service Commissioner should not be a prominent figure on a proposed parliament commission, particularly if that position became a separate appointment, not merely an additional role for the Public Service Commissioner. This 'important' role would then not need to be played 'intermittently' (Parliamentary Service Commissioner 2018). At present, the existing position of joint Parliamentary Service Commissioner/Public Service Commissioner seems to serve little parliamentary purpose, other than to save parliament the cost of funding it.[29]

There will be objections to this proposal. First, the potential promise of a formalised governance structure and a more unified parliamentary service would inevitably be viewed in the Australian Parliament against the spectre of awakening previous proposals for a single parliamentary department (Reid and Forrest 1989; James 1996; NCA 1996; Malcolmson 1999). An alternative approach would be to view a formalised whole-of-parliament governance structure as an opportunity for the parliament to refocus its administration and harness its own efficiencies and reputational gains

---

29   Commentary by Peter Woolcott, Parliamentary Service Commissioner, would suggest his call for a cultural and organisational shift for the Australian Public Service, away from hierarchical rules that discourage innovation and risk, would be similarly useful in the Australian Parliamentary Service. In particular, he advocates career paths for both generalists and specialists, valuing expertise and management capability (Jenkins 2019).

pre-emptively rather than await external intervention. The independence of the clerks and the Parliamentary Librarian is enshrined in the *Parliamentary Service Act 1999*, effectively mitigating past concerns, and the clerks I interviewed (in both parliaments) were not always unwelcoming of the transfer of non-procedural administrative functions to managers, leaving them with more time to exercise their procedural expertise.

Second, the effectiveness of the UK Parliament's formalised governance structures, on which this proposal is based, continue to be widely criticised, both internally and externally (see, in particular, Cox 2018; Ellenbogen 2019; Leslie and Mohr 2021). Indeed, it appears that since the departure of Speaker Bercow, the force and intent of the governance changes to the House of Commons have been wound back (House of Commons 2021). Members of the House of Commons Commission are also considered to be remote from members and not focused on withdrawing or adjusting services in the interests of efficiency.[30] The commission's proposal to abolish the Restoration and Renewal Sponsor Body, supported by the House of Lords Commission, provides strong evidence of political micromanagement and a threat to the success of the previously agreed program (House of Commons Public Accounts Committee 2022). It would be simplistic and defeatist, however, to point to these perceived failures as a reason to not introduce or persist with a structure designed to bring better governance or look to ways of improving it, as difficult as that may prove.

The House of Lords Commission and its members have supported moves to address what is arguably its most pressing management reform in terms of its public standing, that of its size and constitution (Lord Speaker 2017, 2018). Before the 2019 general election, the House of Commons Public Administration and Constitutional Affairs Committee (HCPACAC 2019) was hearing differing views on the administrative role of the Speaker and the future role of the House of Commons Commission.[31] No doubt, the Covid-19 pandemic has resulted in the deferral of many important initiatives. Leaders in the UK Parliament may have to redouble their efforts to engage their own members and encourage their officials

---

30   I. Ailles, pers. comm., 27 October 2021.
31   For example, Lord Lisvane advocated the removal of the Speaker as chair of the commission, which was reported as an attempt to curb the Speaker's power after John Bercow's tenure (Webber 2019). However, further evidence from the Institute for Government, the Hansard Society and Lord Norton favoured further review of the wider governance role after the HOCGC recommendations and argued for a more strategic role for the commission and greater responsibility for all members, including in the restoration of trust in the House of Commons, in line with key arguments in this volume. The inquiry closed pending the general election in December 2019.

in restoring public trust and confidence. In Norton's (2017: 201) terms, they need 'to come [back] out of the bunker, guns firing'.[32] In particular, they need to address not just the structures and processes of effective management but also the skills (HCPACAC 2019; Leslie and Mohr 2021; Jenkins 2021). Proposals to strengthen management capacity should be seen as an opportunity for effective administrative reform. The mechanisms are already in place for collaborative management structures that could help to reduce intra-organisational rivalries, maintain or improve hard-won resources for effective scrutiny and ensure transparent and timely decision-making. A more effectively managed parliament would no doubt also contribute to restoring public confidence.

Returning to the book's third purpose, the case for less 'independent' and defensive thinking can be seen, too, in the context of calls in both countries for wider changes to the way democracy is practised.[33] Parliament should not relinquish any opportunity to re-establish itself as the major player in the democratic space. Both parliaments, through their members and officials, could advocate more effectively to meet the societal challenges they face in collaboration with other democratic institutions. A notable feature of this research has been the discovery of the symbiotic relationships between the UK Parliament and external organisations including the Hansard Society, the UCL Constitution Unit and the Institute for Government, as well as the increasing academic interest in parliamentary administration. Again, I draw attention to the conclusions of the House of Commons Liaison Committee (HCLC 2019) in this regard and the obvious role of each parliament's committee systems as forums for collaboration and deliberation (Hendriks et al. 2019; Hendriks and Kay 2019).

Both parliaments could also capitalise on moves towards greater citizen engagement and participation in public information and discourse.[34] This would call for an extension of outreach and engagement activities

---

32 In this respect, note Chris Bryant's role as Chair of the House of Commons Standards Committee (HC Debates 2021).

33 See, for instance, Gruen (2019), who advocates the establishment of a standing citizens' assembly as an antidote to the partisan self-interest of elected politicians and a departure from Schumpeter's view of electoral democracy as a competition by a political elite for the consent of the governed.

34 See Carson and Elstub (2019) for a comparison of participatory and deliberative democracy. My research steers more towards the latter, whereby participants become better informed and better able to make public judgements. See also Renwick and Palese (2019), who argue for better information and discourse around referendum and election campaigns, or the call from Moran, a former public service head, for a parliamentary policy office to evaluate new policy ideas (quoted in Trounson 2016). Moran proposed a parliamentary policy office akin to the Parliamentary Budget Office. He argued that the public would be well served by policy proposals that had been tested through a 'professional policy process' and that joint parliamentary committees would be ideal to 'thrash out policy ideas'.

and greater cross-sector collaboration to involve both the public and other democratic organisations in restoring trust and confidence in parliament. Again, mechanisms already exist within the committee system; the obvious candidates are the respective procedure committees and those involving electoral or constitutional change. Some would argue these committees are already on task, but greater public involvement could be garnered, including through citizens' assembly–type arrangements. At the very least, greater public participation could lead to new ways to tackle issues in either parliament's too-difficult box—such as electoral reform, parliamentary support and entitlements for members, House of Lords and Senate reform, the eligibility and representativeness of parliamentary candidates, strategic maintenance and renewal of parliamentary buildings and restoring public trust—by experimenting with forms of public discussion in collaboration with other organisations before, rather than after, the next crisis emerges.

Conclusion: Relating public management approaches to parliamentary administration

A major purpose of this book has been to demonstrate the complex management requirements of all parliament's roles and the dilemmas arising from the traditional beliefs and practices of its actors. Perhaps I should have stopped there in my defence of parliament and my explanation of why it is hard to manage. But after highlighting throughout this book a culture of avoidance within parliamentary management, I could not simply leave all these issues in the too-difficult box. Instead, I have put forward public management approaches that might offer an appropriate balance between specialist expertise and management skills and help to establish and embed new beliefs, practices and traditions.

While parliamentary management may never have been a typical example of 'old public administration', it has displayed many of its characteristics. We have seen management reforms occur in both parliaments over several decades, principally in response to calls for greater efficiency, transparency, accountability and responsiveness. These could be classified as NPM reforms, and many of them relate to the more routine (although still important) aspects of operational management. More elusive, however, have been the strategic cultural and behavioural reforms designed to reduce perceptions of incompetence, self-interest, inertia or unrepresentativeness and to win ongoing support and approval for parliamentary democracy while parliament continues to fulfil its primary purposes. The problem is not new; the question of parliament's public standing has been raised through the decades. I have demonstrated that most members are not actively engaged in advocating for institutional reform, either administrative or procedural; in some instances, they are excessively critical; standards of behaviour do not always meet public expectations; and traditional parliamentary administrators are reluctant to cross the political–administrative line into the purple zone—at least publicly. It is important here to reiterate that the actions of parliamentary actors depend heavily on their beliefs about what constitutes effective parliamentary management and that these beliefs are closely tied to their political values and individual conceptions of the public interest. Again, I acknowledge the influence of Bevir and Rhodes (2003, 2006) in this regard. However, also drawing on Bevir and Rhodes, we do not have to accept that the attitudes and practices of parliamentary actors must remain fixed. In the current environment of public distrust and disengagement, we need to look for new ways of energising parliaments, on the one hand, in resolving their internal dilemmas and, in the process, making them more responsive to societal needs.

I have also sought to demonstrate that the problems of both determining and providing public value while seeking public consensus are common to both the public/civil services and parliamentary services and there appears to be little to gain in continuing to proclaim that parliament is 'unique' as a defence against reform. On the contrary, parliament's willingness to seek out ways of making the institution more representative of society as a whole, to collaborate with other actors in the public network to gain the resources it needs, to maintain the highest ethical standards, to work more closely with citizens in representing their collective aspirations and enhancing their efficacy and even to 'co-produce' an effective parliamentary democracy may be the keys to its ongoing relevance.

Epilogue

Overview

From the beginning of this book, I have argued for a greater priority to be given to parliamentary management, taking my cue from Bevir and Rhodes' interpretive approach and, specifically, constructing parliamentary actors as situated agents, garnering stakeholder support for informed management decisions, capable of effective and enduring implementation. At the conclusion of a five-year research period, from 2015 to 2019, I had gathered enough evidence to demonstrate that in comparative terms the United Kingdom's governance arrangements placed its parliament in a better position for the exercise of situated agency and to suggest that the Australian Parliament would benefit from adopting similar arrangements. Such claims may have been diminished by later events that appear to have regressed the advances towards prioritising management and engaging members in collective responsibility. In the same period, events affecting the Australian Parliament, such as the Jenkins review into parliamentary workplace culture (AHRC 2021) and the failure to establish a federal integrity commission thus far (Doran 2021), have also adversely affected public perceptions. But claims of regression and further dents in public confidence should not mean we have to throw up our hands and accept, fatalistically, that path-dependency or management by crisis is the only way for parliaments to evolve. Path-dependency does lead to change Kelso (2009), but there is also a role for situated agency as well as external participation and for understanding that, for parliamentary actors, there are myriad ways of putting the institution first.

I acknowledge that many will see gaps in the issues I have presented. By putting forward new management approaches, I may have entered an intellectual cul-de-sac. This might be unavoidable if one agrees that parliament's responsibilities are far-reaching and characterised by layers of complexity, and that parliamentary effectiveness will always be a contested concept. But culs-de-sac often have pathways out that can be travelled on foot. I have presented a view of parliamentary administration within a public management context, citing an array of contemporary public management literature to encourage further debate or study of how parliament might be managed into the future and, more aspirationally, how it might, by getting its own houses in order, increase its influence in the fields of public policy and democratic reform.

Implications for theory development and new research

This research has built on historical scholarship on parliamentary reform by focusing on the influence of management issues on parliament's effectiveness. It has addressed a large gap in the literature by analysing the complexities and challenges of the many aspects of managing a parliament—a 'constitutional terra incognita'[1]—and the relationships between parliamentary actors. Rather than approaching the subject from a historical institutional perspective, which might have sought to explain administrative reforms using a path-dependent approach, I have used Bevir and Rhodes' (2003, 2006) concept of dilemma to demonstrate and interpret the effects of the conflicting beliefs and practices of parliamentary actors on dilemmas of parliamentary governance, management and procedural and cultural reform. I have taken the research further by advocating public management approaches that could assist in addressing parliament's management dilemmas, challenging conventional claims that parliament is a unique institution for which these approaches are not appropriate. I have suggested that when parliamentary management is viewed through lenses of public management favouring public value, collaboration and co-production, and not solely the pursuit of relentless efficiency, opportunities arise to improve strategic management, build symbiotic and productive relationships, internally and externally, and work collaboratively across organisational boundaries. Competition between parliamentary actors may thereby be reduced, even in a public institution that is defined by contest. Consequently, parliament may be

---

1   M. Flinders, pers. comm., 23 March 2020.

in a better position to fulfil Crick's ideal of parliament as a deliberative forum and a broker of ideas, engaging with an informed public. Further study may help to validate (or moderate) these claims.

Bringing the study of parliament under the public management 'umbrella' opens a range of theoretical opportunities for further study. The boundaries of this research have not permitted an exhaustive analysis of all the public, or non-public, management approaches that could assist parliamentary management, neither have they allowed for a detailed historical and comparative study of management reforms across the parliamentary and public spheres. It is not possible either to conclude that the findings from the study of management effectiveness in two Westminster parliaments can be generalised across other parliaments. But the findings do suggest a direction for further research into how public management practice could help to build a more representative democratic process, with parliament as the key actor. This could include wider studies of the success or otherwise of governance and management arrangements in other parliaments, outside the often narrow and critical confines of parliamentary research—an invitation, perhaps, to 'walk on the bright side of [parliamentary] governance and [parliamentary] service' (Douglas et al. 2021). Studies in the burgeoning field of democratic governance and citizen participation could focus specifically on parliament, thus avoiding the tendency to conflate parliament, politicians and government within public judgements of democracy. Further research might include studies on organisational behaviour in parliaments and contribute, for example, to the limited work on the characteristics and psychological wellbeing of politicians and their staff and the effects of psychological stressors on policymaking (Flinders et al. 2018b; Baldwin et al. 2020; Weinberg 2020). The roles of parliamentary actors, including elected officials, would also provide a rich source for case studies of public leadership. At the very least, surveys of satisfaction with government and public institutions should include parliament to assist in evaluating its efforts in public engagement and education. Advocates of democracy could learn from the UK Hansard Society in this regard.

There is a role, too, for public administration/management scholars to take a greater interest in parliamentary administration and parliament's continuing and potential contribution to public deliberation and subsequent policy development. Again, I note many examples in the United Kingdom such as the Crick Centre, the Hansard Society, UCL's Constitution Unit and the Institute for Government, and collaborations between scholars and practitioners addressing how the UK Parliament is managed and led (HOCGC 2014; HCPACAC 2019). There is little evidence of attention to parliamentary administration in Australian studies of public administration and management, despite its potential to offer a rich field of study. Organisations such as the Institute of Public Administration Australia, the Australasian Study of Parliament Group and the Australia and New Zealand School of Government have great potential to forge new relationships between parliamentary and public management scholars. There is an opportunity for parliament's internal discussion forums to be more open and inclusive.[2] Future public service reviews would ideally include parliamentary departments, as would recently mooted calls for a specialist Australian Public Service college (Easton 2019).

Reflections on unfolding events

When I began my research in 2015, there was little evidence of academic interest in the topic of parliamentary administration or management, although there was a large body of scholarship on procedural and political reform, some of which I have drawn on. Public interest was piqued temporarily by the 'Mills affair', but this was largely stimulated by media embellishment of hostile relationships and a struggle for supremacy between parliamentary actors rather than being of genuine public interest. During the study, I was encouraged by the increasing attention paid to parliamentary administration by parliamentary scholars, particularly in the United Kingdom, and an implicit acknowledgement that administrative outcomes were inherently related to parliamentary effectiveness and parliament's public standing.

Close observers of parliamentary affairs may not have anticipated that the unexpected and unplanned-for result of the Brexit referendum in the United Kingdom would highlight the stark contrast between the role of the government in seeking to implement a perceived mandate and that of the parliament in protecting the perceived public interest, or that it would increase tensions between representative and direct democracy from a premise of 'parliament versus the people' (Russell 2019c). Russell (2020) has since described this relationship as the anatomy of

---

2   Such as the Society of Clerks-at-the-Table and presiding officer and clerks conferences.

a perfect storm. Nor may they have predicted the continuing instability of Australia's Coalition government and its subsequent re-election in 2019, an increasing tendency to elect Independent members, misuse of parliamentary entitlements and heightened criticism of members' personal behaviour. The knock-on effects of these events on the perceptions held by an already disenchanted public, combined with revelations of unacceptable workplace cultures, have influenced the direction of travel of this interpretative study, away from a more routine performance-related concept of parliamentary administration towards the more encompassing dilemma of how to manage parliament's long-term internal and external relationships and purposes.

Increasingly, through the duration of the study, other writers have started to address these issues. For instance, a study by the Institute for Government (Thimont Jack and White 2019: 7) found that in the UK Parliament, after the Brexit referendum, 'where strategic direction is absent and no one is sufficiently in charge to drive it', people with sufficient political capital and buy-in from both government and opposition need to establish new processes and address fundamental questions about parliament's relationship with government. They advocate establishing a joint committee to do just that, as I have advocated a joint parliamentary commission for the Australian Parliament to bring a cross-party approach to addressing strategic administrative issues that cannot be entirely divorced from the political arena. Evidence given to the HCPACAC (2019) inquiry into role of the Speaker has lent further support to claims made in this book. As well, more attention is being paid to parliament's capacity for deliberation and its relationship with the public, more than half a century after Crick expounded these themes.

Similarly, no one could have anticipated the effects of the Covid-19 pandemic, which has seemingly swept away Brexit's predominance in political discussion in the United Kingdom and challenged the capacity of executive government in both countries. One constant of the aftermath of Brexit and the tumultuous and ongoing events linked to the pandemic is, however, increasing alarm about a further threat to parliament's role, and concerns in both countries that parliament has, in fact, been sidelined during the pandemic response by the adoption of emergency government powers (Wright 2020).[3] An Australian scholar, Stephen Mills, claimed the Australian Parliament's lengthy adjournment at the height of the pandemic and 'severely pruned' attendances demonstrated a 'growing capacity and willingness … to govern without parliament, and an acquiescent parliament unable to define a more assertive role for itself' (Mills 2020: 7–8; see also Warhurst 2020). Parliament has been deemed a non-essential service and its deliberative role, which might have contributed to defining the strategic and implementation challenges presented by the pandemic, has been substantially compromised. Anne Twomey, Professor of Constitutional Law at the University of Sydney, advised that there is good reason to ensure that continuing scrutiny and representation within Australia's national parliament can occur by virtual means and, notably, there is no constitutional reason why it should not (Twomey 2020). The Speaker of the NSW Legislative Assembly, concerned about the potential for reduced parliamentary sittings and the number of members in attendance to 'cripple a central pillar of democracy', urged the NSW Parliament to instead meet virtually (O'Dea 2020: 27).

The Australian Parliament has an abundance of administrative and technological capacity to enable it to stand up a robust virtual or hybrid parliament fulfilling all its functions, including voting by electronic means; all it requires is administrative and political will. Here was an opportunity for the parliament to raise its public standing as it led by example in being innovative and adaptive, while also abiding by the significant social restrictions faced by the community, including limited cross-border travel. Instead, the arrangements adopted for the August 2020 sittings (although much heralded by the presiding officers) fell short of the ideal, particularly in the absence of the ability for members to vote remotely, as some of its members have acknowledged (Karvelas 2020).[4] Aversive constitutionalism has continued to dominate and concerns have been expressed about parliamentary privilege and potential interference in the voting process. Former Deputy Prime Minister Barnaby Joyce

---

3   Wright cites former Supreme Court judge Lady Hale, who suggested that in relation to emergency powers during the Covid-19 pandemic, parliament had surrendered its control to the government at a crucial time. Ironically, her views appeared to be supported by backbench members of the Conservative Party rebelling against the extension of emergency powers, in stark contrast to her earlier decision on the illegality of the prorogation of parliament by the Johnson government in 2019. In Australia, rioters protested the extension of emergency powers by the Victorian state government (Thompson 2021).

4   Remote voting might also have enabled the absolute majority vote required to bring on debate on a Private Member's Bill to establish a federal integrity commission (Hitch and Doran 2021).

(Karvelas 2020) claimed the threat to party discipline was a key factor; another appears to be a recurring threat to the capacity of members to continue to assemble in person, despite widespread acceptance of the need to adapt in the wider community (F. Kelly 2020). Associate Professor Tom Daly (2020) from the University of Melbourne provided a compelling argument for pragmatism in terms of keeping parliament running.

In the United Kingdom, parliamentary actors initially responded rapidly to the technological and procedural challenges presented by the pandemic by creating a hybrid parliament that enabled up to 50 MPs to participate from the UK House of Commons chamber, with 120 more joining in virtually and others able to vote remotely. Its acceptance, however, appeared to have been short-lived when the government moved to discontinue virtual proceedings, requiring all members who were able to travel to return to Westminster, at the expense of those who were vulnerable or shielding an at-risk member of their household. The move was criticised as a departure from the principle of equality and the Leader of the House citing a need to progress the legislative program was called an unfounded excuse (White 2020a, 2020b). These events accelerated ongoing division between the modernisers and the traditionalists and led to a group of senior democracy specialists expressing grave concerns about the suspension of the hybrid House of Commons (Russell et al. 2020). On the other hand, the House of Lords continued to use hybrid proceedings to allow its members to participate, particularly those who were vulnerable, and it has been suggested that working from home might become a normal part of its operations (Beamish 2020). The House of Commons Procedure Committee (2020) related examples of ongoing vacillation by the Johnson government, represented by the Leader of the House, in relation to the continuation and expansion of the hybrid system of both physical and virtual participation, despite the obvious capacity of parliament's managers to provide the necessary infrastructure and support. On a brighter note, the 2020 World e-Parliament Report noted that the pandemic had brought about a rise in funds for technology, a shift away from siloed digital strategies and an increase in innovation since the pandemic. However, it also acknowledged that some changes may have been temporary and parliaments would need to make permanent changes to procedural rules, take an institution-wide approach integrated into the fabric and culture of parliament, and proactively retain and adapt realised efficiencies (Williamson 2021).

Further evidence of the UK Parliament's resistance to change is the about-face on the House of Commons' 2019 decision that members should 'decant' from the Palace of Westminster to allow a full restoration to be carried out (Meakin et al. 2020). According to the BBC, the Sponsor Body has freely acknowledged that a change of prime minister and a new set of MPs with different priorities are major factors, quite apart from the expected argument against the project arising from the threat of recession that the pandemic has posed (Wheeler 2020; HC Debates 2020). The ongoing saga of restoration and renewal is a sorry example of an inability to make difficult decisions and implement them. As outlined in a House of Commons Library Briefing Paper (R. Kelly 2022), the Sponsor Body was required to develop an outline of the costs for two 'bookended' objectives: 'do minimum', encompassing essential work, or 'variant', encompassing more aspirational plans. It was hampered by the House of Commons Commission's approval of a requirement for a 'continued presence' in the Palace of Westminster during restoration works, citing the absence of an approved decant strategy for the House of Commons as presenting a significant challenge (R. Kelly 2022). Faced with an unpalatable preliminary estimate of the cost of essential works, halfway through the time previously agreed for developing a detailed and costed restoration plan, the House of Commons Commission (with the implicit agreement of the House of Lords Commission) has called for the abolition of the Sponsor Body and for its work to be brought inhouse (Johnson 2022). Meanwhile, estimates of the ongoing cost of the program vary between £2 million per week (House of Commons Public Accounts Committee 2020) and £10 million per month.[5]

In terms of responses to claims of bullying and harassment and a toxic workplace culture, both parliaments continue to attract criticism (see, for instance, Webber and Calver 2020; Milligan 2020). It is in this area that we can see in both parliaments—if only in response to public outrage—a capacity, through collaborative, cross-party and whole-of-parliament mechanisms, to embed behavioural and cultural change that meets societal expectations. The Independent Complaints and Grievance Scheme operating in the UK Parliament since mid-2018 was reviewed after 18 months, leading to a renewed commitment to build a workplace culture of dignity and respect, with simplified procedures and greater support for complainants (Stanley 2021). In Australia, the Jenkins review

---

5   I. Ailles, pers. comm., 27 October 2021.

into Commonwealth parliamentary workplaces (AHRC 2021) has now provided a comprehensive assessment of a workplace culture based on adversarial and competitive behaviour with manifest examples of bullying and sexual harassment. Resonating with UK inquiries, the AHRC heard that within parliamentary departments people were sometimes placed in leadership positions based on their technical or legal knowledge, rather than their people leadership skills. The DPS was seen as being driven by fear:

> Participants ... told the Commission that DPS employees feared senior leaders in DPS, who in turn feared parliamentarians. Some participants told the Commission that parliamentarians consider DPS a 'whipping boy', especially during Senate Estimates ... [T]he result of this fear was a culture of 'cover up' and silence. (AHRC 2021: 98)

The Jenkins review has taken its cue from the UK Parliament's model and recommended, inter alia, establishing an Office of Parliamentarian Staffing and Culture, reporting to the parliament's presiding officers, to oversee the recruitment and ongoing management of parliamentary staffers; a code of conduct for members and their staff;[6] and an independent Parliamentary Standards Commission with delegated power 'to operate a fair, independent, confidential and transparent system to receive disclosures and handle informal and formal complaints' (AHRC 2021: 25).

The Jenkins review has undoubtedly offered an opportunity for the Australian Parliament to manage its workplace culture on a cross-party, bipartisan and whole-of-parliament basis, envisioning collaborative engagement among the presiding officers, political leaders, parliamentary department heads and external experts. It remains to be seen how its recommendations will be taken up by the new government. Even so, the Australian Parliament will still lack the governing architecture that exists in comparable jurisdictions (Maley 2021; Podger 2022).

The events that have unfolded—and are still unfolding—since the start of this research have increased both the need for and the potential of public management expertise to engender a more nuanced and sophisticated public understanding of parliament's roles, enhance the institution's

---

6   Parliamentary workers employed under the *Parliamentary Service Act 1999* are already subject to the Parliamentary Service Code of Conduct.

public value and build a more effective and sustainable parliamentary institution that has the capacity to contribute to public policy and democratic reform. Retreating to insularity and old arguments in the face of massive challenges will not assist. The key, rather, will be greater internal and external collaboration among parliamentary actors, including scholars and public administrators, managers and procedural specialists, MPs and officials, and between a collective parliamentary leadership and the public.

Bibliography

Act of Union Bill [HL], Bill 132, 2017–19 (United Kingdom).

Adams, J. 2002, *Parliament: Master of its own household?*, Australian Public Service Commission, Canberra.

Agranoff, R. 2012, *Collaborating to manage: A primer for the public sector*, Georgetown University Press, Washington, DC.

Albrow, M. 1970, *Bureaucracy*, Pall Mall Press, London, doi.org/10.1007/978-1-349-00916-9.

Aldons, M. 2001a, 'Performance indicators for the parliament: Sharp or blunt instruments of reform?', *Australasian Parliamentary Review*, vol. 16, no. 2, pp. 27–37.

Aldons, M. 2001b, 'Responsible, representative and accountable government', *Australian Journal of Public Administration*, vol. 60, no. 1, pp. 34–42, doi.org/10.1111/1467-8500.00196.

Alford, J. 2014, 'The multiple facets of co-production: Building on the work of Elinor Ostrom', *Public Management Review*, vol. 16, no. 3, pp. 299–316, doi.org/10.1080/14719037.2013.806578.

Alford, J. 2016, 'Co-production, interdependence and publicness: Extending public service–dominant logic', *Public Management Review*, vol. 18, no. 5, pp. 673–691, doi.org/10.1080/14719037.2015.1111659.

Alford, J., Douglas, S., Geuijen, K. & 't Hart, P. 2017, 'Ventures in public value management: Introduction to the symposium', *Public Management Review*, vol. 19, no. 5, pp. 589–604, doi.org/10.1080/14719037.2016.1192160.

Alford, J., Hartley, J., Yates, S. & Hughes, O. 2017, 'Into the purple zone: Deconstructing the politics/administration distinction', *The American Review of Public Administration*, vol. 47, no. 7, pp. 752–763, doi.org/10.1177/0275074016638481.

Alford, J. & Hughes, O. 2008, 'Public value pragmatism as the next phase of public management', *The American Review of Public Administration*, vol. 38, no. 2, pp. 130–148, doi.org/10.1177/0275074008314203.

Alford, J. & O'Flynn, J. 2009, 'Making sense of public value: Concepts, critiques and emergent meanings', *International Journal of Public Administration*, vol. 32, nos 3–4, pp. 171–191, doi.org/10.1080/01900690902732731.

Allen, N. 2011, 'Dishonourable members? Exploring patterns of misconduct in the contemporary House of Commons', *British Politics*, vol. 6, no. 2, pp. 210–240, doi.org/10.1057/bp.2011.6.

Allen, S. & McKee, R. 2019, 'Why do citizens' assemblies work? Evidence from the citizens' assemblies on Brexit and Social Care', *The Constitution Unit Blog*, 28 February, available from: constitution-unit.com/2019/02/28/why-do-citizens-assemblies-work-evidence-from-the-citizens-assemblies-on-brexit-and-social-care/.

Anckar, C. 2008, 'On the applicability of the most similar systems design and the most different systems design in comparative research', *International Journal of Social Research Methodology*, vol. 11, no. 5, pp. 389–401, doi.org/10.1080/13645570701401552.

Anderson, A. & Meakin, A. 2019, 'A leaky roof and a democratic crisis within: What better time to get serious about redesigning Westminster?', *The Conversation*, 9 April, available from: theconversation.com/a-leaky-roof-and-a-democratic-crisis-within-what-better-time-to-get-serious-about-redesigning-westminster-115050.

Andren, P. 1999, Appropriation Bill (No. 3) 1998–99, Appropriation Bill (No. 4) 1998–99, Appropriation (Parliamentary Departments) Bill (No. 2) 1998–99, Appropriation Bill (No. 4) 1998–99, Appropriation (Parliamentary Departments) Bill (No. 2) 1998–99, Second Reading Speech, 8 March, *House of Representatives Parliamentary Debates*, Parliament of Australia, available from: parlinfo.aph.gov.au/parlInfo/genpdf/chamber/hansardr/1999-03-08/0098/hansard_frag.pdf;fileType=application%2Fpdf.

Ansell, C. & Gash, A. 2008, 'Collaborative governance in theory and practice', *Journal of Public Administration Research and Theory*, vol. 18, no. 4, pp. 543–571, doi.org/10.1093/jopart/mum032.

Ansell, C. & Gash, A. 2018, 'Collaborative platforms as a governance strategy', *Journal of Public Administration Research and Theory*, vol. 28, no. 1, pp. 16–32, doi.org/10.1093/JOPART%2FMUX030.

Appleby, G. & Williams, J. 2009, 'A tale of two clerks: When are appropriations appropriate in the Senate?', *Public Law Review*, vol. 20, no. 3, pp. 194–213.

Appropriation (Parliamentary Departments) Act (No. 1) 2017–2018 (Commonwealth of Australia).

Aschhoff, N. 2018, 'Citizens differ from organizations: Modeling a specific citizen-centered collaborative capacity', *International Journal of Public Administration*, vol. 41, no. 4, pp. 284–296, doi.org/10.1080/01900692.2016.1263657.

Asher, M., Leston-Bandeira, C. & Spaiser, V. 2019, 'Do parliamentary debates of e-petitions enhance public engagement with parliament? An analysis of Twitter conversations', *Policy & Internet*, vol. 11, no. 2, pp. 149–171, doi.org/10.1002/poi3.194.

Attorney-General's Department 2018, *A Commonwealth Integrity Commission: Proposed reforms*, Discussion Paper, December, Australian Government, Canberra, available from: www.ag.gov.au/Consultations/Documents/commonwealth-integrity-commission/cic-consultation-paper.pdf.

Australia, House of Representatives 2018, *Debates*, No. 16, Tuesday, 27 November, Parliament of Australia, available from: www.aph.gov.au/Parliamentary_Business/Hansard/Hansard_Display?bid=chamber/hansardr/fe71afbd-cf96-4da5-a4b4-33913ff9b019/&sid=0000.

Australia, House of Representatives 2021a, *Debates*, Monday, 22 November, Parliament of Australia, available from: www.aph.gov.au/Parliamentary_Business/Hansard/Hansard_Display?bid=chamber/hansardr/25170/&sid=0000.

Australia, House of Representatives 2021b, *Debates*, Thursday, 2 December, Parliament of Australia, available from: www.aph.gov.au/Parliamentary_Business/Hansard/Hansard_Display?bid=chamber/hansardr/25177/&sid=0000.

Australia, Senate 2012, *Debates*, Wednesday, 28 November, Parliament of Australia, p. 10091, available from: parlinfo.aph.gov.au/parlInfo/search/display/display.w3p;db=CHAMBER;id=chamber%2Fhansards%2Fa313cbaa-0111-489d-96e4-ef24e85fa333%2F0139;query=Id%3A%22chamber%2Fhansards%2Fa313cbaa-0111-489d-96e4-ef24e85fa333%2F0000%22.

Australia, Senate 2014, *Debates*, No. 15, 2014, Tuesday, 18 November, Parliament of Australia, available from: parlinfo.aph.gov.au/parlInfo/download/chamber/hansards/0b82d8da-6a2f-49ab-b058-21f890efbee4/toc_pdf/Senate_2014_11_18_3043_Official.pdf;fileType=application%2Fpdf#search=%22chamber/hansards/0b82d8da-6a2f-49ab-b058-21f890efbee4/0000%22.

Australia, Senate 2018, *Debates*, No. 14, 2018, Wednesday, 28 November, Parliament of Australia, available from: parlinfo.aph.gov.au/parlInfo/download/chamber/hansards/c213941c-eb14-4c54-a8dc-11b938aad7dc/toc_pdf/Senate_2018_11_28_6794_Official.pdf;fileType=application%2Fpdf.

Australian Broadcasting Corporation (ABC) 2017, *The House with Annabel Crabb*, ABC TV, available from: www.abc.net.au/tv/programs/house-with-annabel-crabb/.

Australian Human Rights Commission (AHRC) 2021, *Set the standard: Report on the independent review into Commonwealth parliamentary workplaces*, AHRC, Sydney.

Australian National Audit Office (ANAO) 1990a, *The Department of the Parliamentary Reporting Staff*, Auditor-General Report No. 21, ANAO, Canberra.

Australian National Audit Office (ANAO) 1990b, *An investigation of an unofficial account operated by Parliamentary Information Systems Office*, Auditor-General Report No. 25, ANAO, Canberra.

Australian National Audit Office (ANAO) 2006, *Implementation of the parliamentary resolutions arising from the review by the Parliamentary Service Commissioner of aspects of the administration of Parliament: Department of Parliamentary Services*, Auditor-General Report No. 51 2005–06, ANAO, Canberra.

Australian National Audit Office (ANAO) 2009, *Administration of parliamentarians' entitlements by the Department of Finance and Deregulation*, Auditor-General Report No. 3 2009–10: Performance Audit, ANAO, Canberra.

Australian National Audit Office (ANAO) 2015, *Managing assets and contracts at Parliament House: Department of Parliamentary Services*, Auditor-General Report No. 24 2014–15: Performance Audit, ANAO, Canberra.

Aylett, P. 2018, '1979 and all that: An alternative view of select committee reform', *PSA Parliaments*, 11 April, The UK Political Studies Association Specialist Group on Parliaments, London, available from: psaparliaments.org/2018/04/11/alternative-view-of-select-committee-reform/.

Bagehot 2019, 'John Bercow, speaker of the asylum', *The Economist*, 10 January, [Updated 31 May], available from: www.economist.com/britain/2019/01/10/john-bercow-speaker-of-the-asylum.

Bagshaw, E. 2019, 'Legal costs spiral in $14m Parliament House security flop', *The Canberra Times*, 8 April, available from: www.canberratimes.com.au/story/6008690/legal-costs-spiral-in-14m-parliament-house-security-flop/.

Baldwin, A., Pinto, C., Perriard-Abdoh, S. & Weinberg, A. 2020, *Cognitive strain in Parliament: How can we reduce psychological stressors to improve policy-making?*, British Psychological Society, London, available from: www.bps.org.uk/sites/www.bps.org.uk/files/Policy/Policy%20-%20Files/Cognitive%20strain%20in%20Parliament.pdf.

Ballintyne, K. & Mintrom, M. 2018, 'Towards whole-of-government enhancement of public value: An Australian case', *Policy Design and Practice*, vol. 1, no. 3, pp. 183–193, doi.org/10.1080/25741292.2018.1504371.

Barrett, V. 1999, *A study of the impact of public sector reforms on parliamentary administration in Australia, the United Kingdom, Canada and Singapore*, Report to the Australian Public Service Commission, Canberra.

Barrett, V. 2010, 'Publishing the record of parliamentary proceedings: Identifying and controlling the risks', *Journal of Law, Science & Information*, vol. 20, no. 2, pp. 98–118.

Barrett, V. 2014, Presentation to Australia and New Zealand School of Government Round Table on the *Public Governance, Performance and Accountability Act 2013*, Canberra, 25 September.

Barrett, V. 2019, Parliamentary administration: What does it mean to manage a parliament effectively?, Doctoral dissertation, The Australian National University, Canberra.

Barrett, V. 2021, 'The dilemmas of managing parliament: Promoting awareness of public management theories to parliamentary administrators', in T. Mercer, R. Ayres, B. Head & J. Wanna (eds), *Learning policy, doing policy: Interactions between public policy theory, practice and teaching*, ANU Press, Canberra, pp. 129–161, doi.org/10.22459/LPDP.2021.06.

Bartelings, J.A., Goedee, J., Raab, J. & Bijl, R. 2017, 'The nature of orchestrational work', *Public Management Review*, vol. 19, no. 3, pp. 342–360, doi.org/10.1080/14719037.2016.1209233.

Baxter, K. 2015, *Review of the Department of Parliamentary Services*, Senate Finance and Public Administration Legislation Committee, Additional Estimates 2016–17 (February and March 2017), 'Answers to Questions on Notice', No. 111, 13 April 2017, available from: www.aph.gov.au/Parliamentary_Business/Senate_estimates/fapactte/estimates/add1617/parliamentary/index.

BBC News 2019, 'Newspaper headlines: Bercow "out of order" over Brexit?', *The Papers*, [Blog], 10 January, available from: www.bbc.com/news/blogs-the-papers-46818717.

Beamish, D. 2020, 'How has the House of Lords adapted to the coronavirus crisis?', *The Constitution Unit Blog*, 12 June, available from: constitution-unit.com/2020/06/12/how-has-the-house-of-lords-adapted-to-the-coronavirus-crisis/.

Beamish, D. 2021, 'The House of Lords after the pandemic', *Hansard Society Blog*, 8 October, available from: www.hansardsociety.org.uk/blog/the-house-of-lords-after-the-pandemic.

Beetham, D. 2006, *Parliament and democracy in the twenty-first century: A guide to good practice*, Inter-Parliamentary Union, Geneva, available from: archive.ipu.org/PDF/publications/democracy_en.pdf.

Benger, J. 2020, *House of Commons Commission: Clerk's management and team structure review*, 9 November.

Benington, J. & Moore, M. 2010, 'Public value in complex and changing times', in J. Benington & M. Moore (eds), *Public value: Theory and practice*, Palgrave Macmillan, Basingstoke, UK, pp. 1–30.

Bennett, S. 2008, *Parliament House and the Australian people*, Research Paper No. 29 2007–08, 7 May, Parliamentary Library, Canberra, available from: www.aph.gov.au/About_Parliament/Parliamentary_Departments/Parliamentary_Library/pubs/rp/RP0708/08rp29.

Benwell, R. & Gay, O. 2011, *The separation of powers*, Standard Note: SN/PC/06053, 15 August, Parliament and Constitution Centre, House of Commons Library, London.

Bercow, J. 2015, The making of a modern House of Commons, Speech to Policy Exchange, London, 18 August, available from: youtu.be/hn6mN22aXoM.

Besly, N., Goldsmith, T., Rogers, R. & Walters, R. 2018, *How parliament works*, 8th edn, Routledge, London, doi.org/10.4324/9781351251822.

Beswick, D. & Elstub, S. 2019, 'Between diversity, representation and "best evidence": Rethinking select committee evidence-gathering practices', *Parliamentary Affairs*, vol. 72, no. 4, pp. 945–964, doi.org/10.1093/pa/gsz035.

Betts, C. & Wollaston, S. 2018, 'How a citizens' assembly helped select committees find social care consensus', *Hansard Society Blog*, 10 October, available from: www.hansardsociety.org.uk/blog/how-a-citizens-assembly-helped-select-committees-find-social-care-consensus.

Bevir, M. & Rhodes, R.A.W. 2003, *Interpreting British governance*, Routledge, London.

Bevir, M. & Rhodes, R.A.W. 2006, *Governance stories*, Routledge, London.

Bevir, M., Rhodes, R.A.W. & Weller, P. 2003, 'Traditions of governance: Interpreting the changing role of the public sector', *Public Administration*, vol. 81, no. 1, pp. 1–17, doi.org/10.1111/1467-9299.00334.

Blackburn, R., Kennon, A. & Wheeler-Booth, M. (eds) 2003, *Griffith and Ryle on parliament: Functions, practice and procedures*, Sweet & Maxwell, London.

Bond, M. 1958, 'Clerks of the parliaments, 1509–1953', *The English Historical Review*, vol. 73, no. 286, pp. 78–85, doi.org/10.1093/ehr/LXXIII.286.78.

Booth, A. 2021, 'Sir David Amess, Jo Cox and the knotty problem of local constituency security', *The Mandarin*, 18 October, available from: www.the mandarin.com.au/172296-sir-david-amess-jo-cox-and-the-knotty-problem-of-local-constituency-security/.

Boothroyd, B. 2001, *Betty Boothroyd: The autobiography*, Random House, London.

Bottomley, A. 1975, *House of Commons (Administration): Report to Mr Speaker by committee under chairmanship of Mr Arthur Bottomley, MP*, 1974–75 HC 624, HMSO, London.

Boulton, A. 2019, 'Call John Bercow whatever you like, but as Speaker he's given parliament its voice back', *The Sunday Times*, [London], 13 January, available from: www.thetimes.co.uk/article/call-the-speaker-whatever-you-like-but-he-s-given-parliament-its-voice-back-ggst3txjp.

Boulton, C. 1991, 'The organization of the House of Commons Service', in D. Englefield (ed.), *Workings of Westminster*, Dartmouth Publishing Company, Hants, UK.

Bourgon, J. 2011, *A new synthesis of public administration: Serving in the 21st century*, McGill-Queen's University Press, Kingston, ON.

Bradley, A. 2012, 'The Damian Green affair: All's well that ends well?', *Public Law*, vol. 3, pp. 396–407.

Braithwaite, M. 1999, *Review of management and services: Report to the House of Commons Commission*, HC 745, 23 July, UK Parliament, London, available from: publications.parliament.uk/pa/cm199899/cmselect/cmhccom/745/hc745.htm.

Breckon, J., Hopkins, A. & Rickey, B. 2019, *Evidence vs democracy: How 'mini-publics' can traverse the gap between citizens, experts, and evidence*, Report, January, Alliance for Useful Evidence, London, available from: media.nesta. org.uk/documents/Evidence_vs_Democracy_Report_Final.pdf.

Breukel, J., Dosen, I., Grover, C., Lesman, B., Macvean, C. & Rosolen, H. 2017, *Independence of parliament*, Research Paper No. 3, May, Parliamentary Library & Information Service, Department of Parliamentary Services, Parliament of Victoria, Melbourne, available from: www.parliament.vic.gov.au/publications/research-papers/send/36-research-papers/13807-independence-of-parliament.

Brien, A. 1998, *A code of conduct for all parliamentarians?*, Research Paper No. 2 1998–99, 14 September, Parliamentary Library, Canberra, available from: www.aph.gov.au/About_Parliament/Parliamentary_Departments/Parliamentary_Library/pubs/rp/rp9899/99rp02.

British Broadcasting Corporation (BBC) 2015, *Inside the Commons*, BBC Two, available from: www.bbc.co.uk/programmes/b05234h3.

British Broadcasting Corporation (BBC) 2017, *Meet the Lords*, BBC Two, available from: www.bbc.co.uk/programmes/b08h4ch1/episodes/guide.

Brodsky, R.L. 2014, '"Commentary: Public value" and the measurement of government performance: The shift to subjective metrics', *Public Administration Review*, vol. 74, no. 4, pp. 478–479, doi.org/10.1111/puar.12234.

Broinowski, R. 2001, *A witness to history: The life and times of Robert Broinowski*, Melbourne University Press, Melbourne.

Bromell, D. 2012, 'Creating public value in the policy advice role: A reflection from the front line', *Policy Quarterly*, vol. 8, no. 4, pp. 16–22, doi.org/10.26686/pq.v8i4.4432.

Bromhead, P.A. 1958, *The House of Lords and contemporary politics*, Routledge & Kegan Paul, London.

Brown, T. & Evennett, H. 2015, *Principal office holders in the House of Lords*, House of Lords Library Note 2015/007, 19 March, UK Parliament, London.

Bryant, C. 2015, *Parliament: The biography. Volume 2: Reform*, Random House, London.

Bryant, O. & Moffitt, B. 2019, 'What actually is populism? And why does it have a bad reputation?', *The Conversation*, 6 February, available from: theconversation.com/what-actually-is-populism-and-why-does-it-have-a-bad-reputation-109874.

Bryson, J.M., Crosby, B.C. & Bloomberg, L. 2014, 'Public value governance: Moving beyond traditional public administration and the new public management', *Public Administration Review*, vol. 74, no. 4, pp. 445–456, doi.org/10.1111/puar.12238.

Bryson, J.M., Crosby, B.C. & Bloomberg, L. (eds) 2015, *Public value and public administration*, Georgetown University Press, Washington, DC.

Butcher, J.R., Gilchrist, D.J., Phillimore, J. & Wanna, J. 2019, 'Attributes of effective collaboration: Insights from five case studies in Australia and New Zealand', *Policy Design and Practice*, vol. 2, no. 1, pp. 75–89, doi.org/10.1080/25741292.2018.1561815.

Cadwalladr, C. 2016, 'Andy Burnham: "I am ready to leave Westminster and devote myself to Manchester"', *The Guardian*, 31 July, available from: www.theguardian.com/politics/2016/jul/31/andy-burnham-ready-to-leave-westminster-mayor-manchester-interview.

Cameron, S. & McAllister, I. 2016, *Trends in Australian political opinion: Results from the Australian Election Study*, School of Politics and International Relations, The Australian National University, Canberra.

Campbell, R. & Lovenduski, J. 2014, 'What should MPs do? Public and parliamentarians' views compared', *Parliamentary Affairs*, vol. 68, no. 4, pp. 690–708, doi.org/10.1093/pa/gsu020.

The Canberra Times 2017, 'Ring of steel an ugly sign of the times', *The Canberra Times*, 14 September, p. 12.

Capoccia, G. & Kelemen, R.D. 2007, 'The study of critical junctures: Theory, narrative, and counterfactuals in historical institutionalism', *World Politics*, vol. 59, no. 3, pp. 341–369, doi.org/10.1017/S0043887100020852.

Carson, L. & Elstub, S. 2019, *Comparing participatory and deliberative democracy*, newDemocracy Research and Development Note, 21 February, Newcastle University, Newcastle, UK.

Childs, S. 2016, *The good parliament*, University of Bristol, Bristol, UK.

Childs, S. 2019a, 'Necessary baby steps towards The Good Parliament: Proxy voting in the Commons', *British Politics and Policy at LSE Blog*, 30 January, available from: blogs.lse.ac.uk/politicsandpolicy/proxy-voting-scheme-baby-leave/.

Childs, S. 2019b, Twitter post, 31 January, @ProfSarahChilds, available from: twitter.com/profsarahchilds/status/1090858014549118976?cn=ZmxleGlib GVfcmVjc18y&refsrc=email.

Childs, S. 2019c, 'The Good Parliament Report, Brexit politics, and the institutionalisation of a diversity sensitive Commons', *PSA Parliaments*, 23 April, The UK Political Studies Association Specialist Group on Parliaments, London, available from: psaparliaments.org/2019/04/23/the-good-parliament-report-brexit-politics-and-the-institutionalisation-of-a-diversity-sensitive-commons/.

Childs, S. 2019d, 'The Good Parliament: What kind of Speaker do we need?', *The Constitution Unit Blog*, 1 October, available from: constitution-unit. com/2019/10/01/the-good-parliament-what-kind-of-speaker-do-we-need/? amp=1.

Christensen, J.G. 2012, 'Pay and prerequisites for government executives', in B.G. Peters & J. Pierre (eds), *The Sage handbook of public administration*, Sage Publications, London, pp. 101–114.

Church, I. 1991, 'Compiling the record: The making of Hansard', in D. Englefield (ed.), *Workings of Westminster*, Dartmouth Publishing Company, Hants, UK.

Clarke, C. 2014, '"Too-difficult box"', in C. Clarke (ed.), *The too-difficult box: The big issues politicians can't crack*, Biteback Publishing, London.

Clerk of the Parliaments Act 1824 (Chapter 82 5 Geo 4) (United Kingdom).

Climate Assembly UK 2020, *The path to net zero: Climate Assembly UK full report*, House of Commons, London, available from: www.climateassembly. uk/report/read/final-report.pdf.

Coats, D. & Passmore, E. 2008, *Public value: The next steps in public service reform*, Work Foundation, London.

Cocks, B. 1977, *Mid-Victorian masterpiece: The story of an institution unable to put its own house in order*, Hutchinson, London.

Coghill, K., Holland, P., Donohue, R., Rozzoli, K. & Grant, G. 2007, 'Professional development programmes for members of parliament', *Parliamentary Affairs*, vol. 61, no. 1, pp. 73–98, doi.org/10.1093/pa/gsm051.

Coghill, K., Lewis, C. & Steinack, K. 2012, 'How should elected members learn parliamentary skills: An overview', *Parliamentary Affairs*, vol. 65, no. 3, pp. 505–519, doi.org/10.1093/pa/gss031.

Colebatch, H.K. 2019, 'The Section 44 soap opera: Why more MPs could be in danger of being forced out', *The Conversation*, 7 June, available from: theconversation.com/the-section-44-soap-opera-why-more-mps-could-be-in-danger-of-being-forced-out-116955.

Collins, P. 2017, '"Meet the Lords" episode one: The whole institution comes over as absurd', *Prospect*, 27 February, available from: www.prospectmagazine.co.uk/politics/meet-the-lords-episode-one-the-whole-institution-comes-over-as-absurd.

Committee for the Review of Parliamentary Entitlements 2010, *An independent parliamentary entitlements system: Review*, February, Australian Government, Canberra, available from: www.finance.gov.au/sites/default/files/2019-11/independent-parliamentary-entitlements-system-review-feb-2016.pdf.

Committee on Standards in Public Life (CSPL) 2002, *Standards of conduct in the House of Commons*, Eighth report, Cm 5663, HMSO, London.

Commons Press Office 2019, 'Statement re: Sunday Times article', Twitter, 20 January, available from: twitter.com/HoCPress/status/1086940448772505600.

Commonwealth Parliamentary Association (CPA) 2005, *Administration and financing of parliament: A study group report*, CPA Secretariat, London, available from: www.cpahq.org/media/awydqld2/administration-and-financing-of-parliament-study-group-report-1.pdf.

Compton, E. 1974, *Review of the administrative services of the House of Commons*, Report to the Speaker by Sir Edmund Compton, HC 254, HMSO, London.

Connick, S. & Innes, J.E. 2003, 'Outcomes of collaborative water policy making: Applying complexity thinking to evaluation', *Journal of Environmental Planning and Management*, vol. 46, no. 2, pp. 177–197, doi.org/10.1080/0964056032000070987.

Cook, C. 2018, 'Parliament harassment plans fall short of staff hopes', *BBC News*, 10 July, available from: www.bbc.co.uk/news/uk-politics-44788407.

Cook, C. & Day, L. 2018, 'Bullying and harassment at the House of Commons', *BBC Newsnight*, 8 March, available from: www.bbc.com/news/uk-43338305.

Cooper, K. 2014, 'John Bercow Commons Clerk row: What is going on?', *BBC News*, 1 September, available from: www.bbc.co.uk/news/uk-politics-28941205.

Coorey, P. 2018, 'Scott Morrison under pressure to toughen federal ICAC plan', *Australian Financial Review*, 13 December, available from: www.afr.com/news/politics/scott-morrison-under-pressure-to-toughen-federal-icac-plan-20181213-h1936i.

Cowley, J. 2015, 'Andy Burnham thinks he is an outsider but he's really just another member of the Guild', *The New Statesman*, 24 June, available from: www.new statesman.com/politics/2015/06/andy-burnham-thinks-he-outsider-he-s-really-just-another-member-guild.

Cowley, P. & Stuart, M. 2003, 'Parliament: More revolts, more reform', *Parliamentary Affairs*, vol. 56, no. 2, pp. 188–204, doi.org/10.1093/parlij/gsg013.

Cowley, P. & Stuart, M. 2004, 'Parliament: More Bleak House than Great Expectations', *Parliamentary Affairs*, vol. 57, no. 2, pp. 301–314, doi.org/10.1093/pa/gsh026.

Cox, L. 2018, *The bullying and harassment of House of Commons staff: Independent inquiry report*, 15 October, UK Parliament, London, available from: www.parliament.uk/globalassets/documents/Conduct-in-Parliament/dame-laura-cox-independent-inquiry-report.pdf.

Crewe, E. 2005, *Lords of parliament: Manners, rituals and politics*, Manchester University Press, Manchester, UK.

Crewe, E. 2010, 'An anthropology of the House of Lords: Socialisation, relationships and rituals', *Journal of Legislative Studies*, vol. 16, no. 3, pp. 313–324, doi.org/10.1080/13572334.2010.498100.

Crewe, E. 2015, *The House of Commons: An anthropology of MPs at work*, Bloomsbury Academic, London.

Crewe, E. 2017, 'Magi or mandarins? Contemporary clerkly culture', in P. Evans (ed.), *Essays on the history of parliamentary procedure: In honour of Thomas Erskine May*, Bloomsbury Academic, London, pp. 45–66.

Crewe, E. & Walker, A. 2019, *An extraordinary scandal: The Westminster expenses crisis and why it still matters*, Haus Publishing, London.

Crick, B.R. 1968, *The reform of parliament*, 2nd edn, Weidenfeld & Nicolson, London.

Crick Centre 2018, 'The restoration and renewal of the Palace of Westminster', *Parliamentary Briefing*, January 2018, accessed from: www.crickcentre.org/wp-content/uploads/2018/01/D4D-Parliamentary-briefing-January-2018-1.pdf [page discontinued].

Crook, J. & Harrison, D. 2018, 'Westminster restoration and renewal: A wider view', *Hansard Society Blog*, 31 January, available from: www.hansardsociety.org.uk/blog/westminster-restoration-and-renewal-a-wider-view.

Crosby, B.C., 't Hart, P. & Torfing, J. 2017, 'Public value creation through collaborative innovation', *Public Management Review*, vol. 19, no. 5, pp. 655–669, doi.org/10.1080/14719037.2016.1192165.

Crosby, P. 2016, 'Is the architecture of Westminster bad for politics?', *The Conversation*, 1 March, available from: theconversation.com/is-the-architecture-of-westminster-bad-for-politics-55427.

Crowe, D. 2018, '"The last straw": Furious MP Julia Banks to quit parliament over the axing of Malcom Turnbull', *Sydney Morning Herald*, 29 August, available from: www.smh.com.au/politics/federal/the-last-straw-furious-mp-julia-banks-to-quit-parliament-over-the-axing-of-malcolm-turnbull-20180829-p500fk.html.

Curtice, J., Hudson, N. & Montagu, I. (eds) 2020, *British social attitudes: The 37th report*, The National Centre for Social Research, London.

Dahl, A. & Soss, J. 2014, 'Neoliberalism for the common good? Public value governance and the downsizing of democracy', *Public Administration Review*, vol. 74, no. 4, pp. 496–504, doi.org/10.1111/puar.12191.

Dale, I. 2022, 'John Bercow insists he is "empathetic" as he "absolutely denies" bullying MPs', *Leading Britain's Conversation*, 8 March, available from: www.lbc.co.uk/radio/presenters/iain-dale/john-bercow-bullying-report-denies-parliament/.

Daly, T.G. 2020, 'In times of crisis, does parliament really matter?', *Pursuit*, 10 August, University of Melbourne, available from: pursuit.unimelb.edu.au/articles/in-times-of-crisis-does-parliament-really-matter.

D'Arcy, M. 2014, 'Modernising rows', *BBC News*, 21 May, available from: www.bbc.com/news/uk-politics-27505650.

D'Arcy, M. 2015, 'Building for the future', *BBC News*, 8 January, available from: www.bbc.com/news/uk-politics-30728899.

D'Arcy, M. 2018, 'Media scrutiny of parliament', in C. Leston-Bandeira & L. Thompson (eds), *Exploring parliament*, Oxford University Press, Oxford, UK, pp. 207–217.

Davis, J.H., Schoorman, F.D. & Donaldson, L. 1997, 'Toward a stewardship theory of management', *Academy of Management Review*, vol. 22, no. 1, pp. 20–47, doi.org/10.5465/amr.1997.9707180258.

Day, N. 2017, '"Pool fence" shuts out nothing except equality', *The Canberra Times*, 14 September, p. 15.

Defence Abuse Response Taskforce (DART) 2016, *Defence Abuse Response Taskforce: Final report*, March, Australian Government, Canberra, available from: apo.org.au/sites/default/files/resource-files/2016-09/apo-nid67232.pdf.

Department of Finance 2014, *Enhanced Commonwealth performance framework*, Discussion Paper, August, Australian Government, Canberra.

Department of the House of Representatives 2006, *Annual report 2005–06*, Parliament of Australia, Canberra, available from: webarchive.nla.gov.au/gov/20070831040247/http://www.aph.gov.au/house/pubs/ar05-06/index.htm.

Department of the House of Representatives 2007, *Annual report 2006–07*, Parliament of Australia, Canberra, available from: webarchive.nla.gov.au/gov/20080730014510/http://www.aph.gov.au/house/pubs/ar06-07/index.htm.

Department of the House of Representatives 2016, *Annual report 2015–16*, Parliament of Australia, Canberra, available from: www.aph.gov.au/About_Parliament/Parliamentary_Departments/Department_of_the_House_of_Representatives/Annual_Reports/2015-16_Annual_Report.

Department of the House of Representatives 2017, *Annual report 2016–17*, Parliament of Australia, Canberra, available from: www.aph.gov.au/About_Parliament/Parliamentary_Departments/Department_of_the_House_of_Representatives/Annual_Reports/2016-17_Annual_Report.

Department of the House of Representatives 2018a, *Annual report 2017–18*, Parliament of Australia, Canberra, available from: www.aph.gov.au/About_Parliament/Parliamentary_Departments/Department_of_the_House_of_Representatives/Annual_Reports/2017-18_Annual_Report.

Department of the House of Representatives 2018b, *Corporate plan 2017–18*, Parliament of Australia, Canberra, available from: www.aph.gov.au/About_Parliament/Parliamentary_Departments/Department_of_the_House_of_Representatives/Corporate_Plans.

Department of the House of Representatives 2020, *Annual report 2019–20*, Parliament of Australia, Canberra, available from: www.aph.gov.au/About_Parliament/Parliamentary_Departments/Department_of_the_House_of_Representatives/Annual_Reports/2019-20_Annual_Report.

Department of the House of Representatives 2021a, *Annual report 2020–21*, Parliament of Australia, Canberra, available from: www.aph.gov.au/-/media/05_About_Parliament/54_Parliamentary_Depts/542_Dept_of_House_of_Reps/Annual_Reports/2020-21/DHR_Annual_Report-2020-21.pdf?la=en&hash=3FE33B5BBD526B5F85C384F894CCF9516F099259.

Department of the House of Representatives 2021b, *Corporate plan 2021–22*, Parliament of Australia, Canberra, available from: www.aph.gov.au/About_ Parliament/Parliamentary_Departments/Department_of_the_House_of_ Representatives/Corporate_Plans.

Department of Parliamentary Services (DPS) 2004, *Annual report 2003–04*, Parliament of Australia, Canberra, available from: www.aph.gov.au/binaries/ dps/publications/anrep2004/dps_annualreport.pdf.

Department of Parliamentary Services (DPS) 2006, *Annual report 2005–06*, Parliament of Australia, Canberra, available from: www.aph.gov.au/binaries/ dps/publications/dps_areport_05-06.pdf.

Department of Parliamentary Services (DPS) 2012, *Annual report 2011–12*, Parliament of Australia, Canberra, available from: www.aph.gov.au/About_ Parliament/Parliamentary_Departments/Department_of_Parliamentary_ Services/Publications/Annual_Reports/Annual_Report_2011-12.

Department of Parliamentary Services (DPS) 2017, *Annual report 2016–17*, Parliament of Australia, Canberra, available from: www.aph.gov.au/About_ Parliament/Parliamentary_Departments/Department_of_Parliamentary_ Services/Publications/Annual_Reports/Annual_Report_2016-17.

Department of Parliamentary Services (DPS) 2018a, *Annual report 2017–18*, Parliament of Australia, Canberra, available from: www.aph.gov.au/About_ Parliament/Parliamentary_Departments/Department_of_Parliamentary_ Services/Publications/Annual_Reports/Annual_Report_2017-18.

Department of Parliamentary Services (DPS) 2018b, *Corporate plan 2017–18*, Parliament of Australia, Canberra, available from: www.aph.gov.au/About_ Parliament/Parliamentary_Departments/Department_of_Parliamentary_ Services/Publications/Corporate_Plans.

Department of Parliamentary Services (DPS) 2019, *Annual report 2018–19*, Parliament of Australia, Canberra, available from: www.aph.gov.au/About_ Parliament/Parliamentary_Departments/Department_of_Parliamentary_ Services/Publications/Annual_Reports/Annual_Report_2018-19.

Department of Parliamentary Services (DPS) 2020, Operation and management of the Department of Parliamentary Services, Inquiry Submission 5, 21 October, Senate Finance and Public Administration Legislation Committee, Canberra, available from: www.aph.gov.au/Parliamentary_Business/Committees/Senate/ Finance_and_Public_Administration/OperationofDPS/Submissions.

Department of Parliamentary Services (DPS) 2021a, *Annual report 2020–21*, Parliament of Australia, Canberra, available from: www.transparency.gov.au/ annual-reports/department-parliamentary-services/reporting-year/2020-21.

Department of Parliamentary Services (DPS) 2021b, *Corporate plan 2021–22*, Parliament of Australia, Canberra, available from: www.aph.gov.au/About_ Parliament/Parliamentary_Departments/Department_of_Parliamentary_ Services/Publications/Corporate_Plans.

Department of the Parliamentary Library (DPL) 1989, *Annual report 1988–89*, Parliament of Australia, Canberra, available from: parlinfo.aph.gov.au/parlInfo/ search/display/display.w3p;query=Id:%22publications/tabledpapers/HPP032 016004364%22;src1=sm1.

Department of the Senate 2011, *Annual report 2010–11*, Parliament of Australia, Canberra, available from: www.aph.gov.au/About_Parliament/Parliamentary_ Departments/Department_of_the_Senate/Annual_Reports/Annual_Report_ 2010-2011.

Department of the Senate 2012, *Annual report 2011–12*, Parliament of Australia, Canberra, available from: www.aph.gov.au/About_Parliament/Parliamentary_ Departments/Department_of_the_Senate/Annual_Reports/Annual_Report_ 2011-2012.

Department of the Senate 2013, *Annual report 2012–13*, Parliament of Australia, Canberra, available from: www.aph.gov.au/About_Parliament/Parliamentary_ Departments/Department_of_the_Senate/Annual_Reports/Annual_Report_ 2012-2013.

Department of the Senate 2014, *Annual report 2013–14*, Parliament of Australia, Canberra, available from: www.aph.gov.au/About_Parliament/Parliamentary_ Departments/Department_of_the_Senate/Annual_Reports/Annual_Report_ 2013-2014.

Department of the Senate 2015, *Annual report 2014–15*, Parliament of Australia, Canberra, available from: www.aph.gov.au/About_Parliament/Parliamentary_ Departments/Department_of_the_Senate/Annual_Reports/Annual_Report_ 2014-2015.

Department of the Senate 2017, *Annual report 2016–17*, Parliament of Australia, Canberra, available from: www.aph.gov.au/About_Parliament/Parliamentary_ Departments/Department_of_the_Senate/Annual_Reports/Annual_Report_ 2016-2017.

Department of the Senate 2018a, *Annual report 2017–18*, Parliament of Australia, Canberra, available from: www.aph.gov.au/About_Parliament/Parliamentary_ Departments/Department_of_the_Senate/Annual_Reports/Annual_Report_ 2017-2018.

Department of the Senate 2018b, *Corporate plan 2017–18*, Parliament of Australia, Canberra, available from: www.aph.gov.au/About_Parliament/Parliamentary_ Departments/Department_of_the_Senate/Corporate_Plans.

Department of the Senate 2019, *Annual report 2018–19*, Parliament of Australia, Canberra, available from: www.aph.gov.au/About_Parliament/Parliamentary_ Departments/Department_of_the_Senate/Annual_Reports/Annual_Report_ 2018-2019.

Department of the Senate 2020, *Annual report 2019–20*, Parliament of Australia, Canberra, available from: www.aph.gov.au/About_Parliament/Parliamentary_ Departments/Department_of_the_Senate/Annual_Reports.

Department of the Senate 2021a, *Annual report 2020–21*, Parliament of Australia, Canberra, available from: www.aph.gov.au/About_Parliament/Parliamentary_ Departments/Department_of_the_Senate/Annual_Reports/Annual_Report_ 2020-2021.

Department of the Senate 2021b, *Corporate plan 2020–21*, Parliament of Australia, Canberra, available from: www.aph.gov.au/About_Parliament/Parliamentary_ Departments/Department_of_the_Senate/Corporate_Plans.

de Vries, M. & Nemec, J. 2013, 'Public sector reform: An overview of recent literature and research on NPM and alternative paths', *International Journal of Public Sector Management*, vol. 26, no. 1, pp. 4–16, doi.org/10.1108/ 09513551311293408.

Dewey, L., Blackman, D. & Dickinson, H. 2018, *Co-production and innovation: Creating better solutions for future public service implementation*, Public Service Research Group Issues Paper No. 3, 14 November, UNSW Canberra, available from: apo.org.au/sites/default/files/resource-files/2018-11/apo-nid 303221.pdf.

Dickinson, N. 2018, 'Harassment and bullying at Westminster: The independent complaints and grievance policy, parliamentary standards investigations, and the MPs' expenses scandal', *PSA Parliaments*, 23 July, The UK Political Studies Association Specialist Group on Parliaments, London, available from: psaparliaments.org/2018/07/23/harassment-and-bullying-at-westminster/.

Dickinson, N. 2019, 'Sometimes a cigar is just a cigar: (Mis)connecting Brexit and the expenses scandal', *PSA Parliaments*, 3 April, The UK Political Studies Association Specialist Group on Parliaments, London, available from: psa parliaments.org/2019/04/03/misconnecting-brexit-and-the-expenses-scandal/.

Di Francesco, M. 2012, 'Grand designs? The "managerial" role of ministers within Westminster-based public management policy', *Australian Journal of Public Administration*, vol. 71, no. 3, pp. 257–268, doi.org/10.1111/j.1467-8500. 2012.00783.x.

Digital Democracy Commission (DDC) 2015, *Open up! Report of the Speaker's Commission on Digital Democracy*, 26 January, Digital Democracy Commission, London, available from: www.digitaldemocracy.parliament.uk/documents/ Open-Up-Digital-Democracy-Report.pdf.

Disney, J. & Nethercote, J.R. (eds) 1996, *The house on Capital Hill: Parliament, politics, and power in the national capital*, The Federation Press, Sydney.

Donaldson, D. 2017, '"Executive creep" threatening parliamentary independence', *The Mandarin*, 6 June, available from: www.themandarin.com.au/79927-executive-creep-threatening-parliamentary-independence/.

Donaldson, L. & Davis, J.H. 1991, 'Stewardship theory or agency theory: CEO governance and shareholder returns', *Australian Journal of Management*, vol. 16, no. 1, pp. 49–64, doi.org/10.1177/031289629101600103.

Doran, M. 2021, 'Federal anti-corruption commission unlikely to be established this year, as days left to pass legislation tick down', *ABC News*, 23 November, available from: www.abc.net.au/news/2021-11-23/federal-integrity-commission-unlikely-this-year/100640238.

Dorey, P. 2009, 'The House of Lords since 1949', in C. Jones (ed.), *A short history of parliament*, Boydell & Brewer, Woodbridge, UK, pp. 226–248.

Douglas, S., Schillemans, T., 't Hart, P., Ansell, C., Bøgh Andersen, L., Flinders, M., Head, B., Moynihan, D., Nabatchi, T., O'Flynn, J., Peters, B.G., Raadschelders, J., Sancino, A., Sørensen, E. & Torfing, J. 2021, 'Rising to Ostrom's challenge: An invitation to walk on the bright side of public governance and public service', *Policy Design and Practice*, vol. 4, no. 4, pp. 441–451, doi.org/10.1080/ 25741292.2021.1972517.

Doyle, J. 2014, 'Ministers won't block Bercow's "Canberra caterer": Downing Street fears a constitutional crisis if they get involved despite cross-party anger at appointment', *Daily Mail*, [London], 20 August, available from: www. dailymail.co.uk/news/article-2729299/Ministers-won-t-block-Bercow-s-Canberra-caterer-Downing-Street-fears-constitutional-crisis-involved-despite-cross-party-anger-appointment.html.

Dryzek, J. 2009, *The Australian Citizens' Parliament: A world first*, Papers on Parliament No. 51, June, Parliament of Australia, Canberra, available from: www.aph.gov.au/~/~/link.aspx?_id=E03B9D7AA31049C2AD126EBD7AC 3247E&_z=z.

D'Souza, F. 2016, Letter to the Rt Hon. Baroness Stowell of Beeston, 21 January.

Duncan, T. 2004, Benchmarking and measuring the management of parliament, Paper presented to the 35th Presiding Officers and Clerks Conference, Melbourne, July.

Dunleavy, P., Margetts, H., Bastow, S. & Tinkler, J. 2006, 'New public management is dead—Long live digital-era governance', *Journal of Public Administration Research and Theory*, vol. 16, no. 3, pp. 467–494, doi.org/10.1093/jopart/mui057.

Eagles, R. 2017, 'A troubled project—ended by a fire: Restoration and renewal of the Palace of Westminster before 1834', *Hansard Society Blog*, 5 October, available from: www.hansardsociety.org.uk/blog/a-troubled-project-ended-by-a-fire-restoration-and-renewal-of-the-palace-of.

Easton, S. 2017, 'Toughest job in a democracy? Keeping politicians on the level', *The Mandarin*, 27 June, available from: www.themandarin.com.au/80638-toughest-job-democracy-keeping-politicians-level/.

Easton, S. 2018, 'Key case no. 1 and IPEA goes softly-softly on Joyce, Campion travel expenses', *The Mandarin*, 21 March, available from: www.themandarin.com.au/90154-key-case-no-1-ipea-goes-softly-softly-joyce-campion-travel-expenses/.

Easton, S. 2019, 'Why is there no APS college? ASIO head Duncan Lewis says public service needs its own school', *The Mandarin*, 11 September, available from: www.themandarin.com.au/115780-why-is-there-no-aps-college-asio-head-duncan-lewis-says-public-service-needs-its-own-school/.

Edwards, M. 2002, 'Public sector governance: Future issues for Australia', *Australian Journal of Public Administration*, vol. 61, no. 2, pp. 51–61, doi.org/10.1111/1467-8500.00272.

Elder, D. 2006, Discussion paper on governance arrangements in the Parliament of Australia, Unpublished.

Elder, D. 2017, 'Clerk's review', in Department of the House of Representatives, *Annual report 2016–17*, Parliament of Australia, Canberra, available from: www.aph.gov.au/About_Parliament/Parliamentary_Departments/Department_of_the_House_of_Representatives/Annual_Reports/2016-17_Annual_Report/Overviews/Clerks_Review.

Elder, D. & Fowler, P. (eds) 2017, *House of Representatives practice*, 7th edn, Department of the House of Representatives, Canberra.

Elgot, J. 2018, 'Commons bullying inquiry suggests Bercow should consider position', *The Guardian*, 16 October, available from: www.theguardian.com/politics/2018/oct/15/house-of-commons-culture-enabled-bullying-and-sexual-harassment-inquiry.

Ellenbogen, N. 2019, *An independent inquiry into bullying and harassment in the House of Lords: Report by Naomi Ellenbogen QC*, 10 July, UK Parliament, London, available from: www.parliament.uk/globalassets/documents/lords-committees/house-of-lords-commission/2017-19/ellenbogen-report.pdf.

Emerson, K. & Nabatchi, T. 2015, *Collaborative governance regimes*, Georgetown University Press, Washington, DC.

Emerson, K., Nabatchi, T. & Balogh, S. 2012, 'An integrative framework for collaborative governance', *Journal of Public Administration Research and Theory*, vol. 22, no. 1, pp. 1–29, doi.org/10.1093/jopart/mur011.

Engel, C. 2020, 'Restore, renew or start again?', *The Critic*, 22 May, available from: thecritic.co.uk/restore-renew-or-start-again/.

Englefield, D.J. 1985, *The Study of Parliament Group: The first twenty-one years*, Study of Parliament Group, London, available from: www.studyofparliament.org.uk/.

Ercan, S.A., Hendriks, C.M. & Dryzek, J.S. 2019, 'Public deliberation in an era of communicative plenty', *Policy & Politics*, vol. 47, no. 1, pp. 19–35, doi.org/10.1332/030557318X15200933925405.

Esmark, A. 2016, 'Maybe it is time to rediscover technocracy? An old framework for a new analysis of administrative reforms in the governance era', *Journal of Public Administration Research and Theory*, vol. 27, no. 3, pp. 501–516, doi.org/10.1093/jopart/muw059.

European Union (Withdrawal) Act 2018 (United Kingdom).

Evans, G. 1982, 'Scrutiny of the executive by parliamentary committees', in J. Nethercote (ed.), *Parliament and bureaucracy*, Hale & Iremonger, Sydney, pp. 78–92.

Evans, H. n.d., Scrutiny of ministers, Unpublished ms.

Evans, H. 1991, 'Clerk's review', in Department of the Senate, *Annual report 1990–91*, Parliament of Australia, Canberra.

Evans, H. 1999, 'The cost of the Commonwealth Parliament: Amalgamations, values and comparisons', *Australian Journal of Public Administration*, vol. 58 no. 1, pp. 106–111, doi.org/10.1111/1467-8500.00081.

Evans, H. 2002, The Australian Parliament: Time for reformation, Address to the National Press Club, Canberra, 23 April.

Evans, H. 2003, 'Clerk's review', in Department of the Senate, *Annual report 2002–03*, Parliament of Australia, Canberra.

Evans, H. 2004, 'Clerk's review', in Department of the Senate, *Annual report 2003–04*, Parliament of Australia, Canberra.

Evans, H. 2005, 'Clerk's review', in Department of the Senate, *Annual report 2004–05*, Parliament of Australia, Canberra.

Evans, H. 2006, 'Clerk's review', in Department of the Senate, *Annual report 2005–06*, Parliament of Australia, Canberra.

Evans, H. 2007, 'Clerk's review', in Department of the Senate, *Annual report 2006–07*, Parliament of Australia, Canberra.

Evans, H. 2008, 'Clerk's review', in Department of the Senate, *Annual report 2007–08*, Parliament of Australia, Canberra.

Evans, H. 2009, *The traditional, the quaint and the useful: Pitfalls of reforming parliamentary procedures*, Papers on Parliament No. 52, December, Parliament of Australia, Canberra, available from: www.aph.gov.au/-/-/-/-/-/link.aspx?_id=FFC9D73212F84AC0AB2E1936C39B55C4&_z=z.

Evans, M., Halupka, M. & Stoker, G. 2017, *How Australians imagine their democracy: The 'power of us'*, Museum of Australian Democracy and Institute for Governance and Policy Analysis, University of Canberra, Canberra, available from: www.governanceinstitute.edu.au/magma/media/upload/publication/408_Democracy100-report-IGPA.pdf.

Evans, M., Stoker, G. & Halupka, M. 2019, 'Revealed: How Australian politicians would bridge the trust divide', *The Conversation*, 16 October, available from: theconversation.com/revealed-how-australian-politicians-would-bridge-the-trust-divide-125217?.

Evans, M., Stoker, G. & Nasir, J. 2013, *How do Australians imagine their democracy? Australian Survey of Political Engagement findings 2013*, ANZSOG Institute for Governance and Policy Analysis, University of Canberra, available from: www.governanceinstitute.edu.au/magma/media/upload/ckeditor/files/DEMOCRACY%20REPORT-%20UPDATED%20VERSION-27-6-13.pdf.

Evans, P. 2014, A rule to go by: What is the point of parliamentary procedure, UK Parliament Open Lecture, Aberystwyth University, Wales, 7 February.

Evans, P. 2017, 'Introduction: The growth of many centuries', in P. Evans (ed.), *Essays on the history of parliamentary procedure: In honour of Thomas Erskine May*, Bloomsbury Academic, London, pp. 1–18.

Fair Work Act 2009 (Commonwealth of Australia).

Fels, A. 2008, 'Networked governance and collaboration to improve outcomes', in J. O'Flynn and J. Wanna (eds), *Collaborative governance: A new era of public policy in Australia*, ANU Press, Canberra, pp. xi–xiii, doi.org/10.22459/CG.12.2008.

Fels, A. 2015, 'Wanted: An independent umpire to set and enforce clear parliamentary entitlement rules', *The Conversation*, 4 August, available from: theconversation.com/wanted-an-independent-umpire-to-set-and-enforce-clear-parliamentary-entitlement-rules-45571.

Fewtrell, T. 2017, 'Walled-in democracy needs a champion within', *The Canberra Times*, 1 February, p. 17.

Fewtrell, T., Macintyre, C. & Uhr, J. 2008, Architecture and parliament: How do buildings help shape parliamentary business?, Roundtable, Parliament House, Canberra, 22 August, Summaries and Transcript, accessed from: www.aph.gov.au/About_Parliament/Senate/Powers_practice_n_procedures/pops/Papers_on_Parliament_69/Architecture_Power_and_Parliament.

Fisher, J. & vanHeerde-Hudson, J. 2014, 'Conclusions: A very British episode?', in J. vanHeerde-Hudson (ed.), *The political costs of the 2009 British MPs' expenses scandal*, Palgrave Macmillan, Basingstoke, UK, pp. 196–203.

Fledderus, J., Brandsen, T. & Honingh, M. 2014, 'Restoring trust through the co-production of public services: A theoretical elaboration', *Public Management Review*, vol. 16, no. 3, pp. 424–443, doi.org/10.1080/14719037.2013.848920.

Flinders, M. 2002, 'Governance in Whitehall', *Public Administration*, vol. 80, no. 1, pp. 51–75, doi.org/10.1111/1467-9299.00294.

Flinders, M. 2016, 'Saving Westminster from ruin is a chance to rebuild British democracy', *The Conversation*, 12 September, available from: theconversation.com/saving-westminster-from-ruin-is-a-chance-to-rebuild-british-democracy-65191.

Flinders, M. 2019, 'Palace of Westminster is falling down—but government's renewal plans are just as decrepit', *The Conversation*, 8 May, available from: theconversation.com/palace-of-westminster-is-falling-down-but-governments-renewal-plans-are-just-as-decrepit-116766.

Flinders, M. & Anderson, A. 2021, 'MPs' expenses: The legacy of a scandal 10 years on', *British Politics*, vol. 17, pp. 119–143, doi.org/10.1057/s41293-021-00173-9.

Flinders, M., Cotter, L.M., Kelso, A. & Meakin, A. 2018a, 'The politics of parliamentary restoration and renewal: Decisions, discretion, democracy', *Parliamentary Affairs*, vol. 71, no. 1, pp. 144–168, doi.org/10.1093/pa/gsx012.

Flinders, M. & Kelso, A. 2011, 'Mind the gap: Political analysis, public expectations and the parliamentary decline thesis', *The British Journal of Politics and International Relations*, vol. 13, no. 2, pp. 249–268, doi.org/10.1111/j.1467-856X.2010.00434.x.

Flinders, M., Meakin, A. & Anderson, A. 2019, 'The restoration and renewal of the Palace of Westminster: Avoiding the trap and realising the promise', *Political Quarterly*, vol. 90, no. 3, pp. 488–495, doi.org/10.1111/1467-923X.12730.

Flinders, M., Weinberg, A., Weinberg, J., Geddes, M. & Kwiatkowski, R. 2018b, 'Governing under pressure? The mental wellbeing of politicians', *Parliamentary Affairs*, vol. 73, no. 2, pp. 253–273, doi.org/10.1093/pa/gsy046.

Flinders, M., Wood, M. & Corbett, J. 2020, 'Anti-politics and democratic innovation', in *Handbook of democratic innovation and governance*, Edward Elgar Publishing, Cheltenham, UK, doi.org/10.4337/9781786433862.00019.

Forkert, J. 2017, Parliamentary committees: Improving public engagement, Paper presented to the Australasian Parliamentary Study Group Conference, Hobart, 30 September.

Fox, R. 2009, 'Engagement and participation: What the public want and how our politicians need to respond', *Parliamentary Affairs*, vol. 62, no. 4, pp. 673–685, doi.org/10.1093/pa/gsp027.

Fox, R. 2012a, 'Disgruntled, disillusioned and disengaged: Public attitudes to politics in Britain today', *Parliamentary Affairs*, vol. 65, no. 4, pp. 877–887, doi.org/10.1093/pa/gss053.

Fox, R. 2012b, *What next for e-petitions?*, Hansard Society, London.

Fox, R. & Blackwell, J. 2019, 'Hansard Society audit: The public think politics is broken, and are willing to entertain radical solutions', *The Times*, [London], 8 April, available from: www.thetimes.co.uk/article/the-public-think-politics-is-broken-and-are-willing-to-entertain-radical-solutions-x2532pqb2.

Freedom of Information Act 1982 (Commonwealth of Australia).

Freedom of Information Act 2000 (United Kingdom).

Frith, J. (ed.) 2018, *New brooms: Ideas for reforming Westminster from Labour's 2017 intake*, Fabian Society, Joseph Rowntree Trust, London.

Gaines, B.J., Goodwin, M., Bates, S.H. & Sin, G. 2019, 'The study of legislative committees', *The Journal of Legislative Studies*, vol. 25, no. 3, pp. 331–339, doi.org/10.1080/13572334.2019.1662614.

Gains, F. & Stoker, G. 2009, 'Delivering "public value": Implications for accountability and legitimacy', *Parliamentary Affairs*, vol. 62, no. 3, pp. 438–455, doi.org/10.1093/pa/gsp007.

Gammell, C. 2009, 'MPs' expenses: Senior official involved in expenses "unlikely" to play role in future', *The Telegraph*, [London], 14 December, available from: www.telegraph.co.uk/news/newstopics/mps-expenses/6803384/MPs-Expenses-senior-official-involved-in-expenses-unlikely-to-play-role-in-future.html.

Gay, O. 2014, 'The new regime: The role of IPSA', in J. vanHeerde-Hudson (ed.), *The political costs of the 2009 British MPs' expenses scandal*, Palgrave Macmillan, Basingstoke, UK, pp. 175–195.

Gay, O. 2016, 'The restoration and renewal of the Palace of Westminster provides the opportunity to make parliament more user-friendly', *The Constitution Unit Blog*, 29 January, available from: constitution-unit.com/2016/01/29/the-restoration-and-renewal-of-the-palace-of-westminster-offers-an-opportunity-to-make-parliament-more-user-friendly/.

Gay, O. 2017, 'Slumber and success: The House of Commons Library after May', in P. Evans (ed.), *Essays on the history of parliamentary procedure: In honour of Thomas Erskine May*, Bloomsbury Academic, London, pp. 33–44.

Geddes, M. 2016, 'Mary Creagh has become the new chair of the Environmental Audit Committee: Will she be a catalyst or a chieftain?', *PSA Parliaments*, 10 February, The UK Political Studies Association Specialist Group on Parliaments, London, available from: psaparliaments.org/2016/02/10/mary-creagh-has-become-the-new-chair-of-the-environmental-audit-committee-will-she-be-a-catalyst-or-a-chieftain/.

Geddes, M. 2019a, *Dramas at Westminster: Select committees and the quest for accountability*, Manchester University Press, Manchester, UK.

Geddes, M. 2019b, 'The explanatory potential of "dilemmas": Bridging practices and power to understand political change in interpretive political science', *Political Studies Review*, vol. 17, no. 3, pp. 239–254, doi.org/10.1177/1478929918795342.

Geddes, M. & Meakin, A. 2018, Explaining change in parliaments: Dilemmas of managerial reform in the UK House of Commons, Paper presented to the PSA International Annual Conference, Cardiff, 26–29 March.

Geddes, M. & Mulley, J. 2018, 'Supporting members and peers', in C. Leston-Bandeira & L. Thompson (eds), *Exploring parliament*, Oxford University Press, Oxford, UK, pp. 33–42, doi.org/10.1093/hepl/9780198788430.003.0004.

Geddes, M. & Rhodes, R.A.W. 2018, 'Towards an interpretive parliamentary studies', in J. Brichzin, D. Krichewsky, L. Ringel & J. Schank (eds), *The sociology of parliaments*, Springer VS, Wiesbaden, Germany, pp. 87–107.

Godwin, A. 2019, 'CEO Senate estimates opening statement 2019', Media release, 19 February, Independent Parliamentary Expenses Authority, Canberra, available from: www.ipea.gov.au/home-media-centre/senate-estimates-statement.

Goodwin, M. & Atkins, M. 2018, 'Parliament and modernization', in C. Leston-Bandeira & L. Thompson (eds), *Exploring parliament*, Oxford University Press, Oxford, UK, pp. 296–307, doi.org/10.1093/hepl/9780198788430.003.0028.

Grattan, M. 2015, 'Bronwyn Bishop finally resigns as Speaker', *The Conversation*, 2 August, available from: theconversation.com/bronwyn-bishop-finally-resigns-as-speaker-45559.

Griffith, J.A. & Ryle, M. 1989, *Parliament: Functions, practice, and procedures*, Sweet & Maxwell, London.

Gruen, N. 2019, 'When a conversation is not a conversation: Party political discourse in the early 21st century', *The Mandarin*, 19 February, available from: www.themandarin.com.au/104253-when-a-conversation-is-not-a-conversation-party-political-discourse-in-the-early-21st-century/.

Guido Fawkes 2014, 'Has the "Canberra caterer" conceded the clerk fight?', *Guido Fawkes*, [Blog], 22 September, available from: order-order.com/2014/09/22/has-the-canberra-caterer-conceded-the-clerk-fight/.

Haddon, C. & Thimont Jack, M. 2020, 'Minister Andrea Leadsom', *Ministers Reflect*, [Interview], 29 October, Institute for Government, London, available from: www.instituteforgovernment.org.uk/ministers-reflect/person/andrea-leadsom/.

Halligan, J. 2012, 'Leadership and the senior service from a comparative perspective', in B.G. Peters & J. Pierre (eds), *The Sage handbook of public administration*, Sage Publications, London, pp. 115–129, doi.org/10.4135/9781446200506.n8.

Halligan, J., Miller, R. & Power, J. 2007, *Parliament in the twenty-first century: Institutional reform and emerging roles*, Melbourne University Press, Melbourne.

Hansard Society 2005, *Members only? Parliament in the public eye: Report of the Hansard Society Commission on the Communication of Parliamentary Democracy*, Dod's Parliamentary Communications, London.

Hansard Society 2011, *A place for people: A proposal for enhancing visitor engagement with parliament's environs*, Hansard Society, London.

Hansard Society 2014, 'The ramifications of a modest pause in the recruitment of the Clerk of the House', *Hansard Society Newsletter*, 11 September, accessed from: www.hansardsociety.org.uk/the-ramifications-of-a-modest-pause-in-the-appointment-of-the-clerk-of-the-house/ [page discontinued].

Hansard Society 2015, *Audit of political engagement 12: The 2015 report*, Hansard Society, London.

Hansard Society 2017, *Audit of political engagement 14: The 2017 report*, Hansard Society, London.

Hansard Society 2018, *Audit of political engagement 15: The 2018 report*, Hansard Society, London.

Hansard Society 2019, *Audit of political engagement 16: The 2019 report*, Hansard Society, London.

Hansard Society 2021, *Publications and guides: Select committees*, Hansard Society, London.

Hanson, A.H. 1963, 'The purpose of parliament', *Parliamentary Affairs*, vol. 17, no. 3, pp. 279–295, doi.org/10.1093/oxfordjournals.pa.a053913.

Hardman, I. 2015, 'Charles Walker: I have been played for a fool', *The Spectator*, 26 March, available from: www.spectator.co.uk/article/charles-walker-i-have-been-played-for-a-fool.

Harris, I. 2004, 'Clerk's review', in Department of the House of Representatives, *Annual report 2003–04*, Parliament of Australia, Canberra.

Hartigan, J. 2019, 'The tyranny of parliament', *Daily Globe*, [UK], 20 March, available from: www.dailyglobe.co.uk/comment/the-tyranny-of-parliament/.

Hartley, J., Alford, J., Hughes, O. & Yates, S. 2015, 'Public value and political astuteness in the work of public managers: The art of the possible', *Public Administration*, vol. 93, no. 1, pp. 195–211, doi.org/10.1111/padm.12125.

Hartley, J., Alford, J., Knies, E. & Douglas, S. 2017, 'Towards an empirical research agenda for public value theory', *Public Management Review*, vol. 19, no. 5, pp. 670–685, doi.org/10.1080/14719037.2016.1192166.

Hay, C. & Wincott, D. 1998, 'Structure, agency and historical institutionalism', *Political Studies*, vol. 46, no. 5, pp. 951–957, doi.org/10.1111/1467-9248.00177.

Hayne, J. 2018, 'Canberra bubble named 2018 word of the year by Australian National Dictionary Centre', *ABC News*, 13 December, available from: www.abc.net.au/news/2018-12-13/australian-word-of-the-year-canberra-bubble/10611238.

Hayne, K.M. 2019, *Final report: Royal commission into misconduct in the banking, superannuation and financial services industry. Volume 1*, Australian Government, Canberra, available from: static.treasury.gov.au/uploads/sites/1/2019/02/fsrc-volume1.pdf.

Head, B.W. & Alford, J. 2015, 'Wicked problems: Implications for public policy and management', *Administration & Society*, vol. 47, no. 6, pp. 711–739, doi.org/10.1177/0095399713481601.

Heitshusen, V., Young, G. & Wood, D.M. 2005, 'Electoral context and MP constituency focus in Australia, Canada, Ireland, New Zealand and the United Kingdom', *American Journal of Political Science*, vol. 49, no. 1, pp. 32–45, doi.org/10.1111/j.0092-5853.2005.00108.x.

Hendriks, C.M. & Kay, A. 2019, 'From "opening up" to democratic renewal: Deepening public engagement in legislative committees', *Government and Opposition*, vol. 54, no. 1, pp. 25–51, doi.org/10.1017/gov.2017.20.

Hendriks, C.M., Regan, S. & Kay, A. 2019, 'Participatory adaptation in contemporary parliamentary committees in Australia', *Parliamentary Affairs*, vol. 72, no. 2, pp. 267–289, doi.org/10.1093/pa/gsy005.

Higgins, C. 2017, '"A tale of decay": The houses of parliament are falling down', *The Guardian*, 1 December, available from: www.theguardian.com/news/2017/dec/01/a-tale-of-decay-the-houses-of-parliament-are-falling-down.

Hill, A. & Whichelow, A. 1964, *What's wrong with parliament?*, Penguin Books, London.

Hill, C.J. & Lynn, L.E. 2009, *Public management: A three-dimensional approach*, CQ Press, Washington, DC.

Hillman, A.J., Withers, M.C. & Collins, B.J. 2009, 'Resource dependence theory: A review', *Journal of Management*, vol. 35, no. 6, pp. 1404–1427, doi.org/10.1177/0149206309343469.

Hindmoor, A., Larkin, P. and Kennon, A. 2009, 'Assessing the influence of select committees in the UK: The Education and Skills Committee, 1997–2005', *The Journal of Legislative Studies*, vol. 15, no. 1, pp. 71–89, doi.org/10.1080/13572330802666844.

Hitch, G. & Doran, M. 2021, 'Scott Morrison defends blocking proposed federal corruption commission after MP crosses the floor', *ABC News*, 25 November, [Updated 30 November], available from: www.abc.net.au/news/2021-11-25/federal-iac-bill-vote-parliament-helen-haines/100649316.

Holland, E. 1991, 'Reporting select committees: The shorthand writer to the Houses', in D. Englefield (ed.), *Workings of Westminster*, Dartmouth Publishing Company, Hants, UK.

Hood, C. 1991, 'A public management for all seasons?', *Public Administration*, vol. 69, no. 1, pp. 3–19, doi.org/10.1111/j.1467-9299.1991.tb00779.x.

Hood, C. 2005, 'Public management: The word, the movement, the science', in E. Ferlie, L.E. Lynn & C. Pollitt (eds), *The Oxford handbook of public management*, Oxford University Press, New York, NY.

Hope, C. & Krol, C. 2017, 'John Bercow in new Brexit furore over neutrality after admitting he voted Remain', *The Telegraph*, [London], 12 February, available from: www.telegraph.co.uk/news/2017/02/11/john-bercow-new-brexit-furore-neutrality-admitting-voted-remain/.

Horner, L. & Hutton, W. 2010, 'Public value, deliberative democracy and the role of public managers', in J. Benington & M. Moore (eds), *Public value theory and practice*, Palgrave Macmillan, Basingstoke, UK.

Horner, L., Lekhi, R. & Blaug, R. 2006, *Deliberative democracy and the role of public managers: Final report of The Work Foundation's public value consortium*, The Work Foundation, London.

House of Commons 2016, *Director General's Review: Report*, UK Parliament, London, available from: www.parliament.uk/globalassets/documents/commons-governance-office/Director-Generals-Review-Report.pdf.

House of Commons 2017, *The House of Commons: Administration—Annual report and accounts 2016–17*, 19 July, HC 226, UK Parliament, London, available from: www.parliament.uk/globalassets/documents/commons-expenditure/admin-annual-accounts/administration_annual_report_and_accounts_2016_17.pdf.

House of Commons 2018, *The House of Commons: Administration—Annual report and accounts 2017–18*, 23 July, HC 1381, UK Parliament, London, available from: www.parliament.uk/globalassets/documents/commons-expenditure/admin-annual-accounts/administration_annual_report_and_accounts_2017-18.pdf.

House of Commons 2019, *The House of Commons: Administration—Annual report and accounts 2018–19*, 17 July, HC 2434, UK Parliament, London, available from: www.parliament.uk/globalassets/documents/commons-expenditure/admin-annual-accounts/administration_annual_report_and_accounts_2018_19.pdf.

House of Commons 2020, *The House of Commons: Administration—Annual report and accounts 2019–20*, 21 July, HC 580, UK Parliament, London, available from: www.parliament.uk/globalassets/documents/commons-expenditure/admin-annual-accounts/administration_annual_report_and_accounts_2019_20_wav.pdf.

House of Commons 2021, *The House of Commons: Administration—Annual report and accounts 2020–21*, 21 July, HC 316, UK Parliament, London, available from: www.parliament.uk/globalassets/documents/commons-expenditure/admin-annual-accounts/house-of--commons-administration-annual-report-and-accounts-2020-21.pdf.

House of Commons Act 1812 (United Kingdom).

House of Commons (Administration) Act 1978 (United Kingdom).

House of Commons Commission 1979, *Report for 1978–79*, 27 July, HC 177, UK Parliament, London.

House of Commons Commission 1990, 'House of Commons Services: Report to the House of Commons Commission by a team led by Sir Robin Ibbs', *Parliamentary Papers*, 1990–91, vol. IX, HC 30-41, HMSO, London.

House of Commons Commission 1991, *Report for 1990–91*, 25 July, HC 642, UK Parliament, London.

House of Commons Commission 2007a, *Review of management and services: Report by Sir Kevin Tebbit KCB CMG*, 18 June, HC 685, TSO, London.

House of Commons Commission 2007b, *Response to Sir Kevin Tebbit's review of the management and services of the House of Commons*, 19 December, HC 193, TSO, London.

House of Commons Commission 2016, *Strategy for the House of Commons Service 2016–2021: Supporting a thriving parliamentary democracy*, UK Parliament, London, available from: www.parliament.uk/documents/Strategy-for-the-House-of-Commons-Service-2016-2021-long-version.pdf.

House of Commons Commission Act 2015 (United Kingdom).

House of Commons Committee on Issue of Privilege 2010, *Police searches on the parliamentary estate*, 22 March, HC 62 [incorporating HC 1040-i, -ii and -iii of Session 2008–09], UK Parliament, London.

House of Commons (HC) Debates 1943, *House of Commons rebuilding*, 28 October, vol. 393, c. 404, UK Parliament, available from: hansard.parliament.uk/Commons/1943-10-28/debates/4388c736-7e25-4a7e-92d8-eccb751c4f56/HouseOfCommonsRebuilding?highlight=shape%20buildings#contribution-ac4f53c4-1a2a-4782-ab52-39bec4301cad.

House of Commons (HC) Debates 2009, *Debates*, 22 June, vol. 494, cc. 617–624, UK Parliament, available from: hansard.parliament.uk/Commons/2009-06-22/debates/60656796-026e-4bec-96ad-8b1812ddd138/CommonsChamber.

House of Commons (HC) Debates 2013, *Finances of the House of Commons*, 21 November, vol. 570, cc. 1387–1433, UK Parliament, available from: hansard.parliament.uk/commons/2013-11-21/debates/13112168000001/FinancesOfTheHouseOfCommons.

House of Commons (HC) Debates 2014a, *Retirement of the Clerk of the House*, 16 July, vol. 584, c. 904, UK Parliament, available from: hansard.parliament.uk/commons/2014-07-16/debates/14071656000002/RetirementOfTheClerkOfTheHouse.

House of Commons (HC) Debates 2014b, *Speaker's statement*, 1 September, vol. 585, UK Parliament, available from: hansard.parliament.uk/commons/2014-09-01/debates/1409014000001/Speaker%E2%80%99SStatement.

House of Commons (HC) Debates 2014c, *Select Committee on Governance of the House*, 10 September, vol. 585, cc. 1014–1047, UK Parliament, available from: hansard.parliament.uk/commons/2014-09-10/debates/14091048000002/SelectCommitteeOnGovernanceOfTheHouse.

House of Commons (HC) Debates 2015, *Debates*, 26 March, vol. 594, c. 1620, UK Parliament, available from: publications.parliament.uk/pa/cm201415/cmhansrd/cm150326/debtext/150326-0002.htm#15032630000006.

House of Commons (HC) Debates 2016, *Tributes to Jo Cox*, 20 June, vol. 611, cc. 1884–1900, UK Parliament, available from: hansard.parliament.uk/commons/2016-06-20/debates/1606205000002/TributesToJoCox.

House of Commons (HC) Debates 2017a, *Palace of Westminster: Restoration and renewal*, 25 January, vol. 620, cc. 98–121WH, UK Parliament, available from: hansard.parliament.uk/commons/2017-01-25/debates/B64F5EEB-5D57-42D5-B09D-85354A6E6916/PalaceOfWestminsterRestorationandRenewal.

House of Commons (HC) Debates 2017b, *Sexual harassment in parliament*, 30 October, vol. 630, cc. 577–598, UK Parliament, available from: hansard.parliament.uk/commons/2017-10-30/debates/832D011D-F22E-47EB-A7B2-E5062E84AF91/SexualHarassmentInParliament.

House of Commons (HC) Debates 2017c, *Harassment in public life*, 18 December, vol. 633, cc. 787–805, UK Parliament, available from: hansard.parliament.uk/commons/2017-12-18/debates/ED860BED-96F8-40AF-A60C-A19AFFFF4BB5/HarassmentInPublicLife.

House of Commons (HC) Debates 2018a, *Independent complaints and grievance policy*, 28 February, vol. 636, cc. 866–904, UK Parliament, available from: hansard.parliament.uk/Commons/2018-02-28/debates/DDEFA813-D9D0-4F25-B1FA-97799098300D/IndependentComplaintsAndGrievancePolicy.

House of Commons (HC) Debates 2018b, *Independent complaints and grievance policy*, 19 July, vol. 645, cc. 627–661, UK Parliament, available from: hansard.parliament.uk/Commons/2018-07-19/debates/92FF5EA2-68E1-46B5-AC76-B3392609DA66/IndependentComplaintsAndGrievancePolicy?highlight=independent%20complaints%20grievance%20policy#contribution-5FBE418D-D712-416C-8FFC-33F9C24F1F26.

House of Commons (HC) Debates 2019a, *Debates*, 9 January, vol. 652, cc. 364–381, UK Parliament, available from: hansard.parliament.uk/Commons/2019-01-09/debates/fa127de4-8a65-4848-afda-53cb741f2ab2/CommonsChamber.

House of Commons (HC) Debates 2019b, *Proxy voting*, 28 January, vol. 653, cc. 596–614, UK Parliament, available from: hansard.parliament.uk/commons/2019-01-28/debates/950E66E5-D3E9-4A7B-8A80-2E9190087B40/ProxyVoting.

House of Commons (HC) Debates 2019c, *Parliament as a workplace*, 13 June, vol. 661, cc. 898–924, UK Parliament, available from: hansard.parliament.uk/Commons/2019-06-13/debates/102F9B15-FBB1-4641-B95E-5B709D18D4EC/ParliamentAsAWorkplace.

House of Commons (HC) Debates 2020, *Restoration and renewal*, 16 July, vol. 678, cc. 1736–1783, UK Parliament, available from: hansard.parliament. uk/Commons/2020-07-16/debates/9F5BB681-04B9-40D8-AFB9-E229B7 A9D6BA/RestorationAndRenewal.

House of Commons (HC) Debates 2021, *Committee on Standards: Decision of the House*, 8 November, vol. 703, c. 57, UK Parliament, available from: hansard. parliament.uk/Commons/2021-11-08/debates/6E81CD0D-33C6-4796-B224-5D88EFAC8F07/CommitteeOnStandardsDecisionOfTheHouse? highlight=bryant%20standards#contribution-FBD384AB-5EFB-406C-96E2-7CC635D6FE07.

House of Commons Governance Committee (HOCGC) 2014, *House of Commons governance*, 17 December, HC 692, UK Parliament, London.

House of Commons–House of Lords Joint Committee on the Palace of Westminster 2017, *Restoration and renewal of the Palace of Westminster: First report of session 2016–17*, 8 September, HL Paper 41, HC 659, UK Parliament, London, available from: publications.parliament.uk/pa/jt201617/jtselect/ jtpow/41/41.pdf.

House of Commons International Development Committee 2018, *Sexual exploitation and abuse in the aid sector: Eighth report of session 2017–19*, 31 July, HC 840, UK Parliament, London, available from: publications.parliament. uk/pa/cm201719/cmselect/cmintdev/840/840.pdf.

House of Commons Liaison Committee (HCLC) 2019, *The effectiveness and influence of the select committee system: Fourth report of session 2017–19*, 9 September, HC 1860, UK Parliament, London, available from: publications. parliament.uk/pa/cm201719/cmselect/cmliaisn/1860/1860.pdf.

House of Commons Political and Constitutional Reform Committee 2013, *Revisiting* Rebuilding the House*: The impact of the Wright reforms—Third report of session 2013–14*, 18 July, HC 82 [incorporating HC 1062-i to iii, Session 2012–13], UK Parliament, London, available from: publications. parliament.uk/pa/cm201314/cmselect/cmpolcon/82/82.pdf.

House of Commons Procedure Committee 2014, *E-petitions: A collaborative system—Third report of session 2014–15*, 4 December, HC 235, UK Parliament, London, available from: publications.parliament.uk/pa/cm201415/cmselect/ cmproced/235/235.pdf.

House of Commons Procedure Committee 2017, *Matters for the Procedure Committee in the 2017 Parliament—Seventh report of session 2016–17*, 2 May, HC 1091, UK Parliament, London, available from: publications.parliament. uk/pa/cm201617/cmselect/cmproced/1091/1091.pdf.

House of Commons Procedure Committee 2020, *Procedure under coronavirus restrictions: Virtual participation in debate—Sixth report of session 2019–21*, 18 November, HC 905, UK Parliament, London, available from: committees. parliament.uk/publications/3547/documents/34071/default/.

House of Commons Public Accounts Committee 2020, *Restoration and renewal of the Palace of Westminster: Nineteenth report of session 2019–21*, 2 October, HC 549, UK Parliament, London, available from: committees.parliament. uk/publications/2801/documents/27534/default/.

House of Commons Public Accounts Committee 2022, *Restoration and Renewal of Parliament: Inquiry, oral and written evidence*, UK Parliament, London, available from: committees.parliament.uk/work/6485/restoration-and-renewal-of-parliament/publications/.

House of Commons Public Administration and Constitutional Affairs Committee (HCPACAC) 2019, *Oral evidence: The role of parliament in the UK Constitution—Role of the Speaker*, 22 October, HC 32, UK Parliament, London, available from: data.parliament.uk/writtenevidence/committee evidence.svc/evidencedocument/public-administration-and-constitutional-affairs-committee/the-role-of-parliament-in-the-uk-constitution-role-of-the-speaker/oral/106560.html#Panel3.

House of Commons Reform Committee 2009, *Rebuilding the House: First report of session 2008–09*, 24 November, HC 1117, The Stationery Office Limited, London, available from: publications.parliament.uk/pa/cm200809/cmselect/cmrefhoc/1117/1117.pdf.

House of Commons Select Committee on the Modernisation of the House of Commons (Modernisation Committee) 2004, *Connecting parliament with the public: First report of session 2003–04*, 16 June, HC 368, UK Parliament, London, available from: publications.parliament.uk/pa/cm200304/cmselect/cmmodern/368/368.pdf.

House of Lords 2002, *Select Committee on House of Lords Offices: Fifth report*, 14 May, UK Parliament, London, available from: publications.parliament. uk/pa/ld200102/ldselect/ldholoff/105/10502.htm.

House of Lords 2013, *Companion to the standing orders and guide to the proceedings of the House of Lords*, TSO, London.

House of Lords 2016a, *Leader's Group on Governance: Governance of domestic committees in the House of Lords—Report*, 13 January, HL Paper 81, UK Parliament, London, available from: www.publications.parliament.uk/pa/ld201516/ldselect/ldleader/81/8102.htm.

House of Lords 2016b, *Strategy for the House of Lords Administration 2016–2021*, UK Parliament, London, available from: www.parliament.uk/documents/lords-information-office/2017/Strategy%20Implementation%20plan%20 2016%20-%202021.pdf.

House of Lords 2017, *Annual report and resource accounts 2016–17*, 17 July, HL Paper 12, UK Parliament, London, available from: www.parliament.uk/ documents/lords-information-office/2017/HL-Annual-Report-Resource-Accounts-2016-17.pdf.

House of Lords 2018, *Annual report and resource accounts 2017–18*, 17 July, HL Paper 175, UK Parliament, London, available from: www.parliament.uk/globalassets/documents/lords-information-office/2017/2017-18-annual-report-and-accounts-final-cover.pdf.

House of Lords 2019, *Annual report and resource accounts 2018–19*, 18 July, HL Paper 412, UK Parliament, London, available from: www.parliament.uk/ globalassets/documents/hl-management-board/2018-19-annual-report-and-accounts---publication.pdf.

House of Lords 2020, *Annual report and resource accounts 2019–20*, 21 July, HL Paper 110, UK Parliament, London, available from: www.parliament.uk/ documents/HL%20Management%20Board/House%20of%20Lords%20 Annual%20Report%20and%20Accounts%202019-20.pdf.

House of Lords 2021, *Annual report and resource accounts 2020–21*, 19 July, HL Paper 49, UK Parliament, London, available from: www.parliament.uk/contentassets/1258b91f710142e99ed39bddc54f6e43/house-of-lords-annual-report-and-accounts-2020-21.pdf.

House of Lords 2022, *Administration strategy 2019–2025*, UK Parliament, London, available from: www.parliament.uk/globalassets/documents/lords-business-plans/hol-strategy-poster-to-2025.pdf.

House of Lords Debates 2007, *House Committee—First report*, 5 December, vol. 696, c. 1702, available from: hansard.parliament.uk/lords/2007-12-05/debates/07120553000008/HouseCommitteeFirstReport.

House of Lords Debates 2016, *Debates*, 9 May, vol. 771, cc. 1574–1624, available from: hansard.parliament.uk/Lords/2016-05-09/debates/1605099000494/HouseOfLords.

House of Lords House Committee 2016, *Implementing the recommendations of the Leader's Group on Governance: 1st report of session 2016–17*, 6 July, HL Paper 19, UK Parliament, London, available from: www.publications.parliament.uk/pa/ld201617/ldselect/ldhouse/19/19.pdf.

House of Lords Select Committee on the Speakership of the House 2005, *The speakership of the House of Lords: Report with evidence*, HL Paper 92, TSO, London, available from: publications.parliament.uk/pa/ld200506/ldselect/ldsphouse/92/92.pdf.

House of Representatives Standing Committee on Legal and Constitutional Affairs 1997, *Aspects of Section 44 of the Australian Constitution: Subsections 44(i) and (iv)*, 25 August, Parliament of Australia, Canberra, available from: www.aph.gov.au/Parliamentary_Business/Committees/House_of_Representatives_Committees?url=laca/inquiryinsec44.htm.

House of Representatives Standing Committee on Petitions 2018, *Making voices heard: Inquiry into the e-petitioning system of the House of Representatives Petitions Committee*, May, Parliament of Australia, Canberra, available from: parlinfo.aph.gov.au/parlInfo/download/committees/reportrep/024135/toc_pdf/Makingvoicesheard.pdf;fileType=application%2Fpdf.

House of Representatives Standing Committee on Procedure 1999, *It's your house: Community involvement in the procedures and practices of the House of Representatives and its committees*, Parliament of Australia, Canberra, available from: www.aph.gov.au/Parliamentary_Business/Committees/House_of_Representatives_Committees?url=proc/reports/cominv/report.htm.

House of Representatives Standing Committee on Procedure 2005, *History of the Procedure Committee on its 20th anniversary: Procedural reform in the House of Representatives—1985–2005*, 28 November, Parliament of Australia, Canberra, available from: www.aph.gov.au/Parliamentary_Business/Committees/House_of_Representatives_Committees?url=proc/history/report.htm.

House of Representatives Standing Committee on Procedure 2010, *Building a modern committee system: An inquiry into the effectiveness of the House committee system*, 21 June, Parliament of Australia, Canberra, available from: www.aph.gov.au/parliamentary_business/committees/house_of_representatives_committees?url=proc/committees2/report.htm.

House of Representatives Standing Committee on Procedure 2016, *Division required? Electronic voting in the House of Representatives*, 2 May, Parliament of Australia, Canberra, available from: www.aph.gov.au/Parliamentary_Business/Committees/House/Procedure/Divison_required/Report.

House of Representatives Standing Committee on Procedure 2017, *Inquiry into the provisions relating to disorder*, October, Parliament of Australia, Canberra, available from: www.aph.gov.au/Parliamentary_Business/Committees/House/Procedure/DisorderintheHouse/Report_1.

House of Representatives Standing Committee on Procedure 2020, *The House must go on: Report of the inquiry into the practices and procedures put in place by the House in response to the COVID-19 pandemic*, November, Parliament of Australia, Canberra, available from: www.aph.gov.au/Parliamentary_Business/Committees/House/Procedure/ResponsetoCOVID-19/Report.

Houses of Parliament Restoration and Renewal 2020, *A structure for success*, [Online], available from: www.restorationandrenewal.uk/about-us.

Hutchison, J. 1996, 'Setting the scene', in J. Disney and J.R. Nethercote (eds), *The house on Capital Hill: Parliament, politics, and power in the national capital*, The Federation Press, Sydney, pp. 1–11.

Huxham, C. 2003, 'Theorizing collaboration practice', *Public Management Review*, vol. 5, no. 3, pp. 401–423, doi.org/10.1080/1471903032000146964.

Ilbert, C. 1912, *Parliament: Its history, constitution and practice*, Williams & Norgate, London.

The Independent 2017, 'As impartial chair of the House of Commons, John Bercow should not attack Donald Trump', [Editorial], *The Independent*, [London], 7 February, available from: www.independent.co.uk/voices/editorials/john-bercow-bans-donald-trump-from-house-of-commons-theresa-may-conservatives-angry-impartial-chair-a7567671.html.

Independent Expert Panel 2022, *The conduct of Mr John Bercow*, 8 March, HC 1189, UK Parliament, London, available from: www.parliament.uk/globalassets/mps-lords--offices/standards-and-financial-interests/independent-expert-panel/hc-1189---the-conduct-of-mr-john-bercow.pdf.

Independent Parliamentary Expenses Authority (IPEA) 2018, *Travel and travel-related work expenses of the Hon Barnaby Joyce MP: 9 May 2016 to 14 February 2018*, Audit report, July, IPEA, Canberra, available from: www.ipea.gov.au/sites/default/files/travel_and_travel-_related_work_expenses_of_a_parliamentarian_9_may_2016_.pdf.

Independent Parliamentary Expenses Authority (IPEA) 2019, *Corporate plan 2018–19*, IPEA, Canberra, available from: www.ipea.gov.au/sites/default/files/ipea_2018-19_corporate_plan_21_08.pdf.

Independent Review of the APS 2019, *Independent Review of the APS: Priorities for change*, 19 March, Department of the Prime Minister and Cabinet, Canberra, available from: www.apsreview.gov.au/resources/priorities-change.

Innes, J.E. & Booher, D.E. 1999, 'Consensus building and complex adaptive systems: Framework for evaluating collaborative planning', *Journal of the American Planning Association*, vol. 64, no. 4, pp. 412–423, doi.org/10.1080/01944369908976071.

Inter-Parliamentary Union (IPU) & United Nations Development Programme (UNDP) 2017, *Global parliamentary report 2017: Parliamentary oversight— Parliament's power to hold government to account*, 11 October, IPU & UNDP, Geneva & New York, NY, available from: www.undp.org/content/undp/en/home/librarypage/democratic-governance/parliamentary_development/global-parliamentary-report-2017.html.

Inter-Parliamentary Union (IPU) & United Nations Development Programme (UNDP) 2022, *Global parliamentary report 2022: Public engagement in the work of parliament*, IPU & UNDP, Geneva & New York, NY, available from: www.ipu.org/resources/publications/reports/2022-03/global-parliamentary-report-2022.

Jablonowski, A. 2010, *Management Board response to the Tebbit implementation review ('the Jablonowski review'): Report on the implementation of the Tebbit Review recommendations—Paper by the external board member*, August, UK Parliament, London, available from: www.parliament.uk/documents/commons-commission/Commons-Management-Board/Jablonowski-Review-and-Management-Board-response.pdf.

James, D. 1996, *More of the same or a brave new world? The National Commission of Audit*, Current Issues Brief No. 23 1995–96, Department of the Parliamentary Library, Canberra, available from: www.aph.gov.au/About_Parliament/Parliamentary_Departments/Parliamentary_Library/Publications_Archive/CIB/cib9596/96cib23.

James, M., Scott, E. & Tudor, S. 2017, *History of the House of Lords: A short introduction*, House of Lords Library Note 2017/020, 27 April, UK Parliament, London.

Jenkins, S. 2019, 'This APS review will be different, says commissioner', *The Mandarin*, 26 September, available from: www.themandarin.com.au/116772-this-aps-review-will-be-different-says-commissioner/?utm_source=TheJuice&utm_medium=email&utm_source=newsletter.

Jennings, I. 1941, *Parliament must be reformed: A programme for democratic government*, Kegan Paul, Trench, Trubner & Co., London.

Jennings, I. 1961, *Parliament*, Cambridge University Press, Cambridge, UK.

Jennings, W., Stoker, G. & Twyman, J. 2016, 'The dimensions and impact of political discontent in Britain', *Parliamentary Affairs*, vol. 69, no. 4, pp. 876–900, doi.org/10.1093/pa/gsv067.

Johnson, N. 2005, 'What of parliament's future?', in P.J. Giddings (ed.), *The future of parliament: Issues for a new century*, Palgrave Macmillan, London, pp. 12–24, doi.org/10.1057/9780230523142_2.

Johnson, S. 2022, Essential scheme: Initial assessment of cost and schedule; and continued presence—Impact study, Deposited paper, February, UK Parliament, London, available from: assets.ctfassets.net/vuylkhqhtihf/13GvESTY51W brDXnTNmf4O/7599c5a9413402403d26c41cfb8a06b6/Essential_Scheme_ Initial_Assessment_of_Cost_and_Schedule_and_Continued_Presence_ Impact_Study_Final.pdf.

Johnston, N. & Dempsey, N. 2017, *Abuse and intimidation of candidates at general elections*, Debate Pack Number CDP-0161, 13 September, House of Commons Library, London, available from: commonslibrary.parliament.uk/ research-briefings/cdp-2017-0161/.

Joint Committee of Public Accounts and Audit (JCPAA) 2008, *Report 413: The efficiency dividend—Size does matter*, 4 December, Parliament of Australia, Canberra, available from: www.aph.gov.au/parliamentary_business/ committees/house_of_representatives_committees?url=jcpaa/efficdiv/report. htm.

Joint House Department (JHD) 1988, *Annual report 1987–88*, AGPS, Canberra.

Joint House Department (JHD) 2002, *Annual report 2002–03*, AGPS, Canberra.

Joint Standing Committee on Electoral Matters (JSCEM) 2018, *Excluded: The impact of Section 44 on Australian democracy*, May, Parliament of Australia, Canberra.

Joint Standing Committee on the National Capital and External Territories (JSCNCET) 2019, *Telling Australia's story—and why it's important: Report on the inquiry into Australia's national institutions*, April, Parliament of Australia, Canberra.

Judge, D. & Leston-Bandeira, C. 2018, 'The institutional representation of parliament', *Political Studies*, vol. 66, no. 1, pp. 154–172, doi.org/10.1177/ 0032321717706901.

Karvelas, P. 2020, 'Parliament's COVID-19 restrictions undermining democracy, Joyce says', *RN Breakfast*, [ABC Radio National], 31 August, available from: www.abc.net.au/radionational/programs/breakfast/parliaments-covid19- restrictions-undermining/12611978.

Kassam, N. 2019, *Lowy Institute poll 2019*, 26 June, Lowy Institute, Sydney, available from: www.lowyinstitute.org/publications/lowy-institute-poll-2019 #sec37041.

Keane, J. 2010, *Media decadence and democracy*, Papers on Parliament No. 53, June, Parliament of Australia, Canberra, available from: www.aph.gov.au/About_ Parliament/Senate/Public_Information_and_Events/occalect/transcripts/~/ link.aspx?_id=E370A5771E88432DBF3CFC0BA63835E7&_z=z.

Kelly, F. 2020, 'Concern COVID-19 restrictions in Federal Parliament undermine democracy', *RN Breakfast*, [ABC Radio National], 2 September, available from: www.abc.net.au/radionational/programs/breakfast/concern-covid19- restrictions-in-federal-parliament/12619530.

Kelly, G., Mulgan, G. & Muers, S. 2002, *Creating public value: An analytical framework for public service reform*, Public Value Paper, Strategy Unit, Cabinet Office, London, available from: www.academia.edu/23693003/Creating_ Public_Value_An_analytical_framework_for_public_service_reform.

Kelly, R. 2018, *Restoration and renewal of the Palace of Westminster*, Briefing Paper No. 07898, 3 December, House of Commons Library, London, available from: commonslibrary.parliament.uk/research-briefings/cbp-7898/.

Kelly, R. 2020, *The election of a speaker*, Briefing Paper No. 05074, 13 January, House of Commons Library, London, available from: commonslibrary. parliament.uk/research-briefings/sn05074/.

Kelly, R. 2021, *Independent complaints and grievance scheme*, Briefing Paper No. 08369, 27 April, House of Commons Library, London, available from: commonslibrary.parliament.uk/research-briefings/cbp-8369/.

Kelly, R. 2022, *Restoration and renewal: Developments since October 2019*, Briefing Paper No. 08968, 7 April, House of Commons Library, London, available from: commonslibrary.parliament.uk/research-briefings/cbp-8968/.

Kelly, R. & Bochel, C. 2018, *Parliament's engagement with the public*, Briefing Paper No. 8279, 6 April, House of Commons Library, London, available from: www.legco.gov.hk/general/english/library/stay_informed_parliamentary_ news/parliaments_engage_public.pdf.

Kelso, A. 2003, '"Where were the massed ranks of parliamentary reformers?" "Attitudinal" and "contextual" approaches to parliamentary reform', *The Journal of Legislative Studies*, vol. 9, no. 1, pp. 57–76, doi.org/10.1080/ 13523270300660004.

Kelso, A. 2007a, 'The House of Commons Modernisation Committee: Who needs it?', *The British Journal of Politics and International Relations*, vol. 9, no. 1, pp. 138–157, doi.org/10.1111/j.1467-856x.2007.00241.x.

Kelso, A. 2007b, 'Parliament and political disengagement: Neither waving nor drowning', *The Political Quarterly*, vol. 78, no. 3, pp. 364–373, doi.org/10.1111/j.1467-923X.2007.00865.x.

Kelso, A. 2009, *Parliamentary reform at Westminster*, Manchester University Press, Manchester, UK.

Keman, H. 2011, 'Comparative research methods', in D. Caramani (ed.), *Comparative politics*, 2nd edn, Oxford University Press, Oxford, UK, pp. 50–63.

Kennon, A. 2019, 'The business of the House: The role of the clerks in the Speaker's decision on the Grieve amendment', *The Constitution Unit Blog*, 22 January, available from: constitution-unit.com/2019/01/22/the-role-of-the-clerks-in-advising-the-speaker/.

Kenny, C. 2018, *Report to the House of Commons Administration Committee on the findings of the general election 2017 new members induction and service user research*, June, General Election Planning Group, UK Parliament, London, available from: www.parliament.uk/documents/commons-committees/administration/Full-evaluation-report.pdf.

Kettl, D.F. 2006, *The global public management revolution*, Brookings Institution Press, Washington, DC.

Keulen, S. & Kroeze, R. 2014, 'Introduction: The era of management—A historical perspective on twentieth-century management', *Management & Organizational History*, vol. 9, no. 4, pp. 321–335, doi.org/10.1080/17449359.2014.982658.

Key, J. 2017, The Sir Robert Garran Oration, Speech to 2017 IPAA National Conference, Canberra, 15 October, available from: www.ipaa.org.au/wp-content/uploads/2019/06/2017-Garran-Oration-John-Key.pdf.

King, A. 1976, 'Modes of executive–legislative relations: Great Britain, France and West Germany', *Legislative Studies Quarterly*, vol. 1, no. 1, pp. 11–36.

Kouzmin, A. 1979, 'Building (Australia's) new Parliament House: An opera house revisited?', *Human Futures*, vol. 3, no. 1, pp. 51–74.

Laing, R. 2010, 'Clerk's review', in Department of the Senate, *Annual report 2009–10*, Parliament of Australia, Canberra, available from: www.aph.gov.au/About_Parliament/Parliamentary_Departments/Department_of_the_Senate/Annual_Reports/Annual_Report_2009-2010/Clerks_review.

Laing, R. 2013, Here be dragons: The advisory role of clerks, Paper presented to 44th Presiding Officers and Clerks Conference, Canberra, 30 June – 4 July.

Laing, R. 2014, 'Advice from the Clerk of the Senate to Senator Faulkner, tabled during the estimates hearing, 26 May 2014', in Senate Standing Committee of Privileges, *160th report: The use of CCTV material in Parliament House*, 5 December, Parliament of Australia, Canberra, Appendix 1, available from: www.aph.gov.au/Parliamentary_Business/Committees/Senate/Privileges/Completed_inquiries/~/link.aspx?_id=2946091C6D154B518900CE1FAA185ED1&_z=z.

Laing, R. 2016a, 'Clerk's review', in Department of the Senate, *Annual report 2015–16*, Parliament of Australia, Canberra, available from: www.aph.gov.au/About_Parliament/Parliamentary_Departments/Department_of_the_Senate/Annual_Reports/Annual_Report_2015-2016/Clerks_review.

Laing, R. (ed.) 2016b, *Odgers' Australian Senate practice as revised by Harry Evans*, 14th edn, Department of the Senate, Canberra.

Laundy, P. 1964, *The office of speaker*, Cassell, London.

Laundy, P. 1979, 'The Speaker and his office in the twentieth century', in S.A. Walkland (ed.), *The House of Commons in the twentieth century*, Clarendon Press, Oxford, UK, pp. 124–203.

Leslie, K. & Mohr, E. 2021, *House of Lords: External management review*, 27 January, UK Parliament, London, available from: committees.parliament.uk/publications/4441/documents/44971/default/.

Leston-Bandeira, C. 2014, 'The pursuit of legitimacy as a key driver for public engagement: The European Parliament case', *Parliamentary Affairs*, vol. 67, no. 2, pp. 415–436, doi.org/10.1093/pa/gss050.

Leston-Bandeira, C. 2015, 'Reflections on the Speaker's Digital Democracy Commission report', *PSA News*, vol. 26, no. 1, p. 20, available from: eprints.lse.ac.uk/63250/.

Leston-Bandeira, C. & Thompson, L. 2017, 'Integrating the view of the public into the formal legislative process: Public reading stage in the UK House of Commons', *The Journal of Legislative Studies*, vol. 23, no. 4, pp. 508–528, doi.org/10.1080/13572334.2017.1394736.

Leston-Bandeira, C. & Thompson, L. (eds) 2018, *Exploring parliament*, Oxford University Press, Oxford, UK, doi.org/10.1093/hepl/9780198788430.001.0001.

Leston-Bandeira, C. & Walker, A. 2018, 'Parliament and public engagement', in C. Leston-Bandeira & L. Thompson (eds), *Exploring parliament*, Oxford University Press, Oxford, UK, pp. 308–321, doi.org/10.1093/hepl/9780198788430.001.0001.

Levy, R. 2019, 'Populism's problems can be fixed by getting the public better-informed. And that's actually possible', *The Conversation*, 14 January, available from: theconversation.com/populisms-problems-can-be-fixed-by-getting-the-public-better-informed-and-thats-actually-possible-109720.

Lewis, C. 2012, 'Barriers to prioritising education and training for parliamentarians: Role complexity and the media', *Parliamentary Affairs*, vol. 65, no. 3, pp. 699–714, doi.org/10.1093/pa/gss020.

Lewis, R. 2015, 'Mills out of House as rows pile up', *The Weekend Australian*, 25–26 April, p. 9.

Lilley, A., White, H. & Haigh, J. 2018, *Parliamentary monitor 2018*, Institute for Government, London.

Lindquist, E. & Wanna, J. 2011, Co-production in perspective: Parallel traditions and implications for public management and governance, Paper presented to Australia and New Zealand School of Government, Canberra, 1 March.

Lloyd, J. 2015, 'Letter to the presiding officers, dated 14 December 2015', in Parliamentary departments: Answers to questions on notice, Tabled 27 February, available from: www.aph.gov.au/Parliamentary_Business/Senate_estimates/fapactte/estimates/add1617/parliamentary/index.

Lloyd, J. 2016, 'Letter to the presiding officers, dated 10 August 2016', in Parliamentary departments: Answers to questions on notice, tabled 27 February, available from: www.aph.gov.au/Parliamentary_Business/Senate_estimates/fapactte/estimates/add1617/parliamentary/index.

Lloyd, S. 1976, *Mr Speaker, Sir*, Jonathan Cape, London.

Lord Speaker 2017, *Report of the Lord Speaker's committee on the size of the House*, 31 October, UK Parliament, London, available from: www.parliament.uk/documents/lords-committees/size-of-house/size-of-house-report.pdf.

Lord Speaker 2018, *Second report of the Lord Speaker's committee on the size of the House*, 24 October, UK Parliament, London, available from: www.parliament.uk/documents/lords-committees/size-of-house/size-of-house-second-report.pdf.

Lusoli, W., Ward, S. & Gibson, R. 2005, '(Re)connecting politics? Parliament, the public and the internet', *Parliamentary Affairs*, vol. 59, no. 1, pp. 24–42, doi.org/10.1093/pa/gsj010.

Lusoli, W., Ward, S. & Gibson, R. 2006, *Public management: Old and new*, Routledge, New York, NY.

Lusoli, W., Ward, S. & Gibson, R. 2012, 'Public management', in B.G. Peters & J. Pierre (eds), *The Sage handbook of public administration*, Sage Publications, London, pp. 17–31.

Lyn, L. 2006, *Public management: Old and new*, Routledge, New York.

Lyn, L. 2012, 'Public management', in B.G. Peters & J. Pierre (eds), *The Sage handbook of public administration*, Sage Publications, London, pp. 17–31.

Madden, C. & McKeown, D. 2018, *2018 parliamentary remuneration and business resources: A quick guide*, Research Paper Series 2018–19, Updated 6 September, Department of Parliamentary Services, Canberra, available from: parlinfo.aph.gov.au/parlInfo/download/library/prspub/5453769/upload_binary/5453769.pdf;fileType=application%2Fpdf#search=%22library/prspub/5453769%22.

Maer, L. & Kelly, R. 2017, *Hung parliaments*, Briefing Paper No. 04951, 9 October, House of Commons Library, London, available from: commonslibrary.parliament.uk/research-briefings/sn04951/.

Maguire, P. 2018, 'John Bercow's exit timetable allows self-interested Labour MPs to keep having it both ways', *The New Statesman*, 16 October, available from: www.newstatesman.com/politics/staggers/2018/10/john-bercow-s-exit-timetable-allows-self-interested-labour-mps-keep-having.

Maguire, P. & Ellery, B. 2021, 'Tories divided as sleaze row boils over on WhatsApp', *The Times*, [London], 12 November, available from: www.thetimes.co.uk/article/mps-fill-pockets-using-rent-expenses-loophole-v7j5jtls6.

Mahoney, J. & Thelen, K. 2010, 'A theory of gradual institutional change', in J. Mahoney & K. Thelen (eds), *Explaining institutional change: Ambiguity, agency, and power*, Cambridge University Press, Cambridge, UK, pp. 1–37, doi.org/10.1017/CBO9780511806414.003.

Malcolmson, D. 1999, 'Parliament should check its costs', *Australian Journal of Public Administration*, vol. 58, no. 1, pp. 102–105, doi.org/10.1111/1467-8500.00080.

Maley, M. 2021, 'Parliament must lead the way in responding to the Jenkins review', *The Canberra Times*, 30 November, available from: www.canberratimes.com.au/story/7530613/parliament-must-lead-the-way-in-responding-to-the-jenkins-review/.

Marr, A. 2017, 'Andrew Marr: Politicians are easy targets but the work they do really matters', *Evening Standard*, [London], 24 November, available from: www.standard.co.uk/comment/comment/andrew-marr-politicians-are-easy-targets-but-the-work-they-do-really-matters-a3701136.html.

Marsden, P. 1979, *The officers of the Commons, 1363–1978*, HMSO, London.

Marsh, I. 2016, 'The Commons Select Committee system in the 2015–20 Parliament', *The Political Quarterly*, vol. 87, no. 1, pp. 96–103, doi.org/10.1111/1467-923X.12223.

Marsh, I. & Halpin, D. 2015, 'Parliamentary committees and inquiries', in B. Head & K. Crowley (eds), *Policy analysis in Australia*, Policy Press, Bristol, UK, pp. 137–150.

Marsh, I. & Miller, R. 2012, *Democratic decline and democratic renewal: Political change in Britain, Australia and New Zealand*, Cambridge University Press, Cambridge, UK, doi.org/10.1017/CBO9781139198691.

Martin, K. 1982, 'Parliament, information and intelligence', in J. Nethercote (ed.), *Parliament and bureaucracy*, Hale & Iremonger, Sydney, pp. 227–237.

May, E. 2011, *Treatise on the law, privilege, proceedings and usage of Parliament*, 24th edn, Butterworths, London.

McCann, J., Hough, A. & Heriot, D. 2018, *Chronology: The 30th anniversary of Australia's Parliament House*, 9 May, Parliamentary Library, Canberra, available from: parlinfo.aph.gov.au/parlInfo/download/library/prspub/4545 392/upload_binary/4545392.pdf.

McCarthy-Cotter, L., Flinders, M. & Healey, T. 2018, 'Design and space in Parliament', in C. Leston-Bandeira & L. Thompson (eds), *Exploring parliament*, Oxford University Press, Oxford, UK, pp. 24–32, doi.org/10.1093/hepl/9780198788430.003.0006.

McGowan, C. 2018, *National Integrity Commission Bill 2018: Explanatory memorandum and statement of compatibility with human rights*, House of Representatives, Parliament of Australia, Canberra, available from: parlinfo. aph.gov.au/parlInfo/download/legislation/ems/r6217_ems_7c3180fe-5f29-4840-8da8-87fbe13f277d/upload_pdf/18241EMMcGowan.pdf;fileType= application%2Fpdf.

McGuire, M. 2006, 'Collaborative public management: Assessing what we know and how we know it', *Public Administration Review*, vol. 66, pp. 33–43, doi.org/10.1111/j.1540-6210.2006.00664.x.

Mckay, L. 2018, 'When MPs talk, we listen: How communication drives constituents' awareness of their MPs', *PSA Parliaments*, 5 December, The UK Political Studies Association Specialist Group on Parliaments, London, available from: psaparliaments.org/2018/12/05/mps-communication-constit uents-awareness/.

Meakin, A. 2017a, 'Who is in charge of the Palace of Westminster? Big Ben and parliamentary governance', *Hansard Society Blog*, 8 September, available from: www.hansardsociety.org.uk/blog/who-is-in-charge-of-the-palace-of-west minster-big-ben-and-parliamentary.

Meakin, A. 2017b, 'Assault in the corridors of power: Now can we talk seriously about rebuilding Westminster?', *The Conversation*, 3 November, available from: theconversation.com/assault-in-the-corridors-of-power-now-can-we-talk-seriously-about-rebuilding-westminster-86863.

Meakin, A. 2018, 'The Prime Minister and the Palace of Westminster', *PSA Parliaments*, 20 July, The UK Political Studies Association Specialist Group on Parliaments, London, available from: psaparliaments.org/2018/07/20/ prime-minister-and-palace-of-westminster/.

Meakin, A. 2020, 'The new review of restoration and renewal of the Palace of Westminster: Five possible outcomes', *Hansard Society Blog*, 12 June, available from: www.hansardsociety.org.uk/blog/restoration-and-renewal-palace-west minster-possible-outcomes-new-review.

Meakin, A. & Anderson, A. 2019, 'The Parliamentary Buildings (Restoration and Renewal) Act 2019: What next?', *Hansard Society Blog*, 18 September, available from: www.hansardsociety.org.uk/blog/the-parliamentary-buildings-restoration-and-renewal-act-2019-what-next.

Meakin, A., Anderson, A. & Flinders, M. 2020, 'Palace of Westminster restoration and renewal: A new era, or more of the same?', *Hansard Society Blog*, 7 April, available from: www.hansardsociety.org.uk/blog/palace-of-westminster-restoration-and-renewal-a-new-era-or-more-of-the-same.

Meakin, A. & Geddes, M. 2020, 'Explaining change in legislatures: Dilemmas of managerial reform in the UK House of Commons', *Political Studies*, vol. 70, no. 1, pp. 1–20, doi.org/10.1177/0032321720955127.

Megarrity, L. 2017, 'Chipp, Donald Leslie (1925–2006): Senator for Victoria, 1978–86 (Australian Democrats)', in *The Biographical Dictionary of the Australian Senate. Volume 4: 1983–2002*, Department of the Senate, Canberra, pp. 417–423, available from: biography.senate.gov.au/chipp-donald-leslie/.

Members of Parliament (Staff) Act 1984 (Commonwealth of Australia).

Menadue, J. 2019, 'We need a national political summit to promote democratic renewal', *Pearls and Irritations*, 9 January, available from: johnmenadue.com/ john-menadue-we-need-a-national-political-summit-to-promote-democratic-renewal/.

Menhennet, D. & Palmer, J. 1967, *Parliament in perspective*, Bodley Head, London.

Milligan, L. 2020, 'Inside the Canberra bubble', *Four Corners*, [ABC TV], 9 November, [Updated 29 November], available from: www.abc.net.au/ 4corners/inside-the-canberra-bubble/12864676.

Mills, C. 2012, 'Secretary's message', in Department of Parliamentary Services, *Annual report 2011–12*, Parliament of Australia, Canberra, available from: www. aph.gov.au/About_Parliament/Parliamentary_Departments/Department_of_ Parliamentary_Services/Publications/Annual_Reports/Annual_Report_2011-12/Part_1_Secretarys_message.

Mills, C. 2013, 'Secretary's review', in Department of Parliamentary Services, *Annual report 2012–13*, Parliament of Australia, Canberra, available from: www. aph.gov.au/About_Parliament/Parliamentary_Departments/Department_of_ Parliamentary_Services/Publications/Annual_Reports/Annual_Report_2012-13/Part_1_Secretarys_review.

Mills, C. 2014, 'Secretary's review', in Department of Parliamentary Services, *Annual report 2013–14*, Parliament of Australia, Canberra, available from: www. aph.gov.au/About_Parliament/Parliamentary_Departments/Department_of_ Parliamentary_Services/Publications/Annual_Reports/Annual_Report_2013-14/Part_1_Secretarys_Review.

Mills, S. 2020, 'Parliament in a time of virus: Representative democracy as a non-essential service', *Australasian Parliamentary Review*, vol. 34, no. 2, pp. 7–20.

Mintzberg, H. 1973, *The nature of managerial work*, HarperCollins, New York, NY.

Missen, A. 1982, 'Senate committees and the legislative process', in J. Nethercote (ed.), *Parliament and bureaucracy*, Hale & Iremonger, Sydney, pp. 125–134.

Molloy, S. 2019, 'Why would any woman sign up for a life in politics when this is how they're treated?', *News.com.au*, 25 January, available from: www. news.com.au/finance/work/at-work/why-would-any-woman-sign-up-for-a-life-in-politics-when-this-is-how-theyre-treated/news-story/cd5240780c7c 81f5eaf21e04f587507f.

Monk, D. 2009a, *In the eye of the beholder? A framework for testing the effectiveness of parliamentary committees*, Parliamentary Studies Paper 10, Crawford School of Economics and Government, The Australian National University, Canberra.

Monk, D. 2009b, *A statistical analysis of government responses to committee reports: Reports tabled between the 2001 and 2004 elections*, Parliamentary Studies Paper 11, Crawford School of Economics and Government, The Australian National University, Canberra.

Moore, C. 2018, 'If MPs leave while parliament is being restored, I fear they will never be allowed to return', *The Telegraph*, [London], 28 January, available from: www.telegraph.co.uk/news/2018/01/28/mps-leave-parliament-restored-fear-will-never-allowed-return/.

Moore, M.H. 1995, *Creating public value: Strategic management in government*, Harvard University Press, Cambridge, MA.

Moore, M.H. 2013, *Recognising public value*, Harvard University Press, Cambridge, MA.

Moore, M.H. 2016, Recognising public value: Strategic uses of performance measurement in government, Presentation to Australia and New Zealand School of Government Workshop, Melbourne, 25 February.

Moran, T. 2010, *Ahead of the game: Blueprint for the reform of Australian government administration*, Advisory Group on Reform of Australian Government Administration, Department of the Prime Minister and Cabinet, Canberra.

Moroney, T.F. 1997, The rise and fall of the Queensland Parliamentary Service Commission: A study of parliamentary independence vs executive government control, Master's thesis, Department of Government, University of Queensland, Brisbane.

Moynihan, D.P. 2012, 'Identifying the antecedents to government performance: Implications for human resource management', in B.G. Peters & J. Pierre (eds), *The Sage handbook of public administration*, Sage Publications, London, pp. 72–86.

Mulder, D. 2017, 'Parliaments around the world: What can architecture teach us about democracy?', *Hansard Society Blog*, 7 February, available from: www.hansardsociety.org.uk/blog/parliaments-around-the-world-what-can-architecture-teach-us-about-democracy.

Mulgan, R. 2014, 'Carol Mills and the chaos on Capital Hill', *Public Sector Informant*, [Canberra], 2 April, p. 12.

Murphy, K. 2017, 'Speaker vows not to use casting vote to give Coalition a majority in lower house', *The Guardian*, [Australia], 5 May, available from: www.theguardian.com/australia-news/2017/may/05/speaker-vows-not-to-use-casting-vote-to-give-coalition-a-majority-in-lower-house.

Murphy, K. 2018a, 'Australia bans ministers from having sex with staff after Barnaby Joyce scandal', *The Guardian*, [Australia], 15 February, available from: www.theguardian.com/australia-news/2018/feb/15/australia-bans-ministers-having-sex-with-staff-barnaby-joyce-malcolm-turnbull.

Murphy, K. 2018b, 'Compromise is a lost art in Australian politics, Senate president Scott Ryan says', *The Guardian*, [Australia], 29 August, available from: www.theguardian.com/australia-news/2018/aug/29/compromise-is-a-lost-art-in-australian-politics-senate-president-scott-ryan-says.

Murphy, K. 2018c, 'Why parliament still tolerates thuggery not acceptable in broader society', *The Guardian*, [Australia], 28 November, available from: www.theguardian.com/australia-news/2018/nov/28/why-parliament-still-tolerates-thuggery-not-acceptable-in-broader-society.

Murphy, K. 2018d, 'Anthony Albanese on how MPs' loneliness feeds parliament's coup culture', *The Guardian*, [Australia], 5 December, available from: www.theguardian.com/australia-news/2018/dec/05/anthony-albanese-on-how-mps-loneliness-feeds-parliaments-coup-culture.

Murphy, K. 2021, 'Brittany Higgins: Who knew what, and when, about the alleged rape at Parliament House', *The Guardian*, [Australia], 17 February, available from: www.theguardian.com/australia-news/2021/feb/17/brittany-higgins-who-knew-what-and-when-about-the-alleged-at-parliament-house.

Nabatchi, T., Sancino, A. & Sicilia, M. 2017, 'Varieties of participation in public services: The who, when, and what of coproduction', *Public Administration Review*, vol. 77, no. 5, pp. 766–776, doi.org/10.1111/puar.12765.

National Commission of Audit (NCA) 1996, *Report to the Commonwealth Government*, AGPS, Canberra.

National Integrity (Parliamentary Standards) Bill 2018 (Commonwealth of Australia).

Natzler, D. 2018, Letter from Clerk of the House of Commons to staff of the House concerning bullying and harassment, including sexual harassment, 12 March, UK Parliament, London, available from: www.parliament.uk/mps-lords-and-offices/offices/commons/media-relations-group/news/letter-from-the-clerk-of-the-house-to-staff-of-the-house-of-commons/.

Natzler, D. 2019a, 'Statement on the impartial relationship between clerks and members of parliament', 21 January, UK Parliament, London, available from: www.parliament.uk/mps-lords-and-offices/offices/commons/media-relations-group/news/statement-on-the-impartial-relationsip-between-clerks-and-members-of-parliament/.

Natzler, D. 2019b, 'Erskine May online will help demystify parliament', *The Times*, [London], 2 July, available from: www.thetimes.co.uk/article/putting-erskine-may-online-will-help-demystify-parliament-wqqd7vt03.

Negrine, R. & Bull, P. 2014, '"Mr Malik, to represent the people of Dewsbury do you need a £2600 cinema system paid for by the taxpayer?" An analysis of British television news coverage of the 2009 MPs' "expenses scandal"', *Parliamentary Affairs*, vol. 68, no. 3, pp. 573–591, doi.org/10.1093/pa/gsu009.

Nethercote, J. (ed.) 1982, 'Introduction', in J. Nethercote (ed.), *Parliament and bureaucracy*, Hale & Iremonger, Sydney, pp. 1–13.

Newson, N. 2012, *House of Lords: Reform of working practices, 2000–2012*, House of Lords Library Note 2012/033, 11 October, UK Parliament, London, available from: lordslibrary.parliament.uk/research-briefings/lln-2012-033/.

Ng, Y.-F. 2018, 'Emma Hussar allegations show a need for clearer rules about what MPs can—and cannot—do', *The Conversation*, 27 July, available from: theconversation.com/emma-husar-allegations-show-a-need-for-clearer-rules-about-what-mps-can-and-cannot-do-100580.

Nicholls, V. 2010, *Firm foundations for a new politics? The governance of the House of Commons after the MPs' expenses crisis*, Institute for Government, London.

Niven, C.R., Egbuna, E., Doherty, R.A. & Metcalfe, F. 1959, *Notes on parliamentary procedure*, Hansard Society for Parliamentary Government, London.

Northcote, S.H., Trevelyan, C.E. & Jowett, B. 1854, *Report on the organisation of the permanent civil service, together with a letter from the Rev. B. Jowett*, G.E. Eyre & W. Spottiswoode, London.

Norton, P. 1983, 'The Norton view', in D. Judge (ed.), *The politics of parliamentary reform*, Heinemann, London, pp. 54–69.

Norton, P. 1993, *Does Parliament matter?*, Harvester Wheatsheaf, Hemel Hempstead, UK.

Norton, P. 2000, 'Reforming parliament in the United Kingdom: The report of the Commission to Strengthen Parliament', *The Journal of Legislative Studies*, vol. 6, no. 3, pp. 1–14, doi.org/10.1080/13572330008420628.

Norton, P. 2002, 'Parliamentary reform', *French Journal of British Studies*, vol. 11, no. XI-3, pp. 18–30, doi.org/10.4000/rfcb.696.

Norton, P. 2017, 'Speaking for parliament', *Parliamentary Affairs*, vol. 70, no. 2, pp. 191–206.

Norton, P. 2018a, 'Is the House of Commons becoming too powerful?', *The Norton View*, [Blog], 28 December, available from: nortonview.word press.com/2018/12/28/is-the-house-of-commons-becoming-too-powerful/.

Norton, P. 2018b, 'Power behind the scenes: The importance of informal space in legislatures', *Parliamentary Affairs*, vol. 72, no. 2, pp. 245–266, doi.org/ 10.1093/pa/gsy018.

Norton, P. & Wood, D.M. 1993, *Back from Westminster: British members of parliament and their constituents*, University Press of Kentucky, Lexington, KY.

O'Brien, S. 1993, *Dual citizenship, foreign allegiance and s. 44(i) of the Australian Constitution*, Background Paper No. 29, 9 December, Parliamentary Research Service, Canberra, available from: www.aph.gov.au/binaries/library/pubs/bp/ 1992/92bp29.pdf.

O'Dea, J. 2020, 'Socially distant but democratically together: Towards a virtual parliament in NSW', *Australasian Parliamentary Review*, vol. 34, no. 2, pp. 27–53.

Office of the Information Commissioner (OAIC) 2019, 'Part 2: Scope of application of the Freedom of Information Act 1982', *FOI guidelines*, 19 December, OAIC, Sydney, available from: www.oaic.gov.au/freedom-of-information/foi-guidelines/part-2-scope-of-application-of-the-freedom-of-information-act# agencies-subject-to-the-foi-act.

Officer, R. 1996, *National Commission of Audit: Report to the Commonwealth Government*, AGPS, Canberra.

O'Flynn, J. 2007, 'From new public management to public value: Paradigmatic change and managerial implications', *Australian Journal of Public Administration*, vol. 66, no. 3, pp. 353–366, doi.org/10.1111/j.1467-8500.2007.00545.x.

O'Flynn, J. 2008, 'Elusive appeal or aspirational ideal? The rhetoric and reality of the "collaborative turn" in public policy', in J. O'Flynn & J. Wanna (eds), *Collaborative governance: A new era of public policy in Australia*, ANU Press, Canberra, pp. 181–195, doi.org/10.22459/CG.12.2008.17.

O'Flynn, J. 2009, 'The cult of collaboration in public policy', *Australian Journal of Public Administration*, vol. 68, no. 1, pp. 112–116, doi.org/10.1111/ j.1467-8500.2009.00616.x.

O'Leary, R. & Bingham, L. 2009, *The collaborative public manager: New ideas for the twenty-first century*, Georgetown University Press, Washington, DC.

Oliver, A. 2014, *Lowy Institute poll 2014*, 2 June, Lowy Institute, Sydney, available from: www.lowyinstitute.org/publications/lowy-institute-poll-2014.

Oliver, A. 2018, *2018 Lowy Institute poll*, 20 June, Lowy Institute, Sydney, available from: www.lowyinstitute.org/publications/2018-lowy-institute-poll.

Oliver, D. 1997, 'Regulating the conduct of Mps. The British experience of combating corruption', *Political Studies*, vol. 45, no. 3, pp. 539–558, doi.org/10.1111/1467-9248.00095.

O'Malley, N. 2018, 'Total systems failure', *The Canberra Times*, 11 August, p. 6.

Organisation for Economic Co-operation and Development (OECD) 2017, *Skills for a high performing civil service: OECD public governance reviews*, OECD Publishing, Paris.

Osborne, D. & Gaebler, T. 1993, *Reinventing government: How the entrepreneurial spirit is transforming the public sector*, Plume, New York, NY.

Osborne, S.P. 2010, 'The (new) public governance: A suitable case for treatment?', in S. Osborne (ed.), *The new public governance? Emerging perspectives on the theory and practice of public governance*, Routledge, Abingdon, UK, pp. 1–17, doi.org/10.4324/9780203861684.

Osborne, S.P., Radnor, Z., Kinder, T. & Vidal, I. 2015, 'The SERVICE framework: A public-service-dominant approach to sustainable public services', *British Journal of Management*, vol. 26, no. 3, pp. 424–438, doi.org/10.1111/1467-8551.12094.

Osborne, S.P., Radnor, Z. & Strokosch, K. 2016, 'Co-production and the co-creation of value in public services: A suitable case for treatment?', *Public Management Review*, vol. 18, no. 5, pp. 639–653, doi.org/10.1080/14719037.2015.1111927.

Osborne, S.P. & Strokosch, K. 2013, 'It takes two to tango? Understanding the co-production of public services by integrating the services management and public administration perspectives', *British Journal of Management*, vol. 24, pp. S31–S47, doi.org/10.1111/1467-8551.12010.

Parker, J. & Mahy, H. 2007, *Review of the management board of the House of Lords*, Report, April, UK Parliament, London, available from: www.parliament.uk/documents/hl-managmentboard/ReviewoftheMB2007.pdf.

Parkinson, J. 2012, *Democracy and public space: The physical sites of democratic performance*, Oxford University Press, Oxford, UK.

Parliament (Joint Departments) Act 2007 (United Kingdom).

Parliament of Australia 1998–99, *Parliamentary Service Bill 1999: Explanatory memorandum*, Parliament of Australia, Canberra, available from: parlinfo.aph. gov.au/parlInfo/download/legislation/ems/r797_ems_bf3fc237-6e92-4f36-b13f-48843d13e437/upload_pdf/PRLSRVEM.pdf;fileType=application %2Fpdf.

Parliament of Australia 2017a, *The Federation Chamber*, Infosheet 16, Parliament of Australia, Canberra, available from: www.aph.gov.au/About_Parliament/ House_of_Representatives/Powers_practice_and_procedure/00_-_Info sheets/Infosheet_16_-_The_Federation_Chamber.

Parliament of Australia 2017b, *Strategic plan for parliamentary administration*, Parliament of Australia, Canberra, accessed from: www.aph.gov.au/About_ Parliament/Publications/Strategic_Plan_for_parliamentary_administration [page discontinued].

Parliament of Australia 2019, *Australian Parliament digital strategy 2019–2022*, Parliament of Australia, Canberra, available from: www.aph.gov.au/About_ Parliament/Publications/Australian_Parliament_Digital_Strategy.

Parliament of Australia 2020, *Strategic framework: The Parliamentary Service*, Parliament of Australia, Canberra, available from: www.aph.gov.au/About_ Parliament/Publications/Strategic_Framework_-_The_Parliamentary_Service.

Parliamentary Budget Office (PBO) 2013, *Annual report 2012–13*, Parliament of Australia, Canberra, available from: www.aph.gov.au/About_Parliament/ Parliamentary_Departments/Parliamentary_Budget_Office/About_the_PBO/ Corporate_information/Annual_reports/Annual_Report_2012-13.

Parliamentary Buildings (Restoration and Renewal) Act 2019 (United Kingdom).

Parliamentary Corporate Bodies Act 1992 (United Kingdom).

Parliamentary Library 2013, *The hung parliament: Procedural changes in the House of Representatives*, Research Paper Series 2013–14, Parliamentary Library, Canberra, available from: parlinfo.aph.gov.au/parlInfo/download/library/ prspub/2855740/upload_binary/2855740.pdf;fileType=application/pdf.

Parliamentary Precincts Act 1988 (Commonwealth of Australia).

Parliamentary Service Act 1999 (Commonwealth of Australia).

Parliamentary Service Commissioner 2008, *Annual report 2007–08*, Department of Parliamentary Service, Canberra.

Parliamentary Service Commissioner 2010, *Annual report 2009–10*, Department of Parliamentary Service, Canberra.

Parliamentary Service Commissioner 2018, *Annual report 2017–18*, Department of Parliamentary Service, Canberra.

Parpworth, N. 2010, 'The Parliamentary Standards Act 2009: A constitutional dangerous dogs measure?', *The Modern Law Review*, vol. 73, no. 2, pp. 262–281, doi.org/10.1111/j.1468-2230.2010.00793.x.

Patience, A. 2019, 'It's time for a constitutional reform commission', *Pearls and Irritations*, 11 January, available from: johnmenadue.com/allan-patience-its-time-for-a-constitutional-reform-commission/.

Patmore, P. 2017, The independence of the clerk: 'Friendly to all but friends with no one', Paper presented to Thirteenth Workshop of Parliamentary Scholars and Parliamentarians, Wroxton College, Banbury, UK, 29–30 July.

Pattie, C. & Johnston, R. 2014, 'The impact of the scandal on the 2010 general election results', in J. vanHeerde-Hudson (ed.), *The political costs of the 2009 British MPs' expenses scandal*, Palgrave Macmillan, Basingstoke, UK, pp. 88–110.

Peatling, S. 2015, 'Sacked Department of Parliamentary Services secretary Carol Mills accused of misleading parliamentary committee', *Sydney Morning Herald*, 28 April, available from: www.smh.com.au/federal-politics/political-news/sacked-department-of-parliamentary-services-secretary-carol-mills-accused-of-misleading-parliamentary-committee-20150428-1mv0ct.html.

Peatling, S. 2017, 'The House: Annabel Crabb reveals the secrets of Parliament House', *Sydney Morning Herald*, 3 August, available from: www.smh.com.au/politics/federal/the-house-annabel-crabb-reveals-the-secrets-of-parliament-house-20170803-gxockc.html.

Pelling, T. 2017, 'Not me, guv'nor', [Letter to the Editor], *The Canberra Times*, 14 January, [Updated 24 April 2018], available from: www.canberratimes.com.au/national/act/not-me-guvnor-20170114-gtrkxj.html.

Penfold, H. 2004, 'Secretary's review', in Department of Parliamentary Services, *Annual report 2003–04*, Parliament of Australia, Canberra, available from: www.aph.gov.au/binaries/dps/publications/anrep2004/anrep04_secreview.pdf.

Perkins, A. 2019, 'John Bercow's decision endangers the office of Speaker, and our democracy', *The Guardian*, 10 January, available from: www.theguardian.com/commentisfree/2019/jan/09/john-bercow-decision-endangers-the-office-of-speaker-and-our-democracy.

Peters, B.G., Pierre, J. & King, D.S. 2005, 'The politics of path dependency: Political conflict in historical institutionalism', *The Journal of Politics*, vol. 67, no. 4, pp. 1275–1300, doi.org/10.1111/j.1468-2508.2005.00360.x.

Petit, S. & Yong, B. 2018, 'The administrative organization and governance of parliament', in C. Leston-Bandeira & L. Thompson (eds), *Exploring parliament*, Oxford University Press, Oxford, UK, pp. 24–32, doi.org/10.1093/hepl/9780198788430.003.0003.

Pfeffer, J. & Salancik, G.R. 1978, *The external control of organizations: A resource dependence perspective*, Harper & Row, New York, NY.

Photiadou, A. & Dunleavy, P. 2018, 'How democratic is the House of Commons? How effectively does it control the UK Government and represent citizens?', *Democratic Audit UK*, 20 September, available from: www.democraticaudit.com/2018/09/20/audit2018-how-democratic-is-the-house-of-commons-how-effectively-does-it-control-the-uk-government-and-represent-citizens/.

Pierce, A. 2018, 'If John Bercow had any honour he'd have left his Speaker role already', *Daily Mail*, [London], 16 October, available from: www.dailymail.co.uk/debate/article-6279887/ANDREW-PIERCE-John-Bercow-honour-hed-left-Speaker-role-already.html.

Podger, A. 2002, *Review by the Parliamentary Service Commissioner of aspects of the administration of the parliament: Final report*, September, Parliament of Australia, Canberra.

Podger, A. 2018, Submission to the Independent Review of the Australian Public Service, 6 July, Department of the Prime Minister and Cabinet, Canberra.

Podger, A. 2022, 'Clear architecture needed in APH reforms', *The Canberra Times*, 1 March, p. 10.

Pollitt, C. 2003, *The essential public manager*, Open University Press, Maidenhead, UK.

Poulter, D., Votruba, N., Bakolis, J., Debell, F., Das-Munshi, J. & Thornicroft, G. 2019, 'Mental health of UK members of parliament in the House of Commons: A cross-sectional survey', *BMJ Open*, vol. 9, p. e027892, doi.org/10.1136/bmjopen-2018-027892.

Prasser, S. 2019, 'Parliament House in Canberra is the bubble within the bubble', *The Canberra Times*, 8 October, [Updated 28 October], available from: www. canberratimes.com.au/story/6424665/working-at-parliament-house-the-bubble-within-the-bubble/?cs=14246.

Prebble, M. 2012, 'Public value and the ideal state: Rescuing public value from ambiguity', *Australian Journal of Public Administration*, vol. 71, no. 4, pp. 392–402, doi.org/10.1111/j.1467-8500.2012.00787.x.

Prebble, M. 2015, 'Public value and limits to collaboration', *International Journal of Public Administration*, vol. 38, no. 7, pp. 473–485, doi.org/10.1080/0190 0692.2014.949742.

Prebble, M. 2018, 'Is "we" singular? The nature of public value', *The American Review of Public Administration*, vol. 48, no. 2, pp. 103–118, doi.org/10.1177/ 0275074016671427.

Prior, A.M. 2018, 'Getting the story right: A constructivist interpretation of storytelling in the context of UK parliamentary engagement', *Politics and Governance*, vol. 6, no. 4, pp. 83–94, doi.org/10.17645/pag.v6i4.1580.

Public Eye 2017, 'Cup of cronyism? Aussie's cafe and the bizarre attack on public servants who did their jobs', *Sydney Morning Herald*, 6 March, available from: www.smh.com.au/public-service/cup-of-cronyism-aussies-cafe-and-the-bizarre-attack-on-public-servants-who-did-their-jobs-20170306-guru97.html.

Public Governance, Performance and Accountability Act 2013 (Commonwealth of Australia).

Public Service Act 1922 (Commonwealth of Australia).

Pye, R. 2017, 'Clerk's review', in Department of the Senate, *Annual report 2016–17*, Parliament of Australia, Canberra, available from: www.aph.gov. au/About_Parliament/Parliamentary_Departments/Department_of_the_ Senate/Annual_Reports/Annual_Report_2016-2017/Clerks_review.

Raadschelders, J. 1999, 'A coherent framework for the study of public administration', *Journal of Public Administration Research and Theory*, vol. 9, no. 2, pp. 281–304, doi.org/10.1093/oxfordjournals.jpart.a024411.

Rainey, H.G. 2012, 'Public management: Old and new', in B.G. Peters & J. Pierre (eds), *The Sage handbook of public administration*, Sage Publications, London, pp. 13–15.

Reid, G. 1966, *The politics of financial control: The role of the House of Commons*, Hutchinson University Library, London.

Reid, G.S. & Forrest, M. 1989, *Australia's Commonwealth Parliament 1901–1988: Ten perspectives*, Melbourne University Press, Melbourne.

Reilly, T. 1998, 'Communities in conflict: Resolving differences through collaborative efforts in environmental planning and human service delivery', *Journal of Sociology and Social Welfare*, vol. 25, p. 115.

Remeikis, A. 2018a, 'PM changes code of conduct to ban sex between ministers and staffers—as it happened', *The Guardian*, [Australia], 15 February, available from: www.theguardian.com/australia-news/live/2018/feb/15/politics-joyce-turnbull-shorten-australia?page=with:block-5a852054e4b0c73a42840c2a#block-5a852054e4b0c73a42840c2a.

Remeikis, A. 2018b, 'Emma Husar sexual harassment allegations "not supported" investigation finds', *The Guardian*, [Australia], 10 August, available from: www.theguardian.com/australia-news/2018/aug/10/emma-husar-investigation-finds-sexual-harassment-allegations-not-supported.

Remuneration Tribunal 2011, *Review of the remuneration of members of parliament: Initial report*, December, Remuneration Tribunal, Canberra, available from: www.remtribunal.gov.au/sites/default/files/2021-01/2011%20Review%20of%20the%20Remuneration%20of%20Members%20of%20Parliament%20-%20Initial%20Report.pdf.

Renton, T. 2004, *Chief whip: People, power and patronage in Westminster*, Politico's, London.

Renwick, A. & Palese, M. 2019, *Doing democracy better: How can information and discourse in election and referendum campaigns in the UK be improved?*, March, The Constitution Unit, University College London, available from: www.ucl.ac.uk/constitution-unit/sites/constitution-unit/files/184_-_doing_democracy_better.pdf.

Review Body on Senior Salaries (SSRB) 2009, *Review of financial support for members of the House of Lords*, Report No. 71, November, The Stationery Office, London, available from: assets.publishing.service.gov.uk/government/uploads/system/uploads/attachment_data/file/238509/7746.pdf.

Rhodes, R.A.W. 2016, 'Recovering the craft of public administration', *Public Administration Review*, vol. 76, no. 4, pp. 638–647, doi.org/10.1111/puar.12504.

Rhodes, R.A.W. & Wanna, J. 2007, 'The limits to public value, or rescuing responsible government from the platonic guardians', *Australian Journal of Public Administration*, vol. 66, no. 4, pp. 406–421, doi.org/10.1111/j.1467-8500.2007.00553.x.

Rhodes, R.A.W. & Wanna, J. 2008, 'Stairways to heaven: A reply to Alford', *Australian Journal of Public Administration*, vol. 67, no. 3, pp. 367–370, doi.org/10.1111/j.1467-8500.2008.00594.x.

Rhodes, R.A.W. & Wanna, J. 2009, 'Bringing the politics back in: Public value in Westminster parliamentary government', *Public Administration*, vol. 87, no. 2, pp. 161–183, doi.org/10.1111/j.1467-9299.2009.01763.x.

Richards, D. 2019, 'Does Australian democracy need a reboot?', *Article*, 1 February, Australian Institute of Company Directors, Sydney, available from: aicd.companydirectors.com.au/membership/company-director-magazine/2019-back-editions/february/democracy.

Ringeling, A. 2015, 'How public is public administration? A constitutional approach of publicness', *Teaching Public Administration*, vol. 33, no. 3, pp. 292–312, doi.org/10.1177/0144739415573268.

Rittel, H.W. & Webber, M.M. 1973, 'Dilemmas in a general theory of planning', *Policy Sciences*, vol. 4, no. 2, pp. 155–169, doi.org/10.1007/BF01405730.

Roche, M. 2012, *Review of information and communication technology for the parliament*, Report, 30 August, Parliament of Australia, Canberra, available from: apo.org.au/node/31570.

Rogers, R. & Gay, O. 2009, *Suggestions for possible changes to the procedure and business of the House: A note by the clerks*, House of Commons Library Note SN/PC/05110, 18 June, UK Parliament, London.

Rogers, R. & Walters, R. 2015, *How parliament works*, 7th edn, Routledge, London, doi.org/10.4324/9781315730875.

Rosenbloom, D.H. 1983, 'Public administrative theory and the separation of powers', *Public Administration Review*, vol. 43, no. 3, pp. 219–227, doi.org/10.2307/976330.

Rush, M. 2005, 'Career patterns and professionalisation', in P.J. Giddings (ed.), *The future of parliament: Issues for a new century*, Palgrave Macmillan, London, pp. 37–49, doi.org/10.1057/9780230523142_4.

Rush, M. & Giddings, P. 2011, *Parliamentary socialisation*, Palgrave Macmillan, London, doi.org/10.1057/9780230316850.

Rush, M. & Shaw, M. (eds) 1974, *The House of Commons: Services and facilities*, Allen & Unwin, London.

Russell, M. 2000, *Reforming the House of Lords: Lessons from overseas*, Oxford University Press, Oxford, UK, doi.org/10.1093/acprof:oso/9780198298311. 001.0001.

Russell, M. 2011a, *House full: Time to get a grip on Lords appointments*, The Constitution Unit, UCL, London.

Russell, M. 2011b, '"Never allow a crisis to go to waste": The Wright Committee reforms to strengthen the House of Commons', *Parliamentary Affairs*, vol. 64, no. 4, pp. 612–633, doi.org/10.1093/pa/gsr026.

Russell, M. 2013, *The contemporary House of Lords: Westminster bicameralism revived*, Oxford University Press, Oxford, UK.

Russell, M. 2017a, 'Don't abolish the House of Lords. History shows it really can be reformed', *The Guardian*, 24 February, available from: www.theguardian.com/commentisfree/2017/feb/23/dont-abolish-house-of-lords-history-reformed-second-chamber-change.

Russell, M. 2017b, 'The size of the House of Lords: What next?', *The Constitution Unit Blog*, 22 December, available from: constitution-unit.com/2017/12/22/the-size-of-the-house-of-lords-what-next/#more-6290.

Russell, M. 2019a, 'Should we worry if MPs seize control of the parliamentary agenda?', *The Constitution Unit Blog*, 27 January, available from: constitution-unit.com/2019/01/27/should-we-worry-if-mps-seize-control-of-the-parliamentary-agenda-where-could-that-lead-politics/.

Russell, M. 2019b, 'Parliament has exerted its strength and shown its weakness', *UK in a Changing Europe Blog*, 9 April, available from: ukandeu.ac.uk/parliament-has-exerted-its-strength-and-shown-its-weakness/.

Russell, M. 2019c, 'Why a rhetoric of "parliament versus people" is both dishonest and dangerous', *The Constitution Unit Blog*, 5 November, available from: constitution-unit.com/2019/11/05/why-a-rhetoric-of-parliament-versus-people-is-both-dishonest-and-dangerous/.

Russell, M. 2020, 'Brexit and parliament: The anatomy of a perfect storm', *Parliamentary Affairs*, vol. 74, no. 2, pp. 443–463, doi.org/10.1093/pa/gsaa011.

Russell, M. & Benton, M. 2011, *Selective influence: The policy impact of House of Commons select committees*, The Constitution Unit, UCL, London.

Russell, M. & Cowley, P. 2016, 'The policy power of the Westminster parliament: The "parliamentary state" and the empirical evidence', *Governance*, vol. 29, no. 1, pp. 121–137, doi.org/10.1111/gove.12149.

Russell, M. & Cowley, P. 2018, 'Modes of UK executive–legislative relations revisited', *The Political Quarterly*, vol. 89, no. 1, pp. 18–28, doi.org/10.1111/1467-923X.12463.

Russell, M., Fox, R., Keating, M., McEwen, N., Garry, J., Smith, G., Leston-Bandeira, C., Hughes, T. & Zacharzewski, A. 2020, 'Ending of the hybrid House of Commons breached fundamental democratic principles', [Open Letter to Jacob Rees-Mogg], 8 June, *The Constitution Unit Blog*, available from: constitution-unit.com/2020/06/08/ending-of-the-hybrid-house-of-commons-breached-fundamental-democratic-principles/.

Russell, M. & Gover, D. 2017, *Legislation at Westminster: Parliamentary actors and influence in the making of British law*, Oxford University Press, Oxford, UK, doi.org/10.1093/oso/9780198753827.001.0001.

Russell, M., Gover, D. & Wollter, K. 2016, 'Does the executive dominate the Westminster legislative process? Six reasons for doubt', *Parliamentary Affairs*, vol. 69, no. 2, pp. 286–308, doi.org/10.1093/pa/gsv016.

Russell, M. & Paun, A. 2007, *The House rules? International lessons for enhancing the autonomy of the House of Commons*, The Constitution Unit, UCL, London.

Russell, M. & Sandford, M. 2002, 'Why are second chambers so difficult to reform?', *Journal of Legislative Studies*, vol. 8, no. 3, pp. 79–89, doi.org/10.1080/714003926.

Russell, M. & Serban, R. 2020, 'The muddle of the "Westminster model": A concept stretched beyond repair', *Government and Opposition*, vol. 56, no. 4, pp. 744–764, doi.org/10.1017/gov.2020.12.

Rydz, D.L. 1979, *The parliamentary agents: A history*, Royal Historical Society, London.

Ryle, M. 2005, 'Forty years on and a future agenda', in P.J. Giddings (ed.), *The future of parliament: Issues for a new century*, Palgrave Macmillan, London, pp. 3–11, doi.org/10.1057/9780230523142_1.

Saunders, C. 2017, 'Canberra ignored constitutional timebomb for decades', *Australian Financial Review*, 16 November, p. 59.

Savoie, D.J. 2006, 'What is wrong with the new public management?', in E. Otenyo & N. Lind (eds), *Comparative public administration: The essential readings*, Emerald Group Publishing, Oxford, UK, pp. 593–602, doi.org/10.1016/S0732-1317(06)15025-3.

Scott, E. & Newson, N. 2022, 'House of Lords: Timeline of response to Covid-19 pandemic', *In Focus*, 1 March, House of Lords Library, available from: lordslibrary.parliament.uk/house-of-lords-timeline-of-response-to-covid-19-pandemic/.

Scott, T.A. & Thomas, C.W. 2017, 'Unpacking the collaborative toolbox: Why and when do public managers choose collaborative governance strategies?', *Policy Studies Journal*, vol. 45, no. 1, pp. 191–214, doi.org/10.1111/psj.12162.

Seaward, P. 2009, 'The House of Commons since 1949', in C. Jones (ed.), *A short history of parliament*, Boydell & Brewer, Woodbridge, UK, pp. 283–300.

Seaward, P. 2017, 'Reformation to referendum: A new history of parliament', *The History of Parliament Blog*, 6 December, available from: historyof parliamentblog.wordpress.com/2017/12/06/reformation-to-referendum-a-new-history-of-parliament/.

Sedgwick, S. 2011, Submission by the Australian Parliamentary Service Commissioner to the Senate Finance and Public Administration Legislation Committee Inquiry into the Performance of the Department of Parliamentary Services, Canberra, 10 August.

Senate Committee of Privileges 2014, *160th report: The use of CCTV material in Parliament House*, 5 December, Parliament of Australia, Canberra.

Senate Committee of Senators' Interests 2012, *Code of conduct inquiry*, Report 2/2012, 29 November, Parliament of Australia, Canberra, available from: www.aph.gov.au/Parliamentary_Business/Committees/Senate/Senators_Interests/reports/022012/index.

Senate Finance and Public Administration Legislation Committee (SFPALC) 2012a, *The performance of the Department of Parliamentary Services: Interim report*, June, Parliament of Australia, Canberra.

Senate Finance and Public Administration Legislation Committee (SFPALC) 2012b, *The performance of the Department of Parliamentary Services: Final report*, 28 November, Parliament of Australia, Canberra.

Senate Finance and Public Administration Legislation Committee (SFPALC) 2014, 'Department of Parliamentary Services', in *Budget Estimates for 2014–15*, 26 May, Parliament of Australia, Canberra, available from: www.aph.gov.au/Parliamentary_Business/Senate_Estimates/fapactte/estimates/bud1415/index.

Senate Finance and Public Administration Legislation Committee (SFPALC) 2015a, *Department of Parliamentary Services: Interim report*, 28 April, Parliament of Australia, Canberra.

Senate Finance and Public Administration Legislation Committee (SFPALC) 2015b, *Department of Parliamentary Services: Second interim report*, 25 June, Parliament of Australia, Canberra.

Senate Finance and Public Administration Legislation Committee (SFPALC) 2015c, *Department of Parliamentary Services: Final report*, 17 September, Parliament of Australia, Canberra.

Senate Finance and Public Administration Legislation Committee (SFPALC) 2015d, Department of Parliamentary Services: Submission 8, Speaker of the House of Representatives and President of the Senate, 27 November, Parliament of Australia, Canberra.

Senate Finance and Public Administration Legislation Committee (SFPALC) 2018, 'Department of Parliamentary Services', in *Estimates*, 22 October, Parliament of Australia, Canberra, available from: parlinfo.aph.gov.au/parlInfo/search/display/display.w3p;query=Id%3A%22committees%2Festimate%2Fa9 2ee211-b539-4564-bb6d-19d353e0ab7e%2F0000%22.

Senate Finance and Public Administration Legislation Committee (SFPALC) 2019a, 'Department of Parliamentary Services', in *Estimates*, 18 February, Parliament of Australia, Canberra, available from: parlinfo.aph.gov.au/parlInfo/search/display/display.w3p;query=Id:%22committees/estimate/0186e774-64b9-406c-92c1-78150436112e/0000%22.

Senate Finance and Public Administration Legislation Committee (SFPALC) 2019b, 'Department of Parliamentary Services', in *Estimates*, 8 April, Parliament of Australia, Canberra, available from: parlinfo.aph.gov.au/parlInfo/search/display/display.w3p;query=Id%3A%22committees%2Festimate%2F5380c1 ed-2873-4dc9-a34a-af0f6ad4bdd7%2F0000%22.

Senate Finance and Public Administration Legislation Committee (SFPALC) 2021, *Operation and management of the Department of Parliamentary Services*, June, Parliament of Australia, Canberra, available from: parlinfo.aph.gov.au/parlInfo/download/committees/reportsen/024549/toc_pdf/Operationandmanagement oftheDepartmentofParliamentaryServices.pdf;fileType=application%2Fpdf.

Senate Select Committee on Parliament's Appropriations and Staffing 1981, *Parliament's appropriations and staffing: Report of the Senate Select Committee*, Parliament of Australia, Canberra.

Senate Standing Committee on Procedure 2018, *Third report of 2018: Disorder outside formal proceedings*, 19 September, Parliament of Australia, Canberra, available from: www.aph.gov.au/Parliamentary_Business/Committees/Senate/Procedure/2018/Report3.

Senate Standing Committee on Procedure 2019, *First report of 2019: Parliamentary code of conduct*, 3 April, Parliament of Australia, Canberra, available from: www.aph.gov.au/Parliamentary_Business/Committees/Senate/Procedure/2019/Report1/c01.

Senate Standing Committee on Procedure 2021, *First report of 2021: Remote participation in senate proceedings*, 13 May, Parliament of Australia, Canberra, available from: www.aph.gov.au/Parliamentary_Business/Committees/Senate/Procedure/2021/Report.

Shenton, C. 2012, *The day parliament burned down*, Oxford University Press, Oxford, UK.

Shenton, C. 2017, 'Fixing Westminster', *London Review of Books*, vol. 39, no. 22, 16 November, available from: www.lrb.co.uk/v39/n22/caroline-shenton/fixing-westminster.

Shergold, P. 1997, 'The colour purple: Perceptions of accountability across the Tasman', *Public Administration & Development*, vol. 17, no. 3, pp. 293–306, doi.org/10.1002/(SICI)1099-162X(199708)17:3%3C293::AID-PAD950%3E3.0.CO;2-R.

Shipman, T. 2019, 'Theresa May in Brexit meltdown', *The Sunday Times*, [London], 20 January, available from: www.thetimes.co.uk/article/may-in-meltdown-h60z6nx8c.

Shugart, M.S. 2005, 'Semi-presidential systems: Dual executive and mixed authority patterns', *French Politics*, vol. 3, no. 3, pp. 323–351, doi.org/10.1057/palgrave.fp.8200087.

Silvester, J. & Spicer, A. 2014, 'Leading a legislature: A report on findings— Written evidence submitted by Cass Business School City University London', House of Commons Governance Committee, November, GOV 0071, available from: data.parliament.uk/writtenevidence/committeeevidence.svc/evidencedocument/house-of-commons-governance-committee/house-of-commons-governance/written/15731.html.

Simon, H.A. 1977, *Administrative behaviour: A study of decision-making processes in administrative organizations*, 4th edn, The Free Press, New York, NY.

Simons, N. 2015, 'Tory MP Charles Walker gets standing ovation from Labor MPs for defending John Bercow', *The Huffington Post UK*, 26 March, available from: www.huffingtonpost.co.uk/2015/03/26/watch-labour-mps-stand-and-applaud-tory_n_6946996.html?guccounter=1&guce_referrer_us.

Skinner, D. 2017, Independence and reform: The Legislative Assembly for the Australian Capital Territory, Paper submitted to Parliamentary Law, Practice and Procedure Course, University of Tasmania, 12 January.

Sloane, M. 2014, 'The role of the separation of powers and the parliamentary budget setting processes', *Australasian Parliamentary Review*, vol. 29, no. 2, pp. 140–158.

Sloane, M. 2020, '50th anniversary of the establishment of the modern senate committee system', *FlagPost: Parliamentary Library Blog*, 10 June, Parliament of Australia, Canberra, available from: www.aph.gov.au/About_Parliament/Parliamentary_Departments/Parliamentary_Library/FlagPost/2020/June/Fiftieth_anniversary_Senate_committees.

Smith, K. 2018, 'How to restore public trust in government', *The Mandarin*, 17 April, available from: www.themandarin.com.au/91350-restoring-public-trust-in-government/.

Snow, D. & Robertson, J. 2015, '"Choppergate" puts politicians' perks under scrutiny', *Sydney Morning Herald*, 24 July, available from: www.smh.com.au/politics/federal/choppergate-puts-politicians-perks-under-scrutiny-2015 0724-gijj5o.html.

Sowa, J. & Lu, J. 2017, 'Policy and management: Considering public management and its relationship to policy studies', *Policy Studies Journal*, vol. 45, no. 1, pp. 74–100, doi.org/10.1111/psj.12193.

Speake, J. (ed.) 2015, *Oxford dictionary of proverbs*, Oxford University Press, Oxford, UK, doi.org/10.1093/acref/9780198734901.001.0001.

Stanley, A. 2021, *Independent Complaints & Grievance Scheme: Independent 18-month review*, 22 February, UK Parliament, London, available from: www.parliament.uk/contentassets/e3ed0297d92a400bb249c887a30aa59b/icgs-18-month-review_final.pdf.

Stefanic, R. 2018, 'Secretary's review', in Department of Parliamentary Services, *Annual report 2017–18*, Parliament of Australia, Canberra, available from: www.aph.gov.au/About_Parliament/Parliamentary_Departments/Department_of_Parliamentary_Services/Publications/Annual_Reports/Annual_Report_2017-18/Part_1_Secretarys_Review.

St John-Stevas, N. 1959, *Walter Bagehot: A study of his life and thought, together with a selection from his political writings*, Eyre & Spottiswoode, London.

Stoker, G. 2006a, 'Public value management: A new narrative for networked governance?', *The American Review of Public Administration*, vol. 36, no. 1, pp. 41–57, doi.org/10.1177/0275074005282583.

Stoker, G. 2006b, *Why politics matters: Making democracy work*, Palgrave Macmillan, Basingstoke, UK.

Stoker, G., Evans, M. & Halupka, M. 2018, *Trust and democracy in Australia: Democratic decline and renewal*, Report No. 1, Democracy 2025, Canberra, available from: researchprofiles.canberra.edu.au/en/publications/trust-and-democracy-in-australia-democratic-decline-and-renewal.

Streeck, W. & Thelen, K.A. 2005, 'Introduction', in W. Streeck & K.A. Thelen (eds), *Beyond continuity: Institutional change in advanced political economies*, Oxford University Press, Oxford, UK, pp. 1–39.

Sullivan, H., Williams, P. & Jeffares, S. 2012, 'Leadership for collaboration: Situated agency in practice', *Public Management Review*, vol. 14, no. 1, pp. 41–66.

Sutherland, L. & Farrell, S. 2013, The history, workings and future challenges of Hansard, UK Parliament Open Lecture, 16 December, available from: www.youtube.com/watch?v=yaLWV9gfiS0.

Swinford, S. 2017, 'Up to 150 Conservative MPs will support motion to oust John Bercow as Speaker after his comments about Donald Trump', *The Telegraph*, [London], 9 February, available from: www.telegraph.co.uk/news/2017/02/09/conservative-mps-begin-bid-oust-john-bercow-speaker-criticism/.

Sydney Morning Herald (SMH) 2018, 'Husar mess shows change needed in political culture', *Sydney Morning Herald*, 11–12 August, p. 30.

Sylvester, R. & Thomson, A. 2019, 'Anna Soubry on the abuse suffered by MPs', *The Times*, [London], 10 January, available from: www.thetimes.co.uk/article/anna-soubry-on-the-abuse-suffered-by-mps-7p0jmtjtw.

Talbot, C. 2008, *Measuring public value: A competing values approach*, A paper for the Work Foundation, January, London, doi.org/10.13140/RG.2.2.36824.90888.

Talbot, C. 2009, 'Public value: The next "big thing" in public management?', *International Journal of Public Administration*, vol. 32, nos 3–4, pp. 167–170, doi.org/10.1080/01900690902772059.

Tanner, L. 2012, *Sideshow: Dumbing down democracy*, Scribe Publications, Melbourne.

TaxPayers' Alliance 2007, 'Not me guv government', [Blog], 19 September, TaxPayers' Alliance, London, available from: www.taxpayersalliance.com/not_me_guv_government.

Taylor, R. 2019, *Citizens' assemblies: An introductory guide*, Library Briefing, 8 February, House of Lords, London, available from: lordslibrary.parliament. uk/research-briefings/lln-2019-0017/.

The Telegraph 2014, 'Jean-Claude Juncker's most outrageous political statements', *The Telegraph*, [London], 15 July, available from: www.telegraph.co.uk/news/ worldnews/europe/eu/10967168/Jean-Claude-Junckers-most-outrageous-political-quotations.html.

TheyWorkForYou 2017, 'Recent Westminster Hall debates', *TheyWorkForYou*, [Online], mySociety, London, available from: www.theyworkforyou.com/ whall/.

Thimont Jack, M. & White, H. 2019, *Parliament after Brexit*, Report, May, Institute for Government, London, available from: www.instituteforgovernment.org. uk/sites/default/files/publications/parliament-after-brexit-final.pdf.

Thodey, D. 2019, Independent review of the APS: Priorities for change, 19 March, Department of the Prime Minister and Cabinet, Canberra, available from: www. apsreview.gov.au/sites/default/files/resources/aps-review-priorities-change.pdf.

Thompson, A. 2008, 'Secretary's review', in Department of Parliamentary Services, *Annual report and financial statements 2007–08*, Parliament of Australia, Canberra, pp. 3–8, available from: www.aph.gov.au/binaries/dps/publications/ anrep2008/annual_report_final.pdf.

Thompson, A. 2009, 'Secretary's review', in Department of Parliamentary Services, *Annual report and financial statements 2008–09*, Parliament of Australia, Canberra, pp. 11–13, available from: www.aph.gov.au/binaries/dps/ publications/anrep2009/dps_annual_report.pdf.

Thompson, J.D. 2021, 'Are the Melbourne protests Australia's own Capitol riots?', *ABC Religion & Ethics*, 27 September, available from: www.abc.net. au/religion/the-melbourne-protests-and-the-us-capitol-riots/13559334.

Thomsen, M.K. & Jakobsen, M. 2015, 'Influencing citizen coproduction by sending encouragement and advice: A field experiment', *International Public Management Journal*, vol. 18, no. 2, pp. 286–303, doi.org/10.1080/109674 94.2014.996628.

Tomkins, A. 2004, '"Talking in fictions": Jennings on Parliament', *The Modern Law Review*, vol. 67, no. 5, pp. 772–786, doi.org/10.1111/j.1468-2230. 2004.00512.x.

Torfing, J. 2019, 'Collaborative innovation in the public sector: The argument', *Public Management Review*, vol. 21, no. 1, pp. 1–11, doi.org/10.1080/1471 9037.2018.1430248.

Torrance, M. 2017, *Governance and administration of the House of Lords*, House of Lords Library Note 2017/0078, 6 November, UK Parliament, London.

Towell, N. 2014, 'Senate Clerk Rosemary Laing in "extraordinary" attack on parliamentary services boss Carol Mills', *The Canberra Times*, 18 August [Updated 23 April 2018], available from: www.canberratimes.com.au/national/public-service/senate-clerk-rosemary-laing-in-extraordinary-attack-on-parliamentary-services-boss-carol-mills-20140818-105elz.html.

Towell, N. 2015, 'Fit for purpose? Parliamentary services to get full review', *The Canberra Times*, 28 August, [Updated 23 April 2018], available from: www.canberratimes.com.au/national/public-service/fit-for-purpose-parliamentary-services-to-get-full-review-20150827-gj8tkz.html.

Trounson, A. 2016, 'Terry Moran: "We need a parliamentary policy office" to evaluate merit', *The Mandarin*, 24 May, available from: www.themandarin.com.au/65472-terry-moran-we-need-a-parliamentary-policy-office-to-evaluate-merit/.

Twomey, A. 2020, 'A virtual Australian parliament is possible—and may be needed—during the coronavirus pandemic', *The Conversation*, 25 March, available from: theconversation.com/a-virtual-australian-parliament-is-possible-and-may-be-needed-during-the-coronavirus-pandemic-134540.

Uberoi, E. 2017, *Public engagement in the UK Parliament: Overview and statistics*, Briefing Paper No. CBP 8158, 24 November, House of Commons Library, London, available from: commonslibrary.parliament.uk/research-briefings/cbp-8158/.

Uhr, J. 1982, 'Parliament and public administration', in J. Nethercote (ed.), *Parliament and bureaucracy*, Hale & Iremonger, Sydney, pp. 26–66.

Uhr, J. & Wanna, J. 2000, 'The future roles of parliament', in M. Keating, J. Wanna & P. Weller (eds), *Institutions on the edge: Capacity for governance*, Allen & Unwin, Sydney, pp. 10–44, doi.org/10.4324/9781003116127-2.

UK Parliament 2009, 'Speaker calls for a reconnection between parliament and public', *Parliamentary Business*, November, accessed from: www.parliament.uk/business/news/2009/11/speaker-calls-for-a-reconnection-between-parliament-and-public/ [page discontinued].

UK Parliament 2015, 'New education centre to double the number of school children visits', *Parliamentary Business*, July, accessed from: www.parliament.uk/business/news/2015/july/new-education-centre-opened/ [page discontinued].

UK Parliament 2017, 'Westminster Hall and committees', *About Parliament*, [Online], accessed from: www.parliament.uk/about/podcasts/theworkofparliament/house-of-commons-chamber-film/westminster-hall/ [page discontinued].

UK Parliament 2018a, 'Role: Commons Reference Group on Representation and Inclusion', *Parliamentary Business*, [Online], accessed from: www.parliament. uk/business/committees/committees-a-z/other-committees/reference-group-representation-inclusion/role/ [page discontinued].

UK Parliament 2018b, 'Speaker Lenthall defends parliament against the King', *About Parliament*, [Online], accessed from: www.parliament.uk/business/ publications/parliamentary-archives/explore-guides-to-documentary-archive-/ archives-highlights/archives-speakerlenthall/ [page discontinued].

UK Parliament 2018c, *UK gender-sensitive parliament audit 2018: Report of the Gender-Sensitive Parliament Audit Panel to the House of Commons Commission and the House of Lords Commission*, 26 November, Inter-Parliamentary Union, Geneva, available from: www.parliament.uk/documents/lords-information-office/UK%20Parliament_%20Gender%20Sensitive%20Parliament%20 Audit_Report_DIGITAL.pdf.

UK Parliament 2019a, 'Digital strategy for parliament', *MPs, Lords and Offices*, [Online], available from: www.parliament.uk/mps-lords-and-offices/offices/ bicameral/parliamentary-digital-service/digital-strategy-for-parliament/.

UK Parliament 2019b, *Response to the UK gender-sensitive parliament audit: Agreed jointly by the House of Commons Commission and the House of Lords Commission*, June, UK Parliament, London, available from: www.parliament.uk/global assets/documents/lords-committees/house-of-lords-commission/2017-19/ UK_Parliament_Gender_Sensitive_Report_Response_Combined.pdf.

UK Parliament 2019c, 'Televising parliament', *About Parliament*, [Online], available from: www.parliament.uk/about/living-heritage/evolutionof parliament/parliamentwork/communicating/overview/televisingparliament/.

UK Parliament 2022, 'House of Commons chamber proceedings during the Covid-19 pandemic', *About Parliament*, [Online], available from: www. parliament.uk/about/how/covid-19-proceedings-in-the-house-of-commons/.

Van de Walle, S. 2010, 'New public management: Restoring the public trust through creating distrust?', in T. Christensen & P. Laegreid (eds), *Ashgate research companion to new public management*, Ashgate, Aldershot, UK, pp. 309–320, doi.org/10.2139/ssrn.1594042.

vanHeerde-Hudson, J. 2011, 'Playing by the rules: The 2009 MPs' expenses scandal', in D. Wring, R. Mortimor & S. Atkinson (eds), *Political communication in Britain: The leader debates, the campaign and the media in the 2010 general election*, Palgrave Macmillan, Basingstoke, UK, pp. 241–260, doi.org/10.1057/9780230305045_16.

vanHeerde-Hudson, J. 2014, 'Should I stay or should I go?', in J. vanHeerde-Hudson (ed.), *The political costs of the 2009 British MPs' expenses scandal*, Palgrave Macmillan, Basingstoke, UK, pp. 62–87.

vanHeerde-Hudson, J. and Ward, O. 2014, 'The 2009 British MPs' expenses scandal: Origins, evolution and consequences', in J. vanHeerde-Hudson (ed.), *The political costs of the 2009 British MPs' expenses scandal*, Palgrave Macmillan, Basingstoke, UK, pp. 1–26, doi.org/10.1057/9781137034557_1.

Verrier, J. 1995, The future of parliamentary research services: To lead or to follow?, Paper presented to the 61st International Federation of Library Associations and Institutions General Conference, Istanbul, Turkey, 20–25 August.

Verrier, J. 2007, 'Benchmarking parliamentary administration: The United Kingdom, Canada, New Zealand and Australia', *Australasian Parliamentary Review*, vol. 22, no. 1, pp. 45–75.

Verrier, J. 2008, 'An optimum model for the governance of parliaments?', *Australasian Parliamentary Review*, vol. 23, no. 2, pp. 115–134.

Wagenaar, H. 1999, 'Value pluralism in public administration', *Administrative Theory & Praxis*, vol. 21, no. 4, pp. 441–449, doi.org/10.1080/10841806. 1999.11643400.

Wagenaar, H. 2014, 'The necessity of value pluralism in administrative practice: A reply to Overeem', *Administration & Society*, vol. 46, no. 8, pp. 1020–1028, doi.org/10.1177/0095399714550856.

Walker, A. 2019, 'Trust, parliaments, and stability', *PSA Parliaments*, 20 March, The UK Political Studies Association Specialist Group on Parliaments, London, available from: psaparliaments.org/2019/03/20/trust-parliaments/ #more-2782.

Walker, A., Jurczak, N., Bochel, C. & Leston-Bandeira, C. 2019, 'How public engagement became a core part of the House of Commons select committees', *Parliamentary Affairs*, vol. 72, no. 4, pp. 965–986, doi.org/10.1093/pa/ gsz031.

Walker, P. 2019, 'House of Commons suspended after water pours through ceiling', *The Guardian*, 5 April, available from: www.theguardian.com/politics/2019/ apr/04/house-of-commons-suspended-water-pours-through-ceiling.

Walker, P., Asthana, A. & Elgot, J. 2017, 'John Bercow apologises to Lords counterpart amid Trump visit row', *The Guardian*, 8 February, available from: www.theguardian.com/politics/2017/feb/07/john-bercow-accused-of-hypocrisy-over-trump-stance.

Walpole, J., Kelly, R. & Powell, T. 2008, *The Whip's Office*, Library Standard Note SN/PC/02829, 10 October, House of Commons Library, London, available from: commonslibrary.parliament.uk/research-briefings/sn02829/.

Walter, J. 2012, 'Democratic ambivalence? Ministerial attitudes to party and parliamentary scrutiny', in K. Dowding & C. Lewis (eds), *Ministerial careers and accountability in the Australian Commonwealth Government*, ANU Press, Canberra, pp. 67–94, doi.org/10.22459/MCAACG.09.2012.04.

Wanna, J. 2008, 'Collaborative government: Meanings, dimensions, drivers and outcomes', in J. O'Flynn & J. Wanna (eds), *Collaborative governance: A new era of public policy in Australia*, ANU Press, Canberra, pp. 3–12, doi.org/10.22459/CG.12.2008.01.

Warhurst, J. 2018, 'It's not an easy life in parliament', *The Canberra Times*, 16 August, p. 17.

Warhurst, J. 2019, 'Democratic disconnections between big ideas and election politics', *The Canberra Times*, 24 January, available from: www.canberratimes.com.au/national/act/democratic-disconnections-between-big-ideas-and-election-politics-20190122-p50sx4.html.

Warhurst, J. 2020, 'Parliament has been deemed surplus to requirements', *The Canberra Times*, 23 July, [Updated 2 July 2021], available from: www.canberratimes.com.au/story/6843710/parliament-has-been-deemed-surplus-to-requirements/.

Weatherston, J.S. 1975, *Commonwealth Hansard: Its establishment and development*, 3rd edn, AGPS, Canberra.

Webber, E. 2019, 'Speaker's power to run the Commons "must be curbed" after John Bercow's tenure', *The Times*, [London], 23 October, available from: www.thetimes.co.uk/edition/news/speakers-power-to-run-the-commons-must-be-curbed-after-john-bercows-tenure-6g8dl70qn?utm_source=newsletter&utm_campaign=newsletter_119&utm_medium=email&utm_content=119_7563428&CMP=TNLEmail_118918_7563428_119.

Webber, E. & Calver, T. 2020, 'Commons staff "failed" by service to tackle bullying', *The Times*, [London], 13 October, available from: www.thetimes.co.uk/article/commons-staff-failed-by-service-to-tackle-bullying-fdb9q7vb6.

Weerasinghe, A. & Ramshaw G. 2018, 'Fighting democratic decline through parliamentary communications: The case study of the UK Parliament', *PSA Parliaments*, 31 January, The UK Political Studies Association Specialist Group on Parliaments, London, available from: psaparliaments.org/2018/01/31/communications-uk-parliament/.

Wegrich, K. 2019, 'The blind spots of collaborative innovation', *Public Management Review*, vol. 21, no. 1, pp. 12–20, doi.org/10.1080/14719037.2018.1433311.

Weinberg, A. 2013, 'A longitudinal study of the impact of changes in the job and the expenses scandal on UK national politicians' experiences of work, stress and the home–work interface', *Parliamentary Affairs*, vol. 68, no. 2, pp. 248–271, doi.org/10.1093/pa/gst013.

Weinberg, J. 2020, *Who enters politics and why? Basic human values in the UK Parliament*, Policy Press, Bristol, UK.

Wheeler, B. 2009, 'The John Bercow story', *BBC News*, 24 June, available from: news.bbc.co.uk/2/hi/uk_news/politics/8114399.stm.

Wheeler, B. 2020, 'Coronavirus: Will the £4bn parliament refurbishment be scrapped?', *BBC News*, 22 May, available from: www.bbc.com/news/uk-politics-52682922.

White, H. 2015, *Select committees under scrutiny: The impact of parliamentary committee inquiries on government*, June, Institute for Government, London, available from: www.instituteforgovernment.org.uk/sites/default/files/publications/Under%20scrutiny%20final.pdf.

White, H. 2020a, 'Abandoning our virtual parliament could damage our democracy', *Institute for Government Blog*, 14 May, available from: www.instituteforgovernment.org.uk/blog/abandoning-our-virtual-parliament-could-damage-our-democracy.

White, H. 2020b, 'A virtual parliament was well equipped to make progress on the government's legislative agenda', *Institute for Government Blog*, 10 June, available from: www.instituteforgovernment.org.uk/blog/virtual-parliament-was-well-equipped-make-progress-government-legislative-agenda.

Wike, R., Simmons, K., Stokes, B. & Fetterolf, J. 2017, *Globally, broad support for representative and direct democracy: But many also endorse nondemocratic alternatives*, Democracy Report, 16 October, Pew Research Center, Washington, DC, available from: assets.pewresearch.org/wp-content/uploads/sites/2/2017/10/17102729/Pew-Research-Center_Democracy-Report_2017.10.16.pdf.

Wilkins, P. & Phillimore, J. 2019, 'What are the merits of royal commissions and other forms of inquiry?', *The Mandarin*, 18 February, available from: www.themandarin.com.au/104199-what-are-the-merits-of-royal-commissions-and-other-forms-of-inquiry/.

Williams, B.N., Kang, S.C. & Johnson, J. 2016, '(Co)-contamination as the dark side of co-production: Public value failures in co-production processes', *Public Management Review*, vol. 18, no. 5, pp. 692–717, doi.org/10.1080/14719037.2015.1111660.

Williams, I. & Shearer, H. 2011, 'Appraising public value: Past, present and futures', *Public Administration*, vol. 89, no. 4, pp. 1367–1384, doi.org/10.1111/j.1467-9299.2011.01942.x.

Williams, O.C. 1954, *The clerical organization of the House of Commons 1661–1850*, Clarendon Press, Oxford, UK.

Williamson, A. 2021, 'How the Covid-19 pandemic has accelerated parliamentary modernisation', *Hansard Society Blog*, 2 September, available from: www.hansardsociety.org.uk/blog/how-the-covid-19-pandemic-has-accelerated-parliamentary-modernisation.

Williamson, A. & Fallon, F. 2011, 'Transforming the future parliament through the effective use of digital media', *Parliamentary Affairs*, vol. 64, no. 4, pp. 781–792, doi.org/10.1093/pa/gsr028.

Wiltshire, K. 1982, 'Staffing and appropriations of parliament', in J. Nethercote (ed.), *Parliament and bureaucracy*, Hale & Iremonger, Sydney, pp. 302–318.

Winetrobe, B.K. 2013, 'Time for Commons to seize the reform moment', *The Constitution Unit Blog*, 1 September, available from: constitution-unit.com/2013/09/01/time-for-commons-to-seize-the-reform-moment/.

Winetrobe, B.K. 2014, '"The precious centre of our parliamentary democracy": Commons governance after the clerk recruitment affair', *The Constitution Unit Blog*, 1 September, available from: constitution-unit.com/2014/09/01/the-precious-centre-of-our-parliamentary-democracy-commons-governance-after-the-clerk-appointment-affair/.

Winnett, R. & Rayner, G. 2009, *No expenses spared: The inside of the scoop which changed the face of British politics—by the team that broke it*, Bantam, London.

Wintour, P. 2014, 'Retiring Clerk of Commons makes plea for Speaker to remain neutral', *The Guardian*, 25 July, available from: www.theguardian.com/politics/2014/jul/24/retiring-clerk-commons-speaker-sir-robert-rogers-john-bercow.

Wollaston, S. 2015, 'Inside the Commons review: "Cockerell records it all with a mischievous eye"', *The Guardian*, 4 February, available from: www. theguardian.com/tv-and-radio/2015/feb/04/inside-the-commons-review-michael-cockerell.

WPP Government & Public Sector Practice 2019, *The leaders' report: Increasing trust through citizen engagement*, WPP Government & Public Sector Practice, London, available from: marcommnews.com/wp-content/uploads/2019/02/LEADERS-REPORT_digital-final.pdf.

Wright, B. 2011, 'Clerk's review', in Department of the House of Representatives, *Annual report 2010–11*, Parliament of Australia, Canberra, available from: www. aph.gov.au/About_Parliament/Parliamentary_Departments/Department_of_the_House_of_Representatives/Annual_Reports/2010-11_Annual_Report.

Wright, B.C. & Fowler P.E. (eds) 2012, *House of Representatives practice*, 6th edn, Department of the House of Representatives, Canberra.

Wright, O. 2020, 'Parliament surrendered to government in coronavirus pandemic, says Lady Hale', *The Times*, [London], 21 September, available from: www. thetimes.co.uk/edition/news/parliament-surrendered-to-government-in-coronavirus-pandemic-says-lady-hale-t5wmvkfq5?utm_source=newsletter &utm_campaign=newsletter_144&utm_medium=email&utm_content= 144_10579949&CMP=TNLEmail_118918_10579949_144.

Wright, T. 2004, 'Prospects for parliamentary reform', *Parliamentary Affairs*, vol. 57, no. 4, pp. 867–876, doi.org/10.1093/pa/gsh067.

Wright, T. 2014, 'Inside a scandal', in J. vanHeerde-Hudson (ed.), *The political costs of the 2009 British MPs' expenses scandal*, Palgrave Macmillan, Basingstoke, UK, pp. 43–61.

Wright, T. 2015, 'Recalling MPs: Accountable to whom?', *The Political Quarterly*, vol. 86, no. 2, pp. 289–296, doi.org/10.1111/1467-923X.12166.

Wroe, D. 2019, 'Christopher Pyne delivers damning verdict on the state of Australian politics', *Sydney Morning Herald*, 10 February, available from: www. smh.com.au/politics/federal/christopher-pyne-delivers-damning-verdict-on-the-state-of-australian-politics-20190210-p50wt2.html?_ga=2.248259143. 1561386246.1549947679-298088061.1544924570.

www.ingramcontent.com/pod-product-compliance
Lightning Source LLC
Chambersburg PA
CBHW040154270326
41929CB00041B/3394